# Whose National Security?

# Whose National Security?

## CANADIAN STATE SURVEILLANCE AND THE CREATION OF ENEMIES

Edited by Gary Kinsman, Dieter K. Buse, and Mercedes Steedman

✴

Between the Lines
Toronto, Canada

Whose National Security?

First published in Canada by
Between the Lines
720 Bathurst Street, Suite #404
Toronto, Ontario
M5S 2R4

Canadian Cataloguing in Publication Data

Main entry under title:

Whose national security? : Canadian state surveillance and the creation of enemies

Includes bibliographical references and index.
ISBN 1-896357-25-3

1. Subversive activities—Canada. 2. Internal security—Canada. 3. Intelligence service—Canada. 4. National security— Canada. I. Kinsman, Gary. II. Buse, D.K. III. Steedman, Mercedes.

JL86.I58W46 2000          322.4'2'0971          C00-931672-8

Cover and text design by Jennifer Tiberio
Front cover image from I.O.D.E., *Echoes*, Autumn 1948
Back cover image from Democracy Street poster, Democracy Street, Vancouver
Printed in Canada

Between the Lines gratefully acknowledges assistance for its publishing activities from the Canada Council for the Arts, the Ontario Arts Council, and the Government of Canada through the Book Publishing Industry Development Program.

THE CANADA COUNCIL | LE CONSEIL DES ARTS
FOR THE ARTS | DU CANADA
SINCE 1957 | DEPUIS 1957

Canadä

# Contents

## Part III Education under Cover

## Part IV Redefining a Security Threat: Newer Enemies

## Part V The Machinery of State in Action: Means and Consequences

## Part VI Finding Security in the Archives

## Part VII  Old Methods and Recent Trends

## Part VIII The Continuing Surveillance State

# Preface

On November 22–24, 1996, for the first time in Canada, a host of diverse people—critical researchers, scholars, union activists, and members of various other communities from across the country, including activists who had been on the receiving end of Canada's national security campaigns—gathered at Laurentian University in Sudbury for a conference on "national security." The broad-ranging meetings covered the gamut not only of national security campaigns against unions and the left, but also of state surveillance of university campuses, First Nations, immigrants, women's groups, gay men and lesbians, plus supporters of Quebec sovereignty. It addressed the impact of security campaigns on gender relations in the Cold War in a broader sense. The conference included a hands-on session on gaining access to security information. The event as a whole carried all the excitement of sharing ideas, comparing experiences, and exchanging research tips.

The conference had three main objectives: (1) to display the diverse forms of critical research going on across Canada regarding national security and security surveillance; (2) to develop an interdisciplinary focus not only spanning the boundaries of political science, history, sociology, and cultural studies but also moving beyond those disciplines by building critical studies of national security; and (3) to develop awareness among activists and researchers of how to gain access to security information, including the obstacles to access. The conference unanimously passed a motion calling for changes to the Access to Information and Privacy Acts to make it easier for this information to be released to the public and researchers (see p.212).

This book is largely composed of papers originally given at the conference, and it therefore reflects the vibrant presentations and conversations of that event. Most of the papers have been substantially revised, and we have also added six essays, by Dieter K. Buse, Paula Maurutto, Mercedes Steedman, Christabelle Sethna, Zuhair Kashmeri, and Karen Pearlston. The result, we hope, reveals both the breadth of state surveillance in Canada and the impact of the security regime from a personal point of view.

The editors owe debts to many people. Terry Pender worked with us to organize the conference. Joanna Lam and Erika Espinoza were crucial to the running of the conference. We want to thank all the people who took part in and helped to organize the conference. Financial assistance for the conference was provided by INORD (Institute for Northern Ontario Research and Development, Laurentian University), the office of the Vice-President-Academic of Laurentian University, LURF (Laurentian University Research Fund), and SSHRC (Social Sciences and Humanities Research Council). Since the conference, Joanna Lam, Treanor Mahood-Greer, Barb Wendlowski, Rose-May Demoré, Judy Malloy, Erika Espinoza, and Judith Buse have assisted us with this project. A LURF grant has also provided additional support for the publication. We thank our publisher, Between the Lines, in particular Paul Eprile, Peter Steven, and our editor Robert Clarke. We also thank the anonymous reviewers of the manuscript for their suggestions. Finally, we thank *Labour/Le Travail* for permission to reprint Paula Maurutto's revised article, "Private Policing and Surveillance of Catholics," and to James Lorimer and Company for permission to reprint "When CSIS Calls: Canadian Arabs, Racism, and the Gulf War," which is a section from Zuhair Kashmeri's book, *The Gulf Within*.

*Gary Kinsman*
*Dieter K. Buse*
*Mercedes Steedman*

# Contributors

**Kerry Badgley** received his Ph.D. in Canadian history from Carleton University, Ottawa, in 1996 and is employed as an archivist with the National Archives of Canada, Ottawa.

**Geoffrey C. Bunn** is a graduate of the History and Theory of Psychology Program, York University, Toronto. He is British Psychological Society Research Fellow at the Science Museum in London, England.

**Dieter K. Buse** is professor of history at Laurentian University, Sudbury. He co-edited *Modern Germany: An Encyclopedia of History, People and Culture, 1871–1990;* and, with Mercedes Steedman and Peter Suschnigg, *Hard Lessons: The Mine Mill Union in the Canadian Labour Movement.*

**Frank K. Clarke,** who has taught in the Department of History at York University, is working on a study of Cold War society in Toronto.

**Patrizia Gentile** is a Ph.D candidate in the Department of History, Queen's University, Kingston. Her dissertation explores the world of beauty queens and contests in twentieth-century Canada. She is co-authoring a book with Gary Kinsman on the anti-homosexual security purges in Cold War Canada.

**Julie Guard** teaches in the Labour and Workplace Studies Program at the University of Manitoba, Winnipeg. Prior to moving west she taught history, women's studies, Canadian studies, and public policy at York University, University of Toronto, and Trent University. She also participates in the labour movement as an activist and a labour educator.

**Larry Hannant** has a long-time political and scholarly interest in security and intelligence issues. He teaches history at Camosun College, Victoria, B.C., and at the University of Victoria.

**Steve Hewitt** has a Ph.D. in history from the University of Saskatchewan. He is working on a history of RCMP spying on Canadian university campuses.

**Evert Hoogers** has been an elected National Union Representative with the Canadian Union of Postal Workers since 1990, and has researched and written about RCMP surveillance of the union and its activists. From 1980 to 1987 he was president of CUPW's Vancouver local.

**Franca Iacovetta** is a Marxist feminist historian in Toronto and a founding board member of the Ontario Workers' Arts and Heritage Centre. A specialist in the field of immigrant women and workers and the social-gender history of post-World War II Canada, she is involved in a collective project of Italian women workers and radicals across the globe and writing a book with the working title "Making New Citizens in Cold War Canada."

**Zuhair Kashmeri**, a journalist, is the author of *The Gulf Within: Canadian Arabs, Racism and the Gulf War* on the experiences of Arab-Canadians with surveillance and state pressure.

**Gregory S. Kealey** is dean of the School of Graduate Studies and university research professor at Memorial University of Newfoundland. He is the author of *Toronto Workers Respond to Industrial Capitalism, 1867–1892; Dreaming of What Might Be: The Knights of Labor in Ontario, 1880–1900; Workers in Canadian History;* and co-editor with Reg Whitaker of *R.C.M.P. Security Bulletins* (eight volumes).

**Gary Kinsman** teaches sociology at Laurentian University. He is the author of *The Regulation of Desire: Homo and Hetero Sexualities* and a co-author of "'In the Interests of the State': The Anti-Gay, Anti-Lesbian National Security Campaigns in Canada." He is a gay and socialist activist.

**Paula Maurutto** is a SSHRC Postdoctoral Fellow in the Department of Sociology and Anthropology, Carleton University. Her research examines how social science methodologies such as crime mapping, risk assessment, and social surveys transcribe social behaviour into numerical constructs.

**Heidi McDonell** worked for two years as research assistant on a research project on Canadian national security campaigns against gay men and lesbians. For nearly twenty years she lived in Ottawa, where she was active in queer and community politics. She now lives and works in Vancouver.

**Madeleine Parent** has been a labour organizer, social activist, and Quebec sovereignist. She is a member of the National Action Committee on the Status of Women.

**Karen Pearlston** is a doctoral candidate at York University and a veteran of many protest movements.

**Terry Pender**, a prize-winning journalist, has studied at Laurentian University and currently works at the *Kitchener-Waterloo Record*.

**Christabelle Sethna** is a historian of education. She has researched and published in the areas of sex education, teen pregnancy, and birth control history. She has taught at the Ontario Institute for Studies in Education/University of Toronto and is now an assistant professor cross-appointed to the Institute for Women's Studies and the Faculty of Education at the University of Ottawa.

**Geoffrey S. Smith** is professor of physical and health education and of history at Queen's University. His research includes preparation of a monograph with the working title "Contagious Subversion: Sex, Gender, and Disease in the National Security Era."

**Mercedes Steedman** teaches sociology at Laurentian University. She is the author of *Angels of the Workplace: Women and the Construction of Gender Relations in the Canadian Clothing Industry, 1890–1940* and co-editor (with Peter Suschnigg and Dieter K. Buse) of *Hard Lessons: The Mine Mill Union in the Canadian Labour Movement*.

GARY KINSMAN, DIETER K. BUSE, AND MERCEDES STEEDMAN

# Introduction

Would anyone believe that Royal Canadian Mounted Police (RCMP) security operatives, the Canadian version of a secret police, spied upon tea and Tupperware
parties? During the 1950s and 1960s they did. They also monitored high-school
students, gays and lesbians, trade unionists, and left-wing political groups, including Communists, the Co-operative Commonwealth Federation (CCF), and the
New Democratic Party (NDP), as well as feminists and consumer housewives' associations. They watched public servants, members of the military, university students and professors, peace activists, immigrants, Canada Council grant recipients,
Learned Societies meetings, recipients of youth funding initiatives, black community activists, First Nations people and Native Studies programs, plus, of course,
Quebec sovereignists.[1] In its endeavours the RCMP also had some helpers: the state's
collaborators in churches or among social workers and immigrant reception groups
provided another level of monitoring and observing.

    Cold War paranoia is not sufficient—except as an excuse—to account for the
extent of the secret monitoring of Canadians in the twentieth century by their own
government. The massive quantity of this surveillance information, and its use,
raise a number of questions. For instance, who controlled, directed, and oversaw
this extensive national security system? Just whose system was this, and which people was it meant to serve? How did this surreptitious machinery get set into place
in a "democratic" society? Who did it see as a threat, and how did "ordinary"
Canadians become its target?

    Canadian national security surveillance was no accident. It existed not simply
because a few overzealous RCMP officers were "doing their jobs." Instead, it was
organized at the highest levels of the Canadian state through cabinet directives, the
Prime Minister's Office, and discussions on the interdepartmental Security Panel,
which co-ordinated national security efforts across Canada. The Security Panel,
housed under the auspices of the Privy Council Office, was specifically created as
an advisory and co-ordinating rather than an executive body. Chaired by the secretary to the cabinet and reporting directly to the cabinet, the Panel's representatives
included people from the Privy Council, the departments of External Affairs and
National Defence, and the RCMP, the Defence Research Board, and the three

1

branches of the armed forces. The Panel's terms of reference were "to advise on the co-ordination of the planning, organization and execution of security measures which affect government departments, and to advise on other such security measures as may be referred to it."[2] The RCMP was the investigative arm of the panel and was mandated by cabinet to perform security investigations and surveillance.

One specific feature of the Canadian national security state has been its highly secretive character, especially as compared to the more public character of national security campaigns south of the border. The alliances built with the United States, Britain, the North Atlantic Treaty Organization (NATO), and the Western bloc designated a number of groups, including leftists and homosexuals, as "national security risks." These conceptualizations of who was a risk to national security shaped the directives that the bureaucrats gave to the RCMP, while at the same time the RCMP was granted a relative autonomy in its day-to-day operations within the overall directives of the Canadian national security state. The RCMP engaged in extensive spying on individuals and groups in Canada who were perceived as "threats," and it collected extensive information on many of those who opposed the status quo. As a result of this surveillance Canadian state authorities came to know their opposition very well. No one but state authorities regulated the national security bureaucrats, because access to national security information in Canada has never been in the public domain. The members of the political, economic, and social elite who defined Canadian national security were interested in perpetuating social regulation, in ensuring a social stability that would, in the end, be to their own benefit and to the benefit of others like them. The national security campaigns would stir up and maintain a climate of fear directed against those defined as "different" or "other" and thereby also help to maintain the control of people located in positions of power and privilege.

The security activities represented an organized initiative that touched the lives of tens of thousands of people. They were part of a campaign with the full backing of the Canadian state. The campaign also went far beyond the strict confines of state agencies. The RCMP shared information with other social groups, including the Catholic Archdiocese of Toronto, and with employers and government departments. Such groups and others, including social workers and immigrant reception workers, regularly collaborated in providing information to the RCMP, which also regularly relied on and shared information with the U.S. Federal Bureau of Investigation (FBI) and Central Intelligence Agency (CIA). Together, all of these police forces collected very "private" information about the people they spied on.

## The Study of Canadian National Security

Historically there has been a lack of public scrutiny of the state security police in all national contexts. Still, previous path-breaking books on the national security state in Canada, like Reg Whitaker and Gary Marcuse's *Cold War Canada*, Larry Hannant's *The Infernal Machine*, and the writings of Gregory Kealey, have presented some of the main features of how the national security campaigns came to be organized in Canada through the RCMP and the Security Panel.[3] They have focused on the campaigns against the Communist Party, the left, and the union movement—and have therefore largely illustrated the impact of the security campaigns on white, heterosexual-identified men. Although these groups were central targets of the security campaigns, the sweep was much wider. While this book relies on those earlier studies, we also extend our coverage to include cases that demonstrate the role of ethnicity, immigration, race, religion, gender, and sexuality. In doing this we call for a rethinking of the basis of national security, to consider its larger implications. Canadians clearly need to develop a critical analysis of the actions of the RCMP and the Canadian Security Intelligence Service (CSIS), which in 1984 took over many RCMP Security Service operations, but they also need to consider how non-state agencies, such as churches, were often vital in these security campaigns.

Working-class women outside unions, for instance, often became the focus of the national security regime. Security policing was often tied to the "Canadianization" of immigrants and other groups. A characteristic feature of security campaigns was the construction of sexual and gender "deviance" and "normality." The RCMP's attention to gay and lesbian rights organizations continued into the 1970s with surveillance of the Community Homophile Association of Toronto, the Coalition for Gay Rights in Ontario, the first cross-country gay and lesbian rights demonstration in Ottawa in 1971, and early attempts to form a cross-country coalition.[4] High-school students calling for more democracy in the schools and for sex education and birth control came under RCMP scrutiny in the 1960s and 1970s. The continuing surveillance of left activists had an impact on human rights organizations, because many civil libertarians backed off from defending the rights of members of the Communist Party for fear that their own organizations would become tainted by association with the "Red Menace." The RCMP also had a plan to round up, at the outbreak of a third world war, more than one thousand "subversives," including not just members of the Communist Party but also "red diaper babies," the children of alleged subversives. The internment plan, first drawn up in the late 1940s, was revived and expanded after 1969. It was only abandoned in 1983 in the context of the pending creation of CSIS.[5]

The extensive surveillance of people living in Canada violated many people's democratic rights. But, even more, the national security campaigns had a sharp, extensive impact on the social and political fabric of Canada. The surveillance of unionists, political activists, gay men and lesbians, immigrants, working-class women, Quebec sovereignists, young people, and Native and black activists was central to the social organization of the national security state, crucial to its overall organization. As this wide scope makes clear, national security was not only about state regulation, but also included a broader form of social and moral regulation and attempts to define "proper Canadian" subjects.[6]

This book seeks to advance the critical theorization of national security, which we hope explains our title: *Whose National Security?* Researchers and activists have to ask which nation and whose security was being defended, and by whom? The Canadian national security state has mobilized the cause of "national security" against a number of oppressed groups within Canadian society. Often national security has been a code word for the defence of powerful business interests.

Indeed, in the case of the controversial meeting of the Asian Pacific Economic Cooperation (APEC) alliance at the University of British Columbia in November 1997, the defence of the Indonesian dictator Suharto became an integral part of defending Canada's "national security"—but it also became a highly contested part.

Today the national security state in Canada remains very much alive. Its recent endeavours include surveillance of Arabs living in Canada during the Gulf War in 1991, ongoing security campaigns against postal workers, continuing problems of gay men and lesbians in getting security clearances in the public service and military, and, most dramatically perhaps, the RCMP actions against student demonstrators (including pepper-spraying and the profiling of protestors' sexual orientations) at the 1997 APEC summit.[7] In June 2000 we saw a massive police mobilization and the use of pepper-spray against demonstrators in Windsor protesting against the meeting of the Organization of American States and its planned Free Trade Area of the Americas.

Although the national security surveillance campaigns touched the lives of tens of thousands of people in Canada, we also need to keep in mind (as a number of the chapters here indicate) that this surveillance was never total or monolithic. The national security campaigns were never entirely successful. The Canadian national security state never did accomplish the regulation of all people in the country. There was often some space for non-cooperation and resistance. At times people refused to inform on their friends, refused to give names to the RCMP, and fought for their democratic rights—as in the case of the gay men and lesbians who refused to give the names of other homosexuals to the RCMP, the unionists who continued to work with socialists and radicals, and the students who continued to organize for their rights in the face of RCMP surveillance. It is those forms of non-cooperation and resistance that allow us, above all else, to put the ideology of national security in question.

A more inclusive approach to the people affected by the national security campaigns could explore a number of other areas. The important topic of surveillance and secret police activities in Quebec deserves much more detailed coverage than this book has been able to offer. The RCMP national security campaign and "dirty tricks" against the Quebec union, left, and sovereignty movements were more intensive than similar surveillance activities in the rest of Canada in the 1960s and 1970s and took on the added specific dimension of surveillance against a movement for the democratic right to national self-determination. Defence of the national security of Canada was defined during those decades as a matter of clear and active support for Canadian federalism and "national unity" and of opposition to supporters of Quebec independence and sovereignty. Those supporters were defined in turn as being opposed to Canada's national security. The English-Canadian-based "national" dimension of the security campaigns is a unique feature of the phenomenon.

There is also, unfortunately, no chapter here on the security surveillance of the black community in Nova Scotia in the late 1960s and early 1970s. That surveillance was justified on the basis of a supposed connection with the U.S.-based Black Panther Party. The relevant RCMP reports included racist statements characterizing black women as "prolific child-bearers" and black men as layabouts, thieves, and drunks.[8] Although Terry Pender's chapter does address the campaigns against the Native Studies program at Laurentian University, we have not been able to examine the national security campaigns that were directed against First Nations activists because of their supposed connections to the American Indian Movement.[9]

Still, we hope that this book will inspire more exploration in these areas and that future studies will be able to build a more inclusive approach. The developments in computer technology and data processing have opened up greater possibilities for state, and private, observations of individuals' patterns of movement, purchases, and communications. The potential violations of privacy and the massive quantities of data that can be accessed electronically threaten to completely change the way in which surveillance operates—and how it can be studied. This book's offerings are largely empirical in character, because the extent and the actual organization of the security campaigns will have to be more closely defined before a deeper analysis becomes possible.

## What Follows: Themes and Issues

To begin this book, two chapters address the origins of the (in)security state and the structures and personnel employed to gather security information. While Dieter K. Buse outlines the European background and raises questions about citizenship rights, Gregory Kealey looks at the early history of the RCMP to show the role of ethnicity in such forces.

To comprehend the extent of surveillance we have to ask about what, or whom, the state and society saw as a threat. Part II, "Defining a Security Threat: Three Examples," begins to show the breadth of the monitoring of Canadian associations. Paula Maurutto illustrates the extrastate surveillance by the Catholic church on its parishioners in Toronto, Mercedes Steedman considers the surveillance of the Mine Mill women's auxiliaries, and Julie Guard examines the reporting on the Housewives' Consumers' Association. These chapters point out how state surveillance entered into the lives of working-class women, even those who were not members of unions, because of their supposed connection to communists and leftists.

Have Canadian educational institutions threatened to undermine society? In Part III, "Education under Cover," Steve Hewitt examines RCMP spying at the University of Saskatchewan over the period 1920–71, while Terry Pender looks at the surveillance of students, faculty, and the Native Studies program at Laurentian University in Sudbury from the 1960s to the 1970s. Their findings are supplemented by Christabelle Sethna's exploration of RCMP surveillance of high-school students in Toronto in the 1960s and early 1970s.

Spying tried to pinpoint the supposedly deviant or troublesome. The other side of the coin was the establishment of norms to be followed, especially regarding family and social life. The chapters in Part IV, "Redefining a Security Threat: Newer Enemies," look at national security in relation to gender and sexuality, including the campaigns against immigrants. Patrizia Gentile examines the management of gender relations in Cold War Ottawa with the construction of "government girls" and "government men," while Gary Kinsman explores the social organization of the national security campaigns against gay men and lesbians in the late 1950s and 1960s. The national security campaigns relied on laws that criminalized all homosexual activities and on the social consensus that stigmatized homosexuality. The similarity of the tactics of surveillance used by the RCMP against leftists and homosexuals becomes evident here. Franca Iacovetta, in "Making Model Citizens," examines the campaigns for "Canadianization" that took place in the context of the national security reshaping of immigrant reception work and gender relations within immigrant communities. The RCMP activities are seen from a different perspective, as "proper" ethnicity and "Canadianness" became central to the national security campaigns.

Part V, "The Machinery of State in Action: Means and Consequences," explores both the technologies of surveillance and the consequences of surveillance for civil liberties. Frank K. Clarke finds that the security campaigns against communists prevented civil libertarians from defending the democratic rights of communists and led to the division of the civil liberties movement. Geoff Smith offers an auto-biographical account of how the security campaign shaped the daily lives of children growing up in the Cold War atmosphere, while Geoff Bunn looks at the actual and symbolic use of lie detectors in regimes of national security.

Part VI, "Finding Security in the Archives," provides guidance to researchers and other concerned people. Larry Hannant offers reflections on his own attempt to gain access to his files using the Access to Information Act. Kerry Badgley provides an insider's perspective from someone working in the national archives and gives advice on how to get access to security information. Heidi McDonell reflects on her experiences as a researcher from the outside trying to gain access to security information on the campaigns against gay men and lesbians using the Access to Information Act. These chapters reveal, among other things, an important tension between the accounts from "outside" and "inside" the national information archives—a tension that leads to rather different views of the problems with the Access to Information Act. Activists and researchers located "outside" the official institutions of information management argue for changes in legislation and practice to make it far easier to gain access to security information and break down the barriers encountered by many activists and researchers.[10] In June 2000, Toronto lawyer Clayton Ruby won a twelve-year legal battle to find out what information government departments had on him. The Federal Court of Canada ruled that the right of the citizen must be measured against the state's right to collect information. This means that despite exclusions, much of the information collected by state agencies, including CSIS, must be made accessible. How state agencies will operate in the wake of this ruling is not yet clear.

Part VII, "Old Methods and Recent Trends," considers the continuity of left-wing surveillance and the unending state spying. Based on her own experiences, Madeleine Parent looks into the national security investigations of the Quebec student, union, and sovereignty movements, which eventually provoked public protests against RCMP wrongdoings in the 1970s. The public scrutiny and parliamentary review led to the government move to take security surveillance work out of the hands of the RCMP and give it to the new body, CSIS. But similar national security campaigns have continued with CSIS surveillance against the union movement and particularly the Canadian Union of Postal Workers (CUPW), as Evert Hoogers demonstrates. Those surveillance efforts have even been broadened to include Arabs and Muslims living in Canada in the context of the 1991 Gulf War, as Zuhair Kashmeri informs us.

The book's final section, "The Continuing Surveillance State," shows how the campaigns continue today, as Karen Pearlston reminds us in the pepper-spraying and arbitrary arrests of student protestors against APEC at the University of British Columbia. Indeed, security issues, CSIS, and the RCMP have continued to be much in the news. For one thing, CSIS agents appear to have acquired enhanced powers for spying on university campuses. According to one report, the Liberal government has given the spy agency "a greater measure of independence to approve the activities of campus sources."[11] Seemingly, spying on students and staff has once again become, as during the 1960s, a normal espionage activity. What remains unknown is how many of the agency's two thousand staff members or numerous informants participate in such activities.

Meanwhile, evidence has surfaced that the agency is having troubles. Its agents have lost files. They have had computers with classified information stolen from vehicles parked at ball games. Other revelations have come to light about the agency's operations. The parliamentary oversight committee has appeared to have been uninformed and subject to stonewalling. Recently former agents have spoken to the media about internal conflicts, and the agency's labour relations appear to be in a mess.

No sooner had the reports about internal malfunctioning of CSIS died down when a new security scandal surfaced. In May 2000 press reports revealed that the federal government's Human Resources Department had compiled a huge computer database of information on individual Canadian citizens, raising great concerns once again about privacy and state surveillance. The database contained two thousand pieces of personal and financial information on each of thirty-three million Canadians, living or dead, and under existing regulations the RCMP and CSIS could have access to these vast computer files in the normal course of investigating individuals. By the end of May, after considerable public pressure, the government had announced that it would eliminate computer links between the Human Resources database and other government agencies, and the department would only be allowed to release information without personal identifiers. At the same time major concerns continued over the release of personal information by state agencies for "security reasons." Scandal has recently been compounded by illegality at CSIS. Former CSIS agent John Farrell revealed in the summer of 2000 that CSIS continues to be involved in undercover surveillance work against unions, including the Canadian Union of Postal Workers. CUPW is calling for a public inquiry into surveillance of its members and union activities. The "dirty tricks" of the 1960s and 1970s are continuing today.

What theoretical insights do these new studies and the continuing problems surrounding state surveillance support? "How the Centre Holds—National Security as an Ideological Practice" provides a critical summary and reiterates that national security is an ideological practice that needs to be challenged.

## Notes

1. The categories are from the RCMP files index—Finding AID, RG 146, vol. 1–4.
2. Reginald Whitaker, "Origins of the Canadian Government's Internal Security System, 1946–52," *Canadian Historical Review* 65,2 (June 1984), pp.157–58; J.L. Granatstein, *A Man of Influence: Norman A. Robertson and Canadian State Craft 1929–1968* (Ottawa: Deneau, 1981), pp.181–82, 272–76.
3. See Reg Whitaker and Gary Marcuse, *Cold War Canada: The Making of a National Insecurity State, 1945–1957* (Toronto: University of Toronto Press, 1994); Larry Hannant, *The Infernal Machine: Investigating the Loyalty of Canada's Citizens* (Toronto: University of Toronto Press, 1995); and Gregory S. Kealey and Reg Whitaker, *R.C.M.P. Security Bulletins* (St. John's, Nfld.: Canadian Committee on Labour History, various years).
4. This information comes from documents released as part of Steve Hewitt's research. Access Request 98-A-000B5 and National Archives of Canada (NAC), Record of the Canadian Security Intelligence Service (CSIS), RG 146, vol. 3115.
5. Dean Beeby, "RCMP Had Plan to Intern 'Subversives,' Proposal Called for Communists— and Their Children—to Be Rounded up at the Outbreak of War," *The Globe and Mail*, Jan. 24, 2000, p.A2.
6. See Philip Corrigan, "On Moral Regulation," *Sociological Review* 5,29 (1981), pp.313–16. For Canadian explorations using this approach, see Mariana Valverde, *The Age of Light, Soap and Water: Moral Reform in English Canada, 1885–1925* (Toronto: McClelland and Stewart, 1991); and Carolyn Strange and Tina Loo, *Making Good: Law and Moral Regulation in Canada, 1867–1939* (Toronto: University of Toronto Press, 1997).
7. A CSIS spokesperson reiterated in 1998 that security clearances could still be denied to "closeted" gay men or lesbians on the grounds that they were vulnerable to blackmail. Brian K. Smith, CBC Radio, April 14, 1998.
8. See the following Canadian Press stories: Alan Jeffries, April 10, 1994; and Dean Beeby, "RCMP Issues Apology for Spy Reports on N.S. Blacks," July 20, 1994. Thanks to Dean Beeby for these references.
9. See Hewitt and Pender, chapters 6 and 7, in this book. On the surveillance of Native Studies at Laurentian University, see NAC, CSIS, RG 146, vol. 3199, file 95-A, 00094, pp.284–92.
10. Those barriers led to the Sudbury conference's motion calling for changes to the Access to Information Act to make it easier to gain access to information. See p.212.
11. *The Globe and Mail*, Sept. 13, 1999.

# PART I

# ORIGINS OF THE NATIONAL (IN)SECURITY STATE

*Anti-communist ideology at work: Communists depicted as throwing an effigy of Jesus into a garbage pit.* (I.O.D.E., *Echoes*, Spring 1948)

**DIETER K. BUSE**

one ✷ ✷ ✷

# Observing the Political and Informing on the Personal: State Surveillance Systems in a European Context

Spying on opponents has a long, but not an honourable, history. Some countries have taken their penchant for espionage to extreme heights—or, perhaps better, depths—and many people in general remain unaware of the extent and nature of state surveillance. For instance, the incredible extent of spying on political opponents and informing on private life in the German Democratic Republic became known only after the East German state collapsed in 1989/90. That state's system of monitoring citizens and informing on all aspects of personal life—work done even by friends and relatives—generated over two hundred kilometres of personnel files by the Stasi, the state security office.[1] Closer to home, in the United States, the Federal Bureau of Investigation (FBI) enlisted more than three hundred informers, paying them $1.6 million between 1960 and 1976, to spy on three thousand members of the U.S. Socialist Workers Party, a Trotskyist group. In that case, the FBI also used more than one thousand additional unpaid informers.[2]

The extent of secret police observing and informing—as well as its nature and other specifics—has for the most part not been well known, especially in supposedly democratic states. In Canada, for example, a television program aired in early 1998 on the misuse of psychiatry for state security reasons.[3] At issue were events in Montreal during the 1950s, when functionaries in a psychiatric clinic were secretly observing mentally and emotionally distressed persons. The institute director, Dr. Ewen Cameron, later head of the American Psychological Association, was reporting to state agencies on the effects of reprogramming minds. In this case observation supposedly undertaken to help patients medically gave way to observation for state purposes. Privacy and medical confidentiality were being violated for the political use of a foreign security agency, the U.S. Central Intelligence Agency (CIA). In 1977 the CIA acknowledged that "more than 80 institutions including 44 colleges or universities, and 185 non-government researchers were used in the tests," and former officials of the Allan Memorial Institute revealed the CIA funding.[4] The ultimate purpose of this attempt to get into the deepest recesses of citizen minds in the facility's "Sleep Room" remained the same as in all forms of surveillance: the state and its allies sought ever more ways to find out about and to control its citizens.[5]

The extremes in surveillance need to be placed in historical perspective, especially since Canada, like the United States, had only very small foreign and domestic intelligence systems before the twentieth century. Many of the present forms of state surveillance date from the nineteenth century. In Britain, in response to the threat of revolt and organized protests by workers during the early industrial era, the Home Office set up a system of spying to watch machine-breakers (or Luddites), union organizers, and those who questioned the enclosure of common land. E.P. Thompson used those spy reports in his classic study on the making of the English working class.[6] Similarly repressive, and partly in response to the ideas that the French Revolution of 1789 had spread throughout Europe, the Russian Ochrinka, or secret police department, was established under Nicholas I in 1826 to monitor liberals and other "radicals," and many others besides.[7] About the same time, Prince Metternich's Austrian regime established a surveillance system and sent out informers, especially among university students and middle-class radicals seeking to end the strictures (censorship, controlled meetings, and regulations on political groups) of re-established absolutism after 1815. Much of the limited and haphazard Central European domestic surveillance system came to light in studies on the European Revolutions of 1848. Ironically, the new governments that attained power in 1848 continued and expanded the spy system so that their state security decrees "demanded no less than the general surveillance of all political societies by the police."[8] Even earlier, the eighteenth-century absolutist French state had developed an extensive secret police system to spy on its main Enlightenment "opponents,"[9] who undertook such "subversive" measures as publishing encyclopedias and philosophizing on the nature of humans. The strong central state tradition in France resulted in a continuous attempt to watch radicals and dissenters no matter who directed that state or what form it took throughout the nineteenth century.[10]

After the suppression of the Revolutions of 1848 surveillance systems became more structured. For instance, the secret police organizations of the various German states collaborated to share information on supposed radicals during the 1850s.[11] Towards the end of the century all the ministries of the interior of Europe were exchanging information on "anarchists, terrorists and socialists."[12] By then nearly every state had a formalized system of collecting, collating, and reporting information on its real and supposed opponents.

By the end of the nineteenth century most European states were not only collecting information on the political left, but also placing under scrutiny far-right radicals and individuals whose loyalty to the state was considered ambivalent (including prominent Jews in Germany and France). Whether republican or absolute monarchist, the form of state mattered little in the elite's perception of possible left-wing threats to the state and society, and in country after country the political or secret police cast a fine net. For instance, in his research on just one large German city, Hamburg, Richard J. Evans found twenty thousand political reports for the period 1892–1914.[13] The reports came mainly from informers dressed as workers. These special undercover police reported on the public mood by noting what workers said about almost everything: work, unemployment, rents, religion, crime, police, social democracy, unions, imperialism, foreigners, and militarism. In addition to those special constables' pub surveillance, Hamburg's regular political, that is, secret, police systematically collected information on "anarchists and socialists" by keeping dossiers on speakers. They kept records of significant events such as May Day parades and trade union festivals, and gathered information on leftist newspapers, leading personalities, and organizations and clubs associated with Social Democracy. The resulting dossiers numbered in the thousands, and the findings were shared with the Prussian and national counterparts of the Hamburg police.

This type of widespread surveillance became the norm for the modern state in Europe and North America, despite a wide diversity of ideology among the elites. The systems developed usually comprised a central set of personnel files and another set of quarterly and annual summaries. The summaries usually covered each major region or political division of the country. Topping this layered cake of information was an annual situational summary for the whole country drawing upon the local reports and the detailed surveillance of individuals, events, and movements. To provide the information, local police officers worked with informers, collaborators from among the citizenry, and institutions such as the military and churches. Such systems for collecting and collating information became the norm within nearly all European state hierarchies, with the collected surveillance results passed from hand to hand up a bureaucratic ladder. What would change over time was the thoroughness of the spying, some of the technology employed, the professionalization of the police spies, the types of informers, how they infiltrated targeted groups, and the increased diversity of the targets of surveillance. But the bureaucratic model with its pattern of collecting and passing information would remain intact.

These secret police systems and surveillance primarily originated in attempts to gauge the strength and nature of political opponents. During the nineteenth century the secrecy surrounding the establishment and growth of these bureaucracies meant that little public discussion occurred on who was targeted or why. Some individuals, such as the late-nineteenth-century German Social Democratic leader August Bebel, knew they were being followed and their activities monitored. Noticing that one policeman was observing him quite frequently, Bebel called him his "little poodle."[14] Such lampooning of shoddy police methods by the Social Democrats slurred over what they wanted discussed in the weak German parliament: the fundamental issue of citizenship and political rights.

The French and German systems of surveillance, just as in other parts of Europe and North America, were originally set up and operated in secret. Only a select part of the state's officials knew the extent of the spying (not dissimilar to post-World War II Canada or East Germany). Few limits were set to infiltration, and the spies mostly followed the demands of their arbitrary and undemocratic masters. Whether in parliamentary Britain or autocratic Russia, an implicit model seems to have existed in the minds of the European elites: the state represented the mainstream of society, and anyone who sought change was considered to be on the fringe or influenced by foreigners. As Kaiser Wilhelm II proclaimed about the German Social Democrats, they were in his eyes people "without a fatherland." For the elites, who saw themselves as representing the law-abiding centre of society and equated opposition primarily with the political aspirations of labour, unions, and the left, especially socialists and anarchists, obtaining public support or parliamentary legitimacy for secret surveillance was not an issue. Though the main focus of surveillance was the political intentions and numerical strengths of supposedly dangerous opponents, by 1914 the systems included some surveillance of what was then seen as part of the private sphere, with serious implications for cultural controls and norms, such as sexual preferences or family patterns.[15]

How extensive was this system before World War I? In some cases archival materials that would provide a detailed answer are only now becoming available. In others, because the regimes were overthrown or defeated in war, much documentation became accessible in the 1920s and 1950s; though many sources were destroyed or cleansed to protect informers. For instance, in late 1918, when they attained power, the German Social Democrats agreed to the destruction of central police personnel files in Berlin. At that time they tried to protect the identity of informers, some of whom included their own leaders. However, with copies of some documents from the regional or local level combined with other sources, much about the organization, functioning, size, and personnel of the original systems can be reconstructed. Similarly, when the Bolsheviks came to power in Russia they published Tsarist secret police records for the period before 1917; but they did this quite selectively, as recent increased access to former Soviet archives has revealed. In response to attacks on their new regime during the Civil War, the Bolsheviks quickly went beyond the Tsarist model of police repression to spread a system of surveillance with even smaller meshes over the Soviet Union. It was a system that would be copied and extended after World War II in countries under Soviet influence.[16]

World War I witnessed the militarization of foreign and domestic intelligence in many European countries. The military elite set up parallel systems of surveillance or took control of the information emerging from civilian police systems of surveillance.[17] Yet the organizational pattern of collecting at the local level and providing frequent regional and national summaries, plus maintaining extensive dossiers on persons identified as being outside the state's concept of the norm, continued in the same fashion.[18] What changed decisively in the twentieth century was the role of informants. Research on the Gestapo in Nazi Germany as well as on other European secret police systems illustrates the importance of informers' ideological outlook—meaning, the degree of agreement with the regime as opposed to personal or material motivations—to the success of spying on citizens.[19] The number of persons prepared to inform on those identified as "outsiders," people held to be different or unworthy by the state, has been found to be very high, so that only small differences may exist between those who informed for the Nazi and Soviet regime and those who played the same role during the Cold War or any other "crisis" in North America. Not duress by the state, but ideological affinity and cultural homogeneity may be the crucial element in informants' motives.

Documents from the archives of very few countries showing the extent of their systems of surveillance have been published. Fewer still have access to information or privacy legislation that protects the citizen against encroachments by the state.[20] The lingering effects of the Cold War, when state secrecy was legitimized for alleged national security reasons, continue to hide the nature and extent of surveillance. Further, state bureaucrats, whose jobs include defending the ruling elites, control access to that documentation. In all European countries the access rights of citizens remain circumscribed in order to protect the system of surveillance—as opposed to the state protecting its citizens. Journalists and jaundiced former civil servants plus a few idealists have played more important roles than parliamentary review committees in exposing the nature, extent, and arbitrariness of state surveillance of citizens in post-World War II Europe and North America.

A few examples illustrate the pattern during the later part of the Cold War era. In 1961, after the German newsmagazine *Der Spiegel* obtained documents showing that Western troops were not well prepared for a Soviet attack, the German government jailed a number of journalists, had some kidnapped in Spain and shipped back, tapped phones, and followed individuals as it sought to accuse the newspaper of betraying the country. What became known as the Spiegel Affair or scandal would bring down a government but also reveal the extent of state power employed against its own citizens.[21] When a few groups engaged in terror against that state, the German response, in 1972, was a *Radikalenerlass*, or decree against radicals, which excluded thousands from serving in the German civil service, gave the state the right to monitor subscriptions to newspapers and journals, and extended telephone surveillance.[22] In 1973 only 104 cases of telephone tapping were registered, and by 1996 the number was 6,428. Most significantly, the vice-president of the federal secret information bureau supplied his political friends with information gained through surveillance.[23] Still, the related issue of privacy rights led to at least one German census being delayed and restrictions placed on the gathering of electronic data on individuals.

In France journalists revealed that between 1983 and 1986 the president had initiated a system of secret surveillance of alleged opponents—writers, journalists, and lawyers—supposedly in defence of the state.[24] Though receiving much press coverage, the issue died as the right of the state to secrecy took precedence over French citizens' right to know precisely who was spied upon for what reasons. Citizens' rights and civil liberties have few legislative safeguards in Europe. Thus, while, for example, the extent of surveillance in the German Democratic Republic before its demise may seem extreme, we must remember that few other states have had to open their archives and little is known about internal spying except for a few instances that sneak out by accident.

Canada's own extensive system of spying during the twentieth century, which began to be revealed only during the RCMP scandals of the 1970s—barn burnings, thefts of political party records, and smear campaigns against individuals—thus follows a long tradition based on the British and European systems.[25] In response to post-World War I labour unrest the Canadian state reacted much as the European states had done when faced with early industrial unrest. The lateness of industrialization undoubtedly accounted for some of the delay by the Canadian state in transforming part of the RCMP into a secret police surveillance organization, but its system of reporting, collecting, and collating reflects the systems established during the nineteenth century. Ironically, in today's supposedly "open" society based on the rapid spread of communications, this particular form of state knowledge about citizens remains hidden from citizens' eyes. And, in an era when taxes and state expenditures have been called into question, the realm of surveillance is one aspect of state activity that has gone largely uncut, and unexamined.

## Notes

1. Stefan Wolle, "In the Labyrinth of the Documents: The Archival Legacy of the SED-State," *German History* 10 (1992), pp.352ff. More generally, see Nancy Wolfe, *Policing a Socialist Society: The German Democratic Republic* (Westport, Conn.: Greenwood, 1992); and Larry Hannant's chapter here.
2. *The Globe and Mail*, Jan. 21, 1978, p.15. The article reported that court documents revealed that in Chicago alone the FBI paid $2.5 million to more than five thousand spies who reported on residents and organizations. For background, see Natalie Robins, *Alien Ink: The FBI's War on Freedom of Expression* (New York: W. Morrow, 1992).
3. The issue had earlier been publicized by court cases and Anne Collins, *In the Sleep Room: The Story of the CIA Brainwashing Experiments in Canada* (Toronto: Lester and Orpen Dennys, 1988).
4. *The Globe and Mail*, Aug. 4, 1977.
5. Foreign intelligence, by contrast, has been well served by such studies as: Ernest R. May, ed., *Knowing One's Enemies: Intelligence Assessment before the Two World Wars* (Princeton, N.J.: Princeton University Press, 1986); and Jeffrey T. Richelson, *A Century of Spies: Intelligence in the Twentieth Century* (Oxford: Oxford University Press, 1995). Finding out whether such cases are extreme ones or the norms in a larger pattern would require access to all countries' documentation and a thorough international history of security systems. At present none exists.
6. See E.P. Thompson, *The Making of the Working Class* (London: Penguin, 1961), especially pp.530ff. Christopher Andrew, *Secret Service: The Making of the British Intelligence Community* (London: Heinemann, 1986), chap. 1, mentions that background but mainly focuses on espionage and direct violent threats to the state as opposed to systematic surveillance of citizens exercising their rights.
7. Fredric Zuckerman, *The Tsarist Secret Police in Russian Society, 1880–1917* (London: Macmillan, 1996), especially Parts I and II, which provide background on the earlier period.
8. W. Siemann, "The Revolutions of 1848–49 and the Persistence of the Old Regime in Germany (1848–1850)," in *German History since 1800*, ed. Mary Fulbrook (London: Arnold, 1997), p.118; see also J. Sperber, *The European Revolutions, 1848–1851* (Cambridge: Cambridge University Press, 1994).
9. François Moreau, *Le roman vrai de l'Encyclopédie* (Paris: Découvertes Gallimard, 1990), reprints some of the police reports on individuals such as Denis Diderot.
10. A classic study using many secret police files is R.C. Cobb, *The Police and the People: French Popular Protest 1789–1820* (Oxford: Clarendon Press, 1970), which notes the role of the informer but mainly uses the police reports as a source to define popular unrest.
11. The documents relating to this collaboration have been published in I. Materna and H.-J. Schreckenbach, eds., *Dokumente aus geheimen Archiven* (Weimar: Bölhaus, 1987ff), vol. 5. The introductions to this collection provide the best description of the organization and functioning of the German secret police before 1918.
12. Some of the exchanges were preserved in Politisches Archiv des Auswartigen Amts, Bonn, Europa generalia, Nr. 82, Nr. 1, especially for the late 1890s.
13. Richard J. Evans, ed., *Kneipengespräche im Kaiserreich: Stimmungsberichte der Hamburger Politischen Polizei 1892–1914* (Reinbeck: Rowolt, 1989).
14. See his recounting of his experience in his "quiet war" with his observers in *August Bebel: Ausgewählte Reden und Schriften* (Munich: K.G. Sauer, 1995), vol. 6, pp.571–82.

15. See, for example, James D. Steakley, *The Homosexual Emancipation Movement in Germany* (New York: Arno, 1975).

16. Richelson, *Century of Spies*, chap. 4.

17. For Britain and Germany see, respectively: M. Occleshaw, *Armour against Fate: British Military Intelligence in the First World War* (London: Columbus, 1989); and Wilhelm Deist, ed., *Militar und Innenpolitik im Weltkrieg, 1914–1918* (Dusseldorf: Droste, 1970). In the case of France a few examples are available in Jean-Jacques Becker, *The Great War and the French People* (New York: St. Martin's Press, 1986), p.232. Also see D.K. Buse, "Domestic Intelligence and German Military Leadership, 1914–1918," *Intelligence and National Security*, v.15 (2000).

18. Andrew, *Secret Service*, chap. 4, shows the intensification of reporting and the increasing overlap of civilian and military surveillance for Britain.

19. See special issue of *The Journal of Modern History*, 1995, on surveillance and informants; Robert Gellately is preparing a book on denunciation in European history.

20. An excellent overview of the Australian pattern by which archival materials slowly became available, and the extent of surveillance down under became known, is David McKnight, *Australia's Spies and Their Secrets* (St. Leonards: Allen and Unwin, 1994).

21. See R. Bunn, *German Politics and the Spiegel Affair* (Baton Rouge: Louisiana University Press, 1968), pp.51ff.

22. The most comprehensive review of the restrictions placed on civil rights by this decree is in G. Braunthal, *Political Loyalty and Public Service in West Germany* (Amherst: University of Massachusetts Press, 1990); updated summary in Dieter K. Buse and Juergen C. Doerr, eds., *Modern Germany* (New York: Garland Publishing, 1998), pp.306–7. Braunthal finds that the West German government "on numerous occasions infringed on the civil liberties of all residents." The decree illustrates well the attempt to marginalize all who oppose, protest, or even think and behave differently. Contemporaries were well aware of the dangers; see, for instance, *Die Zeit*, April 28 and August 4, 1978. The latter article presents the statistics on the hundreds of thousands of persons reviewed for civil service positions in each federal state as well as what minor acts could make a person to be seen as untrustworthy in the eyes of state officials.

23. *Der Spiegel* 17 (1997), pp.66–69.

24. See, for instance, *Le Monde*, April 12, 1997, pp.6, 15.

25. The British background to the Canadian system has been emphasized in Larry Hannant, *The Infernal Machine: Investigating the Loyalty of Canada's Citizens* (Toronto: University of Toronto Press, 1995), chap. 1.

GREGORY S. KEALEY

two ★ ★ ★

# Spymasters, Spies, and Their Subjects: The RCMP and Canadian State Repression, 1914–39

The Royal Canadian Mounted Police (RCMP) Security Service—for most of the twentieth century Canada's largely secret political police force—is finally being forced out of the historical shadows. The revelations of the McDonald and Keable royal commissions—which led to the creation of the Canadian Security Intelligence Service (CSIS)—and the passage of federal Access to Information legislation have combined to allow historians to begin to penetrate the deep shadows and scrutinize the role of Canada's police spies. This new historical work is not without its controversies, and no doubt more debate will follow.[1]

One thing the historical record now clearly shows is that from its inception the RCMP has equated dissent with the foreign-born. Indeed, the issue of ethnicity is crucial to an understanding of the Canadian security regime. It comes into play both in terms of the people targeted by the RCMP and those doing the targeting. In the period 1914–39 the ethnic identity of not only immigrant workers and communists but also RCMP officers and their spies emerged as a critical factor in the Canadian state's surveillance systems.

From the 1860s to the present, Canada's various secret police agencies have primarily focused their attention on immigrants, labour, and the left.[2] Canada has had a secret service since 1864, when John A. Macdonald, then joint-premier of the Province of Canada, created the office to help protect Canada's borders, both against U.S. incursions related to the Civil War and against the threat of Fenian invasion.[3] The story of the Fenians—Irish nationalist revolutionaries—nicely captures many of the salient themes. As immigrants to North America they simultaneously worked to transform North American industrial capitalism from within and to make revolution against Britain in their native land. They prefigured much of what the Canadian secret service would work against throughout its existence.

While it was initially the Fenians that resulted in a secret police, targets since then have included "foreign agitators," "Reds," and enemy aliens. Significantly, though, the repression of labour and the left neither began nor ended with the state, and even state repression was far broader than the operations of the RCMP Security Service. An array of private and public police forces worked together cooperatively, and non-police institutions, both state and private, also exercised repressive functions.[4]

From 1864 to 1868 the security service was under the authority of Gilbert McMicken's Western Frontier Constabulary, which in 1868 became the Dominion Police. One of Britain's earliest and most famous secret agents, Henri Le Caron, worked in close co-operation with McMicken, Macdonald's spy chief.[5]

In the years from the outbreak of World War I until the start of World War II the major structures of the Canadian Secret Service, as it functioned until the creation of CSIS in 1984, were established, as was its underlying ideological logic. From the outset this ideology was nativist, anti-Semitic, and, above all, anti-communist. Initially imperialist, and closely identified with the interests of the British Empire, the Service later switched metropolitan allegiance from London to Washington.[6]

The outbreak of World War I brought a reorganization of Canadian security and intelligence organization. In the first fifteen years of the twentieth century such matters still rested in the hands of the Dominion Police, the force organized by McMicken in the aftermath of the alleged Fenian assassination of D'Arcy McGee. Primarily a force to provide guards for government buildings, the Dominion Police, under Chief Commissioner Sir Percy Sherwood at the war's outset and then under Acting Commissioner Albert Cawdron after Sherwood's retirement, also co-ordinated intelligence work with the emerging British secret service, another early twentieth-century phenomenon.[7] Under McMicken co-operation with the British included ongoing surveillance of Irish nationalists by secret agent Le Caron. Under Sherwood and after it also included surveillance of Indian nationalists, especially in Vancouver. Thus William Hopkinson, a former Indian police officer, served simultaneously as a Canadian and British secret agent on the west coast from 1909 to 1914, when he was assassinated by Sikh nationalist Mewa Singh in the aftermath of the Komagata Maru incident. (The Komagata Maru, a Japanese-owned freighter, had arrived in Vancouver from Hong Kong in May 1914 carrying 376 natives of the Punjab, primarily Sikhs. This direct challenge to Canada's racist immigration restrictions failed, and the vessel returned to Calcutta after spending months in the Vancouver harbour. After the ship's arrival in India, a riot ensued in which police killed at least twenty passengers.) Hopkinson worked openly as an Immigration inspector and was also paid as a secret operative by both the Dominion Police and Indian intelligence.[8] After his death his secret service mantle passed to Malcolm Reid, his former superior at Immigration in Vancouver. The Dominion Police also played an important Imperial role during the period of U.S. neutrality in the initial years of World War I by functioning as the conduit through which British intelligence material on German subversive activities in the United States was passed on to U.S. authorities. In so doing the Dominion Police aided British intelligence in its successful effort to disguise its active secret service work in the United States before that country's declaration of war against Germany.[9]

While Irish and Indian revolutionaries provided the first targets for Canada's political police, it was the Bolshevik revolution and the domestic labour revolt of 1917–20 that led to a reorganization of Canada's secret service.[10] After an initial flirtation in the fall of 1918 with a civilian security agency—the Public Safety Branch of the Department of Justice under C.H. Cahan—the government of Robert Borden turned to the Royal North-West Mounted Police (RNWMP), which had played a key role in handling the Winnipeg General Strike of 1919. The RNWMP had begun recruiting secret agents in the early days of World War I, and by December 1918 employed eight secret agents and six detectives across Western Canada. Many government officials and much of the Canadian bourgeoisie felt threatened by the rising spectre of Bolshevism, and with the increase in labour agitation in 1917–20 the Borden government amalgamated the Dominion Police and the RNWMP into the RCMP, which quickly assumed responsibility for domestic intelligence and security work, a mandate it would retain for over sixty years, until the creation of CSIS.[11] The RCMP continued the pattern of using secret agents, especially to track so-called subversives, from 1919 onwards. According to a memo from Commissioner A.B. Perry, RCMP secret agents were to become fully acquainted with labour organizations to determine if they had Bolshevik tenden- cies.[12] In these early years the RCMP Security Service began developing its distinct identity, but did not become a separate part of the RCMP until 1936, when the Intelligence Section was officially formed.[13]

Perry was succeeded as commissioner in 1923 by Cortlandt Starnes, who had been in charge of the RNWMP contingent during the Winnipeg General Strike. Starnes ran the Force through the 1920s, a period of stagnation and downsizing. Only the return to provincial policing in Saskatchewan in 1928, where Starnes used the Security Service as a strong pro-RCMP lever, and the election of the Conservative government of R.B. Bennett reversed the tide. Bennett's choice of General J.H. MacBrien to head the Force after Starnes's retirement, combined with the takeover of the Preventive Service (Customs) and the renewal of provin- cial policing in the Maritime provinces, Manitoba, and Alberta, led to a major reinvigoration of the RCMP after 1932. Bennett chose MacBrien as the new com- missioner because he was impressed with MacBrien's fervent anti-communism, military background, and emphasis on the need for a strong political police force. True to form, MacBrien became the first RCMP commissioner to speak out against communism, and he founded the RCMP *Quarterly* as a medium for informing the nation about communist activities.[14] Just as Starnes had used the Security Service to buttress his arguments for the RCMP role in Saskatchewan in 1928, MacBrien did the same in 1932.[15] Indeed, the new commissioner issued a highly unusual General Order to celebrate the Force's expansion. In it he emphasized that the Criminal Investigation Branch (CIB), in which the Security Service resided, was the key element of the RCMP. "It corresponds to the General Staff of the Army," the former chief of the general staff said. Moreover, MacBrien argued:

> The past record of the RCMP is one to be proud of, and it is thought that there is a very special opportunity, at the present time, for the Force to enhance its splendid reputation through the opportunity that now exists to render a very special service to Canada in the present conditions prevailing in the country, due to the eco- nomic depression, and the activities of the Communists.[16]

The increasingly repressive nature of Bennett's response to the Depression also fuelled the growth of the Security Service within the Force. The intelligence functions which for well over a decade had been largely centred on one officer—C.F. Hamilton—became more formal under MacBrien and grew considerably as the Depression continued. World War II and the Gouzenko affair led to its massive growth in the Cold War period.[17] But this growth was not purely a phenomenon of the post-World War II Cold War. To put it more bluntly, the Cold War commenced with the success of the Bolsheviks in 1917.[18]

The RCMP's obsession with communism shows itself starkly in a response to a letter sent to the Prime Minister's Office from businessman A.L. Lawes of Montreal. Writing in late 1938, Lawes had noted that "there will be little disagreement with the suggestion that these three enemies [of democracy] are Nazi, Fascist and Communist, in the order named."[19] Inspector Charles Rivett-Carnac (who would later head the RCMP Security Service) took six pages to refute Lawes's analyses, ultimately concluding:

> The main point which I wish to make in this connection is that while the Communist program embodies the destruction of the state apparatus of the Government and the setting up of a new economic order, the Nazi program which has been brought into being in Germany has retained the principles of the old system to the extent that a modified form of capitalism now exists in that country.[20]

In essence, the RCMP showed more concern in January 1939 about the threat to capitalism than the threat to liberal democracy—even though RCMP officers, including Rivett-Carnac, were sitting on committees concerned with the preparation of war against Germany. Minister of Justice Ernest Lapointe concurred with Rivett-Carnac's memorandum, adding that "regardless of what military pacts were signed," communism was at least as abhorrent as fascism.[21]

By far the fullest picture of Canadian political policing is available for the relatively short period from 1917 until the creation of the RCMP in 1920. For reasons that remain obscure (and were subsequently deemed to be a mistake in 1971), the RNWMP's historical records for those early years were passed to the Public Archives of Canada in the early 1960s.[22] These records include complete registers of the antisubversive (anti-Bolshevik, in the Force's vocabulary) efforts of those early years and the institutional record of the creation of the first secret agent network. Even now, with the deposit in the National Archives of Canada of the vast remaining records of the RCMP Security Service, the nature of the Access to Information process leaves researchers with a far less complete record for the years since 1920.[23]

The major documentation falls into five primary categories: personal history files, subject files, publication files, RCMP personnel files, and the RCMP Security Bulletins. The first three are raw data accumulated by the Mounties from covert and other sources. The personal history files, which commenced in 1919, would, by 1977, at the time of the McDonald Commission inquiry, run to some eight hundred thousand files with a name index of 1.3 million. The subject files, which primarily focus on radical political parties, foreign-language organizations, and labour unions, are equally massive. The publication files are extensive collections of radical newspapers and magazines, sometimes with appended translations and commentaries. The RCMP personnel files sometimes inadvertently provide considerable information about security and intelligence work. The Security Bulletins are weekly or monthly compilations of digested intelligence intended to keep the Force's political and bureaucratic masters up to date on the state of the Canadian left as seen by the Security Service. Unfortunately most of the Bulletins from their origin in 1919 through to 1933 have been lost or destroyed by the Security Service.[24]

## The Spymasters

Who were the spymasters and the spies? Among the spymasters were the last two commissioners of the Dominion Police, the first four RCMP commissioners, and the first four heads of the Security Service.

Sir Percy Sherwood (1854–1940) was Ottawa-born and came from a combined military and police background. A member of the Governor General's Foot Guards, he rose to command the 43rd Regiment with the rank of lieutenant-colonel. He served as Ottawa chief of police from 1879 to 1882, when he joined the Dominion Police as a superintendent; and he was later promoted to commissioner (1885) and chief commissioner (1913). He also served as chief commissioner of the Boy Scouts Association of Canada in 1910–18.[25] His successor, Albert John Cawdron, was also born in Ottawa. He joined the Dominion Police in 1897 and later enlisted in the first Canadian contingent going to South Africa for the Boer War (1899–1902). After returning to Canada he entered the secret service branch of the Dominion Police and succeeded Sherwood in 1918. He joined the RCMP after its creation and rose to assistant commissioner before retiring in 1936.[26]

The first commissioner of the RCMP, A.B. Perry (1860–1956), stemmed from United Empire Loyalist stock in Napanee, Ontario, graduated in the Royal Military College's first class, and joined the RNWMP in 1883 after a brief British military career in the Royal Engineers. As a Mountie he served in the North-West Rebellion and was commissioner of the RNWMP from 1900 to 1920 and of the new RCMP in 1920–23.[27] His successor, Cortlandt Starnes (1864–1934), was born in Montreal, also of Loyalist background. He served with the 65th Regiment in the North-West Rebellion, joined the RNWMP in 1886, and served as commissioner in 1923–31.[28] General J.H. MacBrien (1878–1938) hailed from Myrtle, Ontario. He served briefly as a Mountie at the turn of the century, fought in the Boer War, and served six years in the South African Constabulary before returning to Canada and the military. He rose to the rank of brigadier-general in World War I and served as chief of the general staff in 1920–28. From 1931 until his death in 1938 he headed the RCMP.[29] The last commissioner during the first half of the twentieth century was S.T. Wood (1889–1961), whose father, Zachary, had been assistant commissioner of the RNWMP. Ottawa-born, Wood graduated from Upper Canada College and the Royal Military College, joined the RNWMP in 1912, and served as commissioner from 1938 until his retirement in 1950.[30]

Rounding out this picture is the Force's first intelligence officer, C.F. Hamilton (1869–1933). Born in Roslin, Ontario, and a graduate of Queen's University, Hamilton became a journalist and covered the Boer War for *The Globe*. He was active in the militia and authored many books as an amateur military historian. He joined the RNWMP in 1913, becoming assistant comptroller in 1914 before taking a leave of absence to serve in the militia as deputy chief press censor and director of cable censorship during World War I. Hamilton rejoined the RNWMP in 1919 just in time for its reorganization into the RCMP in 1920, and was quickly appointed secretary of the RCMP, a title later changed to liaison and intelligence officer. He was one of the few RCMP officers whose full-time duties were intelligence and security, and as liaison officer he was the second-highest-paid member of the Force, behind the commissioner, to whom he reported directly.

Hamilton's successors in intelligence followed a slightly different pattern.[31] Arthur Patteson (1887–1934), who had briefly been Hamilton's assistant, was an English immigrant educated at Marlborough, one of the most prestigious schools in England. After an attempt at farming in Alberta he joined the Force in 1914. He made corporal in 1917, enrolled in the RNWMP Cavalry Unit in the Canadian Expeditionary Force, and rejoined the RNWMP in 1919 as a Sergeant. He worked as an orderly room clerk in Edmonton until he made inspector in 1932 and was called to Ottawa as the ailing Hamilton's assistant in late 1931. There Patteson assumed more and more of Hamilton's duties, and with Hamilton's death in 1933 he took over the newly created post of intelligence officer, which replaced the liaison position. As intelligence officer Patteson was responsible for not only Hamilton's old responsibilities but also the Criminal Investigation Branch security work. After his unexpected death by heart attack at age forty-eight, the *RCMP Quarterly* obituary emphasized his British public-school background.[32]

Patteson's immediate successors were also British immigrants. Robson Armitage, an RCMP inspector decorated for his role in capturing an armed bank robber in Ottawa, served for only six months and retired in 1950 as an assistant commissioner. Charles Rivett-Carnac (1935–39 and 1944–45), was born in Eastbourne, Sussex, in 1901. His father was an officer in the Indian police, and he grew up in India until returning to England for public school. He later worked in India in the 1920s after a brief period in France during World War I as an ambulance driver. In the early 1920s he migrated to Canada and joined the Force.[33] Rivett-Carnac served in the Yukon for over a decade before being appointed intelligence officer in 1935 and returning to the post for a year in 1944–45 before being appointed director of criminal investigations and later commissioner.

Hence, of the ten police leaders, seven were Canadian-born of middle-class stock, and two of these claimed Loyalist ancestry. Two were RMC graduates and eight had military experience. Six had prior police experience and one (Hamilton) had experience as the deputy chief press censor. The three English immigrants had public-school backgrounds, First World War experience, and, in one case, Indian police background.

The pattern is clear. The spymasters represented an Anglo-Canadian, Central-Canadian-born, military elite with a few British immigrants with public-school backgrounds thrown into the mix in the 1930s and 1940s. Our spymasters all flourished in what historian Desmond Morton describes as the "moment of Canadian Militarism." That they imported this militarism and its concomitant masculinity into the new RCMP with its paramilitary structure is not surprising.[34] Indeed, an attempt to place the RCMP under the new Department of National Defence in 1922 was avoided only because of Progressive Party opposition. Not only were there no women in the Force in these early years, but marriage was largely prohibited for the rank and file (constables could only marry after twelve years, non-commissioned officers eight years) except in rare cases and then only with the permission of the commissioner upon the recommendation of the officer commanding. Barracks life with military discipline was the lot of the young Mountie recruit. All autobiographical accounts, and RCMP *Annual Reports* as late as 1940–41, emphasize Mountie basic training as being essentially cavalry training with all the accompanying military implications.[35]

## The Spies

Not surprisingly, the rank-and-file Mountie did not share the leadership's background—and the spies shared even less. The regular Mounties who went underground in the time of the labour revolt of 1917–20, some not to surface for years, hardly fit the stereotype of the red-coated hero. The best-documented cases are those of Frank Zaneth (aka Harry Blask), whose cover was blown when he was forced to testify in the Winnipeg Strike trials, and of John Leopold (aka Jack Esselwein), the main witness at the 1931 Toronto show trial of the Communist Party of Canada (CPC) leadership.[36] There were almost certainly many other similar cases that have never surfaced and remain unknown.

Frank Zaneth was born Franco Zanetti in Gombolo, Pavia, southwest of Milan, in 1890, the son of a cabinetmaker. He moved to the United States with an older brother in 1899 and a few years later was joined by the rest of the family in Springfield, Massachusetts. He married in 1910 and the following year migrated with his new wife to Moose Jaw in the hope of acquiring a homestead, which he succeeded in doing in 1912. By 1917 his marriage had ended and he was back in Springfield. From there he applied to join the RNWMP under his newly assumed name, Frank Zaneth, and upon acceptance enlisted at Regina in December. When he completed his basic training, he was immediately sent underground to work as a secret agent, largely because of his ethnic background and language skills. Initially, in spring 1918, he worked in Quebec City seeking out draft evaders after the Easter riots against conscription. In September he moved on to Drumheller, Alberta, to investigate rumours of Industrial Workers of the World (IWW) influence among the immigrant coal-miners there. Here "Harry Blask" first stepped forward. In December he moved on to Canmore and then to Calgary, where he reported to another undercover Mountie, Corporal S.R. Waugh.

In Calgary Blask enjoyed even greater success than he had in the coal camps. He became socialist machinist George Sangster's right-hand man and through him gained access to the Socialist Party of Canada (SPC) and the whole local radical scene. In this capacity he attended the District 18 convention of the United Mine

Workers of America (UMWA) and later in March 1919 the Calgary Western Labour Conference, at which UMWA leader David Rees spotted another RNWMP agent, Robert Gosden, and denounced him as a stool pigeon. In May Blask removed himself to Regina to report personally to Perry, who conveniently arranged to have him arrested to prop up his reputation as a socialist militant. After a conviction and a week in jail, Blask returned to Calgary with his revolutionary reputation reinforced. Throughout the crucial weeks of the Winnipeg General Strike "Blask" continued to report to his RNWMP masters on every radical event in Calgary, including the identity of the radicals' own spy in the anti-strike Citizens' Committee. As the crisis intensified, RNWMP security tightened as well and headquarters sent a new controller, Staff Sergeant Hall, to handle Zaneth for fear that Waugh was too easily identifiable. Throughout the entire crisis, which included a general sympathy strike, Zaneth filed report after report from the centre of Calgary's radical community.[37]

Throughout the summer of 1919 a debate raged within state corridors. A.J. Andrews, the prosecutor for the strike trials in Winnipeg, wanted Zaneth as a star witness; the RNWMP did not want their top labour spy's cover blown. Andrews won the debate, and on December 5, 1919, "Harry Blask" made his last appearance as a key witness against Bob Russell, an SPC and One Big Union (OBU) leader. After a brief spying mission against the OBU in the United States in 1920, Zaneth turned up in Montreal as "James Laplante," allegedly a Québécois immigrant to New England now returning home with U.S. radical credentials. After a summer of undercover work there he was identified by the UMWA's Rees as a spy and denounced in the radical press. Thus ended Zaneth's career as a spy, although he rose through the Mountie hierarchy until retiring in 1951 as an assistant commissioner. His final flirtation with the repression of radicalism came in 1938, when he prepared the groundwork for what would have been the second major national prosecution of the Communist Party of Canada leadership, this time for its role in recruiting volunteers to fight for the Spanish Republic. On this occasion, despite meticulous planning and a large expenditure in preparing the legal background for the prosecutions, the RCMP was persuaded by its political masters to drop the case at the eleventh hour.[38]

John Leopold (aka Jack Esselwein, 1890–1958), who worked undercover as a secret agent in Regina for a decade, joined the Force in 1918 and retired as a superintendent in 1952. Leopold's career mimicked Zaneth's, except for a blown cover, but despite his fame as the leading anti-communist intelligence officer, much of which came in the wake of the Gouzenko controversy, his RCMP career proved far less successful. Bohemian-born Leopold, like Zaneth, was chosen for undercover work because of his ethnicity and language skills. Also like Zaneth, he was diminutive, which no doubt augmented his utility as a secret agent. (They were both under five-foot-five, shorter than the minimum height for normal service in the RCMP.)[39]

Leopold had come to Canada in 1912 and farmed in Alberta before joining the Force. Working undercover in Regina under the name of Esselwein after he finished basic training, he quickly gained the confidence of local radicals and progressed through their ranks, moving from the SPC into the CPC. A case of typhoid fever in October 1920 caused great concern on the part of his handlers, though they were seemingly far more worried about his cover than his health. To maintain the pose, another undercover Mountie, T.E. Ryan, prepared a careful subterfuge through which another left-wing activist removed the radical materials in the patient's possession; and the hospital staff co-operated with an RCMP request by refusing any visitors to the delirious Leopold.[40]

In July 1921, when he had to face a career decision to re-enlist or not, Leopold wrote: "I have no desire to become a 'secret agent' to the RCMP. If I continue my service it would be as an active member of the Force." In that same letter he also indicated what his handlers were planning for him: "If I am pressed to organize the Regina Branch of the Movement [CPC], I will do so with the least amount of effort as possible, and endeavour to get someone else to do the actual work or appear to do it. I will be on my guard against doing anything which could be brought home to me individually."[41]

Apparently the contradiction inherent in the spy who becomes an *agent provocateur* was not lost on either Leopold or his masters. Indeed, in a careful exchange of letters, the Regina officer in command, A.B. Allard, explored the implications of the problem with Commissioner Perry. Gilbert Salt, Leopold's RCMP handler, had written to Allard, who in turn sought the advice of the commissioner, on the question of the role Leopold should play in the new CPC. Salt pointed out: "Should he take an active part, presumably that of leader or organizer he would be liable to most severe punishment when the final breakup comes, as it would be out of the question to uncover him, and even if uncovered he would still be liable, as it would be impossible for him to carry on without doing criminal actions occasionally."[42]

Salt assured Allard that Leopold was willing "to go to any length the Service requires" and that the agent had been exceeding his role as a passive spy:

> He has shown himself capable of neutralizing the efforts of the leaders of the OBU on many occasions, and has not mentioned his efforts in his reports, for instance nearly all the OBU literature, especially the more radical, is sent directly to him, which instead of distributing he has been destroying in large quantities, only parting with sufficient to keep himself above suspicion. He has on many occasions by using diplomacy spoiled meetings, by being unable to find a suitable hall, or neglecting to advertise the meeting etc. He has discouraged organization work by many tricks, has diplomatically wasted OBU funds etc always at the same time being shrewd enough to keep his real object out of sight. I lay stress on this as showing that he may be counted on not to promote the Communist Party in any way on his own initiative, but only when driven or compelled to.[43]

For his part, Allard recommended to Perry that Leopold "pursue his role to the full extent provided it is not anticipated that he would ever be uncovered"—not a particularly useful assumption. Perry showed no hesitation on the matter, instructing Allard that "the opportunity offered of gaining access to Communist plans must not be allowed to escape us." While opining that it was "undesirable that Leopold should actually commit illegal acts himself, or should incite others to commit them," he nevertheless instructed that "he should throw himself into the movement and his aim should be to obtain an appointment as organizer"—which is exactly what Leopold did.[44]

The difficulties of leading a secret life became manifest again in 1922, when Leopold was faced with the loss of his Alberta homestead unless he became naturalized. As he pointed out to headquarters, this was difficult to do given his assumed identity. Ottawa made the appropriate arrangements, as it did later that year when it transferred all his pay arrangements from Saskatchewan to Ottawa to ensure that no paper trail would connect him to Regina. In addition, it arranged that his income tax be paid through Ottawa as well.[45]

In Regina Leopold became the secretary of the local branch of the Workers Party of Canada in December 1921 and at the same time functioned as the key local figure in the secret underground Communist Party. After the CPC decision to undermine the OBU, he became secretary of the Regina local of the International Brotherhood of Painters and in 1924 vice-president and in 1925 president of the Regina Trades and Labour Council. In 1926 he temporarily moved to Winnipeg at Commissioner Starnes's request, because things had become so quiet in Regina that Starnes believed his agent would prove more useful elsewhere.[46] For the first time a note of concern crept into the handlers' comments about Leopold. In direct response to a worried query from Starnes, the officer commanding in Southern Saskatchewan wrote, "This man is somewhat disposed to work alone and without sufficient consultation with his superiors." That note has a cryptic comment scrawled upon it by Starnes: "See Hamilton" (the chief intelligence officer). Hamilton must have calmed the commissioner down, because Starnes then wrote a restrained instruction to Regina suggesting that they chat with Leopold upon his return there and encourage him to stay in closer contact with his control.[47]

In 1927 Starnes moved Leopold to Toronto.[48] While in Winnipeg for the convention of Division 4 of the Railway Running Trades that year, Leopold served as convention chair and subsequently worked on Communist William Kolisnyk's successful campaign for alderman. While Leopold always contended that he had done nothing improper in those years as a communist activist, it seems unlikely that an operative could have risen so high in the CPC and not influenced the outcome of events in which he participated.

In addition to the RCMP's worries about Leopold's activities in 1927, the CPC also began to close in upon him. In November CPC secretary Jack MacDonald informed him that the CPC had received information from two ex-Mounties that identified Leopold as a government agent. Although this storm blew over, clearly CPC suspicions were aroused. Not surprisingly, the value of Leopold's work fell off in the period after the scare about discovery, and as late as April Starnes was considering moving him back to Winnipeg.[49]

After his cover was finally blown by MacDonald in May 1928 and he was expelled from the CPC as a government agent, the RCMP transferred him to the Yukon to get him as far away as possible from his erstwhile comrades.[50] To maintain his secret, even then his pay was maintained on the Ottawa rolls. In April 1931 he was recalled to Ottawa, no doubt in preparation for a planned role as main witness in the Toronto Communist trials, held in November. After working as detective in western Ontario for a time, Leopold was brought back to Ottawa in late 1933 as an expert on Communism to work in the Intelligence Section of the Criminal Investigation Branch.[51] Rather than being a promotion, this move came after a reprimand from his superiors for a series of financial irregularities that included exceeding expenses while testifying in Toronto and a subsequent mishandling of funds while working as a detective in Windsor. In effect Leopold had been demoted to Ottawa and uniform service, forced to make restitution, and given only a one-year service extension instead of the customary three years. The discovery that he had contacted syphilis that year probably also did not impress his superiors.[52] Nor, one suspects, would they have been impressed with the series of letters written over a year-long period from his mother in Czechoslovakia seeking information about his circumstances. The letters went directly to the RCMP because Leopold had not contacted his mother in years.[53]

In 1936 Leopold was twice reprimanded and then demoted for intoxication on duty and insubordination. As in the case of his earlier disciplining, the Force found this a massive embarrassment, especially when it was seized upon by the radical Canadian press as further evidence of the unsavoury character of the RCMP's labour spies. Further embarrassment followed in summer 1937, when M.J. Coldwell, the CCF MP for Regina, revealed that Leopold, or rather Esselwein, had been arrested and convicted in Toronto a decade before during a Communist demonstration against the prosecution of Sacco and Vanzetti, the Italian-American Anarchist martyrs.[54] The RCMP was only slightly reassured by the information that Leopold's fine had been paid by the CPC. Leopold did find a supporter finally in the Force when Rivett-Carnac became Intelligence head. Thereafter Leopold's career unfolded more conventionally, with a return to his previous rank and subsequent promotions. No doubt this related to the increased profile of the Intelligence Section within the RCMP under MacBrien and later Wood.[55]

A vast social distance existed, then, between the spymasters and their spies. Even the underground red coats, the *crème de la crème* of secret agents, possessed ethnic and class backgrounds at total variance from their controllers.[56] While the stories of Zaneth and Leopold tell us much about underground activity, they are only the tip of the iceberg. While information on "human sources" is the most difficult to gain from CSIS and is largely protected under the Access to Information legislation, we do know that the Regina and Calgary pattern was the norm. In addition we know from the old RNWMP records that of some forty-five early agents—both Mounties and civilian—about half were European immigrants with foreign-language skills.[57]

Those from Anglo-Celtic backgrounds included individuals with truly exotic backgrounds, such as the English-born former Wobbly Robert Gosden.[58] Born in Surrey in 1882, Gosden fought in the Boer War before emigrating to North America. After extensive travels, he settled in British Columbia in 1906 and eventually joined the IWW. He spent three months in a Prince Rupert jail after a confrontation between strikers and police. The next year he spent nine months in a San Diego jail after a Wobbly free speech fight there. He gained prominence and a leadership role in the Miners Liberation League during the Vancouver Island coalminer strike. Suggestions that he was an *agent provocateur* began to circulate and were promoted by his involvement in a provincial election scandal in 1916, in which he had organized rampant illegal voting. Certainly by 1919 he was an RNWMP secret agent and, as such, worked in Blairmore, Fernie, Macleod, and Hillcrest in the early months of that year. In March he attended the Western Labour Conference in Calgary, where he was denounced as a police spy by miners' leader Rees. As special agent no. 10, he authored the most extraordinary document of 1919—a letter to Commissioner Perry in which he recommended that the SPC leadership be made to "disappear." Perhaps it is not surprising that Gosden was simultaneously a paid agent and also among the earliest radicals to get a personal history file.

Almost as exciting as Gosden were the two Russian agents, Alexander Durasoff and Barney Roth, who embarrassed the new RCMP terribly in 1920 by getting themselves indicted for perjury after Immigration Department deportation hearings in Vancouver in late 1919 against some twenty or more alleged members of the Russian Workers Union. Commissioner Perry was not amused.[59] Perhaps slightly less exotic than Gosden or the Russian agents was the Petrograd-born Mervyn Black, who had managed cotton mills in the Soviet Union before migrating to South America and later to Saskatchewan. He failed as a farmer and joined the RCMP as a secret agent.

Men with foreign backgrounds thus provided the Anglo-Canadian leadership of the Force with their human sources. However, Leopold's career after his exposure as a spy suggests that this relationship was fraught with tension. The personnel files of other agents often contain poignant reminders that life underground was never easy. The medical file of undercover Mountie T.E. Ryan, Leopold's handler in Regina, for example, offered an explanation from his personal physician for his poor health: "Many years as a plain clothes man with all the temptations that go when there is no uniform."[60]

As the stories of Zaneth and Leopold suggest, the major target of the RCMP Security Service throughout this period was the Canadian left and especially its communist wing, although the RCMP's ability to make discerning distinctions in this regard was never strong. As a result the RCMP security and intelligence archives are filled with materials about immigrants to Canada and their associational life. For instance, the first list of "Chief Agitators in Canada," compiled by the Public Safety Branch of the Department of Justice, contains roughly a two to one ratio of easily identifiable non-Anglo-Celtic immigrant names. Given the propensity of some immigrants to anglicize their names, as Franco Zanetti did, this ratio seems extremely high. As well, the first 2,600 personal history files compiled by the RNWMP and RCMP, while not showing as high a ratio, also demonstrate the Security Service's fascination with Canada's immigrant workers.

The earliest RCMP Security Bulletins offer a similar picture. Among the few early surviving copies, we find in January 1920 considerable coverage of "Ukrainian Propaganda," which surveyed associational and cultural life, and "Finnish Propaganda," which did the same. The Mounties, of course, were quite familiar with the foreign-language press and many of the groups because of the ban on these activities in late 1918 by Order-in-Council. That step was based on the charges of the Public Safety Branch's C.H. Cahan—whom Borden had commissioned to study radicalism, and whose July 1918 report focused on the immigrant threat—and of E.J. Chambers, the chief press censor. Finally, the recently released Finding Aids for RG 146, the CSIS records at the National Archives of Canada, also reveal the extraordinary attention paid to the immigrant community by the RCMP Security Service from its creation in 1920. As General MacBrien remarked in 1932: "It is notable that 99 per cent of these fellows [Communists] are foreigners and many of them have not been here long. The best thing to do would be to send them back where they came from in every way possible. If we were rid of them, there would be no unemployment or unrest in Canada."[61] That sentiment was certainly an article of RCMP faith during this period and beyond.

Any attempt to analyse the nature of state repression in the period from 1914 to 1939, then, must grapple with the duality of ethnicity. Not only was the ethnic identity of the immigrant workers and Reds important, but so too were the national and socio-economic roots of the red-coats, both spymasters and spies. Similarly, gender too is an important category, for the RCMP was a very male institution—a near total institution, as the McDonald Commission noted, which "through its recruiting, training and management practices engulfs its members in an ethos akin to that found in a monastery or religious order."[62] The historical analysis of that ethos, and especially of the even more ingrained Security Service, is in its infancy, but at least it is now possible, thanks to Access to Information legislation, to begin that work. The historical responsibility to do the necessary research and rethinking should be impressed on us all on every occasion—of which there have been many—when CSIS, the Communications Security Establishment (CSE), and the rest of the Canadian intelligence community's current practices are called into question.[63]

## Notes

Thanks for assistance to Michelle McBride, who helped see this paper through to publication, and to the Social Sciences and Humanities Research Council for funding.

1.  Canada, *Commission of Inquiry Concerning Certain Activities of the Royal Canadian Mounted Police* [McDonald Commission] (Ottawa: Queen's Printer, 1981). For information on the Keable Commission, see Robert Dion, *The Crimes of the Secret Police* (Montreal: Black Rose Books, 1982). For recent controversies, see R.C. Macleod, "How They 'Got Their Man,'" *Literary Review of Canada* 5,8 (September 1996), pp.19–21; and Gregory Kealey and Reg Whitaker, "The RCMP and the Enemy Within," *Literary Review of Canada* 5,10 (November 1996), p.22.

2.  Richard Cleroux, *Official Secrets: The Story behind the Canadian Security Intelligence Service* (Montreal: McGraw Hill, 1990); J.L. Granatstein and David Stafford, *Spy Wars: Espionage and Canada from Gouzenko to Glasnost* (Toronto: Key Porter, 1990); Carl Betke and Stan Horrall, *Canada's Security Service: An Historical Outline 1864–1966* (Ottawa: RCMP Historical Section, 1978), Document No. 20, File 117-90-107.

3.  Jeff Keshen, "Cloak and Dagger: Canada West's Secret Police, 1864–1867," *Ontario History* 79 (1987), pp.353–81.

4.  See, for instance, Paula Maurutto, "Private Policing and Surveillance of Catholics: Anti-communism in the Roman Catholic Archdiocese of Toronto, 1920–1960," *Labour/Le Travail* 40 (Fall 1997), pp.113–36, and the shorter version in her chapter here.

5. J.A. Cole, *Prince of Spies: Henri Le Caron* (London: Faber and Faber, 1984). For more on McMicken, see Betke and Horrall, *Canada's Security Service*, pp.82–84, 86–88, 94–96, 126–27.

6. Gregory S. Kealey, "The Surveillance State: The Origins of Domestic Intelligence and Counter-Subversion in Canada, 1914–1920," *Intelligence and National Security* 7,3 (1992), pp.179–210. Evidence of the anti-Semitism is common in documents from the postwar Red Scare.

7. Betke and Horrall, *Canada's Security Service*, pp.183–87; Wayne A. Crockett, "The Uses and Abuses of the Secret Service Fund: The Political Division of Police Work in Canada, 1864–1877," M.A. thesis, Queen's University, Kingston, 1982; Christopher Andrew, *Secret Service: The Making of the British Intelligence Community* (London: Heinemann, 1985); and Bernard Porter, *The Origins of the Vigilant State: The London Metropolitan Police Special Branch before the First World War* (London: Weidenfeld and Nicholson, 1987).

8. Richard Popplewell, "The Surveillance of Indian 'Seditionists' in North America, 1905–1915," in *Intelligence and International Relations, 1900–1945*, ed. Christopher Andrew and Jeremy Noakes (Exeter: University of Exeter, 1987), pp.49–76; Richard Popplewell, *Intelligence and Imperial Defence of the Indian Empire* (London: Frank Cass, 1995); Hugh Johnston, "The Surveillance of Indian Nationalists in North America, 1908–1918," *BC Studies* 78 (1988), pp.3–27; and Hugh Johnston, *The Voyage of the Komagata Maru: The Sikh Challenge to Canada's Colour Bar* (New Delhi: Oxford University Press, 1979).

9. W.B. Fowler, *British-American Relations 1917–1918: The Role of Sir William Wiseman* (Princeton, N.J.: Princeton University Press, 1969).

10. Gregory S. Kealey, "The Early Years of State Surveillance of Labour and the Left in Canada," *Intelligence and National Security* 8,3 (July 1993), p.130; Stan Horrall, "Canada's Security Service: A Brief History," *RCMP Quarterly* 50,3 (Summer 1985), p.43.

11. Gregory S. Kealey, "State Repression of Labour and the Left in Canada, 1914–1920: The Impact of the First World War," *Canadian Historical Review (CHR)* 73,3 (1992), pp. 281–314; Stan Horrall, "The Royal North-West Mounted Police and Labour Unrest in Western Canada, 1919," *CHR* 61 (June 1980), pp.169–90; Gregory S. Kealey and Reg Whitaker, eds., *R.C.M.P. Security Bulletins: The Early Years, 1919–1929* (St. John's, Nfld.: Canadian Committee on Labour History, 1994).

12. "Perry to Officers Commanding," Jan. 6, 1919, National Archives of Canada (NAC), RG 18, vol. 599, file 1328. See also files 1309–1335, circular memos 807, 807A (Jan. 6, 1919), and 807B (Feb. 5, 1919).

13. Betke and Horrall, *Canada's Security Service*, pp.380–83. The staff of the Intelligence Section included six members: Inspector Rivett-Carnac, Sergeant Leopold, two officers—one in charge of agents, the other in charge of the Registry—a stenographer, and a translator.

14. Betke and Horrall, *Canada's Secret Service*, pp.436–37.

15. Macleod, "How They 'Got Their Man,'" pp.19–21; Kealey and Whitaker, "RCMP and the Enemy Within," p.22. Recently the provincial policing function has been glorified at the expense of the Security Service.

16. General Orders, NAC, RCMP Records, RG 146; ATIP request no. 95ATIP-271, 272.

17. Larry Hannant, *The Infernal Machine: Investigating the Loyalty of Canada's Citizens* (Toronto: University of Toronto Press, 1995).

18. Steve Hewitt, "'Old Myths Die Hard': The Transformation of the Mounted Police in Alberta and Saskatchewan, 1914–1939," Ph.D. thesis, University of Saskatchewan, 1997.

19. Michelle McBride, "From Indifference to Internment: An Examination of RCMP Responses to Nazism and Fascism in Canada," M.A. thesis, Memorial University, St. John's, Nfld., 1997; citing Lawes to A.D.P. Heeney, Principal Secretary of the PMO's Office, Nov. 25, 1938, NAC, MG 30, E163, vol. 12, file 137.

20. Rivett-Carnac to Norman Robertson, Undersecretary of State for External Affairs, Jan. 24, 1939, p.1, NAC, MG 30, E163, file 127.
21. Lapointe to S.T. Wood, Aug. 25, 1939, NAC, MG 30, Lapointe Papers, vol. 50, file 50.
22. Gregory S. Kealey, "The Royal Canadian Mounted Police, the Canadian Security and Intelligence Service, the Public Archives of Canada, and Access to Information: A Curious Tale," *Labour/Le Travail* 21 (Spring 1988), pp.199–226.
23. Gregory S. Kealey, "In the Canadian Archives on Security and Intelligence," *Dalhousie Review* 97,1 (1996), pp.26–38. Much of what follows is dependent on either the substantial record for the early years 1917–20 or on the more problematic documentation based on the heavily exempted records acquired via extensive use of the Access to Information legislation.
24. Kealey and Whitaker, eds., *R.C.M.P. Security Bulletins*, 1994. By 2000 the published Bulletins consisted of eight large volumes.
25. Henry Morgan, *Canadian Men and Women of the Time* (Toronto: University of Toronto Press, 1912); Betke and Horrall, *Canada's Security Service,* pp.130–32.
26. Betke and Horrall, *Canada's Security Service*, pp.131, 225–26, 378–79, 384.
27 Ibid. pp.231, 350; Morgan, *Canadian Men and Women.*
28. NAC, RG 18, vol. 3440. See also Starnes entry in Canadian *Who's Who*, 1938–61.
29. Betke and Horrall, *Canada's Security Service*, pp.436–37. See also MacBrien entry in Canadian *Who's Who.*
30. NAC, RG 18, vol. 3450. See also S.T. Wood entry in Canadian *Who's Who.*
31. Betke and Horrall, *Canada's Security Service.* Hamilton made a minimum of $3,000 per annum and was responsible for producing a weekly intelligence summary for government and other officials, for contacts with Scotland Yard and other foreign agencies, and for the secret correspondence of the Department. Morgan, *Canadian Men and Women.* See also Jeffrey A. Keshen, "All the News That Was Fit to Print: Ernest J. Chambers and Information Control in Canada, 1914–1919," *CHR* 73,3 (1992), p.315; Jeffrey A. Keshen, *Propaganda and Censorship during Canada's Great War* (Edmonton: University of Alberta Press, 1996); and Betke and Horrall, *Canada's Security Service*, pp.384–87.
32. Betke and Horrall, *Canada's Security Service*, pp.390–91. The new post of intelligence officer was placed under the director of criminal investigations, unlike the old liaison officer, who reported directly to the commissioner.
33. Charles Rivett-Carnac, *Pursuit in the Wilderness* (Boston: Little, Brown, 1967), esp. chaps. 1, 8; see also Canadian *Who's Who*, 1958–1970. For more information on Armitage see Betke and Horrall, *Canada's Security Service*, pp.391, 465.
34. Mike O'Brien, "Manhood and the Militia Myth: Masculinity, Class and Militarism in Ontario, 1902–1914," *Labour/Le Travail*, 42 (Fall 1998).
35. RCMP, *Annual Reports, 1940–41*, p.135. As late as 1941 initial training was described as consisting of two parts: the calvary/military-style training and the practical policing side, which in 1940 included typewriting, powers of observation, fingerprinting, public speaking, and the use of gas. For an illustration of the calvary training, see C.W. Harvison, *The Horsemen* (Toronto: McClelland and Stewart, 1967).
36. Gregory S. Kealey and Andy Parnaby, "How the 'Reds' Got Their Man: The Communist Party Unmasks an RCMP Spy," *Labour/Le Travail* (Fall 1997), pp.251–66; James Dubro and Robin Rowland, *Undercover: Cases of the RCMP's Most Secret Operative* (Markham, Ont.: McClelland and Stewart, 1991); and Betke and Horrall, *Canada's Security Service*, pp.391–92, 439–40, 449–52.
37. Dubro and Rowland, *Undercover*, esp. chap. 2; CSIS Records, RCMP Personnel file 5743, NAC, RG 146; ATIP 88HR-2533.
38. Dubro and Rowland, *Undercover*, esp. chap. 11; Martin Lobigs, "Canadian Responses to the Mackenzie-Papineau Battalion, 1936–1939," M.A. thesis, University of New Brunswick, Fredericton, 1992; Betke and Horrall, *Canada's Security Service*, p.445.
39. Leopold Medical Record, Sept. 25, 1918 NAC, CSIS Records, RG 146, RCMP Personnel

file 0333, John Leopold; ATIP 88-HR 2533.

40. Leopold Medical Records, Aug. 8, 1921, NAC, CSIS Records, RG 146, RCMP Personnel file 0333, Leopold; ATIP 88-HR 2533; Betke and Horrall, *Canada's Security Service*, pp.392, 439–440.

41. Salt to OC, S. Saskatchewan, July 2, 1921, NAC, RG 146, RCMP Personnel file 0333, Leopold, vol. 3.

42. NAC, RG 146, RCMP Personnel file 0333, Leopold.

43. Ibid. Not surprisingly, that entire passage was deleted from the first released version of this document and was only given to me after a complaint was made to the information commissioner.

44. NAC, RG 146, RCMP Personnel file 0333, Leopold; ATIP 88-HR 2533.

45. Starnes to OC, S. Saskatchewan, April 19, 1923, re: Income Tax Act; Allard to Starnes, Aug. 7, 1923, re: John Leopold, NAC, RG 146, Personnel file 0333, vol. 2.

46. Starnes to R.S. Knight, assistant commissioner, Regina, Aug. 31, 1926, NAC, RG 146, RCMP Personnel file 0333, vol. 2.

47. Starnes to Knight, Oct. 27, 1926, NAC, RG 146, RCMP Personnel file 0333, vol. 2.

48. Kealey and Parnaby, "How the 'Reds' Got Their Man," pp.259–67; Starnes to Knight, March 25, 1927, NAC, RG 146, file 0333, vol. 2.

49. H.M. Newson, Supt, Western Ontario, to Starnes, Nov. 16, 1927 and Starnes to Newson, Nov. 19, 1927, NAC, RG 146, file 0333, vol. 2.

50. Jas. Ritchie, Supt, to Inspector Moorhead, Simpson, NWT, June 9, 1928 NAC, RG 146, file 0333.

51. G.L. Jennings to Commissioner, Oct. 2, 1933, NAC, RG 146, file 0333, vol. 2.

52. Medical history, RCMP Acquaintance of Claim Form, Sept. 21, 1935, NAC, RG 146, file 0333.

53. Mary Leopold to Chief Officer, RCMP, April 2, 1932, NAC, RG 146, file 0333.

54. Memo regarding Sgt. Leopold: Extract from Hansard, April 8, 1937, p.2969; memo to Commissioner, Re: Arrest of J.W. Esselwein (Sgt. J. Leopold), July 27, 1937, NAC, RG 146, file 0333.

55. Jennings to Commissioner recommending re-engaging Leopold given his recent good behaviour, Sept. 11, 1934; and Rivett-Carnac to Director of Criminal Investigation, Oct. 6, 1937, NAC, RG 146, file 0333, vol. 2.

56. For more on the RCMP's use of secret agents, see Michelle McBride, "Fascism, Secret Agents, and the RCMP Security Service, 1939–41: Preliminary Remarks on Three Secret Agents in the Italian-Canadian Community of Montreal," paper presented to CHA/CASIS Panel, Learned Societies Conference, Ottawa, May 31, 1998.

57. Kealey, "Surveillance State."

58. See Mark Leier, "Portrait of a Labour Spy: The Case of Robert Raglan Gosden, 1882–1961," *Labour/Le Travail* 42 (Fall 1998); and Mark Leier, *Rebel Life: The Life and Times of Robert Gosden, Revolutionary, Mystic, Labour Spy* (Vancouver: New Star Books, 2000).

59. NAC, RG 146, RCMP Personnel file 0333.

60. NAC, RG 146, RCMP Personnel file 0333, Leopold; ATIP 88-HR 2533.

61. Lorne and Caroline Brown, *An Unauthorized History of the RCMP* (Toronto: James Lewis and Samuel, 1973); Hewitt, " 'Old Myths Die Hard.'"

62. For an examination of how the RCMP treated female fascists and other women interned during World War II see Michelle McBride, "The Curious Case of Female Internees and the Inter-departmental Committee on Internment during World War II," in *Curious Prisoners*, ed. Franca Iacovetta (Toronto: University of Toronto Press, 2000).

63. For more on the CSE, see James Littleton, *Target Nation: Canada and the Western Intelligence Network* (Toronto: Lester, Orpen Dennys, 1986); and Mike Frost with Michel Gratton, *Spyworld: Inside the Canadian and American Intelligence Establishments* (Toronto: Doubleday, 1994).

# PART II

# DEFINING A SECURITY THREAT: THREE EXAMPLES

**Top:** *Mine Mill unionist Bill Sorenson* (courtesy of Mine Mill/CAW Local 598). **Middle:** *Mine Mill unionists demonstrate at Queen's Park during Steel raids in the 1960s* (courtesy of Mike Solski Collection, Sudbury Public Library). **Bottom:** *Mine Mill Ladies' Auxiliary, Local 117, Sudbury, Feb. 13, 1952* (courtesy of Mike Solski Collection, Sudbury Public Library). [Steedman, chap. 4]

PAULA MAURUTTO

three ☆ ☆ ☆

# Private Policing and Surveillance of Catholics: Anti-Communism in the Roman Catholic Archdiocese of Toronto, 1920–60

"The Holy See is terribly afraid of Communism, the centre of which, in Canada, is Toronto," wrote Toronto's Roman Catholic Archbishop James McGuigan in 1937 upon returning from the Vatican.[1] While this particular claim was exaggerated, such beliefs framed the perceptions of many English-speaking Catholics in the city.[2] Threatened by what appeared to be a profusion of socialist organizing, the Archdiocese of Toronto had by the 1930s developed an infrastructure to seek out and prevent the spread of communism.[3] As the Toronto Red Squad, a branch of the police department, was using coercive tactics to thwart communist-related activities, the Catholic Church was deploying a variety of means to avert this apparent danger, including the surveillance and infiltration of socialist groups and a pervasive moral and educational campaign aimed at newly arriving immigrants. While the Church conducted its own investigations, its endeavours were supported by state officials. It obtained intelligence information from the Red Squad as well as secret Royal Canadian Mounted Police reports. These actions went far beyond religious proselytizing or philanthropic endeavours. The strategies employed by the Church amounted to an active policing of individuals, operating independently from law enforcement agencies but intertwined with state political initiatives.

The activities of the Archdiocese of Toronto, then, reveal a Catholic Church actively involved in the private policing and surveillance of individuals, and these largely anti-communist activities point to a need to extend our notions of the processes and techniques involved in safeguarding national security. Most analyses of political or national security emphasize the state as the apex in the maintenance of social order.[4] The studies of national security rarely consider the role of private philanthropic policing and surveillance.

This oversight might be partly attributed to how private philanthropic institutions enforce discipline—an activity that often does not conform to traditional forms of surveillance and punishment. Public authorities secure social control through the threat and deployment of coercive force, and private corporate police attempt to prevent crime through the knowledge that one is being monitored, as in the use of video cameras. Philanthropic control is more concerned with minimizing social risk by regulating and reforming behaviour,[5] and this concern with moral regulation is what distinguishes philanthropic policing from private corporate policing. Philanthropic institutions are concerned specifically with instilling the "right kind of character." These institutions, as Mariana Valverde's work demonstrates, promise to deliver a subjectivity that will solve social problems by reforming the way in which we govern ourselves.[6] Valverde also proposes that non-state organizations are often more successful than the state in reforming citizens. This reflects the dichotomous public/private relationship in which institutions operating within the private realm, including philanthropic and corporate institutions, are much less confined by the legal boundaries and limits of privacy. Although liberal governments are legally confined to public affairs, as Nikolas Rose and Valverde both note, their administrations often participate in moral reform efforts by providing the legal framework for voluntary action and supporting private campaigns through funding and information.[7]

It is precisely this interaction between private and public institutions, a relationship Valverde terms the "mixed social economy," that is central.[8] This conceptualization disrupts the image of two clearly defined separate spheres. It opens up the possibility of exploring not only how the public sector is linked to private forms of social reform, but also how private policing and surveillance participate in securing public order. By exploring these interconnections, we can deconstruct the idea of the state as the sole guarantor of social order, thereby bringing to light the role of the private charity sector in preserving public order and national security.

## English-Speaking Catholics and the Immigrant "Problem"

By the mid-1920s the established hierarchy of the Roman Catholic Archdiocese of Toronto consisted primarily of Scottish and Irish immigrants. While these Catholics initially encountered hostility and institutionalized bigotry as they settled in a largely Protestant environment, by the late nineteenth century they were embedded within the social and economic mainstream of Ontario society.[9] After World War I they became increasingly rooted within society, developing their own sense of a Canadian identity to the extent that old Irish associations were being replaced by new Canadian organizations.[10] Still, anti-Catholic sentiments continued to prevail among many Protestants. Moreover, as English-speaking Catholics adopted this new Canadian identity, conflicts with French-speaking Catholics began to proliferate. Both sides were vying for status as the official "Catholic" voice in Canada, and the Archdiocese of Toronto often found itself at odds with the Church in Quebec.

Most analyses of the Canadian Catholic response to communism have dealt exclusively with the Church in Quebec. Few works, if any, have studied the activities of Catholics in Toronto. Yet the Catholic Church in Toronto, under the direction of Archbishop Neil McNeil from 1912 to 1934 and Archbishop James McGuigan until 1971, developed strategies and techniques to prevent communist infiltration among newly arriving immigrants and to ensure a loyal English-Canadian Catholic community.[11] Seditious acts that threatened to destroy the Canadian social fabric also challenged the now-entrenched patriotism of English-speaking Catholics. Thus, Catholic anti-communism reflected both a religious ideological opposition and the interests of a privileged class attached to its private property and liberal institutions.

In Toronto the Church was particularly concerned about communism taking hold among the thousands of immigrants arriving yearly from Central and Eastern Europe. The majority of these recent arrivals, many of them practising or nominal Catholics, came from Hungary, Italy, Malta, Poland, Lithuania, and Ukraine. The Catholic population in the Archdiocese of Toronto increased from 85,000 in 1920 to over 164,000 in 1935, and in 1941 Catholics represented 16 per cent of the city's population.[12] Their working-class backgrounds and lack of fluency in English resulted in a concentration in low-paid and unskilled jobs. Deeply rooted prejudices against foreigners and lingering hostility towards Catholics also hampered their employment prospects. The Church viewed their religious devotion, which did not conform to Irish standard practice, as promoting idolatry. Their foreign values and customs were taken as evidence of their predisposition to superstitious beliefs and radical ideologies. By the 1930s, with little relief and few jobs available, Catholic leaders feared these immigrants were potentially ripe for communist organizing. After all, the Communist Party of Canada had been quite successful in recruiting immigrants.[13]

The Communist Party of Canada (CPC) formed in 1921, and although its executive was largely British-born, 95 per cent of the rank and file by 1929 was composed of immigrants, primarily from Finnish, Ukrainian, and Jewish ethnic groups.[14] Despite some gains, by 1929 the Party had only 2,876 members, and in the Ontario provincial election that year it polled a mere 1,440 votes.[15] During the Depression its membership increased, particularly among the poorest elements of society. While the Party did poorly in the 1935 federal election, by 1936 two communists had been elected to Toronto's Board of Control and one to the Board of Education. In the 1939 municipal election, Tim Buck, the Party leader, registered 45,112 votes.[16] Most of those voting for the CPC, however, were not communists, but supported communist attacks against low wages and insufficient government relief. Since few groups were championing the cause of the destitute and the unemployed, many people turned to the CPC for hope. Still, by 1939 its national membership barely exceeded sixteen thousand. As Ivan Avakumovic notes, most of the East European membership "was often unwilling or unable to participate in those Communist activities . . . the CPC considered essential."[17] They tended to limit their participation to communist events within their respective ethnic communities.

## Policing Radicals: The Toronto Red Squad, the RCMP, and the Archdiocese

To the Archdiocese of Toronto, the Party's denunciation of religion as the "opiate of the masses" and its promotion of atheism and, supposedly, free love threatened to undermine the sanctity of the family and eradicate religious freedoms. As such, Catholic leaders were determined to prevent this "evil menace" from taking hold within ethnic communities. The Church's first task in fighting communism was to gain intelligence about the Party's clandestine operations and propaganda techniques, which was not difficult because the Church could rely on a pre-established relationship with the local police. Although the Toronto police force counted many Orangemen on its staff, it collaborated with the Catholic Church on a number of occasions. Often the inspector of police, bypassing official channels, would place delinquent youths under the supervision of Catholic youth leaders to prevent them from appearing before the courts.[18] Moreover, on an ideological level, the anticommunism shared by the two organizations was coloured by fascist overtones (the Vatican was supporting Mussolini's government, and several Catholics leaders in Canada viewed fascism in a favourable light).[19]

Furthermore, the Church defended police attempts to subvert communism.[20] The Toronto Red Squad, a branch of the municipal police department under Chief Constable Brigadier-General Denis C. Draper, was notorious for its brutal treatment of dissidents. The Squad, commonly known as "Draper's Dragoons" for its heavy-handed repression of communists, would club and jail members for distributing propaganda. It prohibited meetings held in "foreign" languages, prevented the Party from campaigning during elections, and used tear gas—for the first time in Canada—to break up meetings. In August 1931 the Red Squad arrested nine of the Party leaders under Section 98 of the Criminal Code, a legislation so broad that strong criticism of the government could merit incarceration.[21] While labour groups demanded a public investigation of the harsh actions deployed by the Red Squad, members within the Catholic Church counteracted public indignation by applauding the police actions. In one *Globe* article Catholic clergy and members of other religious and financial groups sanctioned the Squad's action as an effort to uphold justice and democracy.[22]

The Church endorsement of the Red Squad and RCMP operations enabled it to elicit secret information on communist activity within the city. Confidential RCMP surveillance records compiled in 1923 appear among Archdiocesan files. The files chronicle the range of communist activities throughout Canada and particularly focus on the vulnerability of immigrant groups, specifically Ukrainians and Finns. Page after page reveals the extensive means by which the Party attracted youths into the communist ranks.[23]

> The principal subjects taught are the Ukrainian language . . . revolutionary songs, and such smatterings of history, economics and science as will implant in the children atheistic, revolutionary and communistic opinions and prejudices. Every effort is made to induce the children to regard Russia (including the Soviet Ukraine) as a model country; to hate religion, patriotism, and the government . . . and to desire and expect a revolution by violent methods.[24]

In 1932, when Archbishop McNeil requested information on communist activities in Toronto, Chief Constable Draper readily forwarded intelligence reports compiled by Inspector Douglas Marshall of the Toronto Red Squad. One report documented the range of communist movements in Canada. Other files provided detailed accounts of propaganda techniques and emphasized the Party's success among immigrants. Ethnic societies suspected to be subsidiary organizations of the Party were disclosed (many later appeared listed in the *Catholic Register* as associations for Catholics to avoid). Still other reports exposed how many youth organizations were communist fronts designed to indoctrinate the future generation. The inspector was particularly outraged with the concerted effort to entice youth into the Young Communist League:

> With the training that is being given the children of tender years, to oppose Law and Order, defiance of Police Order, and no check being made on these teachings, the result can only be one thing, revolution. These children will, say in ten years time, be militant and absolutely revolutionary, and unless steps are taken . . . we are going to have a huge population of foreign extraction who will be prepared to go to any length to attain their own ends.[25]

These reports, coupled with the information gathered through the Archdiocese's own surveillance, were taken as confirmation that a communist conspiracy was at hand. According to Archbishop McNeil, twenty-eight thousand Catholics in his Archdiocese had joined the Communist Party, and he was determined to find out the causes of this dissident behaviour.[26]

In the 1930s McNeil commissioned a systematic survey of each Parish in his diocese. Initially the Archdiocese relied on its own informants, lay Catholics who attended ethnic functions. But soon McNeil opted for a more systematic method, hiring his own spy to police ethnic organizations within local parishes. Catherine de Hueck, a Catholic who had fled the Russian Civil War, was an optimal choice.[27] Her Russian heritage and ability to speak several Slavic languages allowed her easy entry into communist organizations. In October 1931, living among the immigrant poor, de Hueck began infiltrating communist organizations and compiling a survey of their activities. Each week she would update the Archbishop on the operations of the Communist Party. Part of her assignment included a visit to New York, the Communist headquarters in North America, to obtain newspapers and periodicals destined for Canada and to elicit information on their activities in Toronto.

In 1932 she presented Archbishop McNeil with a ninety-five-page document on communist activity in Toronto.[28] The report included an analysis of membership profiles, party structure, propaganda techniques, and various schemes to attract immigrants. Communist promotional campaigns in Toronto were successful, she suggested, because they employed systematic planning; the city was divided into sectors, each with its own organizer who was responsible for canvassing the area and attracting workers and the unemployed to communist events. De Hueck recounted how educational and recreational activities, the ethnic press, and foreign-language speeches were designed to appeal to the sentiments of immigrant communities. The Communist Party in Toronto, she claimed, published forty-eight papers in eighteen different languages. All forms of relief, including professional assistance from lawyers, doctors, and dentists, were provided to the poor as a means of luring them to the Party. She described attempts by Party leaders to infiltrate non-communist organizations. What de Hueck found most jarring was their work among school-aged children. Professors and teachers organized debating societies, social newspapers, summer camps, after-hour schools, and underground activities to inculcate radical ideologies among these youth. Moreover, "Atheistic Sunday Schools," as de Hueck referred to them, were held in private homes under the guise of national language Schools. Their location was moved each week in order to avoid police detection. A further tactic, she noted, was the organization of societies such as The League of Youth against War and Fascism, which lacked an outward communist association, but was, in fact, used to draw new members to the Party.[29]

In addition to obtaining this report the Church also conducted a parish-by-parish survey. In one map entitled "Communist Activities in St. Patrick's Parish," thirty-three black dots marked the location of residences, rooming houses, bakeries, restaurants, pubs, theatres, non-Catholic churches, bookstores, and a "suspicious looking store," all thought to be places of communist activity in this downtown area. A good number of these establishments were owned by Finns or Ukrainians.[30] The surveillance reports supported the suspicions of the archbishop, who believed that communists were preying on immigrants who, although not inherently rebellious, were being swayed by cunning and unscrupulous communist propaganda.

The Archdiocese's surveillance and use of spies to police ethnic communities point to how securing citizens, a project undertaken by both the state and voluntary organizations, operated at multiple and intersecting levels. The means adopted to govern individuals, however, were quite distinct.

### Creating a Bulwark against Communism: The Depression Years

While the Toronto Police Department relied on repressive coercion to punish dissidents, the Catholic Church secured its congregation by seeking to reform beliefs and instil a sense of moral fibre. The excessive deployment of force by the Red Squad may have been successful in forcing many communists underground, but it was limited in its ability to effect a conversion of mind and always risked hardening attitudes. The Church specifically sought to morally regulate private behaviour. As McNeil stated in a 1933 brochure, *The Red Menace*: "By intensive action we must educate the people to a conversion of mind. It cannot be done by force or by law. It must be done by the power of the word, written and spoken. Then, and then only, can we hope for a return to Christian ideals and to Christian institutions, where charity and justice reign."[31] During the 1930s the Archbishop successfully launched an anti-communist campaign to ensure a bulwark against communism. In his view, the education of immigrants was paramount.

Sunday sermons warned members to steer clear of subversive organizations, and afternoon radio broadcasts spoke of the ills of communism.[32] Catholic demonstrations reminded audiences that religious gatherings were outlawed in the Soviet Union,[33] and study clubs were formed to educate the unemployed on the ideological dangers lurking in their midst. Services were provided in foreign languages, and new ethnic churches were built to retain the loyalty of immigrant families. To protect the malleable minds of youths, a concerted effort was made to enrol immigrant children in separate schools. The Legion of Decency, a branch of the Catholic Welfare Bureau, was devised to root out indecent and objectionable community events. The Legion protested against stage shows promoting "red propaganda" and denounced communist fund-raising events. It monitored labour organizations, such as the Ontario Federation of the Unemployed and the Federation of Democratic Associations, suspected of being organized by left-wing radicals. Blacklists were compiled of films, books, and magazines promoting socialist ideals.[34]

The Ontario Catholic press regularly printed articles on the persecution of religion in the Soviet Union, as well as clandestine activities within the country. At the same time as the Communist Party newspaper, *The Worker*, promoted Bolshevik ideologies, the *Catholic Worker* was circulated at factories and communist rallies throughout Toronto. Food wrapped in the *Social Forum*, another Catholic paper, was often left behind for workers in factories. The editor of the Catholic *Register*, Henry Somerville, was unrelenting in his editorials on the communist exploitation of immigrant poverty. The Church recruited university students from St. Michael's College to distribute newspapers and leaflets.[35]

Speaking engagements supporting Christian freedom were encouraged among the laity. Catherine de Hueck was often invited to speak publicly on the "Red Menace." As a former spy she was considered an expert on the issue. At one address in 1933, de Hueck, accompanied by lay Catholic Mrs. Harris McPhedran, spoke to over five hundred women from different religious denominations. Their lecture on "What can women do to help in the present crisis" encouraged women to enter the homes of "these homesick lonely foreigners," for only with "a little sympathy and understanding by voluntary workers" could communism be "successfully combatted." This sympathy did not extend to a condemnation of the destitute conditions that many of these immigrants were subjected to during the Depression. Instead, de Hueck and her supporters denounced direct relief for promoting idleness, humiliation, and vagrancy. Rather, they suggested, "how much wiser [it would be] to have each person work for what he or she receives if they only sweep the streets."[36] The dignity and pride of men, they argued, could only be maintained if they were transformed into contributing members of society.

To provide concrete evidence of what "women can do to help," de Hueck, McPhedran, and Catholic reformer Helen McCrea opened a Russian Restaurant, the Tachainick. They boasted that through their efforts, thirty-three people had been removed from the relief rolls in only three weeks. Their success was extended to other business ventures, including a tailor shop, bicycle repair store, and handicraft workshop, all opened in Slavic residential areas. Initiatives such as these, they claimed, reduced men's dependence on society: they restored men's "self-respect and incidentally rescued several of them from communism."[37] Work, not the dole, would prevent contact with the numerous halls spreading left-wing propaganda. The great appeal of these lectures is evidenced by the range of associations seeking de Hueck as a speaker, including the Toronto Board of Trade Club and the Toronto Rotary Club, where she was the first woman to address the organization.[38]

In light of its excessive reaction to left-wing movements, the Church's response to fascism is of particular interest. Throughout the 1930s, the Church maintained a tempered response towards fascism. At one point, in 1938, it issued an apology for having suggested that fascism was a menace equivalent to communism. Even after public opinion in Canada turned against Mussolini following his invasion of

Ethiopia, and despite the clash between the pope and the Italian government over domestic policy in 1936 and the adoption of Nazi-like racial laws in 1938,[39] the Archdiocese of Toronto refrained from taking a strong position against fascism. While the archbishops opposed anti-Semitic activities and participated in mass protests against the persecution of Jews in Germany, they failed to seriously question fascist ideology.[40] When in 1938, for example, the Archdiocese initially proposed a demonstration in Toronto against both communism and fascism, pressure from the German and Italian Catholic congregations convinced Archbishop McGuigan to revoke his stand on fascism.[41] In the end the parade was limited to a protest against communism. In an attempt to prevent any strife with the ethnic parishes, McGuigan forwarded an apology to German and Italian Catholic Legionnaires, stating: "There certainly never was any intention to condemn any particular form of Fascism now existing or to hurt the sensibilities of any of our Catholic people . . . sorry that any misunderstanding has arisen and I'm very eager to dispel it." The apology was also sent to an Italian priest, Reverend Pellicelita, who was later interned by the RCMP during World War II; McGuigan eventually obtained his release.[42] While socialist groups were being condemned, the Archdiocese was, at least indirectly, defending Catholics sympathetic to fascist ideologies.

The most invasive means through which the Archdiocese enforced its moral regulation involved the Catholic Welfare Bureau, a benevolent organization formed in 1922 to administer welfare activities for Catholics. At the onset of the Depression, provincial and municipal governments continued to provide grants to charities. Social welfare, however, was considered a private initiative to be administered through the already existing voluntary agencies. Thus, relief was distributed, for the most part, on a denominational basis, and one of the eight main relief-granting agencies in Toronto was the Catholic Welfare Bureau.[43]

Initially private agencies worked to supplement public relief from the House of Industry and aided those, such as transient men, ineligible for the dole. In 1931, with the establishment of new regulations under the Division of Social Welfare, every welfare recipient had to first apply through a private agency. This new arrangement, designed to root out fraud, had the effect of augmenting the intervention of voluntary agencies in the private lives of individuals. Those in need of relief were now forced to divulge their private selves to philanthropic workers who maintained detailed files on each case. Hence Catholics who relied on benevolent agencies became increasingly vulnerable to the moral reform efforts of the Church.

Given its increased ability to monitor families, the Catholic Welfare Bureau was also able to ensure that children were enrolled in Sunday School and that families were participating in what the Church deemed "appropriate and acceptable" leisure activities.[44] This administration of relief by voluntary agencies on behalf of the state points to how charity operates as a mixed social economy. The state was not directly involved in moral regulation; yet it clearly provided the legal infrastructure for Catholic benevolent agencies to interfere in private lives.

The CPC actively targeted those receiving aid from Catholic charities. It accused the Church of ignoring the unemployed and of further demoralizing and pauperizing those on relief by providing insufficient aid. Members of the Party tried to entice those lined up at Catholic soup kitchens with promises of better relief and services at communist halls. Police reports verified that such tactics were quite successful in luring men away from the Catholic House of Providence. Father Michael J. McGrath, superintendent of the Catholic Welfare Bureau, outraged at the number of men receiving aid from non-Catholic houses of refuge, wrote to the city in 1939 complaining, "Now there [was] no means of offering them work or [to check] whether they [were] involved in any part of the present crime wave."[45]

A settlement house was also formed to provide aid to those who failed to meet the stringent criteria for government relief. In September 1934 St. Francis Catholic Friendship House opened at 122 Portland Street, in a working-class area inhabited mostly by Czechoslovakians, Poles, Russians, Ukrainians, and Jews.[46] Although the formation of the settlement house was first discussed as a means of counteracting Protestant efforts at luring new Canadians, the catalyst for its opening was the growing fear of communist "conversions." The House was strategically positioned across from the Protestant Church of All Nations and a communist hall, a location that enabled Catholics to counteract the appeal of communists among the unemployed. During elections, settlement workers posted "Vote for Christianity" signs across from the "Vote Communist" slogans.[47] The Archdiocese hired de Hueck to run the house.

The Friendship House offered a range of services: soup kitchens, clothing distribution, English-language classes, and a shelter for single men. In the first month it provided 1,200 meals, and by February 1935 it was serving 2,300 per month.[48] Suitable activities to prevent adults from engaging in vice or, worse yet, communist subversion took the form of drama and dance classes, cooking lessons, religious study groups, and book talks. To attract children, the house offered after-school recreation. These activities functioned to inculcate a sense of inner self-improvement and responsibility, with the component of moral education incorporated into every event. Dinner in the soup kitchens was always followed by a discussion of social issues and Catholic teachings. These strategies, de Hueck claimed, averted hundreds of transient workers and poor immigrant families from communism.[49]

In a paradoxical turn of events, de Hueck's accomplishments soon came under attack. Opposed to the Friendship House, several priests called for an inquiry into its canonical status. Many objected to the house's financial status; it obtained funds largely through soliciting donations. Moreover, the clergy disapproved of de Hueck's personal life; she was a single mother, estranged from her husband. Ironically, de Hueck was accused of being a communist: her constant discussions on communism were mistaken by some as evidence of communist sympathies. Furthering these allegations was the accusation that one of the staff at a similar house in Ottawa had been deported as a communist.[50] On August 15, 1936, a commission of five priests was established to look into the matter. The commission concurred, not surprisingly, that the settlement house would be best administered by local priests. Following de Hueck's dismissal, Archbishop McGuigan requested that she continue investigating communist activity, which she did until 1938 when she left to set up settlement houses in the United States.[51]

## Cold War Politics within the Catholic Church

As the federal government pursued collective security through international military alliances, on the home front extrastate institutions were safeguarding national security.[52] During the Cold War the Catholic Church was involved in its own practices of containment. It continued to police suspect communities and maintained its moral and educational campaign designed to curtail internal dangers and preserve freedom and security.[53] The Catholic Church may not have been as influential as the state or business in shaping a political and popular agenda, but it nonetheless was an important force that helped consolidate a postwar outlook. Catholic anti-communism and reform efforts permeated the private lives of thousands of Catholics and non-Catholics living in Toronto. That it had a significant impact on the communist movement is evident in the Party's attempt to defend itself against the archbishop's accusations. In 1949 the Communist paper *The Tribune* reproached McGuigan for his "fascist plot" to destroy democratic freedom and militant trade unionism.[54]

The Cold War was not simply an international, state, or corporate concern: rather, it operated as a mixed social economy in which government interests merged with the goals of private voluntary institutions. The activities of the Catholic Church demonstrate how extrastate institutions were involved in engendering moral behaviour and political values that would consolidate the Cold War agenda. This interlinking between public practices and private initiatives explains, in part, the success of postwar strategies in ensuring a Canadian public that supported an arms race and doctrine of collective security.

During this era federal and provincial interests used Catholic anti-communism to their own benefit. The Catholic vote in Quebec was essential to the federal strategy of collective security and to an increased international role in the North Atlantic Treaty Organization (NATO). Politicians, including Prime Minister Louis St. Laurent and Secretary of State for External Affairs Lester Pearson, as well as Quebec's Union Nationale premier Maurice Duplessis, sought to capture the Quebec electorate by dramatizing the Soviet peril to Catholic audiences. In a 1949 speech at the Richelieu Club in Quebec City, St. Laurent singled out a bishop in the audience and suggested that Soviet domination could result in the bishop's imprisonment, just as had occurred to so many men of the cloth under communist rule.[55] Such Liberal practices, Reg Whitaker and Gary Marcuse note, were successful in convincing Catholics that Canadian troops in Europe and later in Asia "were standing on guard for God, church, and family against the armies of darkness."[56] This federal anti-communist rhetoric, although directed to French-speaking Catholics, gave more legitimacy to the Catholic crusade throughout the country.

In Ontario the Conservative government of George Drew was likewise seeking an ally in the archbishop of Toronto for the war against the "Commies."[57] In a June 1945 letter to Archbishop McGuigan, Drew outlined his concern over the growing momentum of Soviet power within the province: "The fact is that the communists have more votes than ever before. They have an active, vigorous, well financed organization. I believe their propaganda will continue to be as active as ever." As he fuelled the archbishop's fears, Drew encouraged an intensified Catholic moral campaign. For as Drew argued, "There is a very real need for an educational campaign showing what their purpose really is."[58]

Attempts to sway the Catholic vote do not suggest that the Church was a malleable instrument shaped by government interests. Anti-Communism was well-entrenched in the Archdiocese of Toronto before the Cold War. Rather, state initiatives and Catholic goals merged over a common agenda to secure the nation against revolutionary movements. A pervasive pro-Cold War public opinion would not have been achieved without the consent and, more importantly, the participation of extrastate institutions.

As the Gouzenko affair had disclosed how trusted public servants engaged in espionage (see especially chapter 12 here), so too was the Church concerned with disloyalty amidst its own congregation. Rumours that the Church itself was infiltrated by "Commies" intensified the surveillance of ethnic communities. By the late 1940s suspicions were mounting over communist aims to penetrate all aspects of immigrant life, including ethnic parishes and local priests. Within Toronto, allegations regarding the Slovenian community led to a Church commission in 1949 on the "Religious Condition among New Canadians of Slovenian Descent."[59] The investigation concluded that many Slovene families living in Toronto were estranged from the Church, and that this was indeed the outcome of communist propaganda. In addition to the report, the archbishop received a list of names of individuals living in Canada under assumed identities, people who, before emigrating, had been associated with the communists. One of these persons was the president of the Slovenian branch of the Holy Name Society in Toronto. Ironically, the Society was a Catholic devotional confraternity known for its anti-communist activities.[60] Moreover, complaints from parishioners revealed that at least two priests were affiliated with the communist Slovenian People's Party. One reverend was denounced by churchgoers for advocating communist ideals and "basing his treatment [of Slovenians] on their political affiliations." He was also accused of hosting meetings of the Slovenian People's Party in church halls.[61]

In the late 1940s, when concern was mounting over the presence of extreme leftist groups on university campuses, McGuigan promoted the formation of Catholic committees to "quietly size up the extent of communist activities" in universities.[62] Catholic students warned the Archdiocese that university associations were being overrun by the Reds, and reports informed McGuigan that some recent immigrants had obtained teaching posts at Canadian universities for "the explicit agenda of spreading communism in Canada."[63] In response the Canadian Federation of Newman Clubs (CFNC), formed in 1942 to foster unity among Catholic students, resolved in 1947 to combat communism on university campuses. McGuigan encouraged the development of surveillance committees and financed the activities of the University of Toronto Newman Club. The CFNC convinced other student bodies to protest the penetration of communist ideals in the National Federation of Canadian University Students, the main secular student movement.[64]

In addition to policing by Catholics, McGuigan was closely associated with the Toronto Alert Service, a secular organization "dedicated to the task of gathering information" and alerting citizens to subversive operations in Canada and Soviet domination abroad. The Service was, in part, subsidized by the Catholic Women's League.[65] Moreover, McGuigan supported Marjorie Lamb, the director of the Service, by circulating the Service's publications, encouraging Catholics to attend Lamb's anti-communist study clubs, and inviting her to address Catholic gatherings. The Civic Election Alert, a branch of the Alert Service, would inform the archbishop of candidates sympathetic to communism. Not only did McGuigan distribute these names to all the churches in the various wards, but he also requested that pastors encourage their congregations to vote against Labor Progressive candidates.[66]

At the same time as the federal state was ensuring deterrence through an arms race, the Church was participating in containment through its moral and educational campaign. The Archdiocese's strategies, including weekly sermons and social study clubs on "Atheistic Communism," continued to denounce communist threats.[67] The Catholic *Register* exacerbated concern over Soviet domination with such headlines as "Over nine thousand priests and nuns killed or arrested by Reds." The Church organized speakers series, and Watson Kirkconnell, an extreme anti-communist university professor, was invited to speak at one conference. Kirkconnell wrote a government pamphlet on communism in Canada: a distorted analysis of a country about to be overrun by Soviet power.[68] As new evidence of communist penetration surfaced, the Church immediately attempted to quash its success.

In the 1950s, to counteract the communist penetration of unions, the Archdiocese formed labour schools. Involvement in the workers' movement was a priority for the Church. The Vatican encyclicals *Rerum novarum* and, more so, *Quadragesimo anno* encouraged labour associations as a means of protecting workers against unscrupulous capitalists. The development of communism was blamed on the excesses of capitalism, and, as McGuigan noted in 1961, "Communism had had its appeal for one reason: because it presents itself as a solution to the economic problem."[69] Although the Vatican promoted participation in trade unions, it opposed any revolutionary activities; unions were to seek co-operative approaches rather than attempt to dominate business relations.

While a National Catholic Union emerged in Quebec, the expediency of a similar movement for the rest of Canada was a contested issue.[70] Since the early part of the century the Quebec Church had opposed affiliation with the American Federation of Labor or any international labour organization, insisting instead that Catholics participate in confessional unions. Such proposals placed Catholics outside Quebec in a precarious situation. In response, Archbishop McNeil argued that a National Catholic Union was not feasible. His alternative was the formation of labour schools to promote Catholic leadership in the workers' movement. Father Charles E. McGuire, who was placed in charge of the schools, drew on his contacts in the union movement and obtained prominent leaders to address his students. The schools were reasonably popular; they boasted over seven hundred participants and became known for their "leading role in unmasking communism."[71] Several union members, including those affiliated with the International Chemical Workers and the United Packing House of America, sought out McGuire's schools to assist in liberating their unions from communist control.[72] The schools worked, in part, to counter the formation of a strong labour activism, and they reinforced a Cold War outlook.

The goals pursued by the Catholic Church during the Cold War were not dissimilar to those of the state. Internal security in the public sphere was ensured, as Whitaker and Marcuse note, through the "erection of controls to screen out 'security risks' among civil servants and immigrants; the elaboration of internal surveillance techniques to keep watch over dissident political activities; the dissemination of propaganda warning citizens of the dangers of Communism and celebrating the benefits of the Free World."[73] The Catholic Church was pursuing a similar agenda through its spies, informants, and surveillance of immigrants, its university committees to assess subversive activities, and its moral and educational campaign to create a Canadian and Catholic bulwark that would defend not just religious freedom but the nation as a whole.

## The Extrastate Policing of Private Life

The activities pursued by the Roman Catholic Archdiocese of Toronto are evidence of how national security and a political Cold War ideology was ensured through the interplay of a multiplicity of forces extending beyond state or corporate powers. Extrastate organizations have historically participated in the policing of citizens; they are not simply confined to religious devotions or to social welfare.[74] These extrastate forms of surveillance point to the pervasive nature of policing and the extent to which they permeate private life. Policing is not merely a coercive force; it operates at multiple levels. In this sense, private policing is emblematic of Michel Foucault's work on discipline.[75]

Such private means of monitoring and regulating behaviour, however, cannot be subordinated and subsumed under state power or dominant interests. Securing citizens is ensured through the intersection of public and private institutions, and voluntary organizations are capable of making their own claims on the state. For instance, during the 1930s the Toronto Red Squad relied on endorsements from social groups to justify its heavy-handed approach against the Communist Party. As well, the government's Cold War policy would not have been as successful if it were not for groups within civil society that shared the same concerns. State agendas are, in part, shaped by the interests of a plurality of extrastate organizations, while these institutions are simultaneously being influenced by the state.

The mixed social economy between public policy and private initiatives, then, is a key to making sense of the multiple, contradictory, and interlinking techniques and technologies deployed to maintain national security. Policing is not the exclusive property of the state, or limited to private corporate surveillance. Recognizing this wider interaction opens up the possibility of exploring how private life is policed by a plethora of moral, social, and legal bodies.

## Notes

I want to thank Mariana Valverde, Lucy Luccisano, and the other members of the discussion group at the University of Toronto for their insightful comments and encouragement. My thanks also to Gordon Darroch, Lorna Erwin, and the anonymous reviewers for their constructive criticisms, and to Daniel Robinson for his historical insights and continual support. Funding for this research was made available by the Social Sciences and Humanities Research Council of Canada. This is a revised version of a longer article that appeared in *Labour/Le Travail* 40 (Fall 1997).

1.  Archbishop James McGuigan to Archbishop H.J. O'Leary, Toronto, June 1, 1937, McGuigan Papers, Archives of the Roman Catholic Archdiocese of Toronto (ARCAT).
2.  I use the term English-speaking Catholics to differentiate the established hierarchy of the Church—those who arrived from Ireland and Scotland in the nineteenth century—from Catholics who emigrated from Eastern and Central Europe after World War I.
3.  In the 1930s the Church equated socialism with communism. See Gregory Baum, *Catholics and Canadian Socialism: Political Thought in the Thirties and Forties* (Toronto: Paulist Press, 1980). Ontario, and in particular Toronto, was deemed by the Archdiocese as a spawning ground for Bolshevik organizing; the Communist Party of Canada was secretly founded in Guelph in 1921, and the Social Democratic Party of Canada and Socialist Party of North America were gaining momentum in the province. Moreover, by the 1930s, the Co-operative Commonwealth Federation (CCF) was achieving a stronghold within the province.
4.  Gregory S. Kealey, "State Repression of Labour and the Left in Canada, 1914–1920: The Impact of the First World War," *Canadian Historical Review* 73 (September 1992), pp.281–314; Reg Whitaker and Gary Marcuse, *Cold War Canada: The Making of a National Insecurity State, 1945–1957* (Toronto: University of Toronto Press, 1994); Reg Whitaker, "Origins of the Canadian Government's Internal Security System, 1946–1952," *Canadian Historical Review* 65 (June 1984), pp.154–83.
5.  For works on moral regulation, see the special issue of *Canadian Journal of Sociology* 19 (Spring 1994).
6.  Mariana Valverde, *The Age of Light, Soap and Water: Moral Reform in English Canada, 1885–1925* (Toronto: McClelland and Stewart, 1991).
7.  Nikolas Rose, "Beyond the Public/Private Division: Law, Power and the Family," *Journal of Law and Society* 14 (Spring 1987), pp.61–76; Valverde, *Age of Light*.
8.  Mariana Valverde, "The Mixed Social Economy as a Canadian Tradition," *Studies in Political Economy* 47 (Summer 1995), pp.33–60.
9.  See Gordon Darroch and Michael D. Ornstein, "Ethnicity and Occupational Structure in Canada in 1871: The Vertical Mosaic in Historical Perspective," *Canadian Historical Review* 61 (September 1980), pp.305–33, for a detailed study of the 1871 census that reveals that Irish Catholics were well-represented in all occupational categories, although they were significantly overrepresented as labourers.
10.  Mark McGowan, "Toronto's English-Speaking Catholics, Immigration, and the Making of a Canadian Catholic Identity, 1900–1930," in *Creed and Culture: The Place of English-Speaking Catholics in Canadian Society, 1750–1930*, ed. Terrance Murphy and Gerald Stortz (Montreal: McGill-Queen's University Press, 1993), pp.204–45.
11.  Archbishop James McGuigan was appointed Cardinal in 1946.
12.  In the 1930s the Archdiocese of Toronto extended from the Niagara Peninsula to Georgian Bay in the North, and from Long Beach in the West as far as Oshawa in the East. Newman Club of Toronto, *The Ontario Catholic Year Book and Directory* (Toronto, 1920, 1935); Census of Canada 1941, 98-1941.
13.  Jeanne Beck, "Henry Somerville and the Development of Catholic Social Thought in Canada: Somerville's Role in the Archdiocese of Toronto, 1913–1943," Ph.D. thesis, McMaster University, Hamilton, 1977; Brian F. Hogan, "Salted with Fire: Studies in Catholic Social Thought and Action in Ontario, 1931–1961," Ph.D. thesis, University

of Toronto, 1986; McGowan, "Toronto's English-Speaking Catholics."

14. *Report of the Sixth National Convention of the Communist Party in Canada*, May–June 1929, p.12, cited in Watson Kirkconnell, "Communism in Canada and the U.S.A.," *Canadian Catholic Historical Association, Historical Studies*, 1948, pp.41–51. The failure of the Finnish revolution forced many socialists to leave the country after World War I, and many of them came to Canada. The Ukrainian community in Canada was composed of two groups: those emigrating during the Tsarist regime were predominantly pro-Communist, while those arriving in the 1920s were typically anti-communist. The latter group had experienced the failure of an independent socialist Ukraine. Lita-Rose Betcherman, *The Little Band: The Clashes between the Communists and the Political and Legal Establishment in Canada, 1928–1932* (Ottawa: Deneau, 1982), p.10. For other works on the Communist Party in Canada, see Irving Martin Abella, *Nationalism, Communism, and Canadian Labour: The CIO, the Communist Party and the Canadian Congress of Labour 1935–1956* (Toronto: University of Toronto Press, 1973); Ivan Avakumovic, *The Communist Party in Canada: A History* (Toronto: McClelland and Stewart, 1975); Norman Penner, *The Canadian Left: A Critical Analysis* (Scarborough, Ont.: Prentice Hall of Canada, 1977); and William Rodney, *Soldiers of the International: A History of the Communist Party of Canada, 1919–1929* (Toronto: University of Toronto Press, 1968).

15. Avakumovic, *Communist Party*; Betcherman, *Little Band*, pp.11, 75.

16. Watson Kirkconnell, *The Seven Pillars of Freedom* (London: Oxford University Press, 1944).

17. Avakumovic, *Communist Party*, pp.37, 115.

18. Annual Activity Report of the Catholic Big Brothers' Association, Toronto, circa early 1930s, McNeil Papers (ARCAT).

19. Luigi G. Pennacchio, "The Torrid Trinity: Toronto's Fascists, Italian Priests and Archbishops during the Fascist Era, 1929–1940," in *Catholics at the "Gathering Place": Historical Essays on the Archdiocese of Toronto, 1841–1991*, ed. Mark McGowan and Brian Clarke (Toronto: Canadian Catholic Historical Association, 1993), p.234.

20. In response to rumours that Prime Minister William Lyon Mackenzie King had considered disbanding the RCMP in 1926, several members of the Catholic Church wrote to the Honourable Colonel George E. Amyot declaring the necessity of such a force for the security of the country. One letter went so far as to suggest that the RCMP and the Catholic Church were the "two stabilizing institutions in this country." J.B. Maclean to McNeil, Toronto, Aug. 6, 1926, McNeil Papers (ARCAT).

21. Betcherman, *Little Band*; Suzanne Michelle Skebo, "Liberty and Authority: Civil Liberties in Toronto, 1929–1935," M.A. thesis, University of British Columbia, Vancouver, 1968.

22. *The Globe*, Aug. 19, 1929, cited in Betcherman, *Little Band*, p.64.

23. Abbe Philipe Casgarain to McNeil, Toronto, March 7, 1927, McNeil Papers (ARCAT).

24. "No. 210, Notes Respecting Revolutionary Organizations and Agitators in Canada," Toronto, Jan. 31, 1923, Ruthenian Catholics, McNeil Papers (ARCAT).

25. Inspector Marshall's Reports, Toronto, April 21, 1932, May 30, 1932, and Draper to McNeil, Toronto, June 7, 1932, McNeil Papers (ARCAT).

26. Eddie Doherty, *Tumbleweed: A Biography* (Milwaukee: Bruce Publishing, 1948), p.149.

27. For works on Catherine de Hueck, see Jeanne R. Beck, "Contrasting Approaches to Catholic Social Action during the Depression: Henry Somerville the Educator and Catherine de Hueck the Activist," in *Catholics at the "Gathering Place"*, ed. McGowan and Clarke; Shane P. Carmody, "Catherine de Hueck and Catholic Action in Toronto 1930–1936," unpublished paper, May 1985; Catherine de Hueck Doherty, *Fragments of My Life* (Notre Dame, Ind.: Ave Maria Press, 1979); Doherty, *Tumbleweed*; Lorene Hanley Duquin, *They Called Her the Baroness: The Life of Catherine de Hueck Doherty* (New York: Alba House, 1995); Hogan, "Salted with Fire"; Elizabeth Sharum, "A Strange Fire Burning: A History of the Friendship House Movement," Ph.D. thesis,

Texas Technical University, Lubbock, 1977.

28. Catherine Doherty, "Little Mandate," cited in Sharum, "Strange Fire Burning," p.40; Doherty, *Tumbleweed*, p.150.

29. Outline of Communist Activities, 1, 2, Catholic Action Papers (Archives of the Roman Catholic Archdiocese of Ottawa, Ottawa), cited in Sharum, "Strange Fire Burning," pp.42–47; Doherty, *Tumbleweed*, p.150; "Baroness de Hueck Tells of Her Fight against Communism," *Social Forum* 1 (March 1936), p.1; Gustave Sauve, "Moscow in Canada," *Social Forum* 1 (March 1936), p.2.

30. De Hueck's map on Communist Activities in St. Patrick's Parish, Toronto, circa early 1930s, McNeil Papers (ARCAT).

31. McNeil, "The Papal Solution," *The Red Menace*, Toronto, Sept. 8, 1933, McNeil Papers (ARCAT).

32. Pope Pius XI to pastors in Toronto, Nov. 3, 1930, McNeil Papers (ARCAT); Mr. G. Murray, General Manager, Canadian Broadcasting Corporation to McGuigan, Toronto, Jan. 4, 1939, McGuigan Papers (ARCAT).

33. Rev. Joseph H. O'Neill, "Archbishop McGuigan of Toronto and the Holy Name Society: Its Role as a Force against Canadian Communism," *Canadian Catholic Historical Association, Historical Studies*, 1988, pp.61–77.

34. Rev. Michael J. McGrath to McGuigan, Toronto, May 17, 1939, and Financial Reports of the Catholic Adjustment Bureau, Toronto, 1939, McGuigan Papers (ARCAT).

35. Hogan, "Salted with Fire," pp.104–5; Sharum, "Strange Fire Burning," p.81.

36. Mrs. Harris McPhedran to the Honourable J.H. Robb, Minister of Health, Toronto, April 13, 1933, McNeil Papers (ARCAT).

37. Ibid.

38. Baroness' Clippings, Combermere, 1930–1937, Madonna House Files, cited in Sharum, "Strange Fire Burning."

39. Tensions between the Vatican and Mussolini were exacerbated after the conquest of Abyssinia in 1936, when the Italian government, instead of privileging Catholicism as the state religion in the empire, merely adopted a policy of religious toleration. The publication of the government's 1938 manifesto on racial purity and the subsequent anti-Semitic legislation elicited a denunciation from the pope. See Peter S. Kent, "The Catholic Church in the Italian Empire, 1936–38," *Historical Papers*, Canadian Historical Association, 1984, pp.138–50.

40. For the Church's opposition to the persecution of Jews in Germany, see John S. Moir, *Church and Society: Documents on the Religious and Social History of the Roman Catholic Archdiocese in Toronto from the Archives of the Archdiocese* (Toronto: Archdiocese of Toronto, 1991), pp.226–30.

41. Fr. Daniel Ehamn to McGuigan, Toronto, June 10, 1938, McGuigan Papers (ARCAT).

42. McGuigan to Revs. Sanson, Pellicelita, Balo, and Ehman, Toronto, June 11, 1938, McGuigan Papers (ARCAT); Pennacchio, "Torrid Trinity."

43. For a discussion of relief in Ontario during the Depression, see James Struthers, *The Limits of Affluence: Welfare in Ontario, 1920–1970* (Toronto: University of Toronto Press, 1994); Roger E. Riendeau, "A Clash of Interests: Dependency and the Municipal Problem in the Great Depression," *Journal of Canadian Studies* 14 (Spring 1979), pp.50–58.

44. Marion Bell, "The History of the Catholic Welfare Bureau," M.A. thesis, University of Toronto, 1949.

45. Rev. M. J. McGrath to McGuigan, Toronto, circa October 1938, and McGrath to McGuigan, Toronto, circa January 1939, McGuigan Papers (ARCAT).

46. De Hueck to McNeil, Toronto, July 1, 1934, McNeil Papers (ARCAT).

47. John Fitzgerald, retiring editor of the Montreal *Beacon*, Toronto, circa 1934, McNeil Papers (ARCAT).

48. Sharum, "Strange Fire Burning," pp.68–70.

49. Ibid.; Hogan, "Salted with Fire," p.104.

50. Rev. Francis to McGuigan, Toronto, Dec. 18, 1936, McGuigan Papers (ARCAT).

51. Hogan, "Salted with Fire," pp.123–25.
52. For an analysis of how the private family sphere was involved in promoting "domestic containment" in the United States, see Elaine Tyler May, *Homeward Bound: American Families in the Cold War Era* (New York: Basic Books, 1988).
53. Accounts of the Cold War era, which tend to be framed by a state-centred approach, largely ignore these activities. For example, Whitaker and Marcuse's extensive work on the Cold War includes a detailed discussion of extrastate and non-corporate institutions, but their analysis maintains a state-centred bias. See Whitaker and Marcuse, *Cold War Canada*. See also Reg Whitaker, "Fighting the Cold War on the Home Front: America, Britain, Australia and Canada," *The Socialist Register* (London, 1984), pp.23–67. In this article Whitaker does present an analytical distinction between "state repression" and "political repression," the latter referring to a wider "political system" outside the state, typified by "McCarthyism" in the United States. This political system, however, is still characterized as an extension of or as propelled by the state. Those extrastate institutions that participated in a Canadian version of "McCarthyism"—right-wing groups, the media, and avid anti-communists such as Watson Kirkconnell and Pauline McGibbon and the Toronto Alert Service, to name a few—are characterized as having played a rather minor role in the formation of a Cold War outlook. As Whitaker and Marcuse, *Cold War Canada*, p.272, suggest, "It is hard to know how much, if any, influence such services actually had, since the numbers and importance of their subscribers is unknown. Certainly, they had little influence relative to comparable groups in the United States at this time."
54. J. Bacon to McGuigan, Toronto, Aug. 22, 1949, McGuigan Papers (ARCAT).
55. R.D. Cuff and J.L. Granatstein, *Ties That Bind: Canadian-American Relations in Wartime, from the Great War to the Cold War* (Toronto: Samuel Stevens Hakkert, 1977), p.149.
56. Whitaker and Marcuse, *Cold War Canada*, p.266.
57. Premier Drew, notorious for his red-baiting ideology, had been maintaining a secret Special Branch of the Ontario Provincial Police, a "Gestapo," based on the old Red Squad. See Gerald L. Caplan, *The Dilemma of Canadian Socialism: The CCF in Ontario* (Toronto: McClelland and Stewart, 1973), pp.168–90.
58. Ontario Premier George A. Drew to McGuigan, Toronto, May 31, 1945, June 14, 1945, McGuigan Papers (ARCAT). In the 1940s, two members of the Communist Party were voted into the Ontario legislature: Joe Salsberg in the Jewish Spadina district (1943–55) and Alex MacLeod in the Bellwoods riding (1943–51). Also, a number of communists were elected to the Toronto Board of Education.
59. "Report on the Religious Conditions among New Canadians of Slovenian Descent," Toronto, circa 1949, McGuigan Papers (ARCAT).
60. See Father Joseph H. O'Neill, "Archbishop McGuigan of Toronto and the Holy Name Society: Its Role as a Force against Canadian Communism," *Canadian Catholic Historical Association* 55 (1988), pp.61–77.
61. Fr. Jakob Kolaric to McGuigan, Toronto, July 31, 1952, confidential correspondence to McGuigan, Toronto, July 14, 1951, F. Turk to McGuigan, Toronto, April 5, 1955, and Rudolf Cujs to McGuigan, Toronto, March 6, 1955, McGuigan Papers (ARCAT).
62. McGuigan to Robert Lindsay, CFNC President, Toronto, Jan. 16, 1947, and Toronto Newman Club to McGuigan, Toronto, Nov. 22, 1948, McGuigan Papers (ARCAT).
63. E. Dubois to McGuigan, Toronto, Dec. 8, 1947, McGuigan Papers (ARCAT).
64. McGuigan to Robert Lindsay, CFNC President, Toronto, Jan. 16, 1947, Toronto Newman Club to McGuigan, Toronto, Nov. 22, 1948, and Catherine D. McLean, CFNC External Affairs Chairman to McGuigan, Toronto, Jan. 30, 1947, McGuigan Papers (ARCAT). For information on the communist infiltration of university campuses, see Paul Axelrod, "Spying on the Young in Depression and War: Students, Youth Groups and the RCMP, 1935–1942," *Labour/Le Travail* 35 (Spring 1995), pp.43–63.
65. "She's a Redhead Who's Out to Beat the Reds," *Toronto Telegram*, Jan. 30, 1959; Marjorie Lamb, "Opportunities Unlimited: A Time of Choice," *Vital Speeches of the*

*Day* (New York) 26,11 (March 15, 1960).

66. Lamb to Wall, Archdiocese of Toronto Chancellor, Toronto, 1949–1958, and Lamb to McGuigan, Toronto, 1958–1960, McGuigan Papers (ARCAT); Marjorie Lamb, *Communism and You* (Toronto), Jan. 28, 1962.

67. "'Atheistic Communism' Study Clubs," *Register*, Oct. 18, 1947; "HNS Central Study Club on Atheistic Communism," *Register*, Nov. 1, 1947.

68. *Register*, July 8, 1950; Kirkconnell, "Communism in Canada and the U.S.A."; and Whitaker and Marcuse, *Cold War Canada*, pp.277–79.

69. Article by McGuigan, Toronto, circa 1961, McGuigan Papers (ARCAT).

70. For a discussion of the union movement in Quebec, see Fraser Isbester, "A History of the National, Catholic Unions in Canada, 1901–1965," Ph.D. thesis, Cornell University, Ithaca, N.Y., 1968.

71. "Toronto Labour Schools Noted for Unmasking Communism," *Register*, Aug. 31, 1957.

72. Hogan, *Salted with Fire*, p.263; Beck, "Henry Somerville."

73. Whitaker and Marcuse, *Cold War Canada*, p.22.

74. See, for example, Kelly Hannah-Moffat and Mariana Valverde, "Saving the Prisoner or Prison? Private Philanthropy and State Punishment in Turn-of-the-Century Ontario," *Canadian Journal of Law and Society*, forthcoming; Margaret Little, "The Blurring of Boundaries: Private and Public Welfare for Single Mothers in Ontario," *Studies in Political Economy* 47 (Summer 1995), pp.89–109.

75. Michel Foucault, *Discipline and Punish: The Birth of the Prison* (New York: Vintage Books, 1977).

four ⋆ ⋆ ⋆

# The Red Petticoat Brigade: Mine Mill Women's Auxiliaries and the Threat from Within, 1940s–70s

*If you have in any police of a nation, a secret force investigating individuals at all times, including active and true patriots in trade unions and in parliament, then I say that is a gestapo.*

Harold Winch, M.P., House of Commons Debates, June 25, 1959.

In 1969 the RCMP filed its last surveillance report on the Ladies' Auxiliary of the Mine, Mill and Smelter Workers union of Sudbury, Ontario.[1] The report closed a file on the local that dated back to the 1940s. Why would the RCMP be interested in this women's organization?

During the postwar period, whenever an auxiliary local in Rossland, British Columbia, or Port Colborne, Ontario, held a tea party, local RCMP officers would report the event to the Security and Intelligence Branch in Ottawa. When the Timmins, Ontario, local of the Mine Mill Ladies' Auxiliary held a Christmas raffle of Avon cosmetics in fall 1962, the local police dutifully reported the information to the town's RCMP detachment. One typical 1963 report on Sudbury activities noted that the auxiliary locals of the International Union of Mine, Mill and Smelter Workers (IUMM&SW) were "continuing to hold rummage sales, bake sales and draws to raise funds for various charitable organizations," apparently considering this fact to be worthy of the attention of those watching out for the nation's security.[2]

At first glance, perhaps, it may seem ridiculous for the Mounties to be spending their time, year after year, reporting on the success or failure of what often amounted to teas, bazaars, and Tupperware parties, yet for decades the RCMP Special Branch kept files on all the activities of Mine Mill women's auxiliaries across the country. In Northern Ontario it was standard procedure for local Security and Intelligence officers to file the initial report. The information was then processed in North Bay and sent on to the Ottawa headquarters.[3] Each main local of Mine Mill had a separate file, usually with the caption "Subversive Activities in . . ." The all-encompassing character of this surveillance is astounding.

By the end of the Cold War the Canadian spy machine had a detailed record of these women's activities.

During the Cold War nearly everyone became a suspect, and women's organizations closely linked to left-led unions such as the United Electrical Workers (UE) and Mine Mill were obvious targets for surveillance. In a way, the RCMP were reframing apparently harmless tea parties as threats to national security not because of what the women were doing, but because of whom the women had married. Still, the rationale for surveillance involved more than simple guilt by association. If the women were suspect only because they were linked to other Mine Mill activities, then surely reports would have been less frequent. Reports would have focused on Mine Mill women's activities, such as strike support or visits to classified countries, that tied them to left activism. But watching out for rummage sales, bake sales, and draws, often held to support local charities? Tea parties? Was that not extreme? Not according to the RCMP mandate.

The security responsibilities of the RCMP were defined by the 1939 Official Secrets Act. The Force was to discover and prevent espionage and subversion, to screen government employees and to screen applicants for visas and citizenship. By 1953 the RCMP Security and Intelligence division's efforts to carry out this mandate had resulted in twenty-one thousand active files on individuals and twenty-three hundred on organizations.[4] The pursuit of subversive elements in the civil service, the unions, and social groups did not abate. While the Cold War search for "the enemy within" required a broad definition of subversion, the RCMP focus on communists and their so-called front groups predominated in most of the surveillance work. The shifts in Canadian government policy towards the Soviet Union directed some of this work, but by and large the RCMP was left to its own devices. By the 1950s the RCMP focus was on "a Communist Party build up within our borders."[5]

The major countersubversive action undertaken by the Security Service was the collection and processing of information gathered from informants, secret agents, and public documents. As the RCMP's own analysts Carl Betke and Stan Horrall noted, "The RCMP preferred to employ as far as possible, agents who were not members of the force. Their association with it was temporary, less direct and their employment could be discontinued once their usefulness was over."[6] To supplement its own surveillance reports the RCMP relied on information from local media and sympathetic friends in churches, unions, and cultural associations. The officers did not have to look far afield for their soldiers in the Cold War.

There were no RCMP officers at Ladies' Auxiliary meetings. Surveillance was carried out by concerned citizens who acted as occasional informants. One facet of community surveillance, for instance, was co-operation between the RCMP and the Catholic Church (see Paula Maurutto's chapter here). These extrastate forms of surveillance served to complete the circle of surveillance.

The development of a postwar social consensus that accepted this level of surveillance may seem odd to us now, but to understand why these women's groups were seen as potentially dangerous to the Canadian state, one has to look at the broader Cold War culture. After the Depression of the 1930s and World War II, emotional issues and family relations took on a greater significance in most people's lives. As Mary Louise Adams points out in her study of postwar gender politics:

> In the years following the Second World War, the heterosexual family was valued as the "traditional" foundation of the Canadian social structure. The family was reified as a primary stabilizing influence on both the individual and the nation as a whole. . . . Mainstream discourses suggested that dissent and difference could weaken the face of democracy in the ideological fight against communism. Canadians were called upon to show an impressive social cohesiveness as evidence of their dedication to the superiority of the Western way of life. A commitment to the family was central to the social homogeneity necessitated by this display.[7]

We are just now beginning to understand the political and cultural ramifications of the Cold War, but it is clear that family life was an ideologically contested site. Putting life back together after the war required a change in gender roles both at home and in the workplace. The war had drawn many working-class women into the waged labour force, and many of them held well-paying jobs for the first time. With the demobilization of soldiers and the dismantling of war production, women were dismissed from most of these jobs. Yet married women continued to enter paid work, and by 1961 they accounted for 22 per cent of the female labour force (during the war married women accounted for only 4.5 per cent of the female labour force).[8] After the war women moved back into either low-paid work or unpaid work as wives and mothers, but keeping them in the home and keeping them happy represented a real political challenge. Cold War discourse overlaid a changing discourse on gender roles.

The patriotic virtues of a stable family life, with women back in the home as dutiful wives and mothers, were constantly reaffirmed by the state, the media, and the church. Elaine Tyler May points out that women's position in the home is central to the political stability of capitalism. In her study of U.S. families during the Cold War, May outlines the 1959 "kitchen debate" between Nixon and Khrushchev, describing Nixon's response to the communist way of life. Nixon insisted that the superiority of the American way of life "rested not on weapons, but on a secure, abundant family life of modern suburban homes. In these structures, adorned and worshipped by their inhabitants, women would achieve their glory and men would display their success. Consumerism was not an end in itself; it was the means of achieving individuality, leisure and upward mobility."[9] Postwar democratic discourse espoused a more egalitarian civil society in which men and women shared the fruits of the new consumerism, which itself frequently required an extra income. The contradiction between the renewed domesticity and the increase in married women's labour-force participation made it harder to marginalize women's political voice. Postwar popular culture's hierarchical familialism of the 1950s "Father Knows Best" variety co-existed with another increasingly prevalent point of view. While acknowledging the importance of family, this view saw wives and husbands as partners in both the marriage and the community.

While this society still maintained separate domestic and public spheres, the postwar years continued the transformation of earlier forms of domestic ideology.

The Cold War message contained a certain ambivalency. When Nixon contrasted the mass dictatorship of communism with the capitalists' rights to free political expression, he was praising individual freedom and familial patriotism as the bulwark of an abundant family life in capitalist societies. If free, individually based political expression was to be one of the defining features of the free world, then the ideology would also reaffirm women's rights as "free" political agents in the postwar gender order. While the postwar domestic feminism was cloaked in Cold War rhetoric, it also opened the political space for women's continued participation in public life.

Indeed, the free-world discourse opened up spaces for political activism, and working-class women made the most of them—even though the Cold War narrative of communist conspiracies attempted to control the meaning of democratic struggle and to challenge the left's attempt to remake life in working-class communities during the 1940s and 1950s. As Dorothy Sue Cobble notes in her re-evaluation of the significance of postwar working-class feminism, "Working class feminists bore the torch of gender equality and justice in the 1940s and 1950s,"[10] and many working-class women, though recognizing their commitment to family life, pushed at the same time for gender equality and social justice in the broader society. For their part, Mine Mill women developed their political and social critique of the postwar economy and social recovery from their standpoint as wives and mothers. Their democratic struggles for postwar reform questioned the normative hold of the Canadian political and social elites on the shape of postwar Canadian life. As "wives and mothers of wage-earners," Mine Mill women frequently sent letters of protest to the Canadian government about rising consumer prices, the lack of available working-class housing, and the need for a national health-care system. On one level the RCMP reports on tea parties may seem a bit ludicrous, then, but on another they were part of a broader national security campaign that viewed all forms of political opposition as a threat to the state.

## Cold War Canada: The Sudbury Experience

Support for RCMP surveillance was woven into Sudbury's community. In the 1950s Sudbury was a typical company town. Mining companies employed almost 40 per cent of the working population in 1951.[11] The paternalistic control of the two main employers, Inco and Falconbridge, reached far into community life, and the local elite expected loyalty and trust in their ability to lead the community. Postwar labour demands increased the local labour force, housing shortages were common, and the immigrants recruited to assist mining-company production added to the unstable aspects of the community.[12]

In the 1940s and 1950s the Sudbury basin ore deposits accounted for close to 90 per cent of all nickel production in the non-communist world.[13] When the local Sudbury union successfully certified in 1944, Local 598 of Mine Mill at Inco became the largest local in the international organization.[14] This left-led union was large enough to pose a threat to the stability of capitalism, and Mine Mill became a central target of Cold War politics. In Sudbury Mine Mill's social unionism challenged the hegemony of a local political and social elite that had long assumed the right to take care of the community. Ruth Reid, an auxiliary activist, long-time volunteer at the Mine Mill summer camp, and widow of Mine Mill's recreational director described the social climate in Sudbury: "This was a Mine Mill town in the 1950s. All the community activities were run by Mine Mill. Everyone from the Mayor and his family to the local doctors' wives and children were at the Mine Mill hall for some activity or another."[15] The centrality of family life to the post-war recovery made it a potential site for subversion, and local elites were quick to recognize the significant influence that Mine Mill men and women were having on local family life. Hence the popularity of Mine Mill's social unionism soon became part of a larger political and cultural struggle for the hearts and minds of Sudbury's working class.

## The Organization of Women's Auxiliaries in Northeast Ontario

Sexist assumptions that women, like children, were gullible and susceptible to communist influence meant that women and children were a central site for the battle against communism at home. In the April 1949 issue of *Chatelaine* Ronald Williams warned Canadian women not to be stooges for Communists. He argued, "You have to give the Communists credit for one thing: they have never underestimated the power of women." Williams continued, "The order has gone out here and in all free democracies: *infiltrate into any women's, youth or cultural organization you can find.* . . . This accent on women and youth, this constant drive to tap the tremendous latent power of women in all kinds of activity—churches, homes and school and fraternal clubs, art and culture—is by no means new."[16] These sentiments were echoed by members of the local elite, who believed it was their duty to keep an eye on all of the union's activities. Were women in the Mine Mill auxiliaries dupes of communism or were they communists themselves? Suspicion of even the most innocuous gathering prevailed.

The Mine Mill ladies' auxiliaries had been actively recruiting members since the late 1930s, and by the 1950s they existed in most of the mining centres across Canada. The Mine Mill auxiliaries in both Canada and the United States were part of an international organizational structure under the leadership, by the late 1940s, of Kay Carlin, the Mine Mill auxiliaries' first women's organizer in northeastern Ontario, and the wife of Mine Mill organizer Bob Carlin. Through this organization the auxiliaries pushed for recognition as full partners in the Mine Mill union movement.[17] But most locals were never more than a few hundred strong. While the Sudbury auxiliary signed up several hundred women in the first few years after its charter was granted in 1944, with a union membership of over fourteen thousand men the women's group remained small. The main function, according to Agnes Gauthier, president of Sudbury's Local 117 Ladies' Auxiliary in 1950, was to be of assistance to the local wherever and whenever it was needed, to further the cause of labour, and to strive for improved living conditions for miners and their families.[18] The Mine Mill constitution outlined the main purpose of the ladies' auxiliaries as "the education and training of women in the labour movement and to assist their Local Unions in time of need and labour disputes, to support the union in its legislative efforts and to provide educational and cultural activities for our members and their children."[19]

While the male-dominated trade union tried to make a place for its women-folk in the union, the space the women were able to claim still tied them to conventional gender roles. In the auxiliaries, family loyalty to husbands and children now extended to loyalty to the political aims of the Mine Mill union. Anything else would have been seen as inappropriate and unfeminine.

In her examination of postwar mass culture, Joanne Meyerowitz points out the problematic and contradictory nature of women's political position. She argues:

> Historians sometimes contend that the Cold War mentality encouraged domesticity, that it envisioned family life and especially mothers as buffers against the alleged Communist threat. But Cold war rhetoric had other possible meanings for women. In the *Ladies Home Journal,* authors often used the Cold War to promote women's political participation. . . . Senator Margaret Chase Smith made the case most strongly: "The way to reverse this socialistic, dictatorial trend and put more *home* in the government is for you women, the traditional homemakers, to become more active in your government." In this line of argument, the Cold War made women's political participation an international obligation.[20]

The contradictory and competing mores of Cold War family values restrained Mine Mill women from stepping outside of those cultural confines at the same time as it extended women's right to political activism. Public service was an important component of auxiliary work. As Ruth Reid puts it, "Someone once referred to the Ladies' Auxiliary as social workers because they supported so many things in the community."[21] The women raised funds for hospitals and schools and worked with the Red Cross. They also organized cultural activities—play schools and movie shows, dance school, drama groups. As Reid says, "At the children's camp the women were there as mothers, cooks, and at the beginning of the summer the parents and Ladies' Auxiliary always helped get the camp cleaned up for the new season."[22]

The women walked a fine line between unfeminine behaviour and pushiness on the one side and supportive militancy on the other. The women who chose to become active were usually left-of-centre, working-class women with a strong sense of trade-union consciousness. Many women who became leaders in the auxiliary had previously been political activists. "I think the ones of us who were really prominent, if you want to use that word, were people who had a base in union activity, that knew something about it," observed one auxiliary executive member. "Because it really wasn't a popular thing. The society didn't really accept it. Not at that time."[23]

Given the view of family life as the centre of postwar peace and stability, the church and local business people or elite tended to see women as the gatekeepers of these values, and women's loyalty to the established order was key. Women who joined the union auxiliary were seen as disrupting both the community and the domestic order. As one auxiliary member suggested: "At the time the union was not a socially accepted thing. Not in 1958. I mean, when I was working with the church auxiliary you said that very freely, but you didn't as far as being in the union auxiliary. Because they just, they didn't accept it, society didn't accept it to the extent that they probably would now."[24]

Some of the Mine Mill women understood the political nature of their work in the auxiliaries, but many members were ill-prepared to face the anti-communist backlash and RCMP surveillance that marked their years of activism in the union.

## RCMP Reports on Mine Mill Women

RCMP records show continual reporting on all Canadian auxiliaries of Mine Mill. One report from the Timmins detachment provides a glimpse of the RCMP's attitude towards the Mine Mill women:

> It may also be of interest to record that the undermentioned mailing list is maintained by this Ladies Auxiliary and although there is no doubt some innocent trade unionists listed herein, there are a good number who are known to be definitely connected with subversive movements and their correct address may be of interest at Div. H.Q. or for certain individual files . . . [three lines deleted].[25]

RCMP security was intent on keeping track of the movements of any Mine Mill women who might at some future time become "subversively inclined."[26] For example, a November 22, 1952, report from the Fort Erie detachment security officers noted, "The writer has endeavored to find out if [deleted] holds any prominence in the Ladies Auxiliary." On February 27, 1956, an officer at the same RCMP detachment observed that the Auxiliary appeared to be "only a social group that do not take an active interest in the affairs of the union." He added, "However, should there be any indication of their interest in that regard in the future, a report will be submitted immediately."[27] Names of conference delegates were routinely submitted to central headquarters so that Special Branch officers could monitor women identified as Communists or seen as being sympathetic to the Communist cause. As a result, all women holding official positions in any local of the Ladies' Auxiliary came under RCMP scrutiny. Like their male counterparts, national leaders, such as Dorothy McDonald, national co-ordinator of the women's auxiliaries, were detained by U.S. police when they tried to attend international meetings of the union. McDonald's response to her arrest in Chicago in 1949 illustrates her resistance to this infringement of her civil rights. In an open letter to the International board meeting, McDonald outlined her response to the RCMP role in curtailing her travel to the United States. "The mere fact that I am not allowed to enter your country will not stop me from speaking my mind whenever and where ever I see fit and certainly it will not stop me from protesting against tyranny no matter in what form, because I am a firm believer in real democracy."[28]

The Security and Intelligence reports drew information from Mine Mill newspapers, Auxiliary newsletters, and informants who appear to have attended occasional Auxiliary meetings. The RCMP reports frequently included attachments:

copies of Mine Mill newspapers, convention reports, and other documents prepared by Mine Mill. Local community members were only too willing to pass along samples of these materials.

While all reports were forwarded to Ottawa, they were also circulated to other units that might be interested in the information. For example, reports on the Timmins and Kirkland Lake locals frequently made their way into the Sudbury detachment files. When co-ordinator Dorothy McDonald announced the call for the Eighth Annual Mine Mill Convention, to be held in Sudbury in February 1956, the South Porcupine RCMP detachment forwarded the information and the accompanying newsletters to the North Bay Security division and on to Ottawa for review. The names of the women attending the convention were duly noted.[29]

RCMP officers also monitored other left-wing newspapers to gain information on Mine Mill women. For example, when the National Congress of Canadian Women conducted a survey of women's opinions on family allowances, health insurance, and housing, McDonald presented the views of Timmins women. The report, carried in the *Canadian Jewish Weekly*, made its way into RCMP clipping files and more than likely into McDonald's personal file.[30]

While RCMP officers reporting on the Sudbury Ladies' Auxiliary frequently mentioned that the activities of the organization were "*confined* to non-subversive endeavors," the surveillance never stopped.[31] The "rummage sales, bake sales and draws" cited in Constable J. Wiebe's September 16, 1963, report on Sudbury Auxiliary activity are typical of the somewhat less than "subversive" nature of the activities uncovered. These events, Wiebe noted, were in aid of raising funds "for various charitable organizations such as the Canadian National Institute for the Blind, the Children's Aid Society and the Cancer Society."[32] Even such benign reports did not result in an end to the surveillance. What the Mounties wanted was information that would add to the files of "suspected and known Communists" and election to any office in the Auxiliary immediately made one suspect. When the local RCMP detachments tracked the names of all women delegates to the 1956 convention, this information made its way to Ottawa to become part of the growing list of potential subversives.[33]

In May 1962 J.L. Forest, officer in charge of "A" Division of the Security and Intelligence Branch in Ottawa, wrote to the RCMP commissioner suggesting that a file be opened on the Timmins Ladies' Auxiliary. He outlined his reason as follows:

> Local 312 I.U.M.M. & S.W. Ladies Auxiliary in Timmins, Ontario is presently quite active. It is noted in the Mine Mill Ladies Auxiliary Newsletter for April 1962 (forwarded on [deleted] re: Mine Mill Auxiliary Newsletter—General Information) that Local 312 was represented by a delegate at the International Convention of the I.U.M.M. & S.W. held in Toronto, Ontario, March, 1962.[34]

The file was duly opened. A follow-up note on June 1, 1962, directed the records office to create a file entitled "International Mine Mill and Smelter Workers Union, Local 312, Ladies Auxiliary—Communist Party activities within—Timmins, Ontario." It would seem that attendance at any Mine Mill meeting made a person suspect. A successful recruitment drive by any local of the women's auxiliaries was sure to draw the interest of the RCMP. By December 1962, Timmins Security and Intelligence officers were dutifully reporting on all the activities of the local. Clearly, a portion of their reports made use of information from McDonald's Ladies' Auxiliary newsletters.[35] In 1967, after four years of reporting on the Timmins women of Mine Mill, the reporting officer commented, "There has been no activity of importance during the past four years." Still, the surveillance continued.

RCMP reports were not so much interested in the content of the women's political activism as they were in the ever-widening search for potential subversives. The RCMP saw the women as duplicitous stooges for a communist movement, even though, according to the Force's own records, the women were doing nothing that could be remotely construed as a threat to national security. Cold War discourse reframed Mine Mill women's call for peace, justice, and equality for working people as a threat to the patriotic normative culture of the masculine elite. The scope of state surveillance, the criteria of "threat to national security," was wide indeed, running from anyone who was a communist, to anyone who was friendly with communists, to anyone who could potentially be a stooge for communism.

This wide scope made the RCMP job more difficult, and Security and Intelligence officers learned to be creative. In their review of RCMP activities, internal analysts noted how the RCMP collected information: "From informants and secret agents and from every bit of public information the Section compiled its description of the multi-faceted Communist activity." From the RCMP's point of view this meant:

> A knowledge of Communist membership was crucial, in addition, to discovery of Communist activities in organizations not designated Communist: "front groups, labour organizations and mass language groups." The front groups were in the main dedicated to the international "Cominform" strategy of a "peace" campaign launched in the late 1940s. Organizations like the Canadian Peace Congress and various Peace Councils, certain women's and youth groups, and those who advocated "Ban the Bomb" petitions, would appeal to many who were not Communists. . . . The only way to know the Communist influence in front groups was to keep track of the identities of open and secret Communists who held membership in them.[36]

### The Catholic Connection

The fight against communism extended well beyond RCMP record-keeping. The Catholic Church community actively organized against suspected communist infiltration of Mine Mill. Because the communists were able to use unsuspecting citizens to promote their causes, everyone had to be vigilant and everyone was suspect. The local press ran items declaring Mine Mill communist, and by 1959 the recently created Catholic University of Sudbury was offering courses on anti-communism. Professor Alexandre Boudreau warned unsuspecting Sudbury citizens:

> Most people distrust the Communist Party and would never *knowingly* have anything to do with it. Since the Communists are relatively few in members, this

poses a serious problem for them. Alone and by themselves, they can do practically nothing and you would be surprised to discover how few Communists there are in a city like Sudbury and at the same time what great influence they can exert on the whole population.[37]

In his radio broadcasts and university extension courses Professor Boudreau suggested strategies to Sudburians for "upsetting the communist applecart." He advised, "We can interfere with their recruiting by helping youth work, Scouts, Guides and Church Youth groups and by showing a film on Communism from time to time. We can refuse co-operation or publicity to Communist fronts. We can be sure that no Communist gets elected to office because there is nobody to run against him."[38]

Of course, if you were going to fight communists, you needed to know where they were located. Otherwise the situation could create a climate of fear. This point was made in the House of Commons debates of November 28, 1963. Several members of parliament wanted the government to release a list of subversive organizations. The government refused, arguing that such disclosures would inhibit the RCMP's work. Instead the state practices allowed the climate of suspicion and fear to persist. In Sudbury and many other Mine Mill mining communities the Cold War discourse was sustained by the media, church, and local chamber of commerce attacks on the union.

The local press sent fear into all good Christians, Protestant and Catholic alike, by running stories about the atheism of communism. Popular Cold War discourse produced a steady diet of anti-communist sentiment and rumours about the possibilities of communist infiltration into everyday life. The Cold War propaganda fed on those rumours, as Irene Haluschak, a member of the Ladies' Auxiliary for Local 117, explained:

> The women believed that if it was in the *Sudbury Star* then it was true. When the *Sudbury Star* wrote that the Reds had taken over the Mine Mill hall and had put up a communist flag—who had done it was a right-wing group from the Ukrainian community on Frood Road. A lot of women told me, "Well Jesus, Irene, they had put up the communist flag!" I said, "No, they didn't. They [the people who did that] came from Toronto, it said right in the *Sudbury Star*." I said, "You read your paper a little more carefully and you'll see they said alleged." . . . The women believed that under communists you would be a slave, they would take everything, they would take their house, you wouldn't have anything, you wouldn't be able to go to church. A communist was like a bogeyman, and the women were frightened of them.[39]

The newspaper articles on communism asserted its subversive nature, the way it could spread its tentacles into the family, the school, and the media. Such forms of subversion gave every citizen the responsibility for combating this evil. It placed everyone on guard.

## Extending the Scope of Surveillance: Building an Anti-Communist Consensus

The prevailing climate of fear and mistrust provided a compliant populace ready to assist the RCMP in its work. Catholic women, through their Church association, were especially receptive to this propaganda as local priests frequently spoke of the need to combat the spread of communism. At the Fortieth Annual Convention of the Catholic Women's League (CWL), held in Sudbury in 1960, a motion was passed to "recommend that the Justice Department in Ottawa take immediate steps to outlaw the Communist Party of Canada and make known to the public all societies which are communist organized or controlled."[40]

In 1961 the RCMP deputy commissioner publicly identified Mine Mill as one of several unions whose leading executive and policies were associated with the communist movement. He pointed to Sudbury as a community facing bitter strife as a result of the union's presence there. The local Catholic Church papers were quick to pick up on his comments. Reverend R.F. Venti's editorials in the *Catholic Register* focused on the revelations. He noted, "A small group of Communists is trying to take control of the majority. The Sudbury miners need the public support of every citizen in order to win the fight." He continued, "When democracy is attacked, we are attacked. We must speak out; we must protect against any Red force that attempts to take us over; we must show on whose side we are."[41] In the anti-communist discourse, loyalty to the local elite and the church was loosely linked to loyalty to the nation. But Mine Mill women had clearly tied their "loyalties" to the union movement, and this public stance made them immediately suspect.

Irene Haluschak recalled her experience:

> Oh, you could hear some crazy stories! One time somebody said about me, that I was head of the Communist Party in the district and that I had organized cells and I was running this big thing, you know, that was so dangerous. That had come during a local union election. We had won. They said, "Well, why wouldn't they win! Irene's running the whole thing. They have got cells working and Irene's in charge of it." I thought, oh god, to have that power! It was really ridiculous, it was really crazy.[42]

Catholic Church leaders and members fed the fears of communism, encouraging the view that godless elements in the Mine Mill were attempting to subvert the men and women.[43] The anti-communist forces within the Church were able to mobilize lay women in the community through successfully tapping the resources of the CWL.[44] In a community in which about 60 per cent of the inhabitants were Catholic, the Church offered an extensive infrastructure to back the forces for the war against communism.[45] Police reports on Mine Mill activities made much use of citizens' observations. Local alderman, priests, and members of the CWL all provided information. An RCMP report of June 12, 1959, advised the central office that "[name deleted] approached the force asking for assistance in 'cleaning up' his local."[46] The state security system could rely on the loyalty of local people for reports on union activities.

The intense anti-communism had the effect of suppressing radical activism in the union and fuelled the internal rivalries in the union and its auxiliaries. During the raids on Mine Mill made by the United Steelworkers of America in the early 1960s, Mine Mill women's auxiliary members were referred to as the "Red petticoat brigade." The prevailing attitude made many people cautious about lending their support for views that would go against the grain of supposed postwar harmony and prosperity. Mine Mill members Stan and Peggy Raciot recalled their experience of red-baiting:

> This onslaught of propaganda that we were communists. What does this horrible communist look like? And it seems nobody can describe them and yet they said it was a horrible thing. To me it is just a word. At the churches they said to get rid of the communists, because there were members [of Mine Mill] that were communist. People didn't say look at all the good things Mine Mill did for us.[47]

As part of their day-to-day surveillance work the RCMP frequently visited the homes of "suspects." While the experienced activists were aware of being targets of RCMP surveillance, others were more easily intimidated. Patricia Chytuk, a founding member of Ladies' Auxiliary Local 117 in Sudbury, recalls receiving a visit:

> I didn't know who they were. They said they were the secret police. If it was now I would have asked them to identify themselves, but then you heard so much. Then they were visiting other people's houses too. A woman phoned me, she was reading an English-language Ukrainian newspaper, she liked it. She was active in our organization. She said, "Oh, what am I going to do? These people came and said I am not supposed to read the paper, it's against the law!" I said, "Come on!" "Well, she said, "these men said they were secret police."
> When they came to the house, my goodness, I was frightened. My late husband came in from work as they were leaving. He said, "Who were they?" I said, "They said they were the secret police." He said, "What the heck do they want here? . . . Just ignore them." Well, I said, "I had two women phone me this week, I didn't tell you because I didn't want to disturb you, but this is what is going on." Finally we had a meeting and they were saying, "Some guy gets paid ten bucks to go and visit you, just ignore them." But it scared a lot of people to leave the paper, not to read the paper.[48]

The RCMP expected compliance among the men and women they threatened and intimidated, and the Force seemed certain that it would not be publicly questioned for such intrusions into the private lives of working-class citizens. It was a no-win situation for those who received a visit from the plain-clothed agents, for if they admitted publicly to having received such a visit, in the eyes of the community they would be as good as guilty. Only an economically and socially secure individual would be able to withstand these paid agents' efforts of intimidation, and many immigrant working-class people were not in that position.

## Women's Resistance, and the Reframing of Activism

The Cold War discourse reframed women's socialist and community activism as "communist," and because the state was unwilling to outline exactly what it considered to be subversive, a wide range of activities continued to be suspect. When Doug Fisher, a Co-operative Commonwealth Federation (CCF) Member of Parliament for Port Arthur in the late 1950s, challenged the government to clarify its surveillance practices, he was met with government resistance. Fisher argued, "I am in the liberal tradition and always suspicious of any police activities which are protected from the knowledge of the communality." He warned, "Any time we give an organization authority and work to do that we cannot examine openly and know how they are working, we have to watch very closely; we have to check on it on occasion to make sure it is needed; that the dangers are so severe and terrible that we allow this particular type of police organization to be free from the surveillance of elected representatives."[49] His advice went unheeded, and with no "standard definition of subversive" the RCMP continued to have a free hand to decide who and what was considered subversive. Justice Minister E. Davie Fulton outlined the government's position:

> As to laying down a standard definition alleged to be a Communist front organization. I do not think it is possible to arrive at such definitions. The methods of the Communists are so infinitely various or devious or skillful I should think you would have to have a 100 page book before you could define everyone of the members they might have and therefore every type of organization that could be deemed to be suspect on security grounds.[50]

That the government was unwilling to make public either the organizations it considered subversive or the criteria upon which it made this judgement fuelled public suspicions that anyone who said anything critical of the ruling political party in public was subversive. With no boundaries placed on what constituted "communist activities," there were therefore to be no boundaries on the Mounties' efforts to disclose those activities. RCMP spying merely reflected and monitored the political activities of anyone who was designated by the state and the mainstream political culture as a possible threat to national security.

The postwar conflict between communism and Christian civilization was not actively regulated through state law. In 1950 Prime Minister St. Laurent best expressed the state strategy during the Cold War:

> I firmly believe that some years ago communist leadership was, to a regrettable degree, influential in some labour unions and the question arose as to whether or not some action should be taken by legislative authority in Canada to purge the labour unions. That was not done. We relied on the good sense, good judgement, patriotism and Christian traditions of the labouring people themselves to see that they got rid of these obnoxious influences.[51]

The RCMP surveillance of innocuous social groups was part of a larger social construction of Cold War culture, one that turned neighbour against neighbour and generated a general climate of suspicion. In this way RCMP surveillance served to constrain the character of working-class postwar activism for both men and women. For working-class women activists, these constraints of postwar "normalcy" meant that women who openly advocated women's equality and social justice were immediately suspect, even when they were holding tea parties. Yet Mine Mill women did actively promote a greater voice for women of the day. Through the auxiliary movement, working-class women worked for the cessation of weapons testing, for full disarmament, and for the creation of conditions that, as Dorothy McDonald reported, "would enable women to fulfill their roles in society, as mothers, workers, and citizens which includes the right to work, the protection of motherhood, equal rights with regards to marriage, children and property."[52] The picture of 1950s suburban affluence and family life in the age of *Leave It to Beaver* suggested a cultural ideology in which working-class people fulfilled their consumer dreams and became home owners with stay-at-home moms. Mine Mill women held a different vision of postwar economic and social recovery, and in the immediate postwar years, week after week, year after year, they continued to organize around that vision and build on it, despite constant RCMP intimidation and surveillance.

## Notes

1. RCMP, Security and Intelligence Branch, "International Union of Mine, Mill and Smelter Workers—Ladies Auxiliary—Local 117, Sudbury, Ontario," report, April 30, 1969, National Archives of Canada (NAC), Ottawa, Record Group (RG) 146.
2. RCMP, Security and Intelligence Branch, "International Union of Mine, Mill and Smelter Workers—Ladies Auxiliary—Local 117, Sudbury, Ontario," report, Sept. 16, 1963, NAC, RG 146.
3. The file system for these reports was multilayered. In addition to the specific local files, the RCMP kept a file entitled Mine Mill, Northern Ontario, and another national-level file system for national convention and general national surveillance on the union. Thus reports at a local level were frequently forwarded to head office to become part of yet another system of files. These files systems are complex, and the maze of evidence can be difficult to decipher. For example, information on Mine Mill women could be located in a file by that name but could also appear as an entry in any of the other file systems. Files on the Labor Progressive Party, ethnic associations, and other union files are all part of the net of information kept by the RCMP on Mine Mill activists.
4. Carl Betke and Stan Horrall, *Canada's Security Service: An Historical Outline, 1864–1966* (Ottawa: RCMP Historical Section, 1978), chap. 6, "From Royal Commission on Espionage to Royal Commission on Security, 1946–1966," Document No. 20, File 117-90-107, obtained through Access to Information Act.
5. Ibid., chap. 4.
6. Ibid.
7. Mary Louise Adams, *The Trouble with Normal: Postwar Youth and the Making of Heterosexuality* (Toronto: University of Toronto Press, 1998), p.38.
8. Canada Census, as cited in Pat Connelly, *Last Hired, First Fired: Women and the Canadian Work Force* (Toronto: Women's Press, 1978), p.64.
9. Elaine Tyler May, *Homeward Bound: American Families in the Cold War* (New York:

Basic Books, 1988), pp.17–18.

10. Dorothy Sue Cobble, "Recapturing Working Class Feminism: Union Women in the Postwar Era," in *Not June Cleaver: Women and Gender in Postwar America, 1945–1960*, ed. Joanne Meyerowitz (Philadelphia: Temple University Press, 1994), p.75.

11. C.M. Wallace and A. Thomson, eds., *Sudbury: Rail Town to Regional Capital* (Toronto: Dundurn Press, 1993).

12. Ibid., chaps. 8, 9.

13. John Deverell and the Latin American Working Group, *Falconbridge: Portrait of a Canadian Mining Multinational* (Toronto: James Lorimer and Company, 1975), p.14. See also Wallace Clement, *Hardrock Mining; Industrial Relations and Technological Changes at INCO* (Toronto: McClelland and Stewart, 1981). Nickel is a key resource, because it is an essential ingredient in making stainless steel, structural steel, and machine parts. The economic prospects for nickel production are closely tied to military and heavy machinery production.

14. Irving Abella, *Nationalism, Communism and Canadian Labour* (Toronto: University of Toronto Press, 1973), p.90. When a certification vote was held in December 1943 at Inco, 6,913 votes were cast for Mine Mill and 1,187 for the company union; at Falconbridge 765 voted for Mine Mill and 194 voted for the company union. Local 598 was certified as the bargaining agent at Inco on Feb. 4, 1944, and at Falconbridge on March 7, 1944. Jim Tester, "The Shaping of Sudbury: A Labour View," paper presented to the Sudbury Historical Society, April 18, 1979.

15. Interview with Ruth Reid, Sudbury, May 1993.

16. Ronald Williams, "Are You a Stooge for a Communist?" *Chatelaine*, April 1949, pp.90–94.

17. The Ladies' Auxiliaries of IUMM&SW were, at least technically, autonomous from the main union. They were chartered by the National Executive Board of Mine Mill and awarded their own local numbers and held their own local and national conventions, as well as sending representatives to local, national, and international Mine Mill meetings and conventions.

18. Radio Talk by Agnes Gauthier, Mine Mill Ladies' Auxiliary, April 23, 1950.

19. Bylaws of the Ladies Auxiliaries' of the International Union of Mine Mill and Smelter Workers in Canada, adopted Feb. 27, 1956. Canadian autonomy for Mine Mill was established in 1955. Clement, *Hardrock Mining*, p.103.

20. Joanne Meyerowitz, "Beyond the Feminine Mystique: A Reassessment of Postwar Mass Culture, 1946–1958," *Journal of American History*, March 1993, p.1469.

21. "'We're Still Here': A Panel Reviews the Past and Looks to the Future," in *Hard Lessons: The Mine Mill Union in the Canadian Labour Movement*, ed. Mercedes Steedman, Peter Suschnigg, and Dieter K. Buse (Toronto: Dundurn Press, 1995), p.152.

22. Ibid., p.151.

23. Interview, Ladies' Auxiliary member (name withheld), Sault Ste. Marie, Ont., March 1992.

24. Ibid.

25. "Subversive Activities in Mine Mill—Local 241," Oct. 10, 1952, RCMP Reports, NAC, RG 146, volume and file number deleted.

26. "Subversive Activities in Mine Mill, Fort Erie Report re National Convention, Feb. 27, 1956, RCMP Reports, NAC, RG 146, volume and file number deleted.

27. "Subversive Activities in Mine Mill—Local 241," Nov. 22, 1952, and Fort Erie RCMP report re National Convention in Sudbury, Feb. 27, 1956, RCMP Reports, NAC, RG 146, volume and file number deleted.

28. Dorothy McDonald, "Talk to Convention," no date, IUMM&SW Archives, University of British Columbia, Vancouver.

29. "Mine Mill Auxiliary Newsletter," Jan. 6, 1956, RCMP Reports, NAC, RG 146, volume and file number deleted.

30. Re: Mine Mill (Women's Auxiliary) Clipping, *Canadian Jewish Weekly*, Ottawa Headquarters, Sept. 18, 1952, RCMP Reports, NAC, RG 146, volume and file number

deleted.

31. International Union of Mine Mill and Smelter Workers—Ladies' Auxiliary—Local 117—[deleted]—Sudbury, Ont., Feb. 24, 1964, four pages, RCMP Reports, NAC, RG 146, volume and file number deleted. Emphasis added.

32. International Union of Mine, Mill and Smelter Workers—Ladies' Auxiliary—Local 117—Sudbury, Ont., Sept. 16, 1963, RCMP Reports, NAC, RG 146.

33. Today, even though delegate names are a matter of public record, the report released under the Access to Information Program (ATIP) still deleted the names of delegates. The RCMP were not always successful in their efforts to regulate the movements of Mine Mill activists crossing the Canada-U.S. border. Timmins Auxiliary members Pat Fournier and Dorothy McDonald, delegates to the 1949 Chicago convention, had been overlooked. "Owing to the fact that it was felt that Local 241 was too impoverished to send a delegate, let alone two. In fact, even now the suspicion is aroused, but it is as yet only a suspicion, that the Labour Progressive Party are footing the bill." Constable G.M. Beaton, Timmins, Security and Intelligence officer, Sept. 15, 1949.

34. J.L. Forest, to the Commissioner, RCMP, May 29, 1962.

35. RCMP Report, "International Mine Mill and Smelter Workers Union, Local 312, Ladies' Auxiliary—Communist Party activities within—Timmins, Ontario," Timmins, S.I.S., Dec. 18, 1962. Most of these investigators' comments are still held as exemptions under the Access to Information Act. Furthermore, most of the information in the file obtained under an access to information request is still exempted. Since the RCMP's bank of suspects was compiled from newspapers and informants who passed on information concerning newly elected officials or on delegates to conventions, most of this information was already in the public domain, yet today the heavy hand of censorship still prevails and in documents released under ATIP much of this public information is still blacked out.

36. Betke and Horrall, *Canada's Security Service*, chap. 6.

37. Prof. Alexandre Boudreau, Program of Courses, 1959–1960, University of Sudbury—Extension Division, Box F43.2, Laurentian University Archives. Boudreau's activities came to the attention of the RCMP. In 1960 the RCMP reported on Boudreau's efforts to extend his anti-communist teachings to the miners. "A steward's school is to be held by Local 598 in Sudbury, on the 15-2-60. . . . Professor Boudreau [deleted] from the University of Sudbury will give four hours of lectures. Boudreau [deleted] is the individual who carried out the intense campaign on behalf of Don Gillis and his slate during the recent Local 598 elections. [deleted] it is the intention of the CPC, Sudbury—to have as many Party members as possible attend the school. Special attention is to be given to [deleted] lectures and attempts are to be made to disrupt these lectures and [deleted] is to be heckled constantly." RCMP Security Service Records, Report on International Union of Mine Mill and Smelter Workers—Local 598—Communist Activities Within, Sudbury, Ont., Feb. 17, 1960, NAC, RG 146.

38. Ibid.

39. Interview with Irene Haluschak, Sudbury, Ont., June 5, 1993.

40. *40th Annual Convention of the Algoma Diocese Catholic Women's League*, May 19, 1960, Christ the King Church, Sudbury, Ont., Archives of the Algoma Diocese, North Bay, Ont.

41. Reverent R.F. Venti, "No Place for Neutral," *Catholic Register*, Oct. 14, 1961.

42. Interview with Irene Haluschak, Sudbury, Ont., May 1993.

43. The strongest anti-communist rhetoric came from within the English Catholic community. The French Catholic Church was less anti-union, as priests in the region supported the Christian labour-movement encyclicals. Interview with Yvonne Obonsawin, Elliot Lake, Ont., April 1995. The French section of the Church, under the direction of Father Albert Régimbal, offered labour studies classes in the parish. Most Reverend Bishop Alexander Carter, circular to the diocese, vol. 2, no. 1, Sept. 15, 1958.

44. The Catholic Women's League dates back to 1932, when the first Church women's organizations were formed in the Algoma diocese. Minutes of the Annual Meetings,

Catholic Women's League, May 1932, Archives of the Diocese of Algoma, North Bay, Ont.

45. At the 1960 meeting of the Catholic Women's League, members were congratulated on the work they had done during the strike. Minutes of the Fortieth Annual Convention, Catholic Women's League, Algoma Diocese, May 16, 1960, p.110.

46. RCMP Report, transit slip, June 12, 1959, Constable Northcott to Inspector Parent, NAC, RG 146, access file number 1025-9-91043, part 4, vol. 7. Parent's reply on June 15th stated, "Attached please find subject's personal file. It is noted that extract number 3 and 5 concern very good items of open information but under subjects' alias of [deleted]."

47. Interview with Stan and Peggy Raciot, Mine Mill members, Sudbury, Local 598. Interview conducted by Bea Hart, CBC Radio, no date.

48. Interview with Patricia Chytuk, Sudbury, Ont., May 1997.

49. Quoted in Betke and Horsell, *Canada's Security Service*, chap. 6.

50. Canada, *House of Commons Debates*, June 25, 1959, pp.5149–50.

51. Canada, *House of Commons Debates*, May 2, 1950, p.2087.

52. Report by Co-ordinator Dorothy McDonald on Mine Mill Auxiliaries, Eleventh Annual Convention, IUMM&SW, Sept. 14, 1959.

*Mrs. Rae Luckocks of the Housewives Consumers' Association, bearing 750,000 petitions calling for price controls, intercepted by RCMP officers before gaining admission to the House of Commons, Ottawa, 1947* (National Archives of Canada, C146269). [Guard, chap. 5]

JULIE GUARD

five ★ ★ ★

# Women Worth Watching: Radical Housewives in Cold War Canada

Post-World War II Canada is typically depicted as prosperous and politically complacent. But like most generalizations, this characterization obscures a more complex reality. As historian Alvin Finkel points out, a significant minority of Canadian families were poor or almost poor throughout the 1950s. Nor was it immediately apparent to most Canadians that the postwar period would bring prosperity; on the contrary, many feared a postwar economic recession, like the one that had followed World War I.[1] When the federal government's disengagement from wartime control over the economy resulted in steeply increasing prices and rising inflation in 1946 and 1947, people's worst fears seemed to be confirmed.[2] A political response emerged quickly, led by a group of left-wing women who began organizing consumers across the country to demand a change in federal policy.

Between 1947 and 1950 the Housewives Consumers' Association organized a series of well-publicized campaigns protesting government inaction and calling for the reimposition of price and rent controls.[3] A number of the leading members of the Housewives were affiliated politically with the Communist left, and this perspective clearly informed their claim that the government used economic policy to protect business profits at the expense of ordinary Canadians. Yet the authority with which they articulated their concerns derived from their position in the home, as mothers and homemakers. Rising prices, coupled with declining real and relative wages, they stated, were driving up the cost of basic necessities so that even the most creative shoppers were having difficulty providing their families with a healthy, nourishing diet. They reminded the ruling Liberals of their wartime promises of a high and rising standard of living and called on them to adjust their policies in the interests of the family.[4]

In contrast to their male counterparts in the labour and political left, who relied for support on a limited constituency composed mainly of union members and committed socialists, the Housewives enjoyed broad popular appeal. Industrial reconversion to peacetime production and the removal of the strictures that had stabilized the economy during the war were affecting everyone, both middle and working class. Families across the country encountered reduced purchasing power as a result of rising prices, declining wages, and inflation. This diversity was

73

reflected in the Housewives' support. In addition to support from various trades and labour councils, labour unions, the Labor Progressive Party (LPP), and the left-wing press, the Housewives' campaigns were endorsed by a number of city councils, home and school associations, middle-class women's groups, veterans' associations, professional social workers, and clergymen.[5] Few of these groups and individuals would have joined an organization that called for working-class struggle against capital, but they supported the Housewives' implicitly class-conscious demands for policies that more equitably balanced the needs of ordinary families against the interests of big business.[6]

As an organization with links to the Communist movement, in which a number of leading activists were known or suspected Communists, the Housewives Consumers' Association was among the thousands of organizations monitored by the Security Service of the RCMP, which was responsible for domestic security. Yet RCMP files on the Housewives, obtained through requests to the National Archives under the Access to Information Program, suggest that these women, who conformed so thoroughly to prevailing constructions of respectable femininity, presented the Mounties who watched them with a dilemma. Both Communism and domesticated womanhood played important, but conflicting, roles in the symbolic economy of Cold War culture.

As the linchpin of the nuclear family, the housewife represented safety and security, the very things that communism, as the embodiment of foreignness and danger, threatened.[7] Cold War political culture justified police surveillance of Canadians who were active in the Communist movement by portraying Communists as dangerous radicals who advocated violent revolution. Yet the Housewives were active community members who advocated stronger government control over the market. Authorities warned Canadians that Communists wanted to destroy the social institutions that democracy protected, one of the most important of which was the family.[8] Yet the Housewives campaigned for policies to protect the interests of ordinary families and to ensure an adequate standard of living for their children.

Following past practice, the Mounties designated the Housewives, like any organization in which Communists were active, as subversive, and proceeded on the assumption that they were engaged primarily in disseminating communist ideas. Yet diligent investigation turned up no concrete evidence to support these presumptions. On the contrary, the Housewives' proposals were endorsed by a broad cross-section of Canadians, and their criticisms of government policy were consistent with the views expressed in newspaper editorials across the country.[9]

The Security Service's continued identification of the Housewives as subversives, despite the complete absence of corroborating evidence, exemplifies how accusations of political subversion were used during the Cold War to discredit and silence dissent. Anti-communism was deployed to justify surveillance of virtually any organization on the political left that criticized government policies by labelling it a potential or actual threat to the state. Political analysts have argued compellingly that liberal democracies minimize resistance through the use of coercion while maintaining popular consent through their democratic structures.[10] Recent scholarship on Cold War political culture suggests that, in Canada, the balance between these mechanisms shifted towards coercion in the late 1940s, when the Housewives were active.[11] This predisposition, together with the equation of political dissidence with disloyalty, justified the RCMP's surveillance of anyone who demonstrated, or who was suspected of harbouring, an inclination towards socialism.[12]

As active participants in organizations identified by the Mounties as Communist, including the Labor Progressive Party, which replaced the banned Communist Party of Canada (CPC), a number of the most prominent members of the Housewives Consumers' Association fell automatically into the category of subversives. Several provincial presidents of the Housewives, including Florence Theodore in Saskatchewan, Mrs. Ben Swankey in Alberta, and Margaret (Peggy) Chunn in Manitoba, as well as active members such as Alice Maigis in Toronto, were LPP members.[13] A number of leading members, such as Pat (Pearl) Chytuk, Lil Ilomaki, and Sinefta Kizema, were active in cultural organizations such as the Association of United Ukrainian Canadians, the Finnish Organization of Canada, and the United Jewish People's Order, all of which were sympathetic to communism.[14] Others, like Mona Morgan and Audrey (Staples) Mozdir, were involved in women's auxiliaries of Communist-led trade unions such as the International Woodworkers (IWA) and the United Electrical, Radio and Machine Workers (UE). Some were active in more than one of these organizations. Pat Chytuk, for instance, was a founding member of the Mine Mill and Smelter Workers local women's auxiliary in Sudbury, and many of the Housewives were active in union auxiliaries and cultural organizations as well as the LPP.[15]

While some of the leading members of the organization were certainly Communists, the Housewives were undeniably women. Identifying rising prices as not only a family problem but also a social issue, they enlisted the support of other women in their campaigns, calling for policies to protect the well-being of their families in terms that resonated with the prevailing cultural ideal of domestic femininity. As mothers and homemakers, they explained, their primary commitment was to their families. When postwar inflation, rising prices, and declining wages threatened the comfort and security of their families, they said, maternal responsibility compelled them to act. In the name of the family, therefore, they called for a return to the wartime policies that had created economic stability by controlling prices and profits.[16]

These women perceived no contradiction between their concerns as housewives and mothers and their political views. On the contrary, they believed that the Marxist interpretation of capital's exploitation of waged workers, which they shared with their comrades in the communist movement, lent clarity to the problems they confronted at home. The communist argument that social inequality was the result of opposing class interests seemed consistent with their struggles as homemakers to stretch diminishing wages while corporate profits rose. Housewives and wage-earners confronted the same class enemy, and were thus linked in the same struggle. When the state failed to establish countervailing mechanisms to restrain the power of capital, they contended, the result was not only exploitative wages, but also unfair prices.[17]

These ideas distinguished the Communist members of the Housewives from society's mainstream majority, but materially their lives were very much like those of other women. Their many meetings, demonstrations, and other political events frequently drew them out of their homes, so they probably relied more heavily than others on extended family, neighbours, and husbands for child care. But their daily reality was nonetheless shaped by the domestic labour of caring for homes, husbands, and children. Most of the Housewives were married women with children and, as practical women with limited access to babysitters, they quite naturally combined their domestic responsibilities with their political activities. Babies in carriages were brought to protest rallies, and public events were structured to include mothers and children.[18]

Neither the domestic details of the Housewives' daily lives nor the fluidity between their identities as housewives and their political views were treated as noteworthy by the Special Branch agents who watched them. Instead, the Mounties concentrated their efforts on determining how many, and which, of the Housewives had links to the Communist movement. Much of the evidence contained in the RCMP's secret files on the Housewives Consumers' Association consists of names (although the censor has deleted many of these), including lists of members who were known or suspected Communists, the names of known or suspected Communists with whom they associated, and other organizations in which they were involved.

The RCMP's search for linkages between the Housewives and other individuals and organizations designated by themselves as subversive was consistent with the Cold War myth that domestic Communists were engaged in an international conspiracy to overthrow capitalism by means of violent revolution. Despite the absence of any hard evidence, the notion of an international Communist plot was supported by the media, political pundits, political figures, and religious and community leaders to the extent that its existence became accepted as a fact. Although the fear of a Communist "fifth column" was demonstrably unfounded, the journalists and local authorities who contributed to the general climate of fear-mongering and intolerance that anti-communism evoked did not simply imagine the Communist threat. On the contrary, as Reg Whitaker and Gary Marcuse have demonstrated, popular anti-communism was a deliberate strategy designed to achieve specific political goals. The "Communist conspiracy" of the Cold War, they contend, was manufactured by government and corporate elites to facilitate the public acceptance of policies that contained labour strife and suppressed political dissent.[19]

The definition of Communists as potential spies and conspirators was totally at odds with contemporary understandings of womanhood. As feminist theorists have amply demonstrated, "woman" has long been a heavily defined and overdetermined category of identity, and this was particularly the case between the late 1940s and the early 1960s.[20] This period, colloquially identified as "the fifties," was characterized by repressive social norms, one of the most restrictive of which concerned gender identities and gender relations. Women in particular had a limited range of acceptable life choices, and virtually all of them revolved around the family. Normative womanhood meant marriage, motherhood, and homemaking. Conceivably, the boundaries of acceptable female behaviour could be stretched to include paid work, but authorities were divided on this issue, which was debated regularly in the pages of women's magazines. Even those who expressed themselves in favour of "working mothers" agreed, however, that paid work should not interfere with women's primary responsibilities in the home. Motherhood was widely perceived as women's natural role, and full-time homemaking was endorsed by secular and religious authorities, government, and the media as essential to a happy, socially productive family.[21]

Full-time motherhood and homemaking were also construed as the foundation of a healthy society. A mother who stayed home was lauded as the best protection against the new social ills, such as juvenile delinquency, homosexuality, and divorce, that social commentators identified as presaging social disintegration.[22] The U.S. historian Elaine Tyler May contends, moreover, that a healthy society, made up of healthy families in which everyone was properly adjusted to their prescribed gender, sexuality, and social functions—the maintenance of which depended on the presence of a stay-at-home mother—was understood to be an effective antidote against opportunistic political ills, the most virulent of which was communism. The full-time homemaker was thus both a normative model for real women and a powerful cultural symbol of stability, security, and democracy.[23]

The transformation of the Housewives from respectable mothers and homemakers into a threat to national security provides an illuminating illustration of how the Cold War construction of Communism was deployed in the interests of the state. As homemakers, the Housewives, firmly grounded in their authority as respectable wives and mothers, were able to mount a credible challenge to the Liberal government. Indeed, popular endorsements of the Housewives' proposals threatened to mobilize popular opinion in opposition to existing policy. It was therefore clearly in the Liberals' interests to define the Housewives as Communists rather than as housewives. This redefinition, encouraged in public statements by prominent politicians and graphically depicted in the mainstream media, dramatically undermined the respectability and authority that the Housewives claimed as women, redefining them as dangerous subversives and thus neutralizing them as a political threat.

## Seeing Red

Newspaper accounts of the Housewives' activities reveal that, initially, the mainstream press did not treat the Housewives' political affiliations as being especially remarkable. In March 1947 a group of twelve delegates from Manitoba, Saskatchewan, Alberta, and British Columbia travelled to Ottawa to confront the finance minister and present their proposals for revising economic policy.[24] They advocated a return to milk subsidies and federally legislated price controls, which had existed during the war and were then in the process of being lifted. Their appeal was unsuccessful. Newspaper accounts of the event describe Finance Minister Douglas Abbott as listening politely to their suggestions and then proceeding to implement established policy.[25]

Although many members of the delegation were publicly known as members of the LPP, newspaper reports of their effort were uniformly sympathetic. Reporting in advance of their trek, the *Winnipeg Free Press* applauded their effort, presenting as fact the Housewives' statement that they represented "the hopes of about 70 per cent of Manitoba's housewives" and detailing the Housewives' proposed program for reform. The *Leader Post* (Regina) was similarly positive, noting that the CCF government in Saskatchewan endorsed and supported the Housewives' goals. Both articles named the delegates, but neither mentioned their political affiliations, although these were a matter of public record.[26]

The *Montreal Standard* opined that the failure of the Housewives to achieve their objective could be attributed in part to the fact that eight of the twelve delegates were Communists. Despite this, the account was sympathetic, noting that the reporters covering the event could see clearly that the Housewives were "getting a run-around" from the finance minister, Reconstruction Minister C.D. Howe, and Conservative opposition leader John Bracken.[27]

Within a month the tenor of the reports on the Housewives had changed dramatically. The *Winnipeg Free Press*, which had so recently praised Manitoba Housewives' president Margaret Chunn for leading the struggle against rising prices, ran a series of three articles on April 22, 23, and 24, identifying her and several others as Communists and accusing the Housewives of being nothing but a "Communist front." Under headlines proclaiming "Hundreds of Unwary Women Duped: Communist Officials Head Up Housewives Consumers' Group" and "Winnipeg Central Headquarters for Communist-led Housewives," the unnamed writer dealt out conspiracy theory with a heavy hand. Reminding readers of the recent spy scandals, in which Fred Rose, Canada's only Communist Member of Parliament, had been convicted of espionage, he portrayed the Housewives as merely a vehicle for recruiting "unsuspecting women" to Communism. Unnamed former members purportedly alleged that, at meetings, they were "inculcated with Communistic ideals." Believing they had joined an "apolitical" organization, they'd had "a rude awakening," they said, when the Communists took over and began using meetings to proselytize for Communism.[28]

The clear implication behind these accusations was that, if the Housewives were Communists, and thus members of the international Communist conspiracy, they could not be genuine housewives. Although these women represented themselves as housewives, the article explained, they were actually Communists, who "do not care a straw about price control or about any other genuine public issue. . . . Their one ambition is to stir up trouble, to spread discontent, and to exploit a genuine public grievance for their own selfish and dangerous ends." Their only loyalty was to Russia, and as agents of the Soviet Union, "Communists are eager to exploit the freedom of everyone who does not obey the Communist dogmas." These people, "remorselessly and ceaselessly . . . weaken and destroy our democratic society." In these articles and others that followed, "responsible" and "loyal" but "unwary" housewives were contrasted with Communists, who were "slippery . . . conspirators" who "cannot be trusted."

The articles, and others like them, received national coverage, despite the egregious hyperbole of their argument. Over the next several weeks, newspapers across the country published accusations about similar Communist infiltration in the local Housewives' associations. Housewives in Vancouver, Edmonton, Regina, Saskatoon, Toronto, and Montreal, as well as the targeted Winnipeg Housewives Consumers' Association, acknowledged that their membership included Communists, but they denied vehemently that the organization was "Communist-dominated." Both Communist and non-Communist members spoke strongly on behalf of free speech and freedom of political belief, insisting that their cause was a good one and that the political affiliations of the members were irrelevant.[29]

Although committed in principle to protecting civil liberties, elected politicians saw in these revelations opportunities for discrediting and silencing the dissenting voices animated by the Housewives' campaigns. In the following months a number of provincial and local politicians attacked the Housewives publicly. In May 1947 Ontario Conservative Premier George Drew, who less than two years later would run for federal office on an anti-Communist platform,[30] red-baited the Housewives in a speech to the Ottawa Women's Canadian Club. In an obvious reference to the Housewives, Drew warned the women present to be wary of groups that "mask" their actions "under the mantel of public service, but are acting, if not for the total disintegration of Canada, at least for disunity and discord among Canadians." Although they may claim to be working only for social reform and lower prices, he cautioned, "we must realize that we are up against a highly organized program of propaganda," and that these organizations are not as harmless as they seem.[31]

In September of the same year, in the run-up to the Winnipeg civic election, mayoral candidate C.E. Simonite played the "red card" in a dispute with school board candidate and Housewives' president Chunn. A delegation of Housewives, led by Chunn, had embarrassed Acting Mayor Simonite by appearing en masse at city hall to suggest that he "wire the federal government immediately to demand that price control be re-established." Simonite not only refused to accede to the women's demands, but also subsequently denounced Chunn as a member of a political faction that thrived "on the misfortune . . . of those in misery . . . for the sake of propaganda."[32]

A few cautious voices urged Canadians to resist the emotive appeal of anti-communism and think critically about the issues that, they pointed out, were still relevant. Few of these commentaries, which appeared in daily newspapers and magazines, challenged the Cold War orthodoxy that communism was, at best, a misguided political view. They merely suggested that, if their proposals were sound, the political views of the Housewives were irrelevant. The most sympathetic of these appeared in the *Ottawa Citizen*, whose editorialist contended that the Housewives were "on the right side of the issue" and suggested that their implicit critique of "the profit motive" enjoyed "a good deal of popular sympathy." More typical was the argument presented in *The Ottawa Journal*, which called the exposure of the Housewives as Communists a "minor hullabaloo" and a "red herring," and urged readers not to be distracted from the real issue, which was the need for government to act, as it had during the war, to control prices and profits.[33]

Even *The Financial Post* and *Saturday Night*, both of which later published some of the most virulent anti-communist pieces, recommended moderation.[34]

*The Financial Post*, although unwilling to overlook the Housewives' Communist associations, suggested that, since many of the Housewives' members were not Communists, it was "not fair to brand the whole movement a communist front." Indeed, several of the groups were led by anti-Communists, the *Post* argued, and their delegations to Ottawa had been endorsed by organizations, such as the Toronto Labour Council, the Ontario Federation of Labour, and the Canadian Congress of Labour, which had a reputation of actively opposing Communism. At least some of the Housewives, the *Post* implied—those who were demonstrably not "under the thumb of the communists"—were the genuine article.[35]

*Saturday Night* magazine declined to endorse either the Housewives or their demands, but its editorial writer cautioned against sacrificing civil liberties in the war against communism. The price campaign, he held, was "undoubtedly a Communist racket," but the political views of an issue's supporters should be treated as irrelevant. Canadians should not be alarmed at the prospect of "joining hands with the Communists in any cause which deserves the support of liberal and progressive thinkers." On the contrary, "The danger lies in the possibility that liberal and progressive thinkers will be frightened out of such activities by the fact that there are two or three Communists engaged in them, and will thus leave the conduct of the nation's affairs to be run entirely by illiberal and unprogressive thinkers." These retrograde thinkers, he concluded, are always "delighted at the opportunity" to disguise their ideas as anti-communism.[36]

Some of the clearest insights were, not surprisingly, articulated by the Housewives themselves. Mrs. A.C. Latham of Moose Jaw, Saskatchewan, observed, "You can't raise your voice in protest about anything anymore without having a charge of Communist levelled at you." Mrs. Anne Arland of Toronto suggested that the persecution of the Housewives was a reflection of their popularity, quipping, "If we are Communists, then there are a lot of Communists in Canada."[37]

## The Mounties' Dilemma

Authors who examined opinion polls found over half of Canadians at this time regarded communism as a "serious threat" to the nation, and moderate voices were largely overshadowed by anti-communist fear-mongering.[38] The popular anxieties, encouraged by respected politicians and other authorities, shaped the political culture in which the Mounties fulfilled their assigned tasks. Within this context the Housewives' political affiliations guaranteed their designation as subversive. Yet in almost a decade of surveillance, agents were unable to find concrete evidence linking the Housewives to the LPP, despite constant exhortation from superior officers to do so. Their failure to substantiate the assumption that the LPP provided either financial support or direction, together with the information that not all of the Housewives' members and relatively few of their supporters were members of the Communist LPP, led some agents to conclude that the Housewives were not, in fact, a Communist "front" organization, but only an organization of women.

In their reports, field agents pointed out the tenuousness of the links between the Housewives and the Communist Party on the basis of the available evidence.

One such memorandum was prompted by a specific question from RCMP Superintendent McClellan: "Is this communistic organization endeavouring, or planning to endeavour, to infiltrate the Canadian Association of Consumers?" The agent, Sergeant R.D. Robertson, reported that, in his view, the Housewives were not a serious threat to national security. The assertions of another agent that the "Communist Party is taking leadership in the Hamilton Housewives Association" and that there was "little doubt" that the Communists were "behind the scenes," were, in his view, "purely supposition." On the basis of his close observation of the organization, Robertson concluded that the Housewives constituted no threat of subversion, and recommended that the investigation be abandoned. Although there were undoubtedly Communists active in some of the Housewives Consumers' Associations, he asserted, neither the members nor the affiliated organizations were subversive.[39]

Others considered the organization's soft links to the communist movement sufficient evidence that the Communist Party "ran" the Housewives, apparently agreeing with the popular view, articulated by a *Winnipeg Free Press* editorial writer, that "a few trained Communist agitators and organizers, in key positions, are usually enough to enable the Communist party to capture any organization it wishes to dominate."[40] For these operatives, the Housewives' presence in Communist-identified "ethnic" organizations, such as the Association of United Ukrainian Canadians, the United Jewish People's Order, and the Finnish Organization of Canada, and at public events sponsored by the LPP, was sufficient evidence that the Housewives Consumers' Association was only a "front" for the Communist Party.[41]

Two RCMP inspectors, Leopold and Shakespeare, seemed especially insistent that agents persevere in their efforts to find hard evidence that the Housewives were a "Communist front" organization that was "run by the Party" for its own purposes. Leopold evinced particular willingness to condemn the Housewives on the basis of their association with known Communists or their participation in events supported or organized by the Communist Party. Indeed, if the Housewives were to be deemed guilty by association with Communists, ample evidence was uncovered by surveillance. For instance, the Housewives played a prominent role in a celebratory rally held at Toronto's Massey Hall in January 1948, dubbed "The 100th Anniversary of Marxism," commemorating the hundredth anniversary of the publication of the Communist Manifesto. At the rally, a representative of the Housewives delivered a speech from a podium she shared with well-known Communist luminaries, including national party leader Tim Buck as well as Stewart Smith, A.A. MacLeod, Leslie Morris, and Fred Collins. The Housewives' "Roll Back Prices" petition was circulated among the fifteen hundred supporters—plus at least one police informer and a Mountie—who were in attendance.[42]

By contrast, several agents assigned to watch the various Housewives associations readily identified a number of leading members as Communists, but were prepared to abandon both the search for hard links to the Communist Party and their surveillance of the Housewives themselves as unpromising and unnecessary. Often, the recommendation that the file on the Housewives be closed was based simply on the local organization's inactivity, but occasionally agents' reports hint at the frustration that searching for potential spies among the Housewives must have generated.

One agent, reporting on a meeting of the Housewives in Ottawa, expressed disbelief that the Housewives constituted a genuine security risk: "There was nothing properly organized, everyone wanting to speak at the one time, nobody seems to take the movement seriously at the moment and the whole affair could be termed as semi-comedy." Although several of those present were Communists, these were clearly not the masters of international intrigue who were so skilled at manipulation and persuasion that they constituted a threat to the nation. Such women, in the opinion of a number of agents, represented no danger to the state and thus did not warrant continued surveillance.[43]

In short, careful investigation by the Mounties revealed that the Housewives were, indeed, active in the organizations of the communist left. Several held executive posts in their provincial LPPs. But the Mounties found no evidence supporting the contention that the Housewives were involved in any sort of conspiracy. On the contrary, all the evidence suggested that the Housewives were exactly what they claimed to be: an organization of women representing various positions on the left but sharing a traditional view of gender relations and the family and a critical perspective on the state. Yet despite the absence of evidence, surveillance of the Housewives continued. The common-sense belief in a Communist conspiracy, moreover, was reinforced by the Cold War political culture within the RCMP. The ranking officers in the Security Service were not only ideologically committed to anti-communism, but had also built their careers on their success as red-hunters. Thus both common sense and the organizational imperatives of the RCMP dictated continued surveillance of the Housewives.

## A Threat to Whom?

The determination to label the Housewives as a Communist "front" also reflected prevailing political imperatives. The Housewives' demands that government intervene in the economy to protect working-class families from exploitation by big business focused critical public attention on the discrepancy between wartime promises and postwar policy. They pointed to the success of wartime price and rent controls, along with ceilings on profits and subsidies for basic necessities, as proof that government could intervene effectively in the market when it so chose. That it had failed to impose similar controls on the postwar economy, they suggested, was indicative of a deliberate policy decision, one that permitted capital to prosper at the expense of ordinary people.

The Liberals' ability to contain this political threat was dependent on discrediting the Housewives and other progressive, left-wing organizations. The myth of an international Communist conspiracy was central to this process. In March 1948 the Housewives were subjected to a renewed bout of red-baiting, beginning with the publication of an editorial in the Windsor *Daily Star* bearing the headline, "Canadians Duped to Aid Red Fifth Column." The article, part of a series, was applauded by the *Star*'s editor as "the most complete account ever written of

Communists in Canada." Don Cameron, the intrepid researcher, asked his readers to consider, "Are you an involuntary marcher in the Communist fifth column organized for the violent seizure of Canada's material and human resources to enrich the world's most tyrannical dictatorship?" The Housewives Consumers' Association was one of the "front" organizations whose sole purpose, according to Cameron, was to lure unsuspecting Canadians into situations where they would fall under communist influence and to trick them into participating in subversive activities. Despite its obvious hyperbole and incredible premise, the article was deemed newsworthy enough to be reprinted elsewhere, and similar attacks on the Housewives appeared in rival newspapers.[44]

These accusations, however ridiculous, had a powerful impact on the Housewives. Their vilification in the mainstream press undermined their popular support, and the suggestion that they were part of an international conspiracy against democracy was sufficient excuse for the Liberals to successfully ignore their concerns. In April 1948, when the Housewives mustered yet another delegation to Ottawa to confront the finance minister, the effect of this sustained red-baiting was apparent. Previously, Abbott had only managed to evade the Housewives' pointed questioning of his policies, but on this occasion he refused to receive them. He justified this refusal by direct reference to the accusations against the Housewives. He explained, "I came to the conclusion, as did my colleagues . . . that the primary purpose of these delegations was to foster Communistic propaganda. . . . I do not think it is the duty of myself or any of the ministers to facilitate that sort of propaganda and that is the reason why we refused to see them."[45]

Even while he admitted that not all the delegates were Communists, Abbott used the identity of "communist" to discredit the entire group by association. The strategic value of such a label in discouraging non-communists from participating in a stigmatized organization was emphasized in a report on the episode in *The Globe and Mail*: "The great body of the women, as Mr Abbott pointed out, are not Communist. Some have been profoundly shocked at being classed with Reds. One Toronto Sunday School teacher yesterday admitted she did not know how she was going back to face her class."[46] As this example suggests, common-sense ideas about communism, once in place, could be used to great effect by elected officials to silence criticism of government policies and stifle dissent. Indeed, during the Cold War those who spoke out against the state placed themselves at such risk of public identification as communists that, not surprisingly, few people other than communists were willing to do it.

The dilemma encountered by the Mounties does not appear to have troubled elected officials, including the members of the federal cabinet. The contradictions that complicated the Mounties' definition of the Housewives as a political threat were not an issue for these political elites, whose perception of the Housewives as a danger was not dependent on theories of international conspiracies. On the contrary, as their willingness to use the coercive apparatus of the state to silence the Housewives indicates, they recognized the Housewives as a serious political threat, not because they were communists but because, as a popular movement supported by public opinion, they constituted a viable challenge to the power of the state.

## Notes

I am grateful to Dieter Buse, Gary Kinsman, and Mercedes Steedman for their helpful and insightful comments on an earlier draft of this paper. Thanks also go to York University for supporting this research with a Major Research Grant.

1.  Alvin Finkel, *Our Lives: Canada after 1945* (Toronto: James Lorimer and Company, 1997), pp.5–14; Robert Bothwell, Ian Drummond, and John English, *Canada Since 1945: Power, Politics, and Provincialism*, rev. ed. (Toronto: University of Toronto Press, 1989), pp.44–51.
2.  Dominion Bureau of Statistics, *Canada Year Book 1948–49* (Ottawa: King's Printer, 1949), pp.iii–xliii, 945–56.
3.  The exact number of women who were active members of the Housewives Consumers' Association is almost impossible to determine, in part because of the episodic nature of the organization. At a given moment, the RCMP's recorded estimates of the number of people who considered themselves members varies from a low of fifty to a high of fifty thousand. At one point the Housewives themselves recorded their estimated membership as one hundred thousand. National Archives of Canada (NAC), CSIS Records, RG 146, vol. 3353, part 2A.
4.  Alvin Finkel, "Paradise Postponed: A Re-examination of the Green Book Proposal of 1945," *Journal of the Canadian Historical Association, 1993*, pp.120–42; David Slater, "Colour the Future Bright: The White Paper, the Green Book, and the 1945–1946 Dominion-Provincial Conference on Reconstruction," in *Uncertain Horizons: Canadians and Their World in 1945*, ed. Greg Donaghy (n.p.: Canadian Committee for the History of the Second World War, 1997), pp.191–201.
5.  "Partial List of Sponsors Received to Date, 10 April 1948," NAC, CSIS Records, RG 146, Housewives and Consumers Federation of Canada (HCFC), vol. 3353, part 2, items 831, 833, 834; "Roll Back Prices Petition Drive Nears 200,000 Mark," *The Westerner*, March 20, 1948, NAC, CSIS, RG 146, Housewives Consumers' Association (HCA), Toronto, vol. 3440, part 1, item 1278; "To Call Open Conference in Ottawa," *The Westerner*, Feb. 28, 1948, HCA, vol. 3440, part 1, item 1293; "Will Sign up Million to Make Ottawa Move Symbol 2 Rolling Pins," *The Toronto Daily Star*, Jan. 21, 1948, HCA, vol. 3440, part 1, item 1331.
6.  One group that did not support the Housewives was the Provincial Women's Committee of the Ontario Co-operative Commonwealth Federation (CCF). See Dan Azoulay, "'Ruthless in a Ladylike Way': CCF Women Confront the Postwar Communist Menace," *Ontario History* 89, 1 (March 1997), pp.23–52.
7.  The symbolic importance of normative femininity in the Cold War has been demonstrated by a number of scholars. Two useful treatments of this topic are Deborah A. Gerson, "'Is Family Devotion Now Subversive?' Familialism against McCarthyism," in *Not June Cleaver: Women and Gender in Postwar America 1945–1960*, ed. Joanne Meyerowitz (Philadelphia: Temple University Press, 1994), pp.151–76; and Franca Iacovetta, "Making 'New Canadians': Social Workers, Women, and the Reshaping of Immigrant Families," in *A Nation of Immigrants: Women, Workers, and Communities in Canadian History, 1840s–1960s*, ed. Franca Iacovetta, with Paula Draper and Robert Ventresca (Toronto: University of Toronto Press, 1998), pp.482–513.
8.  Susan Prentice, "Workers, Mothers, Reds: Toronto's Postwar Daycare Fight," *Studies in Political Economy* 30 (1989), pp.115–41.
9.  "Among Those Women from the West," *The Ottawa Journal*, April 7, 1947, NAC, CSIS Records, RG 146, HCFC, vol. 3353, Supplement 1, vol. 1, item 1056; clipping [no headline], *The Globe and Mail*, April 17, 1947, HCFC 3353, Supplement 1, vol. 2, item 1124; "Housewives' Agitation," *The Ottawa Journal*, April 25, 1947, HCFC, vol. 3353, part 1, item 666; "Consumers in Trouble," *The Toronto Daily Star*, Dec. 12, 1947, HCFC, vol. 3353, Supplement 1, vol. 2, item 1147; "Consumer Federation Will Trek to Ottawa," *Montreal Gazette*, Dec. 12, 1947, HCFC, vol. 3353, Supplement 1, vol. 2,

item 1146; "The Housewives' Petition," *The Citizen* (Ottawa), April 1948, HCFC, vol. 3353, Supplement 1, vol. 2, item 1115. Two exceptions to this trend are: "The Housewives Go on Strike," *The Albertan*, May 1947, HCFC, vol. 3353, part 1, item 643; "Good Women with a Bad Case," *The Ottawa Journal*, 1949, HCFC, vol. 3353, Supplement 1, vol. 2, item 1113.

10. For one of the classic articulations of this argument, see Leo Panitch, ed., *The Canadian State: Political Economy and Political Power* (Toronto: University of Toronto Press, 1977).

11. Paul Axelrod, "Spying on the Young in Depression and War: Students, Youth Groups, and the RCMP 1935–1942," *Labour/Le Travail* 35 (Spring 1995), pp.43–64; Larry Hannant, *The Infernal Machine: Investigating the Loyalty of Canada's Citizens* (Toronto: University of Toronto Press, 1995); Gary Kinsman, "'Character Weakness' and 'Fruit Machines': Towards an Analysis of the Anti-Homosexuality Security Campaign in the Canadian Civil Service," *Labour/Le Travail* 35 (Spring 1995), pp.133–62; Paula Maurutto, "Private Policing and Surveillance of Catholics: Anti-communism in the Roman Catholic Archdiocese of Toronto, 1920–1960," *Labour/Le Travail* 40 (Fall 1997), pp.113–36; Daniel J. Robinson and David Kimmel, "The Queer Career of Homosexual Security Vetting in *Cold War Canada*," *Canadian Historical Review* 75,3 (September 1994), pp.319–45.

12. For a fascinating popular treatment of this phenomenon, see Len Scher, *The Un-Canadians: Stories of the Blacklist Era* (Toronto: Lester, 1992), and a film, "The Un-Canadians," NFB, Montreal, 1996.

13. "Demand March on Ottawa to Protest Prices," *The Ottawa Journal*, Feb. 7, 1947, NAC, CSIS Records, HCFC, vol. 3353, Supplement 1, vol. 1, item 1093; "Protesting Housewives," *The Leader Post* (Regina), March 1, 1947, HCFC, vol. 3353, Supplement 1, vol. 1, item 1092; RCMP secret memorandum re: Florence (Mrs. Alex) Theodoré, Regina, Saskatchewan, April 2, 1947, HCFC, vol. 3353, part 1, item 679; interview with Margaret (Peggy) Chunn, Mona Morgan, and Audrey (Staples) Mozdir, July 24, 1998.

14. Transcript of item published in *Ukrainske Zhitya* (Ukrainian Life), May 15, 1947, NAC, CSIS Records, RG 146, HCFC, vol. 3353, part 1, item 628, vol. VII, no. 20 (302), p.10; RCMP secret memorandum re: CP Activity in Housewives Consumers' Association, Canada Generally, Toronto, Feb. 28, 1948, HCFC, vol. 3353, part 1A, item 691; RCMP secret memorandum re: Housewives Consumers' Associations and Leagues, Feb. 20, 1948, item 700; RCMP secret memorandum re: CP Activity in the Housewives Consumers Association, Toronto, Ont., July 21, 1948, HCA, vol. 3440, part 2A, item 1377; RCMP secret memorandum re: Association of United Ukrainian Canadians, June 5, 1948, item 1382; RCMP secret memorandum re: Canadian Congress of Women, Toronto, Ont., May 17, 1948, item 1391; RCMP secret memorandum re: CP Activity in the Housewives Consumers Association, May 7, 1948, items 1396–97; RCMP secret memorandum re: Housewives Consumers' Association, Toronto, Ont., Feb. 25, 1948, HCFC, vol. 3440, part 2, item 1298; summary and translation of items from *Vapaus*, issues of Jan. 20–Jan. 31, 1948, HCA, vol. 3440, part 2, item 1374; copy of minutes of All-Canadian Women's Conference and Financial Report of Conference Committee, held March 11, 1950, HCFC, vol. 3353, part 3, items 926–7; interview with Pat (Pearl) Chytuk, Feb. 27, 1997; interview with Lil Ilomaki and Alice Maigis, Dec. 12, 1996.

15. Interview with Margaret (Peggy) Chunn, Mona Morgan, and Audrey (Staples) Mozdir, July 24, 1998.

16. For example, "Build More Homes Restore Price Controls Women's Meet Asks," *Daily Tribune*, Oct. 18, 1947, NAC, CSIS Records, RG 146, HCA, vol. 3440, part 1, item 1348.

17. Interview with Lil Ilomaki and Alice Maigis, Dec. 12, 1996; interview with Pat (Pearl) Chytuk, Feb. 27, 1997; interview with Margaret (Peggy) Chunn, Mona Morgan, and Audrey (Staples) Mozdir, July 24, 1998.

18. "Housewives to Protest Here on High Prices," *The Citizen* (Ottawa), May 13, 1947, NAC, CSIS Records, RG 146, HCFC, vol. 3353, part 1, item 634.

19. Reg Whitaker and Gary Marcuse, *Cold War Canada: The Making of a National Insecurity State, 1945–1957* (Toronto: University of Toronto Press, 1994), pp.355–60.

20. For example, Judith Butler, *Gender Trouble: Feminism and the Subversion of Identity* (New York: Routledge, 1990); Linda J. Nicholson, ed., *Feminism/Postmodernism* (New York: Routledge, 1990); Denise Riley, *'Am I That Name?' Feminism and the Category of 'Women' in History* (Minneapolis: University of Minnesota Press, 1988).

21. Katherine Arnup, *Education for Motherhood: Advice for Mothers in Twentieth-Century Canada* (Toronto: University of Toronto Press, 1994); Joan Sangster, *Earning Respect: The Lives of Working Women in Small-Town Ontario, 1920–1960* (Toronto: University of Toronto Press, 1995); Joan Sangster, "Doing Two Jobs: The Wage-Earning Mother, 1945–70," in *A Diversity of Women: Ontario 1945–1980*, ed. Joy Parr (Toronto: University of Toronto Press, 1995), pp.98–134; Veronica Strong-Boag, "Their Side of the Story: Women's Voices from Ontario Suburbs, 1945–60," in *Diversity of Women*, ed. Parr, pp.46–74; Veronica Strong-Boag, "Home Dreams: Women and the Suburban Experiment in Canada, 1945–1960," *Canadian Historical Review* 72,4 (1991), pp.471–504; Veronica Strong-Boag, "Canada's Wage-Earning Wives and the Construction of the Middle Class, 1945–60," *Journal of Canadian Studies* 29,3 (Fall 1994), pp.5–25.

22. Mary Louise Adams, *The Trouble with Normal: Postwar Youth and the Making of Heterosexuality* (Toronto: University of Toronto Press, 1997); Mariana Valverde, "Building Anti-Delinquent Communities: Morality, Gender, and Generation in the City," in *Diversity of Women*, ed. Parr, pp.19–45.

23. Elaine Tyler May, *Homeward Bound: American Families in the Cold War Era* (New York: Basic Books, 1988). See also Joanne Meyerowitz, ed., *Not June Cleaver: Women and Gender in Postwar America* (Philadelphia: Temple University Press, 1994).

24. "Western Women Find Trip to Ottawa Futile," *Montreal Standard*, April 5, 1947, p.2, NAC, CSIS Records, RG 146, HCFC, vol. 3353, Supplement 1, vol. 1, item 1070; "Second Prices Delegate Named," *The Leader Post* (Regina), March 27, 1947, "Government Denies Delegation Grant," *The Leader Post*, March 28, 1947, "Controls Sought," *The Leader Post*, March 29, 1947, HCFC, vol. 3353, Supplement 1, vol. 1, item 1067; "Housewife Convoy Going to Ottawa," *Winnipeg Free Press*, March 27, 1947, item 1068; "Protesting Housewives," *The Leader Post*, March 1, 1947, item 1092; "Demand March on Ottawa to Protest Prices," *The Ottawa Journal*, Feb. 7, 1947, item 1093; interview with Lil Ilomaki and Alice Maigis, Dec. 12, 1996; interview with Pat (Pearl) Chytuk, Feb. 27, 1997; interview with Margaret (Peggy) Chunn, Mona Morgan, and Audrey (Staples) Mozdir, July 24, 1998.

25. "Western Women Determined to See Finance Minister," *The Evening Citizen* (Ottawa), March 31, 1947, NAC, CSIS Records, RG 146, HCFC, vol. 3353, Supplement 1, vol. 1, item 1052; "Women Fail to Have Controls Restored," *Winnipeg Free Press*, April 3, 1947, item 1057; "Western Women Find Trip to Ottawa Futile," *Montreal Standard*, April 5, 1947, items 1070–71.

26. "Second Prices Delegate Named," *The Leader Post* (Regina), March 27, 1947, "Government Denies Delegation Grant," *The Leader Post*, March 28, 1947, "Controls Sought," *The Leader Post*, March 29, 1947, NAC, CSIS Records, RG 146, HCFC, vol. 3533, Supplement 1, vol. 1, item 1067; "Housewife Envoy Going to Ottawa," *Winnipeg Free Press*, March 27, 1947, item 1068.

27. "Western Women Find Trip to Ottawa Futile."

28. "Hundreds of Unwary Women Duped: Communist Officials Head up Housewives Consumers' Group," *Winnipeg Free Press*, April 22, 1947, NAC, CSIS Records, RG 146, HCFC, vol. 3353, part 1, item 676; "Winnipeg Central Headquarters for Communist-led Housewives," *Winnipeg Free Press*, April 23, 1947, item 659; "The Pattern of Communist Tactics," *Winnipeg Free Press*, April 23, 1947, item 660; "Communist Strategy Is Exposed," *Winnipeg Free Press*, April 24, 1947, item 662.

29. RCMP secret memorandum re: Housewives Consumers' Association, Saskatoon, Sask., commentary and transcription of article, "Claims Housewives Group under Communist Control," *Star Phoenix* (Saskatoon), April 24, 1947, NAC, CSIS Records, RG 146, HCFC, vol. 3353, part 1, items 646–48; "Don't Need 'Red' Price Fight Aid, Labour Chiefs Say," *Montreal Star*, April 24, 1947, item 653; "Do Reds Guide League? 'No' Says Leader's Wife," *The Edmonton Journal*, April 23, 1947, item 672; "Wives Duped by Reds," *Calgary Herald*, April 23, 1947, item 673; "Union Will Fight Communists' 'Help,'" *The Gazette* (Montreal), April 24, 1947, item 656; "Says Housewives Not Communists," *The Ottawa Journal*, April 24, 1947, item 668; "Housewives Indignant," *The Leader Post* (Regina), April 24, 1947, item 664; "Housewives Protest 'Communist' Label," *The Toronto Daily Star*, April 24, 1947, item 651; "Housewives Deny Press Allegations of Red Domination of Organization," *Star Phoenix*, April 1947, item 652; "Housewives Indignantly Deny Association Communist-Directed," *Winnipeg Free Press*, April 24, 1947, item 654; "Women Deny Domination by Communists," *The Citizen* (Ottawa), April 24, 1947, item 667; "Communist Boycotts Attacked," *Daily Province* (Vancouver), May 9, 1947, item 630.

30. Bothwell, Drummond, and English, *Canada Since 1945*, pp.116–18.

31. "Drew Asks Women to Check Moves of Political Groups," *The Citizen* (Ottawa), May 29, 1947, NAC, CSIS Records, RG 146, HCFC, vol. 3353, part 1, item 640.

32. "Simonite, Housewives Clash," *Winnipeg Free Press*, Sept. 22, 1947, private collection, Margaret Chunn.

33. "Housewives' Agitation," *The Ottawa Journal*, April 29, 1947, NAC, CSIS Records, RG 146, HCFC, vol. 3353, part 1, item 666; "Rolling-Pin Economics," *The Citizen* (Ottawa), June 25, 1947, HCFC, vol. 3353, Supplement 1, vol. 1, item 1013.

34. Whitaker and Marcuse, *Cold War Canada*, pp.276–79.

35. Censored transcript, "Will 'Fellow-Travellers' Control Housewives' Cavalcade to Ottawa?" *The Financial Post*, June 7, 1947, NAC, CSIS Records, RG 146, HCFC, vol. 3353, Supplement 1, vol. 1, items 997–99; underlined transcript, "Will 'Fellow-Travellers' Control Housewives' Cavalcade to Ottawa?" *The Financial Post*, June 7, 1947, HCFC, vol. 3353, part 1A, items 772–4.

36. "Call it Anti-Communism," *Toronto Saturday Night*, June 28, 1947, NAC, CSIS Records, RG 146, HCFC, vol. 3353, part 1A, item 761.

37. "Housewives Deny Press Allegations of Red Domination of Organization," *Star Phoenix* (Saskatoon), April 24, 1947, NAC, CSIS Records, RG 146, HCFC, vol. 3353, part 1, item 652.

38. Whitaker and Marcuse, *Cold War Canada*, pp.283–84.

39. RCMP secret memorandum re: Consumers Federated Council, Feb. 9, 1948, NAC, CSIS Records, RG 146, HCFC, vol. 3353, part 1A, items 717–18.

40. "The Pattern of Communist Tactics," *Winnipeg Free Press*, April 23, 1947, NAC, CSIS Records, RG 146, HCFC, vol. 3353, part 1, item 660.

41. Special Section File Distribution Slip from Inspector Leopold, NAC, CSIS Records, HCFC, vol. 3440, part 2A, item 1394; RCMP secret memorandum re: CP Activity in the Housewives Consumers' Association, May 7, 1948, item 1396; RCMP secret memorandum re: Housewives Consumers' Association, Toronto, Ont., March 6, 1948, HCA, vol. 3440, part 1, item 1291; RCMP secret memorandum re: CP Activity in the Housewives Consumers' Association, March 17, 1948, HCA, vol. 3440, part 2, item 1282; Special Section File Distribution Slip from Inspector Leopold, June 10, 1947, HCFC, vol. 3353, part 1, item 627; handwritten note, signed by "L," HCFC, vol. 3353, part 1A, item 758.

42. RCMP secret memorandum re: CP Activities in the LPP, Toronto, Ont., Feb. 17, 1948, NAC, CSIS Records, RG 146, HCA, vol. 3440, part 1, items 1302–3.

43. RCMP secret memorandum re: Housewives Consumers' Association, Toronto, Ont., June 26, 1947, NAC, CSIS Records, RG 146, HCFC, vol. 3353, part 1A, items 769–70; RCMP secret memorandum re: Consumers Federated Council, Feb. 3, 1948, item 725; RCMP secret memorandum re: Housewives' Union, Toronto, Ont., Nov. 19, 1937,

HCA, vol. 3440, part 1, item 1274; RCMP secret memorandum [title deleted], Saskatoon, Sask., April 15, 1947, HCFC, vol. 3353, Supplement 1, vol. 1, items 1047–8.

44. RCMP extract re: Housewives Consumers' Association, "Canadians Duped to Aid Red Fifth Column," *Halifax Herald*, March 13, 1948, NAC, CSIS Records, RG 146, HCA, vol. 3440, part 1, item 1283; "Some Enlightenment," *The Hamilton Spectator*, Jan. 24, 1948, item 1297.

45. "Cabinet Refuses to See Women March Planned," *Toronto Daily Star*, April 14, 1947, NAC, CSIS Records, RG 146, HCFC, vol. 3353, Supplement 1, vol. 2, item 1133; "Cabinet Refused Housewives Meet," *The Citizen* (Ottawa), April 14, 1947, item 1134; "Housewives' Group Said Propagandists for Reds; Denied Cabinet Hearing," *The Globe and Mail*, April 15, 1948, item 1127; "Abbott Tells Why Cabinet Wouldn't See Housewives," *Toronto Daily Star*, April 15, 1948, item 1128; "Abbott Charges Housewives Inspired by Communists," *The Ottawa Journal*, April 15, 1948, item 1129; "Charges Group Is 'Fostering Communism,'" *The Citizen* (Ottawa), April 15, 1948, item 1130.

46. [No headline], *The Globe and Mail*, April 17, 1948, NAC, CSIS Records, RG 146, HCFC, vol. 3353, Supplement 1, vol. 2, item 1124.

# PART III

# EDUCATION UNDER COVER

*Young Socialists contingent at an antiwar demonstration, Toronto, late 1960s or early 1970s* (courtesy of Deborah Fraleigh). [Sethna, chap. 8]

STEVEN HEWITT

six ★ ★ ★

# Spying 101: The RCMP's Activities at the University of Saskatchewan, 1920–71

*The reason there are so few historical certainties is that so much of history is done in secret.*

Bernard Porter, *The Origins of the Vigilant State: The London Metropolitan Police Special Branch before the First World War*, 1987

RCMP Security Service activities initially surfaced in the media in relation to surveillance of the Quebec sovereignty movement as well as the world of spying and espionage.[1] Battling spies and sovereignists was, however, only part of the history of RCMP Security Service operations. The Force's security intelligence activities in other areas in Canada have largely gone unnoticed and unreported. While sovereignists and communists occupied the top of the list of targets for the attention of the RCMP Security Service, other groups did not escape police scrutiny. Indeed, no institution with even a hint of radicalism escaped the tentacles of the RCMP, and this is certainly true of the University of Saskatchewan, which has never been a hotbed for sovereignists and not ordinarily a place where people have gathered to discuss ideas that would directly challenge the status quo of Canadian society. Almost entirely unbeknownst to the faculty, staff, students, and chroniclers of the university, their institution had a secret and intricate relationship with the Mounties for well over fifty years. The nature of that association offers an insight into both the operations of the RCMP and the security of civil liberties in Canada.

In the 1960s student protest had erupted in France and the United States, with a spillover effect in Canada. In 1969 retired RCMP deputy commissioner William Kelly wrote that because some sympathetic students might be recruited by the Soviet Union, the Force needed to keep a close watch on them. A year earlier Kelly had called protests by students, labour, and black and Native groups part of a "coherent movement."[2] But according to historian Michael Hayden, there was more smoke than fire when it came to student dissent at the University of Saskatchewan:

> Anyone who reads the administrative correspondence of the University of Saskatchewan gets, at first, the impression that the university was deeply involved in the North American and European explosion of discontent. . . . In Saskatoon, despite the reaction of administration and some faculty, the outbreak was very mild—a few picketings, several speeches, a few tentative invasions of faculty meetings, one short strike, and one almost friendly sit-in do not a revolution make.[3]

Close to fifteen hundred pages of recently released RCMP documents related to the prairie university suggest that Canada's national police force believed otherwise. The records reveal a great deal about the paranoia of an institution of the Canadian state and the persistence of that mentality over several decades.[4]

Mountie attention to universities like the University of Saskatchewan, however, stretched back well before the Second World War. It was in connection with radicalism and the Winnipeg General Strike that the University of Saskatchewan first gained the attention of a member of the RCMP. The specific event was a lecture given at the university in 1920 by J.S. Woodsworth, a church minister and prominent labour activist, and one of those arrested less than a year earlier during the Winnipeg General Strike. In the aftermath of Woodsworth's talk on the outlawed One Big Union, a student in the class approached the *Saskatoon Daily Star* with the story.[5] The newspaper's report prompted Detective-Sergeant C.T. Hildyard to investigate. He obtained the student's name and proceeded to interview him, finding "him to be an absolutely reliable youth of about 23 years of age."[6] Hildyard reported on the professors involved in Woodsworth's appearance[7] and noted that the lecture had been given without the knowledge or approval of the university administration. But his main concern was with its impact on the students. This fear of youth being indoctrinated would be a repeated theme in the RCMP's espionage activities at Canadian universities. Youth were perceived as naive, essentially a blank slate on which anyone could leave his or her intellectual imprint. Their naiveté made them, by nature, according to Commissioner S.T. Wood, "radical and therefore receptive to subversive propaganda promising social and economic reforms."[8]

In this case the concerned Mountie was reassured by his source: "While there were quite a few young boys of 17 and 18 years of age present, he did not think that any harm had been done," although "he would discuss this address with the rest of his class and find out as to whether any harm had been done or not."[9] Hildyard quickly discovered that many of the parents of the students did not share his fear about the persuasive power of Woodsworth's lectures. In telephone calls to the newspaper and personal conversations with the RCMP officer, several parents stated that "it was only right that they as students should hear both sides of the industrial questions of the day, and it was preferable for them to hear the Radical side under such circumstances than for them to hear these views from agitators on the street corners or at labour meetings."[10] Even the sympathetic newspaper editor who had supplied Hildyard with the student/informant's name turned against the Mountie. He ran an editorial entitled "Liberty of Speech" that questioned why the RCMP were investigating lectures at the university.[11] Faced with this general acceptance of Woodsworth's speech, a chastened Hildyard in the end argued only that the students had no choice in whether or not to hear the labour activist's address.[12] Some three years later Hildyard, during a report on a speech given in Saskatoon by Communist activist Becky Buhay, found it necessary to note that the audience was composed of "a large crowd of Ukrainians and Russians and a sprinkling of English speaking people, including a few students from the Saskatchewan University."[13]

Mountie activities at the university did not begin in a substantial way until 1935 and 1936. After the 1930 election of R.B. Bennett and his Conservative Party, the government's attempts to cure Canada's economic ills quickly proved futile in the face of the rapidly worsening Depression. As protest increased, the government's main recourse became repression. The prime minister boasted of employing "iron heels" to stamp out the spectre of communism.[14] In such an atmosphere the RCMP, under the leadership of Conservative appointee Major-General J.H. MacBrien, gained new power and prominence. MacBrien, like the prime minister, believed fervently that the real problem of the 1930s was communism: "It is notable that 99% of these fellows [communists] are foreigners and many of them have not been here long. The best thing to do would be to send them back where they came from in every way possible. If we were rid of them there would be no unemployment or unrest in Canada."[15] His police force echoed that view.

Such an approach seemed even more applicable in 1935, a pivotal point in the decade. Bennett had promised to bring radical change to the Canadian political and economic systems. Midway through the year over a thousand unemployed men set off for Ottawa to take their grievances directly to the prime minister, only to find their journey, known as the "On to Ottawa Trek," halted in Regina by the RCMP and themselves dispersed in the aftermath of a police-provoked riot on July 1. In October 1935 the Bennett government was swept from power by the Liberals under William Lyon Mackenzie King. The Mounties, however, remained in place and their gaze on communists in Canada proved unflinching.

The target of RCMP attention at the University of Saskatchewan in 1935 and 1936 appears on the surface rather innocuous; it was the student newspaper, *The Sheaf.* M.F.A. Lindsay, a Mountie who would later become commissioner, was on campus taking law classes; he read several articles that contained unflattering comments about the Mounted Police, the Canadian state, and the British Empire.[16] For example, the February 28, 1936, issue of the newspaper carried material that a Mountie sergeant "respectfully suggested, amounts to a criminal libel."[17] Specifically he objected to an editorial and a cartoon that contained a dangling figure with the name "Leopold" on his sleeve—a reference to RCMP Sergeant John Leopold, who, as Jack Esselwein, a Regina house painter, had infiltrated the Communist Party in the 1920s before having his real identity exposed in 1928. (See chapter 2 here.) Leopold renewed his connection with Regina on July 1, 1935, during the Regina Riot, having arrived with evidence implicating the Trek leaders.

The first article to bring *The Sheaf* to the attention of the Mounted Police had appeared in November 1935 just before Armistice Day. The editorial, entitled "Thanksgiving Day," attacked the British Empire as having "a record of rapine, savage murder, diplomatic deviltry, cold-blooded bargaining, wholesale stealing, unholy alliances and general aggrandizement unequalled by any other nation in the world's history."[18] Obviously written to generate a reaction, the editorial prompted one war veteran to "bet my last dollar that 50 percent of those who voiced their opinions never did a day's work in their short lives and do not know anything except what they read in books, and another thing, I do not think they have a drop of British blood in their veins."[19] Lindsay, the Mountie/student on campus, went on to investigate "the source of the apparent radical activities of a Communist nature, and the authorship of the attached articles in particular" and discovered that one of the authors was indeed "of Anglo-Saxon parentage" but also "an avowed supporter of the Communist Party of Canada."[20] Three days after this report S.T. Wood, officer in charge of RCMP units in Saskatchewan, sent the attorney general of the province the offending article, noting that it was "not calculated to imbrue [sic] the susceptible minds of the youthful reader with healthy and prideful views of our British Empire, its history, traditions, and institutions."[21]

The Mountie on campus investigated the source of The Sheaf's funding, in particular what body or individual had the power to remove its staff, and noted that the faculty did not become involved in the matter because "the paper has always *delighted in attacking* [them] on any pretext and causing trouble amongst the students." The matter was brought to the attention of the university president, Walter Murray, who replied that the students were free to publish such articles.[22] The only course of action open to Wood was to instruct members of the Saskatoon detachment that future copies of The Sheaf "be obtained and forwarded to this office as soon as they become available in order that the tendencies of this publication may be followed consecutively."[23] Some three years later there would be less tolerance of criticism of patriotic symbols, as the Student Representative Council fired The Sheaf's editor over an article attacking the commemoration of Armistice Day.[24]

The Mounted Police's interest in activities at the University of Saskatchewan was not unique; throughout this era the RCMP became more aware of what was happening on the campuses of Canadian universities.[25] The Mounties spied on student groups such as the Canadian Youth Congress (CYC) and the Canadian Student Assembly (CSA), and MacBrien stated his desire for university officials to control professors more tightly.[26] A dire warning was issued in a weekly RCMP Security Bulletin:

> When a disease spreads until it affects a vital organ it is time for strong remedial action. The virus of Communism, long coursing, almost unopposed, in our social blood-stream has now reached the heart of our educational system as represented by undergraduates and even college professors in several of our leading universities. . . . Evidence of a Communist "drive" upon our College youth is steadily accumulating. As yet the majority in every student body is loyal to Democracy but it appears to be waging an unequal fight against well organized foreign-controlled disruption and disaffection.[27]

Although the communist involvement in student organizations was minimal, the Mounties continued to cast a wary eye upon any student activism. When the 1939 Royal Tour's stop at the campus in Saskatoon coincided with a provincial CYC meeting, the RCMP decided it was "advisable that plain clothes men be detailed to mingle with the youth congress" during the Royal visit. Later, in 1940, Dave Bowman, the national chairman of the CYC, resigned his position shortly after being interviewed by RCMP officers in Saskatoon. The event in question became more controversial when Bowman died soon after the meeting.[28]

The Mountie files on the University of Saskatchewan then show nothing until 1946, when they resume with attention focused squarely on faculty and students. The gap is perhaps explained by the thinly spread RCMP resources during the Second World War and the high priority placed on prevention of sabotage. Also, the Communist Party of Canada had been outlawed in 1940 and many leading Communists found themselves interned for part of the war.[29] With the end of the war the Cold War had begun, in part triggered by the 1945 defection in Ottawa of Igor Gouzenko, a Soviet Embassy cipher clerk.[30] The Gouzenko revelations only confirmed the RCMP's perspective, because the Force had always considered communism to be a greater threat to the Canadian state than fascism. At the university the Force until the 1960s focused on the Communist Party of Canada and its various guises, specifically the Labor Progressive Party (LPP). The RCMP was also extremely wary of any criticism of the United States, Canada's ally in the Cold War, and of any praise for the Soviet Union, Canada's Cold War enemy.[31]

The concentration on the university made sense. Where else in Saskatoon could members of the Mounted Police find a ready supply of radicals? The men in scarlet decided in November 1947 that radicalism at the University of Saskatchewan was of enough interest to be included in a monthly national RCMP bulletin on such activities. Despite their belief that the total number of "Leftists" on campus stood at no more than thirty, the police began collecting files, including photographs, on anyone or any event considered to have radical connections.[32] Often the material consisted solely of clippings from *The Sheaf,*[33] but undercover Mounties and informants also attended meetings. An October 19, 1949, Mountie report described a debate between campus members of the LPP's Karl Marx University Club and the Co-operative Commonwealth Federation (CCF), although the individual making the report was careful to point out, "No notes were taken during the C.C.F. version of the debate."[34]

Mock parliamentary elections occurred yearly on campus, and the Mounted Police seemed concerned when the LPP captured eight seats and 174 votes in 1940, having only taken two seats the previous year. That concern was heightened by a brief article in *Saturday Night* that alluded to the election results and noted, "The university elections in past years have provided a good bellwether for Saskatchewan opinion."[35] To the local Mounties, communism seemed to be making inroads among the cream of Saskatchewan youth. The Saskatoon detachment forwarded LPP election material to Ottawa and investigated a member of the Karl Marx Club, noting in a report his place of residence and his re-enrolment for another year. One member of the LPP, a student with the last name of Bardal, had his activities carefully documented by Mountie surveillance in 1950 and 1951. Searches knew no boundaries. While looking for a woman connected with radical activities, a member of the Saskatoon Special Branch gained access to university records to see if she was either a teacher or a student.[36]

The meetings of other groups also turned up in RCMP reports. Holding a debate in Convocation Hall entitled "Is the United States a Warmongering Nation?" sufficed to get the Student Christian Movement reported on.[37] This organization, which dated from the 1930s and had helped start the Canadian Student Assembly, would be the subject of Mountie enquiries well into the 1960s.[38] In 1952 the Little Theatre of Wynyard, affiliated with the university's extension department, was investigated because it had been allegedly infiltrated by a "Communist element." Noted the inspector in charge of the Yorkton Subdivision, "It will be of interest to see to what extent the Communists will use this group to further their aims and activities."[39]

All of these RCMP activities pale in comparison to the Force's work in the 1960s. During that decade of radicalism, universities and specifically university students were at the forefront of protest movements throughout the Western world. The Mounties had a difficult time coping with the various forms of social protest, because, although most of the protests were still leftist in origin, they were not necessarily Communist-inspired. The "new left" offered a strong critique of American society and values, but unlike the "old left" its proponents were not as beholden to Marxist orthodoxy or the Communist Party line.[40]

To deal with the 1960s upsurge in radicalism the Mounties accelerated their activities on campus, all the while denying such a course of action. In 1961 Commissioner George McClellan assured the Canadian Association of University Teachers "that there was no general surveillance on university campuses" and "the RCMP did not ask . . . either faculty or students to act as informants."[41] Previously recruitment had occurred, and no new restrictions prevented individuals from volunteering their services to the Mounted Police. In 1964 a University of Saskatchewan student walked into RCMP headquarters in Saskatoon and offered his services as an informant. The officer who interviewed him was suspicious of the individual's motivation and apparently nothing came of the offer.[42] Still, other informants were used, although their identities remain the ultimate secret protected by the Access to Information Act.

Restrictions placed on the RCMP's recruitment and use of informants on campus did not please Superintendent H.G. Langton of the Saskatchewan branch of the 1960s version of the Security Service, the Security and Intelligence Service (SIS). In 1965 he expressed frustration that a certain individual connected with the University of Saskatchewan could not assist the force further regarding a "Teach-in" and other radical activities and suggested that his file "should be studied and a complete new look taken at the possible ways and means of gaining or obtaining the services [deleted] to report on Communist activities within these groups. It is realized that existing policy in relation to enquiries at educational institutions brings about some problems in this respect, however the necessity of having available [deleted] in all fields of endeavour cannot be overemphasized."[43]

The limitations of informants would be overcome through the use of undercover surveillance teams that spied on individuals and groups both on and off campus. Those spied on included individuals and organizations at the university, such as Students for a Democratic University (SDU), and visitors to the campus. For example, a September 1966 film presentation on the guerrilla struggle in Venezuela led to the use of a five-man RCMP surveillance team that followed the four members of Vanguard Tours all over Saskatoon and watched as they set up a table in front of Marquis Hall. The report concluded on a comforting note with the reassurance that most students had been either indifferent to the radical appeal or even openly hostile, offering ridicule. (See the Appendix to this chapter for the surveillance report.) Later a team of six Mounties spied on three members of the Black Panther Party who visited the Saskatoon campus in November 1969.[44]

Often surveillance related to the university occurred off campus. At Prince Albert in October 1968, John Gallagher, a member of the university's Student Representative Council, spoke on issues of concern to students at the Saskatchewan Federation of Labour's annual convention. In the audience was an RCMP "source," who depicted the speech as "of a low-key nature [which] did not make any demands or threats of student revolution."[45]

Even social-democratic campus groups could not escape the attention of the Mounted Police. The RCMP, using information gleaned from *The Commonwealth*, the official newspaper of the New Democratic Party, took an interest in a New Democratic Youth (NDY) meeting in November 1968, at which "The Need for Radical Youth" was the scheduled topic. Even though the NDP was well within the Canadian political mainstream, two Mounties monitored the meeting, watching those who entered and reporting on their identities, although they were only able to identify one individual. An informant present at the meeting offered a detailed description of the discussion that took place. These findings were included in a report titled "Trotskyist Activities in Political Parties—Saskatchewan."[46] In an era that just preceded that party's expulsion of its Waffle faction, this work reflected the police fear that those of the more radical left were seeking to infiltrate the NDP.

The RCMP followed events on campus with an intensity that would have put all but the most dedicated student to shame. Even the most obscure political references did not escape their gaze as they faithfully clipped articles from *The Sheaf* and collected political pamphlets and handouts. At the end of most reports the officers listed the sources for the information contained within, much the way a bibliography concludes an essay. The sources consisted of printed material, such as clippings from student publications, and human resources, including the names or code names of informants and undercover Mounties. The more important the occurrence, the more sources employed in creating a report.

In 1969 the Security and Intelligence Section of "F" Division in Saskatchewan was asked by headquarters in Ottawa to assess radical threats connected with educational institutions, to provide a sort of summary in the form of a scorecard of radicals. The report to the commissioner did not express concern about the potential for university-inspired disorder:

> 3. These institutions [the university's Saskatoon and Regina campuses] have, in the past, been controlled to a degree at the top level by academics who have held a conservative point of view. Changes that have been necessary as it related to University/Student problems have been made by the University by sitting down with the students and the necessary changes made prior to any unrest becoming evident. . . . These have had their share of student radicals and professors, but, in

our opinion, they have been controlled fairly well by the university, as it is apparent the administration is well aware of those who have leftist viewpoints.

4. The usual demonstrations, along the anti-U.S. involvement in Vietnam theme, as well as those of a more local nature such as the university budgetary problems with the Saskatchewan Provincial Government over student loans, cutbacks in grants to various colleges, and student voice on the Board of Governors, etc., will likely take place again. However, through our liaison [deleted] we have learned that little or no violence is expected. It is apparent the University is aware that changes must be made in certain areas of the educational process and endeavours are being made in this direction without losing control to some of the demands being put forth to most campuses across Canada.

5. We are aware that the Saskatoon City Police have a riot squad which has been specially trained to handle any problems that may occur on Saskatoon campus. It is our understanding complete liaison between the Saskatoon campus and Saskatoon City Police has been established and are of the opinion that force can handle any problems which might arise.[47]

The report included a list of individuals, both students and faculty, and organizations, such as the SDU, likely to be the sources of disorder on campus. The report continued, "Experience has shown these people to be 'talkers' and behind-the-scenes manipulators and not of a violent type nature other than [deleted] a well-known Red Power advocate, has, to this date, confined his activities off-campus, although he solicits and receives support from campus leftists."[48]

The section on the Regina Campus of the University of Saskatchewan contained lengthy comments on specific faculty members:

> The leading activist both as an organizer of students and the radical left faculty. Has a strong influence over both. His effectiveness would be overwhelming should an occasion arise.
>
> Close associate [deleted]. Considered that he will be a leading activist should trouble result. Will probably be effective with the radical left students.
>
> A leading figure in the New Left. Has influence over students as a lecturer and from living and social contact. Would probably have good effect over the radical left students.[49]

The RCMP accurately viewed the Regina Campus, which in the 1970s would become the University of Regina, as more radical than its Saskatoon equivalent. Regina was a newer institution with younger faculty members, many of whom had experienced the radicalism of U.S. university campuses.[50] On at least one occasion members of the RCMP apparently tried to interfere with the hiring of a faculty member at Regina. A June 10, 1965, report noted, "It is indeed unfortunate that notwithstanding the views [deleted] the Regina Campus Board of Governors have approved the appointment of [deleted] to the University of Saskatchewan, Regina Campus. [section deleted] It therefore becomes more evident that the Regina Campus will bear close watching."[51]

By the end of the decade the RCMP's university gaze was increasingly directed at Native and Métis organizations and their connections with radical black organizations in the United States. Police closely monitored a student-organized seminar series that included controversial campus appearances by black activist Dick Gregory and members of the Black Panther Party; they were especially interested in any references to Canadian Natives and their political activities.[52] Members of the RCMP also spied upon campus meetings connected with the Métis Society of Saskatchewan and speculated about connections between Native activists and radical student organizations:

> The lot of native people in Saskatchewan remains very poor and if conditions do not improve there will most certainly be trouble. . . . The universities throughout Canada have taken an interest in Indian problems. . . . This interest, however, has sparked many university groups, particularly the radical groups, to become involved. Here in Saskatoon, at the University of Saskatchewan [deleted] the Students for a Democratic University (SDU) . . . have had a great deal to say about the Indian situation. They have also attempted to influence Indian and Métis students from this campus in their programs and activities.[53]

The Mountie making this report felt particularly indignant that a speaker at the university in Saskatoon had stated that Indians experienced starvation in the north. He felt it necessary to offer a dissenting opinion in his report: "The talk about people starving in La Loche is unjustified. Hunting and fishing in the area is good and food is plentiful; enough so that when these people receive their welfare cheques they spend the money on liquor. As an example, if a person receives a $90 cheque, he will charter a plane from La Loche to Buffalo Narrows for $60 and return with $30 worth of liquor."[54]

The social tensions in Canadian society, which had been building throughout the 1960s, finally erupted during October 1970 with the Front de Libération du Québec (FLQ) crisis. Several rallies related to the imposition of the War Measures Act occurred on both campuses of the University of Saskatchewan, and the RCMP covered all of them, reporting on participants and the speeches made and collecting pertinent articles and letters from *The Sheaf* and the Saskatoon *Star Phoenix*.[55]

One final event grabbed the attention of the RCMP in the early 1970s. In the spirit of sit-ins that had transpired throughout the university community, some of them ending with vandalism, students occupied the eighth floor of the University of Saskatchewan's Arts Building to protest the failure of the Department of Economics and Political Science to renew the contract of John Richards, an assistant professor. Many students felt that Richards's contract had not been renewed because of his leftist views.[56] As during the previous year's October Crisis, the local RCMP intelligence contingent gathered relevant newspaper articles, listed some material regarding Richards, and speculated as to the outcome of the sit-in, correctly noting that the peaceful demonstration was losing momentum and would probably end when final exams began. The report concluded with a promise of continued vigilance: "Should future demonstrations be staged by local student activists . . . [they] will be duly reported."[57]

What do these documents disclose about the RCMP view of universities? A 1967 comment scrawled on a Department of External Affairs document seems particularly revealing. During that year External Affairs decided it needed a greater presence on university campuses across Canada, so an official was despatched to meet with faculty members at several Canadian universities, including Saskatchewan.[58] In turn an External Affairs official, noting the Force's "own involvement from time to time with the university authorities," sent a copy to the RCMP and asked for comments. One police official wrote that there was "nothing of particular interest to the RCMP, except that it is gratifying to note [that the] author realizes the ideological hostility that prevails throughout the university community."[59]

To many Mounties the university must have seemed like a strange and hostile place. Sometimes the police felt the hostility directly, as when the RCMP attempted to recruit future members on campus. Assistant Commissioner W.L. Higgitt issued a memo on the subject:

> 2. We would suggest that in future when "On Campus" interviews are contemplated at Universities, the member/members responsible for conducting the interviews also liaise directly with S.I.S. [Security Intelligence Service] personnel at the local level, who would be in a position to brief these members on conditions on a particular campus, i.e., personalities to be wary of, etc.[60]

The Saskatoon office of the SIS reported that it did not expect any "unfavourable incidents" during recruiting at the University of Saskatchewan.[61]

The RCMP's relationship with higher educational institutions was complicated by the limited education of many of the Mounties. Prior to 1974 (when it was raised to Grade 12) the minimum educational requirement for a Mountie was Grade 11, and even lower levels in earlier years. In 1963, after being asked how many Mounties had university degrees, Commissioner Cliff Harvison responded, "I don't have time for all that research."[62] Some sixteen years later a high-ranking Mountie estimated that 15 per cent of the Force had a university degree.[63] Even in the 1990s a Mountie drill instructor at "boot camp" in Regina felt it necessary to tell a group of incoming recruits, "This is not a university campus. . . . There is no place here for free-thinking and individuality."[64] The university and its values were truly foreign to the RCMP as an institution.

The secret Mountie work at the University of Saskatchewan, which supposedly ended with the death of the RCMP Security Service in the 1980s, raises as many questions as it answers.[65] First, there is the matter of the complicity of the university administration. The records are unclear as to what role, if any, administrators played in either assisting members of the RCMP or in initiating their work. It is difficult to believe that administrators had no knowledge of Security Service work, especially when RCMP officers on occasion gained access to student records. Then there is the question of how typical was the Security Service work in Regina and Saskatoon. Journalist Paul Palango, in *Above the Law*, suggests that the Security Service, unlike the crime-fighting wing of the RCMP, was highly centralized with all initiatives coming from the highest levels.[66] Again the evidence for this does not appear in the records. Directives seemed to flow from top down, but it also appears that local Mounties initiated their own investigations. Significantly, at least six Mounties worked in Security and Intelligence in Saskatoon in the 1960s.

Did their very presence lead to the construction of radicals, because as employees for any organization they needed to justify their own existence, to demonstrate that they were performing useful and important work? Whatever the case, more work needs to be done on the basic operations of an important component of Canada's security state.

# Appendix

ROYAL CANADIAN MOUNTED POLICE

DIVISION "F"
DATE 11 OCT. 66
SUB-DIVISION SASKATOON
DETACHMENT S.I.B.

Re: Workers Vanguard—General Information, Toronto, Ontario.

INFORMATION

1. [passage deleted under Access] placing advertisements on
bulletin boards on the Saskatoon Campus, University of
Saskatchewan, Saskatoon, Sask. These advertisements,
attached in duplicate, advertised a film on the guerilla
struggle in Venezuela, to be presented by the Vanguard
Tours, 8:00 p.m., 29-9-66, Union Centre, 416—21 St.,
Saskatoon, Sask.

2. Surveillance Report....

<u>29-9-66</u>

7:00 am.
(B & C)—Surveillance set up covering the [deleted] back yard.
The [1962 Volkswagen] van was still parked therein....

8:00 a.m.—After leaving [deleted] drove to Evan Hardy
Collegiate ... where [deleted] left the van carrying books
and pamphlets.

8:10 a.m.—Subjects arrived in front of Walter Murray
Collegiate ... [deleted] left the van carrying books and
pamphlets.

8:13 a.m.—Van continued on to Aden Bowman Collegiate ...
where [deleted] left the vehicle.

8:20 a.m.—[deleted], alone, drove to Nutana Collegiate ...
and parked.

8:25 a.m.—[deleted] drove away from in front of Nutana
Collegiate, east on Taylor St., then stopped, turned around
and returned west on Taylor and stopped in front of Queen
Elizabeth School, Taylor St. and Eastlake Ave. Proceeded on
to Aden Bowman Collegiate and picked up [deleted]. After
driving to both Walter Murray and Evan Hardy Collegiate,

all four subjects returned to [deleted], parked the van in
the back yard and entered the house.

9:00 a.m.—[deleted] left the house and walked to the van.
He could be seen looking around the immediate area as if
looking for surveillance, then returned into the house.

9:15 a.m.—[deleted] arrived in his car, parked in the back
yard and entered the house.

9:45 a.m.
(B & C)—[deleted] left the house, walked to the van opened
the rear door and appeared to be rummaging for something.

9:50 a.m.—He returned to the house and entered, meeting
[deleted] who walked to the van got something from inside,
then returned to the house.

9:55 a.m.—[deleted] left the house and walked to a trash
barrel, walked to the van then returned to the house.

10:30 a.m.
(B, C & E)—[deleted] left the house and walked to the back
door of the van and stood talking. Joined shortly
[deleted].

10:45 a.m.
11:00 a.m.
(B, C, D, E)—All four entered the van and drove directly to
Saskatoon Campus, University of Saskatchewan and parked in
the Public Parking lot. After locking the vehicle, the four
split up, [deleted] to Marquis Hall, [deleted] to a main
path between buildings were he started to sell copies of
the Young Socialist Forum. [deleted] walked to the
Administration Office, left that building and lost from
sight near Alumni Association Bldg. [deleted] went to St.
Andrews Hall and was lost from sight inside.

11:00 a.m.
12:00 noon—All three subjects could be seen attempting to
sell the Y.S.F. on campus. [deleted], in the meantime, had
set up a table in the main lobby of Marquis Hall and had
placed copies of Y.S.F., War and Revolution in Vietnam and
announcements regarding the forthcoming film and discussion
that evening (29-9-66) at the Union Centre. In addition,
pamphlets announcing the Canadian Student Days of Protest,
Nov. 11-12, 1966 were available for those interested.

12:00 noon
4:30 p.m.—All four subjects attempt to sell subscriptions
and the Y.S.F. to students going back and forth. At the
same time, [deleted] got a discussion going with students
who were taking the time to stop at the table. The following persons were identified as being near the table while
the group were [*sic*] there:

[section deleted]

COMMENT:
The main lobby of Marquis Hall is the entrance to the cafeteria for a large segment of the student body who take
their meals there during the noon hour. Consequent it is
estimated that the Vanguard group had access to seeing at
least 2000 or more students who would have been going to
and from the cafeteria and classes. There were from 20 to
100 students at any given time crowding around the table
listening and arguing with the four subjects, although the
majority of students usually moved on, laughing or making
snide remarks, after hearing the Vanguard "pitch."

3:30 p.m.
4:00 p.m.
(B & C)—[deleted] left Marquis Hall, walked to the van and
returned to the University of Saskatchewan Bookstore carrying a small suitcase and a binder. She entered the bookstore, browsed, checked the magazine racks, then left the
store. After leaving the bookstore, she walked upstairs and
entered room 236. After talking to an U/F receptionist, she
left and went to the main library, sat there a short while
then returned to Marquis Hall.

[several pages deleted]

SOURCES:

16.  (1): Cst. D.I. MacKenzie.
     (2): Surveillance teams—   (A)—Sgt. A.M. KUIACK.
                                (B)—Cst. J.C. DUDLEY.
                                (C)—Cst. J.S. RAE
                                (D)—Cst. D.I. MacKENZIE
                                (E)—Cst. A.H. GODIN.

[section deleted]

INVESTIGATOR'S COMMENTS:

17. It would appear this group left Saskatoon during the
early a.m., 30-9-66 after surveillance was ended.

18. Although they confined themselves to the University of Saskatchewan, Saskatoon Campus and the Union Centre, we cannot, at the present time give an accurate assessment of subscriptions sold or new followers gained while here.
19. The fact that they visited high schools in this City is of interest, however, whether or not high school students attended the meeting cannot be reported upon at this time.
20. Although this group were in proximity of approximately 2000 students during the time on Saskatoon Campus, it is our opinion the discussion did not go over very well with the students as it appeared that the majority who stopped at the table did so only to kill time during the noon hour, most appearing to take part only to heckle or to get an argument going which at times became heated between [deleted] and whoever he happened to be talking to.
21. We are presently endeavouring to further identify those who attended the meeting held at the Union Centre. Information we received will be reported.
22. Information has just recently been received regarding the Canadian Student Days of Protest. A movement has just been organized on Saskatoon Campus for this protest and information concerning it can be expected shortly from this office, caption, Saskatoon Student Committee for Protest Against the War in Vietnam.
23. Information as supplied in paras (14) and (15) would indicate the Vanguard Tour has been travelling extensively and is submitted for informational purposes.

Cst. J.C. Dudley, #19419

**Source:** Report of Cst. J.C. Dudley, Oct. 11, 1966, National Archives of Canada, RG 146, vol. 2774, File 94-A-00057, Part 4.

# Notes

Special thanks to Bill Waiser, Michael Hayden, Joan Champ, Stan Hanson, Moira Harris, and the archivists who handle RG 146 access requests at the National Archives of Canada.

1.  See, for instance, Richard Cleroux, *Official Secrets: The Story Behind the Canadian Security Intelligence Service* (Toronto: McGraw-Hill Ryerson, 1990); Robert Dion, *Crimes of the Secret Police* (Montreal: Black Rose Books, 1982); John Sawatsky, *Men in the Shadows: The Shocking Truth about the RCMP Security Service* (Toronto: Totem Books, 1982); and Jeff Sallot, *Nobody Said No* (Toronto: James Lorimer and Company, 1979).
2.  Greg Marquis, *Policing Canada's Century: A History of the Canadian Association of Chiefs of Police* (Toronto: University of Toronto, 1993), p.303. The revelation that the Mounted Police had spied on black activists in Nova Scotia sparked an outcry when it was discovered that on several instances the recording Mounties employed racist terminology and engaged in activity designed to disrupt the black organizations. "RCMP Apologizes for Racist Comments," *The Globe and Mail*, July 21, 1994, p.A2.
3.  Michael Hayden, *Seeking a Balance: The University of Saskatchewan 1907–1982* (Vancouver: University of British Columbia Press, 1983), p.257.
4.  The records acquired under the Access to Information Act are those listed under the file "University of Saskatchewan." Other records related to the same institution, however, exist under various other headings.
5.  "J.S. Woodsworth in Address Tells the 'Inside' Story of Strike," *Saskatoon Daily Star*, March 23, 1920, pp.3, 9. For more on the Winnipeg General Strike, see David Jay Bercuson, *Confrontation at Winnipeg: Labour, Industrial Relations, and the Winnipeg General Strike* (Montreal: McGill-Queen's University Press, 1974).
6.  Report of C.T. Hildyard, March 24, 1920, Royal Canadian Mounted Police Personnel Records, Records for Cecil Thoroton Hildyard.
7.  Ibid. Hildyard dealt with the loyalty of the three. Only one was listed as "absolutely reliable and quite beyond any suspicions of radical leanings." He raised the possibility of approaching the university's administration over the conduct of the three professors, but nothing seems to have been done.
8.  S.T. Wood, "Tools for Treachery," *RCMP Quarterly* 8,4 (April 1941), pp.394–97.
9.  Report of C.T. Hildyard.
10. Ibid.
11. "Liberty of Speech," *Saskatoon Daily Star*, March 27, 1920, p.4. W.F. Herman, the editor of the *Daily Star*, had apparently promised to keep the Mountie's investigation confidential.
12. Report of C.T. Hildyard.
13. Report of Det. Sergt. Hildyard, Feb. 22, 1923, p.7, National Archives of Canada (NAC), Record Group (RG) 146, RCMP Records Related to Becky Buhay, vol. 10, file 92-A-000012.
14. John Herd Thompson, with Allen Seager, *Canada: 1922–1939: Decades of Discord* (Toronto: McClelland and Stewart, 1990), p.226.
15. Lorne and Caroline Brown, *An Unauthorized History of the RCMP* (Toronto: James Lorimer and Company, 1978 [1973]), p.63.
16. The attendance of Lindsay and six others (six of the seven already had university degrees) at university was sponsored by the Mounted Police; all studied law. William and Nora Kelly, *The Royal Canadian Mounted Police: A Century of History, 1873–1973* (Edmonton: Hurtig Publishers, 1973), p.175.
17. Report of Sergt. H.W.H. Williams, March 19, 1936, NAC, RG 146, RCMP Records Related to the University of Saskatchewan, vol. 2774, file 94-A-00057, part 1.
18. "Thanksgiving Day," *The Sheaf*, Oct. 25, 1935.
19. *Regina Leader*, Nov. 25, 1935.
20. Report of Constable M.F.A. Lindsay, Nov. 6, 1935, NAC, RG 146, vol. 2774, file 94-A-

00057, part 1. For a discussion of Mounted Police attitudes towards ethnicity, see S.R. Hewitt, "Malczewski's List: A Case Study of Royal North-West Mounted Police-Immigrant Relations," *Saskatchewan History* 46,1 (Spring 1994), pp.35–41.

21. S.T. Wood to the Attorney General of Saskatchewan, Nov. 9, 1935, NAC, RG 146, vol. 2774, file 94-A-00057, part 1.

22. Report of Cst. Lindsay, Nov. 6, 1935, p.2, emphasis in original; and Wood to Commissioner J.H. MacBrien, March 30, 1936, NAC, RG 146, vol. 2774, file 94-A-00057, part 1. MacBrien scratched his signature in the margin, indicating that he had read Wood's message.

23. Wood to the O.C., Saskatoon Detachment, March 14, 1936, NAC, RG 146, vol. 2774, file 94-A-00057, part 1.

24. Stan Hanson and Don Kerr, "Pacifism, Dissent and the University of Saskatchewan," *Saskatchewan History* 45,2,4 (1993). This article details several prominent cases, including the one of Professor Carlyle King, surrounding freedom of speech at the University of Saskatchewan during the final years of the 1930s and the period of the war. There is no evidence that the Mounted Police played a role in any of these cases, although clearly the Force would have approved of the silencing of any dissent against the war effort or Canada's war capability.

25. Such attention to universities was also certainly not unique to Canada. A similar pattern was occurring in the United States, where J. Edgar Hoover's Federal Bureau of Investigation (FBI) began to collect information about campus activities. For more information on Hoover and the FBI, see Richard Gid Powers, *Secrecy and Power: The Life of J. Edgar Hoover* (London: Hutchinson, 1987). For more information on the FBI's secret work on campuses in the 1930s, see Robert Cohen, *When the Old Left Was Young: Student Radicals and America's First Mass Student Movement, 1929–1941* (New York : Oxford University Press, 1993).

26. Paul Axelrod, "Spying on the Young in Depression and War: Students, Youth Groups and the RCMP, 1935–1942," *Labour/Le Travail* 35 (Spring 1995), pp.44–46.

27. "Intelligence Bulletin, Weekly Summary February 12, 1940," in *R.C.M.P. Security Bulletins: The War Series, 1939–1941*, ed. Gregory S. Kealey and Reg Whitaker (St. John's, Nfld.: Canadian Committee on Labour History, 1989), pp.140–41.

28. Axelrod, "Spying on the Young," pp.56, 58.

29. For a study of the origins of the Defence of Canada Regulations, see Daniel Robinson, "Planning for the 'Most Serious Contingency': Alien Internment, Arbitrary Detention, and the Canadian State, 1938–39," *Journal of Canadian Studies* 28,2 (1993), pp.5–20. For a history of anti-communist repression during the Second World War, see Reg Whitaker, "Official Repression of Communism during World War II," *Labour/Le Travail* 17 (Spring 1986), pp.135–66. For specific examples of those interned, see William Repka and Kathleen M. Repka, *Dangerous Patriots: Canada's Unknown Prisoners of War* (Vancouver: New Star Books, 1982).

30. C.W. Harvison, *The Horsemen* (Toronto: McClelland and Stewart, 1967), pp.147–67.

31. For a study of Canada's role in the early years of the Cold War, see Reg Whitaker and Gary Marcuse, *Cold War Canada: The Making of a National Insecurity State, 1945–1957* (Toronto: University of Toronto Press, 1994).

32. Report of Cst. J.A. MacKenzie, Dec. 16, 1947; report of Insp. T.W. Chard, i/c CIB, Nov. 7, 1947, NAC, RG 146, vol. 2774, file 94-A-00057, part 1. For examples of earlier RCMP Security Bulletins, see Kealey and Whitaker, eds., *R.C.M.P. Security Bulletins: The War Series*; Kealey and Whitaker, eds., *R.C.M.P. Security Bulletins: The Depression Years, Part I, 1933–1934* (St. John's, Nfld.: Canadian Committee on Labour History, 1993); and Kealey and Whitaker, eds., *R.C.M.P. Security Bulletins: The Early Years, 1919–1929* (St. John's, Nfld.: Canadian Committee on Labour History, 1994).

33. The clippings included any stories related to the LPP and even letters written on the subject of technocracy.

34. For a long time the RCMP was careful to avoid spying on democratic socialist organizations. This policy can be traced back to 1925 when word came down from on high to

end surveillance activities against J.S. Woodsworth, who by that time had been elected to parliament.

35. Report of Cst. S.J. Anderson, RCMP Special Branch, Nov. 17, 1949, NAC, RG 146, vol. 2774, file 94-A-00057, part 1; and "Saskatchewan: A Bellwether," *Toronto Saturday Night*. A copy of the latter was included in the RCMP's University of Saskatchewan records.

36. Reports of Cst. S.J. Anderson, Oct. 21, 1949, June 12, 1951, and Oct. 7, 1950, NAC, RG 146, vol. 2774, file 94-A-00057, part 1.

37. Report of Cst. J.A. MacKenzie, i/c Saskatoon Special Branch, March 11, 1949, NAC, RG 146, vol. 2774, file 94-A-00057, part 1. The following week's topic, "Is the Soviet Union a Warmonger?" was also reported on, as was the topic the week after that, "Can We Believe What We Read in the Newspapers?"

38. Axelrod, "Spying on the Young," p.47; report of Sgt. R.L. Firby, Aug. 14, 1965, NAC, RG 146, vol. 2774, file 94-A-00057, part 5.

39. Insp. H.C. Forbes to the O.C. "F" Division, May 9, 1952, NAC, RG 146, vol. 2774, file 94-A-00057.

40. Richard E. Peterson, "The Student Left in American Higher Education," in *Students in Revolt* (Boston: Houghton Mifflin Company, 1969), ed. Seymour Martin Lipset and Philip G. Altbach, p.206.

41. Edward Mann and John Alan Lee, *RCMP vs. the People: Inside Canada's Security Service* (Don Mills, Ont.: General Publishing Co., 1979), p.191.

42. Report of Cpl. R.L. Firby, Feb. 2, 1964. The individual "was told that should he obtain information which causes him concern and he felt this force should be made aware of he should feel free to contact myself [Firby] at any time. . . . This individual's true motive for coming to this force at this time cannot be properly assessed, however this matter is being reported under this reference for future informational purposes."

43. Report of Supt. H.G. Langton, i/c "F" Div. Security and Intelligence, Aug. 27, 1965, NAC, RG 146, vol. 2774, file 94-A-00057, part 5.

44. Report of Cst. J.C. Dudley, Oct. 11, 1966, p.4; report of Cpl. W.G. Andrew, Dec. 2, 1969, NAC, RG 146, vol. 2774, file 94-A-00057, part 5.

45. RCMP Report, Dec. 3, 1968, NAC, RG 146, vol. 2774, file 94-A-00057, part 7. Gallagher's name was deleted from the RCMP material under the Access to Information Act. His name, however, was easily obtainable from newspaper accounts of the labour meeting.

46. Report of Cst. W.P. Lozinski, Nov. 27, 1968, NAC, RG 146, vol. 2774, file 94-A-00057, part 7.

47. Supt. R.J. Ross, i/c "F" Division Security and Intelligence Section, to the Commissioner, Aug. 18, 1969, NAC, RG 146, vol. 2774, file 94-A-00057, part 7.

48. Ibid.

49. Ibid.

50. Hayden, *Seeking a Balance*, pp.244–46.

51. Supt. H.G. Langton to the Commissioner, June 10, 1965, NAC, RG 146, vol. 2774, file 94-A-00057, part 5. Another report apparently connected with the same event mentioned, "Although it was known the appointment . . . had been approved prior to the interview [deleted] on the 10-6-65, this open information, was relayed to [deleted] in an effort to show good faith on the part of the force." Report of Sgt. R.L. Firby, June 10, 1965, NAC, RG 146, vol. 2774, file 94-A-00057, part 5.

52. Gregory's visit disturbed the Saskatoon chief of police, Jim Kettles, who complained to the federal government about Gregory's entrance into Canada. Marquis, *Policing Canada's Century*, p.303. See also Terry Pender's chapter in this book.

53. Report of Cst. J.S. Rae, Dec. 5, 1969, Aug. 20, 1969, NAC, RG 146, vol. 2774, file 94-A-00057, part 7.

54. Ibid.

55. Report of Cst. B.W. Traynor, Nov. 26, 1970, NAC, RG 146, vol. 2774, file 94-A-00057, part 7.

56. For a detailed description of the events, see Hayden, *Seeking a Balance*, pp.262–63.
57. Report of Cst. B.W. Traynor, March 25, 1971, NAC, RG 146, vol. 2774, file 94-A-00057, part 7.
58. L.A.D. Stephens to the Undersecretary, External Affairs, Oct. 25, 1967, NAC, RG 146, vol. 2774, file 94-A-00057, part 6. The faculty members interviewed at the University of Saskatchewan, Saskatoon Campus, were Norman Ward, Fred C. Barnard, David G. Smith, John C. Courtney, John Cartwright, and David Kwavnik of Political Science, Kenneth Laycock, Kenneth Rea, and Harold Bronson of Economics, John McConnell, Geography, and Joseph Fry, History.
59. J.J. McCardle, Defence Liaison for External Affairs, to Dep. Com. W.H. Kelly, RCMP, and responding comments, Nov. 9, 1967, NAC, RG 146, vol. 2774, file 94-A-00057, part 6.
60. Memo of Asst. Com. W.L. Higgitt, March 14, 1969, NAC, RG 146, vol. 2774, file 94-A-00057, part 7.
61. Ibid.
62. *Toronto Telegram*, June 14, 1963, as cited in Mann and Lee, *RCMP vs. the People*, p.123.
63. Mann and Lee, RCMP vs. the People, p.123. This level of education in the RCMP contrasts with the Federal Bureau of Investigation, which since 1947 has required that every applicant have a university degree with honours.
64. Corporal Bernie Lajoie, as quoted in James McKenzie and Lorne McClinton, *Troop 17: The Making of Mounties* (Calgary: Detselig Enterprise, 1992), p.19.
65. The Security Service's death was brief, since it was resurrected as the Canadian Security Intelligence Service. Some 95 per cent of the Mounties in the Security Service simply transferred to the new spy agency. Some did not even have to change desks. Cleroux, *Official Secrets*, p.82.
66. Paul Palango, *Above the Law: The Crooks, the Politicians, the Mounties, and Rod Stamler* (Toronto: McClelland and Stewart, 1994), pp.55–56.

TERRY PENDER

seven ★ ★ ★

# The Gaze on Clubs, Native Studies, and Teachers at Laurentian University, 1960s–70s

Whatever the RCMP Security Service was doing on the Laurentian University campus in Sudbury, the officers commanding did not like it. A secret memorandum of March 23, 1972, instructs the Sudbury detachment of the Security Service to immediately stop an operation at Laurentian:

> 1. If in fact the foregoing is the case, the intelligence gained in this instance hardly justifies the risk investigators took in possibly placing this force in an embarrassing position. You can no doubt appreciate that should the Canadian Association of University Teachers (CAUT) [deleted] be provided with this type of ammunition, they would waste little time in bringing it to the attention of the government.

> 2. The initiative of your investigators in Sudbury is recognized, however, please bring this matter to their attention with the request that further incidents of this nature be curtailed forthwith.[1]

Exactly what the Security Service was doing that could embarrass the RCMP cannot be determined. The files indicate that the potentially embarrassing activities were associated with a meeting of the Young Socialist League (a Trotskyist group).[2] The Cold War was still on, and in their search for communist influences of any kind the state's secret police entangled much of the university community in a widespread program of political surveillance.

Decades after that memorandum was written, most of the information relating to these events remained censored and held in secret by the Canadian Security Intelligence Service (CSIS), until the National Archives of Canada released some of the documents under a 1995 Access to Information Act request. Ultimately, 289 pages of files were released. The declassified documents demonstrate that political surveillance on the Laurentian University campus occurred against student organizations, the Native Studies Program, a Marxist Study Group, teach-ins, demonstrations, and the Canadian Association of University Teachers, among others. The RCMP had informers on campus, conducted surreptitious surveillance operations, and collected publicly available information on its Laurentian-related targets. The

Cold War fear of communist influence intensified such surveillance. A report on the International Student Service of January 23, 1975, was typical with its claim: "Due to the nature of this organization, it provides an excellent field for Communist infiltration."[3] The RCMP monitored all groups that it categorized as "vulnerable" to "infiltration" by the Communist Party.

## The Native Studies Program

The University of Sudbury, one of Laurentian University's affiliated colleges, started a Native Studies Program in the 1975–76 school year. The program immediately attracted the attention of the RCMP Security Service. Members of the American Indian Movement (AIM) were associated with the program, and the Security Service viewed this course of study as a "hotbed" of radicalism, tangible proof of "extremism," and a site for the "brainwashing of young minds" vulnerable to infiltration by other "subversive" organizations.[4] A report of July 12, 1976, asserted: "Information received [names deleted] indicates that the program has an enrolment of approximately one hundred and ten (110) students with an average age of twenty-five (25). In view of the fact that the average age is relatively young, the group is being readily swayed by [censored] a brainwashing process."[5]

As the summer of 1976 ended the Sudbury detachment's Security Service advised RCMP headquarters that surveillance associated with the Native Studies Program would be expanded into Native communities. The RCMP wanted "to monitor the effect of the aforementioned program as it pertains to the native people in our area."[6] A report from March 3, 1977, noted that the enrolment was ninety-three students, and that the program was vulnerable to infiltration: "The aforementioned information clearly illustrates potential infiltration of this program by such organizations as the National Black Coalition of Canada (NBCC) . . . [censored] . . . and the previously mentioned Marxist Study Group. The situation is being monitored on an on-going basis . . . [censored] . . . both at Laurentian University . . . [censored] . . . and the University of Sudbury."[7] Other reports demonstrate that the Security Service was highly concerned about any presence of AIM in the area.

AIM was founded in July 1968 by Clyde Bellecourt and Eddie Benton Banai in Minneapolis, Minnesota. Inspired by the struggle for fishing rights and land claims, AIM evolved as thousands of Native people found themselves faced with racism and discrimination in cities. Jobs, housing, education, Native culture and tradition, and protection of civil rights were priorities for the group. Imitating the success of the Black Panther Party for Self-Defence, AIM organized street patrols to witness and film arrests of Indians in Minneapolis and elsewhere to combat police brutality and harassment.[8] In February 1973 members of AIM occupied South Dakota's Wounded Knee, the site of the last Indian massacre by the U.S. Calvary in 1890. AIM demanded an investigation into broken treaty promises, advocated improved conditions on reservations, and espoused "sovereignty" over Indians' own affairs.[9] During the occupation, which lasted about seventy days, gun battles between the AIM occupiers and the Federal Bureau of Investigation killed one Native and paralyzed one FBI agent.

In August 1974 AIM members visited Anicinabe Provincial Park in Northwestern Ontario in support of Native protestors who had occupied the area. The park was part of an unresolved land claim, and the protestors wanted to draw attention to the plight of First Nations in the area. The drastic situation included near total unemployment, a high rate of suicide, alcoholism, poor health, and a traditional fishery polluted by mercury from a pulp mill.[10] Although AIM was started by urban Natives to help other Natives living in cities and grew out of the activism of the consciousness raised by black civil rights and antiwar activists, its social understanding changed over time. At first AIM emphasized traditional spirituality, but the movement quickly realized that the problems of urban Indians were often an outgrowth of problems on reservations.[11]

By the mid-1970s the security intelligence bureaucracy was using the phrase "Native extremism." A Security Service report headed "Native Extremism in Northern Ontario," of August 11, 1976, singled out the Laurentian program. The program was allegedly "the focal point for Indian activity," which since its introduction had "expanded immensely."[12] The report called Sudbury "a breeding ground for AIM radicals" because of the large First Nations population in the area and the semi-isolated location of the city, which allowed "transient AIM people" to go there for "sweat lodge" ceremonies away from larger cities where "pressure has been exerted upon them by local law enforcement officials." The sensational report continued:

> AIM support in the area has been growing steadily as has been evidenced by the increased enrolment in the university programs as well as local activities. To date there has been no evidence to support militancy amongst the local natives, however, it is felt that a situation such as the one that presently exists in Treaty #9 could conceivably precipitate an armed confrontation.

The report equated enrolment in the Native Studies Program with AIM support. The mention of the Treaty Nine situation referred to a national campaign by members of the White Dog First Nation to draw attention to the mercury contamination of their traditional fishery, and to unresolved land claims. This document, unlike most Security Service reports, raised the spectre of violence. The Security Service found "the possibility of another confrontation, i.e., Anacinabe [*sic*] Park, is certainly within the realm of possibility. The missing ingredient would appear to be a vital issue affecting native people which in the opinion of the writer, would in all likelihood culminate in an armed rebellion."

Just like the universities, the surveillance of the Native Studies Program was part of a continent-wide operation. As the occupation of Wounded Knee came to an end, the FBI telexed the RCMP, advising the Mounties to investigate border crossings by AIM members.[13] Prior to that the RCMP had never heard of AIM, but surveillance of Native groups increased during the next two years, according to writer Johanna Brand:

AIM leaders in Alberta, for example, are aware of covert attempts by the RCMP Security Service to obtain information about individuals. False and irresponsible reports have been issued about the activities of AIM leaders. . . . The Security Service also attempted to recruit strategically placed individuals to act as spies on perfectly legitimate organizations. In one such instance, Ronald Pankiw, Robert Gordon and Lindsay Welch, members of the Security Service, then working in Toronto, attempted to recruit a clergyman who frequently travels across Canada and maintains contact with a wide variety of native organizations.[14]

Incredible as it sounds, the RCMP justified its surveillance of the Native Studies Program, in part, by saying it was vulnerable to infiltration by the Marxist Study Group, a handful of students who met once a month, for a few months.

### The Marxist Study Group

As part of its surveillance the RCMP collected articles or letters about the Marxist Study Group that appeared in the student newspaper, *Lambda*. The name of one group member, Maurice Proulx, is underlined on those documents, most likely indicating that the Security Service maintained a separate file on him. By his own admission he was then a member of the Communist Party of Canada.[15] An RCMP report from May 7, 1976, mentioned a split in the Marxist Study Group that had developed after the resignation of some members who claimed that Proulx was using the group to foist his ideology on others.[16] It appears that the group dissolved soon after the split. A telex from the Sudbury detachment stated: "A review of Laurentian University newspaper, Lambda, during the current 1977/78 school term has failed to reveal the existance [*sic*] or continuance of a Marxist Study Group."[17]

The chilling effect of secret files can still be felt long after the Cold War ended. A former member of the Marxist Study Group does not want to be publicly identified with it more than twenty years after the RCMP closed its file on the tiny band of undergraduates who met and argued into the night. That former group member says: "I still feel that some twenty-odd years later there could be some ramifications because I work for the federal government. . . . I finally have a good job, and I want to keep it."[18] The Marxist Study Group, says this source, met a couple of times a month, and literature on Marxism, historical materialism, and current events was made available. A guest speaker often addressed the group, which also organized protests against cuts to education, tuition increases, and wage and price controls. Says the source, "I think a lot of it was just to bring some political awareness to the campus."

Proulx had no qualms about using his name during an interview. The study group worked to expose undergraduates to a Marxist interpretation of events and history, he says.[19] The group did "solidarity work" with refugees from the CIA-backed coup in Chile, South African blacks, and unions opposed to the federal government's wage and price controls. "I thought it was very important that people like myself do what they could to change society," Proulx says. "To people who benefit and want to preserve the status quo I guess that's subversive. I certainly hope I was subversive. I liked to think of myself as a subversive then. I'd be disappointed if they didn't think so. It was my goal and purpose at the time."

While Proulx views himself as subversive, and it seems the Security Service shared his opinion, it is hard to see the threat to national security that warranted surveillance. The study group had no influence on the student body, and ultimately ended in dissension.

Was infiltration of university groups truly viewed as a threat to national security by the RCMP, or was it used as an excuse to monitor large numbers of people who wanted to bring about peaceful social change? By the 1960s the Security Service knew that the Communist Party of Canada had little or no influence in Northern Ontario.[20] Given this knowledge, why would the Security Service continue to equate possible infiltration of an organization by the Communist Party as a national security threat?

## A New Focus on Universities

The RCMP told the Royal Commission on Security in the late 1960s that universities had become increasingly important for security intelligence. For the Counter Subversion Branch, or Anti-Communist Section, "This meant a new focus and a new field in which to develop informants," the Royal Commission stated. "The unique opportunities for intellectual influence coupled with the university backgrounds of a number of Soviet agents in Canada, the United States and Great Britain, made universities another special concern of the Anti-Communist Section."[21]

By the 1960s the Canadian Association of University Teachers was sufficiently alarmed by Security Service activities on campuses to start a nationwide campaign to resist this "special concern" of the postwar period. The campaign resulted in the government issuing directives that did nothing to protect universities from the Cold Warriors in the RCMP.

In June 1961 Justice Minister E. Davie Fulton instructed RCMP Commissioner C.M. Harvison "to suspend the RCMP's investigations of subversive activities in universities and colleges" until security needs were reviewed. RCMP headquarters advised all divisions to suspend investigations connected with "Communist penetration" of universities, but "long established and reliable agents and contacts should be permitted to continue to report upon developments."[22] In other words, the Security Service kept its university-related informants and agents. Another letter makes it clear that RCMP headquarters' main concern was the possible embarrassment associated with publicly exposed operations on a university campus. If anyone in the Security Service thought that the justice minister wanted to get the Mounties away from universities, the RCMP headquarters advised otherwise in a letter. The letter, the justice minister commented,

> should not be interpreted as meaning that we have waived our interest in
> Communist activities within educational institutions, but rather we must under-

take a careful review of our approach to problems which could result in critical and somewhat embarrassing reflections upon the intentions of the Force. It should be made clear that no action of any kind which could result in public discussion or complaints to the Minister is to be undertaken until the review.[23]

For its objections to Security Service activities CAUT earned a permanent place in the files. By the fall of 1962 CAUT was asking faculty associations to pass a resolution protesting against Security Service actions on campuses:

Resolved, that the Canadian Association of University Teachers express its disapproval of questions concerning the political or religious beliefs, activities or associations of students or colleagues. Members of the Association are advised not to answer such questions, even when they are part of the security investigation of persons seeking government employment.[24]

CAUT stated that intellectual inquiry, academic consultation, and discussion must occur in an atmosphere of "the most complete freedom." This freedom, CAUT said, is a necessary condition of higher education, and "it is the duty of every university, and of every university teacher, to preserve that freedom." The Security Service followed CAUT's campaign closely, even though the Service did not classify the effort as "subversive." A heavily censored RCMP report on the campaign concluded: "It is realized that the criticism and activities herein are not to my knowledge by [*sic*] subversive organizations. This material is, nevertheless, submitted for the information of headquarters. A copy is being placed on our file, [name censored], Laurentian University, Sudbury, Ont., Communist Activities Within."[25]

Someone at the RCMP Headquarters refiled the report under "General Conditions and Subversive Activities in Canadian Universities."[26] Another field report on the CAUT campaign said that the Laurentian faculty opposed the resolution and it looked like the University of Ottawa faculty would do likewise. "Both however, are Catholic universities and as such take a more militant anti-Communist stand."[27] This report added that information on how the resolution fared at other universities would be forwarded, and it singled out Queen's University: "Correspondence concerning the current situation at Queen's University is being forwarded to you under the caption 'Queen's University—Communist Activities Within.'"

It appears that little more than sustained criticism of the RCMP Security Service was all that was needed to initiate widespread, general surveillance by the Service. Indeed, one report filed by the Sudbury detachment of the Security Service was captioned: "Criticisms and Actions by Subversive Organizations Against the RCMP."[28] Within months of taking office in 1963, Liberal Prime Minister Lester B. Pearson met with CAUT representatives and issued a statement, saying:

There is at present no general RCMP surveillance of university campuses. The RCMP does, in the discharge of its security responsibilities, go to the universities as required for information on people seeking government employment in the public service or where there are definite indications that individuals may be involved in espionage or subversive activities.[29]

In September 1971 the Liberal cabinet issued a directive on university-related wiretaps and informants. It declared that no wiretaps or informants "will be used on university campuses except where the Solicitor General has cause to believe that something specific is happening beyond the general free flow of ideas on university campuses."[30]

If anyone thought that was too restrictive, the solicitor general eased up on the regulatory oversight in December 1971, just months after announcing his first "restrictions." These "restrictions" would not apply in cases of emergency as long as a report was made to the solicitor general within two days, and in cases in which informers volunteered information and were not paid for it.[31] Unpaid informants on university campuses could operate for the RCMP, and there was no requirement that elected leaders be kept informed.

## Covering All Corners and Events

In February 1969 the Sudbury Security Service reported the results of the recent elections for the Students General Association (SGA)—the English-speaking undergraduate government at Laurentian University. The RCMP was most interested in the results of a referendum vote on the SGA's affiliation with the Canadian Union of Students (CUS) and the Ontario Union of Students (OUS): "As this report contains information pertaining to the CUS and the OUS copies are being placed on files [censored] and [censored] at this point. We are attaching as many extra copies as possible in the event similar action is concurred with at other levels."[32]

Surveillance became more extensive in August 1969 with a report on "student unrest," and the SGA figured prominently: "The SGA, because of its position vis-a-vis the university was regarded as the main force insofar as any possible student unrest is concerned."[33] The SGA's continued associations with CUS and OUS were noted: "This coupled with the recent 1969 annual CUS convention which, incidentally, was held at Laurentian University, may have a bearing as to the future politics and activities of the S.G.A. and students in general at the University." Detective-Sergeant P.T. Legare, who wrote the report, did not expect Laurentian to be a hotbed of "student unrest" in the fall of 1969, but added, "The situation could change swiftly with arrival of new students and faculty members." And the situation did change.

By the spring of 1970 protests hit Laurentian. About six hundred students occupied different buildings on campus, sympathetic faculty refused to teach, and final examinations were cancelled. The protests were part of a dispute between Laurentian's Senate and Board of Governors. The Senate, on which faculty and students had some representation, fought with the president and Board of Governors over the governing structure and administration of the university. The Senate and students noted that the board was dominated by business interests generally, and the Inco and Falconbridge mining companies, specifically. The Board of

Governors eventually conceded a key demand, and asked university president Stanley Mullins for his resignation. During the ninth day of the sit-in a Security Service report observed, "Flyers advertising a march on Ottawa on 18 April 1970 and sponsored by the Sudbury Vietnam Committee . . . were much in evidence in the few University buildings where the sit-in is staged."[34]

An earlier event provides further insight on the extent of surveillance. In November 1968 a detailed, seven-page report was filed on a teach-in about the Soviet Union. The report included attendance figures, start and finish times, and names of leaders, speakers, and session chairs. It also related parts of conversations and disagreements among the delegates. The information was so detailed that it appears to have been written by an informant or officer who attended the teach-in: "The most significant feature of the Teach-in, it is felt, is the apparent unsolicited or unscheduled participation of the trotskyists [sic]. It is noteworthy . . . that the trotskyists [sic] then had plans or intentions of taking part in the Teach-in [sic]; however, from what transpired at the sessions, they had obviously not been invited."[35]

Later, when the student newspaper carried articles about the Sudbury Committee for a Democratic Chile, the Security Service clipped the publication. In 1973 the Central Intelligence Agency had backed a coup in Chile that brought General Augusto Pinochet to power. The victims of repression and those who sought to aid the victims became targets of security monitoring. Chilean-refugee communities in Canada and Canada-Chile friendship committees became surveillance targets for the Security Service, which reported "Laurentian University's *Lambda* carried a two page spread on Chile showing various articles which are leftist and anti-American in nature."[36] That comment was in a file captioned: "Communist Party of Canada, policy and activity, re, peace and friendship-Chile."

While that information came from the student newspaper, some bits came from denouncers and informants. Some individuals on campus volunteered information to the RCMP Security Service. The Sudbury detachment was no doubt pleased when someone "provided this office with a leaflet which had been posted throughout Laurentian University. The leaflet stated that the Socialist Society of Laurentian [deleted] would be holding a meeting on 19-OCT-72."[37] What action the Security Service took in response to this information is not known, because the next five pages in the file were completely removed by the CSIS censors. The meeting was most likely observed, because that is what happened when the Young Socialists League visited Laurentian on January 21, 1972. Security Service officers noted the attendance at that meeting (nineteen) and filed a three-page report.

Surveillance of student organizations could be very general. A heavily censored version of a Security Service report from April 3, 1975, dealt with the International Student Organization. The Sudbury Security Service passed on the report "for record purposes and the existence of such a student organization in Canada. We attach no Security Service interest to the operation of ISO or the individuals involved."[38] Just a few months earlier a report on the ISO had characterized the organization as "vulnerable to Communist infiltration."

## The Files

Peter Marwitz is a former RCMP officer who was with the Security Service from 1969 to 1984, when he transferred to the civilian CSIS. He retired in 1989. In an interview Marwitz said the field reports filed by the Sudbury Security Service were sent to the head office of A Division, which had jurisdiction over Western Quebec, Eastern Ontario, and Northern Ontario, and then the information "would be matched up against other things by readers."

> The material would have been looked at, and the original copy would have been forwarded on to headquarters where it would have gone to the Counter-Subversion Branch. They, of course, would have carded all the names [mentioned in the report]. Carding means they underline and indicate whether or not there is a file [on the person named] if it hasn't already been indicated on the report. And then they would make copies and put it on that particular file. Then those files would go out to readers in headquarters, to the analysts, who would read it and review what's on it. If they wanted something to be done by Sudbury they would write back to A Division, and A Division would tell Sudbury: "Go and do this." These reports [on Laurentian] were part of a larger process. Our net was nation-wide, it wasn't just Northern Ontario.

Censors with CSIS allowed very little to pass through the mesh of this nationwide net. The Laurentian University file is so heavily censored that it is impossible to determine if the RCMP surveillance ever became disruptive. It is difficult to know what impact the university-related surveillance had on students and faculty. Sometimes the surveillance was very open, as on February 22, 1963, when RCMP Inspector Wiebe came calling on the Rev. J.W.E. Newberry, the president of Huntington College, one of Laurentian's affiliated colleges.[39] Wiebe asked about two Vancouver students taking part in a "peace walk" to Berlin, about "Communist tendencies" within the Canadian Peace Research Institute, and about any "Communist tendencies" among staff or students at Huntington. "I had the feeling that during the interview that I more than any other person at the university was the one being investigated," Newberry said. He believed that the RCMP was trying to intimidate him, and, through him, the faculty and students. Did it work?

Surveillance just in itself can be effective social control, and maybe Inspector Wiebe was counting on that. Wiebe's visit occurred long before Michel Foucault was writing about the "gaze" and its effects: "An inspecting gaze, a gaze which each individual under its weight will end by interiorising to the point that he is his own overseer, each individual thus exercising this surveillance over, and against, himself."[40]

The Security Service and the federal government justified intrusive questions about individuals on campus by saying that the people under scrutiny had to be cleared for government-related work. CAUT believed that even this approach was unacceptable, and it is easy to see why. A latent function of this screening process is to restrict the country's political life. As Larry Hannant puts it:

Pressure to conform came from the fear of a pervasive and omnipresent panoptic eye, the very type of surveillance system implemented in security screening. Whether or not they read Foucault, security-intelligence forces appear to understand this knowledge. Their usual practice is to maintain a high level of surveillance but only rarely to act upon the intelligence gained by it. Implicitly they grasp that placing people under scrutiny tends to constrain their actions. It may also alter the ideological climate in society by legitimizing one set of political ideas and rendering other views unacceptable.[41]

The narrowing of public discourse can serve to maintain existing social relations. On a university campus, which should be a redoubt of uninhibited thinking, enquiry, and learning, there should be no room for the "panoptic eye" of security intelligence officers. This practice has an additional dimension of ideological control, according to James Littleton: "The knowledge that someday one will have to be 'cleared' has a remarkable ability to induce intellectual self-censorship. The inevitable consequences is that basic assumptions about the international relations and about the political process tend to remain unchallenged. Thus the scope of public discourse is narrowed."[42]

The validity of the theorizing by Foucault and others is demonstrated by the experiences of a former member of the Laurentian Marxist Study Group. Even today that individual is worried that previous public association with the Marxist group could cause problems with his employer, the federal government. Says the former surveillance target: "It's really awful, but I'm concerned about my job. . . . It's awful. There's nothing significant in what I did. But there's still a cloud that hangs over you from all of that."[43] Just a gaze . . .

## Notes

1. National Archives of Canada (NAC), CSIS Records, Ottawa, RG 146, vol. 2770, file 95-A-00094, p.160.
2. Ibid., p.166.
3. Ibid., p.88.
4. NAC, RG 146, vol. 3199, file 95-A-00094, pp.284–92.
5. Ibid., p.292.
6. Ibid., p.291.
7. Ibid., p.284.
8. See Peter Matthiessen, *In the Spirit of Crazy Horse* (New York: Viking, 1981).
9. See Terry H. Anderson, *The Movement and the Sixties: Protest in America from Greensboro to Wounded Knee* (Oxford: Oxford University Press, 1995).
10. See Johanna Brand, *The Life and Death of Anna Mae Aquash* (Toronto: James Lorimer and Company, 1978).
11. Brand, *Life and Death*, p.35. In Sudbury Art Solomon was a spiritual leader/adviser to AIM and a guest lecturer at the Native Studies Program at Laurentian University. Although almost every name is removed from the RCMP files, the Security Service's demonstrated interest in AIM could only mean that Solomon was a surveillance target.
12. NAC, RG 146, vol. 3199, file 95-A-00094, p.289; also for following quotations.
13. Brand, *Life and Death*, p.154.
14. Ibid., pp.156–57.

15. Interview with Maurice Proulx, June 4, 1997.
16. NAC, RG 146, vol. 3189, file 95-A-00094, p.278.
17. Ibid., p.276. This Security Service report is the most recent one—that is, last dated—released by the CSIS censors and the National Archives relating to Laurentian University.
18. Interview, unnamed, Oct. 3, 1997.
19. Interview with Maurice Proulx, Nov. 3, 1997.
20. Interview with Peter Marwitz, June 4, 1997.
21. Canada, *Report of the Royal Commission on Security* [Mackenzie Commission] (Ottawa: Queen's Printer, 1969), chapter 6, p.57.
22. Canada, *Commission of Inquiry Concerning Certain Activities of the Royal Canadian Mounted Police* [McDonald Commission], Second Report, vol. 1 (Ottawa: Queen's Printer, 1981), p.341.
23. Canada, *Commission of Inquiry*, p.342.
24. NAC, RG 146, vol. 2770, file 95-A-00094, vol. 1, pp.78–79; also for following quotations.
25. Ibid., p.75.
26. Ibid., p.77.
27. Ibid.
28. Ibid., p.74.
29. Canada, *Commission of Inquiry*, p.342.
30. Ibid., p.347.
31. Ibid., p.348.
32. NAC, RG 146, vol. 2770, file 95-A-00094, p.15.
33. Ibid., p.113.
34. Ibid., p.242.
35. Ibid., p.218.
36. Ibid., p.38.
37. Ibid., p.119.
38. Ibid., p.133.
39. *Maclean's*, April 20, 1963, p.15; also for following quotations.
40. Michel Foucault, *Power/Knowledge: Selected Interviews and Other Writings 1972–1977*, ed. Colin Gordon (Toronto: Random House, 1980), p.247.
41. Larry Hannant, *The Infernal Machine: Investigating the Loyalty of Canada's Citizens* (Toronto: University of Toronto Press, 1995), p.247.
42. James Littleton, *Target Nation: Canada and the Western Intelligence Network* (Toronto: Lester and Orpen Dennys, 1986), p.166.
43. Interview, unnamed, March 10, 1997.

CHRISTABELLE SETHNA

eight ✳ ✳ ✳

# High-School Confidential: RCMP Surveillance of Secondary School Student Activists

On January 21, 1971, as the Toronto Board of Education debated the merits of extending its Grade 7 to 12 Family Life Education program to include the topics of birth control, family planning, and abortion, it received a delegation of about twenty students.[1] The delegation's spokesperson, one fifteen-year-old Debbie, not only argued in favour of the extension of the program but also insisted that secondary schools provide students with contraceptive information and devices. Debbie explained:

> The high school is where we really need birth control. . . . It's hard for high school women to get it anywhere else. Students get pregnant and are forced to resign from school. Their whole lives are botched up just because they didn't have access to birth control. They lose their chance for an education, for a decent job, and often end up having to get married when they don't want to.[2]

This attempt to address the disproportionate price that girls paid for one uncontained ejaculation fell short. The majority of trustees voted to give principals the power to decide whether or not to implement the extended version of the Family Life Education program, and then only to students from Grade 11 on up.

In June 1995 I was able to interview Debbie about her activities for my postdoctoral study on sex education at the Toronto Board of Education between 1950 and 1980.[3] In preparing for the interview I learned that she had won her school's campaign for student council president on a platform that included freedom of student assembly, an end to the Vietnam War, and access to contraceptive devices. She had become a founding member of her school's Women's Liberation Club and had been a member of an array of left-wing organizations. When I asked her to recall her teachers' reaction to her activism, she was charitable about what she termed their "opposition." She remembered being suspended for calling a teacher by his first name and for coming to school braless and barefoot. Yet because of two of her teachers' involvement in left-wing radicalism and her own ability to be "strongly forthright," she believed she had been able to carry on with her activities, as she put it, "without interference."[4]

It was only after I turned off my tape recorder that she said with a smile, "One teacher told me: 'Be careful or the Mounties will get you!'" I smiled back. Under a hot summer sun at a lazy Bloor St. café the teacher's remark appeared offhand and amusing. But after Ruth Pierson, my doctoral supervisor, drew my attention to the spring 1995 issue of *Labour/Le Travail*, which documented the RCMP surveillance of a wide range of individuals considered subversive, the teacher's comment no longer seemed a quaint anachronism from a paranoid age.[5] Rather, it became a signpost for my investigation into RCMP surveillance of Ontario high-school students during the heyday of the student power movement.

High-school student activism between 1960 and 1975 was overshadowed by unrest at Canadian universities and continues to be overlooked by contemporary Canadian scholarship on old- and new-left campus radicalism.[6] But it did not escape the attention of the RCMP. The Force identified the province's high schools as sites for real or potential political insurgency and targeted high-school political activists—individually and collectively—for secret surveillance.

Although the RCMP appeared willing to acknowledge that student-power activists were, in general, a tiny minority of the total student population, it insisted that "it would be foolish to dismiss [them] as having no great potential for mischief because of their lack of numerical strength."[7] This small group, it was feared, assisted in promoting the international spread of communism, possibly by violent means, both by recruiting students as members or as sympathizers to penetrate key sectors of society and by encouraging large numbers of students to participate in demonstrations that were—unbeknownst to the demonstrators—driven by Marxists.[8]

In Ontario the RCMP was particularly concerned about the seeming success of left-wing radicals in meeting their aims for recruitment and demonstrations—not just in universities but in high/schools as well. The RCMP speculated that university students would form a revolutionary alliance with labour and high schools to seize the jewel in the province's crown—the University of Toronto—in order to begin structuring a classless society. Officers suspected that, because of their work with labour and university and high-school students, Trotskyist organizations would be openly or clandestinely involved in this activity.[9]

While Trotskyist organizations in Canada were known for their old-left vanguard support for the destruction of capitalism and the building of socialism, they portrayed themselves as anything but old hat. Keen to capitalize on the 1960s new-left tenet that students, not just workers, could be agents of social change, Trotskyists were quick to understand the ideological promise of adolescent alienation. They encouraged members to harness not just university but high-school rebels to their cause. Trotskyist youth leaders advised making high schoolers, regardless of their economic status, aware of the "frustration, deceit, ignorance, hypocrasy [*sic*], and ignobility" of industrial capitalist society.[10] Trotskyists had, and continued to have, a stormy relationship with the New Democratic Party (NDP). But it was hoped that high-school recruits would not only assume leading roles in clubs like the New Democratic Youth (NDY) but also help to politicize classmates by taking on issues such as the lack of democracy in the schools.[11]

By the mid-1960s the lack of democracy in schools had become an issue that many secondary school students could identify with. In high schools across Ontario students appeared to be jettisoning the three Rs in favour of the ABCs (anger, back talk, and confrontation).[12] Walkouts, marches, strikes, and sit-ins to protest school bans of political clubs, principals' control over the editorial content of school newspapers, and school dress codes concerning the length of boys' hair and girls' skirts rocked secondary schools to the chants of "We Shall Overcome." Some students undoubtedly participated in these demonstrations because of their left-wing political beliefs. Others did so out of personal dissatisfaction with schools' authoritarian attitude towards the student body.[13] Regardless of their motivation, pupils were not only suspended and threatened with expulsion but also inevitably red-baited. "They fling around these names—Socialism, Communism, Leftists, Rightists," noted Lee Akens, who had struck to protest the disruption of her classes by construction at Toronto's Malvern Collegiate, "and that's what made me mad, first of all. You see, our strike, if you can say that it was organized at all, was organized entirely by ourselves."[14]

RCMP investigators were interested in keeping tabs on the tumult at schools to ascertain the extent of Trotskyist involvement. For example, on March 15, 1965, two officers took note of an evening demonstration by the Toronto High School Federation of Students (THSFS) outside the administrative offices of the North York Board of Education:

> At 7:00 pm there were approximately 52 students picketing in front of the building, all within the 15–18 year bracket, none of whom were recognized. They carried signs which read:
> "Democracy Rules Except in High Schools"
> "Majority Rules Except in High Schools"
> "Politics is a part of education"
> "New Democratic Youth."
> At 8:00 pm the students entered the administration building and stayed inside until 9:15 pm at which time they dispersed on foot.[15]

The author of the surveillance report noted pointedly, albeit weakly, that the founding meeting of the THSFS was "supposedly" held at the home of well-known Trotskyists.[16]

Apart from on-site surveillance, the RCMP drew upon information received from informants, who were likely to be teachers, principals, or school-board trustees.[17] But it was not unknown for the RCMP to have teenagers on its payroll, and youths may also have been used to gather intelligence at Trotskyist meetings and conferences pertaining to their peers.[18] Informants passed along to the RCMP the names of high-school students who were present. They also recorded Trotskyists' plans for interesting high-school students in joining their organizations. Informants appeared to confirm the RCMP's suspicions that high schools were hothouses for left-wing revolutionaries. The spies reported variously that Trotskyists stated that high schools contained "the cadres who will lead in the future," that Trotskyist youth workers were buoyed by the "positive progress" they had made in schools, and that Trotskyists wanted to concentrate on attracting students from "the lower grades so that activity can be continued from year to year."[19]

Newspapers also served to keep the RCMP abreast of high-school student political activism. Deposited in the Force's files were clippings from the Canadian mainstream press headlined: "'Beatle' bangs shorn student unrepentant" and "Trustees won't let student speak." Both dealt with student concerns—such as freedom of dress and speech—that Trotskyist organizations were believed to "exploit."[20] Most likely because Trotskyists encouraged politicizing students via the NDY, letters to the editor from students expressing dismay at schools' refusal to sanction political clubs were also deposited.[21] So too were articles on individuals such as Joe Young, a self-identified "Trotskyite."[22] Young began a career rattling the establishment at the ripe age of fifteen, when he formed a Ban the Bomb club at his high school during the Cuban Missile Crisis of 1962. Young's continuing agitation for peace at age twenty-three as a member of the Young Socialists (YS) presumably proved to the RCMP that age did little to temper youthful student activism.[23]

The YS was officially founded on July 8, 1967, at a Toronto conference. Although the YS identified itself as an "independent socialist organization built of youth and by youth," it was intended to serve as a Canada-wide training ground for adult membership in the League for Socialist Action (LSA). The average age of members was twenty-one, with twenty-seven being the upper limit. The organization was most active in Toronto and Vancouver, with a core membership of about 150 to 200 across the country.[24] From its inception, the YS broadcast its solidarity with young Canadians in the hip youthspeak of the day. "Our generation," noted one of the organizers for the Toronto branch, "is bugged by the whole scene. . . . But just rebelling, just dropping out, is no answer. It leads nowhere."[25] The YS's success on university campuses was open to debate, but its popular appeal to high-school students was quite evident, possibly because the group pledged to work for a national campaign to democratize high schools. Schools, proclaimed the YS, were "run like prisons—run in the interests of the tiny elite that controls Canada."[26]

A far more stinging indictment of schools began circulating in Canada the following year. In his incendiary underground pamphlet *The Student as Nigger*, Jerry Farber, a white college teacher from the United States, drew upon the example of slavery in the U.S. south and upon the lexicon of the black power movement to equate schools with plantations, students with slaves, and teachers with masters. Arguing that "educational oppression is trickier to fight than racial oppression," Farber concluded that schools psychically neutered white and black students in order to program them for passive obedience to the state.[27] Farber's piece made the rounds of Canadian university newspapers, including *The Varsity* at the University of Toronto, and also appeared in publications as diverse as *This Magazine is About Schools* and the Senate *Hansard*.[28]

Farber failed, however, to take into account that black students in universities and high schools in North America were almost always relegated to the margins of curricula, classrooms, and councils in ways that white students never could be. The systematic racist isolation of black students within institutions of learning was precisely the issue that triggered several well-publicized campus riots and schoolyard mêlées in Canada and the United States.[29] The RCMP viewed white and black student activism very differently. The former was associated with the new left, the latter with militant African-American groups such as the Black Panthers, leading the RCMP brass to warn of dangers posed by any co-operation between black militants and left-wing radicals.[30]

*Living and Learning: The Report of the Provincial Committee on Aims and Objectives of Education in the Schools of Ontario* (1968) appeared about the same time as Farber's pamphlet and caused another stir in Canada. The authors of the Hall-Dennis Report—as it was popularly known—called for child-centred education intended to help students cope with the rapid social change of the late twentieth-century.[31] Remarking that teenaged students "express a growing concern about worldly problems, and show a desire to share in the decisions of the community," the authors appeared to advocate a much softer approach to the regulation of student political activism than the hard line usually taken by schools.[32] But the RCMP could hardly have been less sympathetic, particularly when it came to the YS. Although there was no indication that the YS engaged in illegal or violent acts, YS members were watched, their meetings and conferences infiltrated and interfered with, their headquarters staked out, their papers and pamphlets collected, and their protests surreptitiously photographed. No demonstration with YS members present was considered unworthy of surveillance:

> On 3-10-68, approximately 45 students picketed the Toronto Board of Education offices protesting student rights in the secondary school system. Representatives from the Young Socialists [deleted] who utilized a bull horn to shout slogans. Approximately 12 students returned to a 3:00 pm Board meeting where they stood up and identified themselves as representatives of Etobicoke, Vaughn Road, Superschool, Ontario Union of Students and [?] four from Castle Frank high schools. This last group is currently embroiled in a controversy over disciplinary measures regarding long hair, no untoward incidents occurred.[33]

By 1970, as part of an expanded political platform encompassing support for women's liberation, the YS came out in favour of school-based co-educational sex education programs, which included information on birth control and abortion. The move was timely. Media pundits had repeatedly cited the shift in sexual mores in combination with ignorance about sexual matters as the reason for a rise in the rates of single teen pregnancy. Sex education in schools was touted as a means of combatting the problem. Yet despite the new mood of progressivism, officials at the Ontario Department of Education remained extremely hesitant about the matter.[34]

In contrast to those women's liberationists who argued that the roots of women's oppression lay in patriarchy, women involved in the YS viewed capitalism as the source and a socialist revolution as the solution. Alongside the family, the school was blamed for playing a key role in oppressing women because it denied them a knowledge of their bodies. "Health courses," stated a YS committee in a brief to the Royal Commission on the Status of Women, "which provide detailed, diagrammed information about the functioning of the pituitary gland tell the young girl nothing about birth control."[35]

High-schools girls who participated in the women's rights campaigns in which YS members were involved were also drawn into the RCMP's surveillance net:

> It was learned that there are approximately 18 members of the Y. S. in Newmarket, largely made up of female students at Newmarket High School. They are believed to meet on Thursday evenings in Richmond Hill, Ontario, and seem to be concerned a great deal with Women's Liberation items, although the Quebec issues, anti-war and in general anti-establishment trends are part of their program. It is believed that at least one member of the Y. S. attends Huron Heights High School, located in Newmarket as well. The following students are the most vocal Y. S. members and leaders at Newmarket High School: [deleted].[36]

As YS women grew increasingly involved with issues of women's liberation, many of them joined the Toronto Women's Caucus (TWC). Intended to accommodate women of diverse political backgrounds, the TWC made safe, free, accessible abortion its main goal. The group's literature often highlighted the "tragedy" of pregnant high-school women whose life plans were derailed "by one unfortunate accident."[37] The base of the TWC was made up of university students, but the group attracted a sprinkling of high-school students, many of whom had already been radicalized in the YS. The RCMP now stretched its surveillance net to encompass TWC members, because it was through women's liberation in high schools, as one informant recorded, that "the Trotskyists intend to organize and cause dissension."[38]

True to her teacher's warning, Debbie, the high-school student referred to earlier, did come to the attention of the RCMP after she joined the YS and the TWC. A YS handbill announcing both her election to student council president as well as an upcoming conference for high-school students on birth control was deposited on file. Informants kept track of her speaking engagements. Teachers at her school were watched because some of them were identified as "instrumental" in recruiting students to the "Trotskyist Movement." Ironically, the YS's public denouncements about the RCMP's penchant for spying on students also made their way into classified RCMP files.[39]

The relationship between the RCMP spying on high-school students and the shifting constructions of subversion and adolescence is complex, and calls for further study. Adolescence in this society is considered inherently subversive.[40] But such an essentialist approach does little to open up to exploration exciting theoretical and practical territories for evaluating the state's historical capacity for regulating adolescents' sexual—and, quite clearly now, political—agency as mediated by their gender, race, and class.

## Notes

I am grateful to the Social Sciences and Humanities Research Council of Canada for their financial assistance. Ruth Roach Pierson, Steve Hewitt, and Edgar-Andre Montigny deserve my thanks for their input and encouragement. A slightly different version of this paper was presented at a session sponsored jointly by the Canadian Historical Association and the Canadian Association for Security Intelligence Studies, University of Ottawa, May 31, 1998.

1. Toronto Board of Education, *Minutes of the Board of Education*, Jan. 21, 1971, pp.20–21.
2. "High School Women Demand Liberation," *Young Socialist* 2,2 (March 1971), p.4.
3. Christabelle Sethna, "Compromising Positions: Sex Education at the Toronto Board of Education, 1950–1980," SSHRC postdoctoral fellowship, 1995–97.
4. Interview with Debbie, June 13, 1995.
5. *Labour/Le Travail* 35 (Spring 1995).
6. For example, see Doug Owram, *Born at the Right Time: A History of the Baby Boom Generation* (Toronto: University of Toronto Press, 1996), pp.217–47; Paul Axelrod, "Spying on the Young in Depression and War: Students, Youth Groups and the RCMP, 1935–1942," *Labour/Le Travail* 5 (Spring 1995), pp.43–63; and Steve Hewitt, "Spying 101: The RCMP's Secret Activities at the University of Saskatchewan, 1920–1971," *Saskatchewan History* (Fall 1995), pp.20–31. Contemporaneous writing on high-school student activism was primarily American. See Irving G. Hendrick and Reginald Jones, eds., *Student Dissent in the Schools* (Boston: Houghton Mifflin Co., 1972); G. Louis Heath, ed., *The High School Rebel: Readings in Adolescent School Rebellion* (New York: MSS Educational Publishing, 1969); Kenneth L. Fish, *Conflict and Dissent in the High Schools* (New York: The Bruce Publishing Co., 1970); Marc Libarle and Tom Seligson, eds., *The High School Revolutionaries* (New York: Random House, 1970); Beatrice M. Gudridge, *High School Student Unrest: Education U.S.A., Special Report* (Washington, D.C.: National School Public Relations Association, 1969). For the Canadian scene, see Charles Hobart, "The Implications of Student Power for High Schools," *Education Canada* 9,2 (June 1969), pp.21–32; H.L. Willis and Gerald Halpern, "A Survey of How High School Students Perceive Their High Schools," *Education Canada* 10,2 (June 1970), pp.29–33; Tim and Julyan Reid, eds., *Student Power and the Canadian Campus* (Toronto: Peter Martin Associates, 1969), pp.175–226; and Robert Stamp, *The Schools of Ontario, 1876–1976* (Toronto: University of Toronto Press, 1982).
7. "Student Activism—Metropolitan Toronto," in *Young Socialists, Toronto, Ontario*, part 19, Toronto S.I.B., October 1968, p.1488, National Archives of Canada (NAC), CSIS Records, RG 146, vol. 3691.
8. Ibid., pp.1484–1509.
9. Ibid., pp.1501–2. Trotskyists are followers of Leon Trotsky, one of the main leaders of the 1917 Russian Revolution, who came to oppose Joseph Stalin's dictatorship of the Soviet Union.
10. "Youth Discussion Bulletin," in *Young Socialists Toronto, Ontario*, part 3, Oct. 31, 1963, p.112, NAC, RG 146, vol. 3690.
11. Ibid., p.114.
12. Gudridge, *High School Student Unrest*, p.3.
13. Harry Kopyto, "Students Demand Rights," *Young Socialist Forum* 2,4 (Early Summer 1965), pp.1–2; "High School Protest I: Toronto," *This Magazine is About Schools* 1,1 (April 1966), pp.20–36; Stamp, *Schools of Ontario*, pp.227–29; Pierre Berton, *The Smug Minority* (Toronto: McClelland and Stewart, 1968), pp.33–37.
14. "High School Protest I," p.23.
15. *Young Socialists*, part 7, pp.388–89, NAC, RG 146, vol. 3690.
16. Ibid., p.390.
17. *Young Socialists, Toronto, Ontario*, part 19, p.1530, NAC, RG 146, vol. 3691.
18. Stanley McDowell, "Goyer Denies Funds Paid to Teen-agers for Tips to RCMP," *The Globe and Mail*, Aug. 16, 1971, pp.1–2. My thanks to Steve Hewitt for this reference.
19. *Young Socialists, General Information, Toronto, Ontario*, part 2, p.35554, NAC RG 146, vol. 352; *Young Socialists, Toronto, Ontario*, part 14, p.886, NAC, RG 146, vol. 3691; *Young Socialists, Toronto, Ontario*, part 10, p.535, NAC, RG 146, vol. 3690.
20. "'Beatle' Bangs Shorn Student Unrepentant," *The Toronto Star*, March 22, 1965, and "Trustees Won't Let Student Speak," *The Toronto Star*, March 16, 1965, in *Young Socialists*, part 7, pp.391–93, NAC, RG 146, vol. 3690.

21. *The Globe and Mail,* March 26, 1965, in *Young Socialists, Toronto, Ontario,* part 9, p.503, NAC, RG 146, vol. 3690.
22. Ivan Prokopchuk, "Youth: Mighty Joe Young Likes to Rattle the Establishment," *The Toronto Star,* Sept. 5, 1970, in *Young Socialists, Toronto, Ontario,* part 23, p.2015, NAC, RG 146, vol. 3691.
23. Ibid.
24. "Join the YS-LJS," *Young Socialist Forum,* August–September 1967, p.4; *Young Socialists, Toronto, Ontario,* part 14, p.892, NAC, RG 146, vol. 3691; interview with Gary Kinsman, July 14, 1998.
25. "Join the YS-LJS," p.4.
26. "Join the YS-LJS," p.4. For an assessment of YS success on university campuses, see Andy Wernick, "A Guide to the Student Left," *The Varsity,* Sept. 24, 1969, p.8.
27. Jerry Farber, *The Student as Nigger* (New York: Pocket Books, 1970), p.99.
28. Jerry Farber, "The Student as Nigger," *The Varsity,* Jan. 29, 1968, pp.6–7; Jerry Farber, "The Student as Nigger," *This Magazine is About Schools* 2,5 (Winter 1968), pp.108–16; and Farber, *The Student as Nigger* (New York: Pocket Books, 1970), p.14.
29. Gudridge, *High School Student Unrest;* Fish, *Conflict and Dissent in the High Schools;* Sarah Spinks, "Notes on McGill and Sir George," *This Magazine is About Schools* 3,2 (Spring 1969), pp.139–44.
30. "Campus Unrest Linked to U.S. Source," *Canadian News Facts* 3,4 (May 19, 1969), p.263.
31. Stamp, *Schools of Ontario,* p.217.
32. *Living and Learning: The Report of the Provincial Committee on Aims and Objectives of Education in the Schools of Ontario,* Toronto, 1968, p.35.
33. *Young Socialists, Toronto, Ontario,* part 19, p.1530, NAC, RG 146, vol. 3691.
34. June Callwood, "It's Time We Taught Sex in Our Schools," *Canadian Weekly,* Jan. 23, 1965, p.3.
35. "From Human Being to Dancing Doll—in 16 Short Years," *Young Socialist,* May–June 1968, p.5.
36. *Young Socialists, Ontario,* part 2, p.2793, NAC, RG 146, vol. 3685.
37. Canadian Women's Movement Archives Toronto Women's Caucus Herstory, "Abortion: A Woman's Right to Choose," (circa 1970). For more information on the TWC, see Francie Ricks, George Matheson, and Sandra W. Pyke, "Women's Liberation: A Case Study of Organizations for Social Change," *Canadian Psychologist* 13,1 (January 1972), pp.34–35; and Becki L. Ross, *The House That Jill Built: A Lesbian Nation in Formation* (Toronto: University of Toronto Press, 1995).
38. *Young Socialists, 1971 Cross Canada Socialist Educational Conferences, Waterloo, Ont., Aug. 20–25, 1971,* part 3, p.4300, NAC, RG 146, vol. 3700.
39. *Young Socialists, Ontario,* part 2, p.2797, NAC, RG 146, vol. 3685; *Young Socialists, Toronto, Ontario,* part 25, p.2305, NAC, RG 146, vol. 3691; *Young Socialists, Toronto, Ontario,* part 24, p.2128, NAC, RG 146, vol. 3691; *Young Socialists, 1971 Cross Canada Socialist Educational Conferences, Waterloo, Ont., Aug. 20–25, 1971,* part 3, pp.4401–2, 4410, NAC, RG 146, vol. 3700.
40. For example, see Constance Nathanson, *Dangerous Passage: The Social Control of Sexuality in Women's Adolescence* (Philadelphia: Temple University Press, 1991); Christabelle Sethna, "The Facts of Life: The Sex Instruction of Ontario Public School Experience, 1900–1950," unpublished Ph.D. dissertation, University of Toronto, 1995; and Marie Louise Adams, *The Trouble with Normal: Postwar Youth and the Making of Heterosexuality* (Toronto: University of Toronto Press, 1997).

# PART IV

# REDEFINING A SECURITY THREAT:
## NEWER ENEMIES

*"'Miss Civil Service, 1959', Joan Carey cuts the ideal figure of a 1950s classy woman as she poses in front of tulips. A popular Ottawa tourist attraction, the annual Tulip Festival also had a beauty contest, 'Miss Tulip' throughout the postwar era. 'Miss Civil Service' was often chosen as 'Miss Tulip'."* (National Archives of Canada, "Miss Civil Service", Joan Carey, Ted Grant Collection, PA206633). [Gentile, chap. 9]

PATRIZIA GENTILE

nine ✲ ✲ ✲

# "Government Girls" and "Ottawa Men": Cold War Management of Gender Relations in the Civil Service

During the Second World War, "moral restraints" were loosened as new social spaces were opened, encouraging women and gays and lesbians to establish more of a collective sense of legitimacy.[1] During the Cold War, however, various state and other committees were established to ferret out "subversive" and "evil" elements and to reconstruct patriarchal and heterosexist relations. The committees mobilized to tighten orthodox and conventional ideals of masculine men, domesticity, and the family.[2] These seemingly extreme efforts to homogenize the cultural and social ideals of sexuality and gender have led historians to characterize the 1950s and 1960s as a time of social insecurity or anxiety.[3] For example, David Johnson argues that the anti-homosexual purge of the McCarthy era in the United States had "little to do with national security. . . . Instead, it reflected an underlying anxiety over the bureaucratization and urbanization of Washington, changes largely precipitated by the New Deal and World War II."[4]

Similarly, in Canada there has been a tension between the systemic efforts to homogenize and "stabilize" social relations and the gender/sexual anxieties that have been part of the national security state. These "efforts" took an especially imaginative turn within the federal bureaucratic work culture with the creation of "Miss Civil Service"/"Mister Civil Service" beauty contest titles, along with an idealized image of the "Ottawa Man." The creation of these model images of a civil servant was an integral aspect of the cultural environment in which the national security state operated. Indeed, the very establishment of this typical Ottawa Man and Government Girl exemplifies how the federal bureaucracy dealt with the growing gender anxiety that resulted from the so-called "reintegration" of traditional gender values in the 1950s and 1960s and the "security" issues that affected the Canadian state internally.

The cultural and national insecurity of the Cold War era led to a rallying cry for the strengthening of the family and heterosexuality. Family stability was considered the only "antidote" to "moral fallout."[5] The result of this conceptualization of the family made the lives of people who did not conform difficult:

131

> According to the common wisdom of the [1950s], "normal" heterosexual behav-
> ior culminating in marriage represented "maturity" and "responsibility"; there-
> fore, those who were "deviant" were, by definition, irresponsible, immature, and
> weak. It followed that men who were slaves to their passions could easily be duped
> by seductive women who worked for the communists. Even worse were the "per-
> verts" who, presumably, had no masculine backbone.[6]

One of the greatest anxieties was the fear that women would refuse to go back into
the home and that "women would achieve sexual independence outside the para-
meters of marital/familial relations."[7] The notion of "deviance," then, was a way to
identify not only gays and lesbians but also women who resisted or challenged the
gender norms and social order prescribed by political and medical experts.

In North America women were called upon to "embrace domesticity in service
to the nation."[8] Accepting a place in suburbia, which pushed women to the periphery of a privatized social life, and the accompanying notions of "domestic bliss"
were characterized as the ultimate duty to your country. Women were told that if
they did not embrace domesticity and dedicate their lives to becoming good wives
(that is, serving their husbands' emotional and sexual needs) and mothers, they
would be held to blame for "a host of society's problems," such as "homosexual
sons, juvenile delinquents, mental cripples, wandering and alcoholic husbands, and
school truants."[9] Because the notion of national security was linked to the idea that
a strong nation is a nation based on family, in which young men grow up to be
responsible, virile citizens and young women become dutiful and submissive wives,
the maintenance of "the happy united family" was constructed as the most important single goal for women.[10] It was within this context of family as the microcosm
of the nation that issues of loyalty and reliability were considered paramount to the
struggle against subversive elements.

The growing numbers of faceless civil servants that accompanied the rapid
expansion of the modern bureaucratic state meant that the fear of the unknown
"Other" heightened existing anxieties about the tenuous state of international relations. The anti-communist and anti-homosexual purges and the complex surveillance systems established to carry out those purges were a direct response to this
fear of the Other emerging from within. The spectre of the Government Girl and
Ottawa Man as symbols of the ideal government workers should not be seen as
ridiculous caricatures or stereotypes when we consider that by the late 1950s,
homosexuals in the federal civil service were seen as "security risks."[11] Although
they were created to posit a clear definition of proper gender and sexual practices,
the figures were implicitly responding to the government's need to ensure that its
employees were loyal and reliable in all facets of their lives. In the Cold War era,
workplace productivity and loyalty were not considered separate from loyalty to a
shared value system in "personal" life. The civil service beauty contests and the
Ottawa Man stereotype served both to establish what was considered appropriate
behaviour for civil servants and to ferret out "undesirable" elements. Of course,
once those elements are discovered and identified, the state can then take "legitimate" action against them.

The Miss Civil Service beauty contests would solidify the ideology of femininity and beauty that was at the core of the Cold War cult of domesticity, while justifying the gender division of labour. The Mister Civil Service contest and the Ottawa Man would reveal how the national security state and all the gender and sexual anxieties that it generated translated into a renegotiation of masculinity and masculine sexuality. Indeed, both these examples show how gender relations undergo continuous flux and reinvention.

### "Miss Civil Service": Defining the Feminine Boundaries of Conformity

The crowning of the first "queen" of the civil service occurred during the Recreational Association's snow carnival in 1950. Theresa Nugent won the title "Miss RA" that year and was crowned the first official "Miss Civil Service" in 1951. The civil service beauty contests became annual events lasting until 1973. Through those years the contests and the messages they created enforced "proper" codes of femininity, beauty, and sexuality in the federal community.

In the 1965 edition of *RA NEWS*, the editor made specific references to the important role of the RA Queen or Miss Civil Service as the representative of the "Ideal Government Girl":

> The RA Queen of the year contest differs from the ordinary beauty contest in that the girl who is selected reflects credit not only on herself but also on all of the thousands of girls who work for the Federal Government. . . . Having chosen its Queen for the year, the RA proudly requests that she represents them at many public appearances so that as many as possible can see the person whom you might meet any day in any office—the Ideal Government Girl.[12]

As the official ambassador of the "Ideal Government Girl," the civil service beauty queen was a symbol of pride for the RA and the federal government. Consequently, being chosen "Miss Civil Service" or, after 1960, "RA Queen of the Year" was considered a great honour. For many of these chosen women, serving as Miss Civil Service meant instant fame, popularity, and respect.

But by the 1950s, for some, the image of the Government Girl was considered to be a dangerous vision. Alan Philips, a writer for *Maclean's* magazine, certainly felt that way. In his article "The Government Girl," Philips provided a dismal picture of what happens to "girls" who left their warm, protective homes and families to live alone in the big city as a government worker.

> As a national figure, the Government Girl . . . is a shadowy presence, sensed but seldom seen, behind regulations and services that touch us all. Federal officials are a helpless crew until 'their girls'—Glee and about twenty thousand others— hastily sign in at 9 a.m., relax, powder their noses, open files, and start the typewriters, calculators, dictaphones and duplicators piling up the paper in quadruplicate.[13]

For Philips, young girls who took jobs as stenographers or typists were just looking for "adventure" and "independence," leaving behind their proper life back at home as dutiful daughters. There was an assumption that these women had no legitimate reason to quit their homes and families, leaving readers to believe that the thousands of women who did uproot their lives did so for frivolous reasons. It did not seem to occur to Philips that the women might have wanted, or needed, to search for careers or work for economic survival in a rapidly urbanizing world. There was also an assumption that the young women were becoming socially mobile, acculturating themselves to big-city life and its endless possibilities of social and sexual choice or danger.

In the article Philips traces the life of the aptly named Glee Jesse "of Calgary, a tall good-looking brunette" who "turned her back on her steady boyfriend, her parents and the well-paid job as a secretary to an oil-company executive."[14] Indeed, the story Philips constructs is one in which a perfectly "good" girl was taking a big risk by moving to Ottawa. One of the risks is the dead-end nature of a job as stenographer or typist. In Ottawa, too, women outnumber men, and the "freedom" they get in living away from home could lead many of "these girls" to inappropriate social behaviour, such as drinking, buying on credit, and having sex. When asked about how her parents felt about her leaving home, Glee said her father did not approve but her mother did not seem to mind and, in fact, encouraged her because, "After all, Glee was going to Ottawa, where respectability is almost as rampant as vice is believed to be in Montreal."[15]

The article continues in this vein, emphasizing the potential ruin of these Government Girls due to the man shortage in Ottawa. The piece suggests that these "innocent" girls are the lustful targets of hoards of bachelors who roam the streets looking for sex. Laurentian Terrace, a residence built by the government for the young women flooding into the city during the Second World War, is considered one of those "targets." According to Winifred Moyle, the residence's in-house dietician, the lust-crazed bachelors "call up almost every night for dates." Moyle complains, "Even the hotels give them our number. . . . It's extremely annoying, and we certainly don't encourage it."[16]

The image conjured up leaves the impression that the young women working in Ottawa were easy prey for the oversexed and lonely bachelors looking for dates. The concentration of single women at the Laurentian Terrace and the YWCA supposedly made it easier to locate these unsuspecting "girls." The message was that if you sent your innocent daughter to Ottawa you were sending her to her demise, and Philips made several attempts to debunk the notion of Ottawa as a "respectable" city.

But until Glee and the thousands of other secretaries and typists found a home and a husband, they continued to work at their low-paying, dead-end jobs. With the influx of women into the federal service by the mid-1950s, there seemed to be a need to define and create an image of the "typical government girl."[17] Each government department would organize an internal competition to select the "girl" who would represent the department at the "Night of Stars," the event at which the actual judging for Miss Civil Service took place. Judging from the profiles provided of the winners by the RA NEWS, the typical government girl was a woman who worked in an administrative support position and had lots of charm and poise, and a good personality. She was preferably single with no children, heterosexual, well-groomed, tall, thin, and "beautiful," with shiny hair.[18] Indeed, to emphasize this ideal the articles announcing the winner for a particular year would publish the beauty queen's height, weight, and measurements, along with her address.

Although advice on how to dress and sit and where to look for a man could be found scattered throughout the RA newspaper, the woman's page, better known as "Feminine Fancies" (a feature in the 1950s), was where most of the crucial information on proper feminine behaviour could be found. The page included recipes, fashion advice, points on etiquette, advice on how to organize a wedding, articles featuring "beauty hints," and news on the latest engagements. A 1959 article in "Feminine Fancies" entitled "How to Meet a Man" offered advice on where women should go to meet their future boyfriends and husbands. It suggested, "If you have not found the RA a happy hunting ground, try the YWCA or better still the YMCA dances and co-ed clubs, or your church's young people's groups."[19] If Ottawa proved unsuccessful as a "hunting ground," then a trip to Montreal was the next best option.

The article is an example of the need to enforce heterosexual dating activity while maintaining some control over the sexual possibilities and sexual danger that dating entailed. Although women were needed in administrative support positions, their work pattern was seen as temporary. Marriage and having children were their true destiny. To reinforce the link between beauty, popularity, and marriage, the *RA NEWS* featured civil service beauty queens who had boyfriends, got engaged, or, once married, had babies. A letter to the *RA NEWS* written by Marie Rochon, Miss Civil Service 1956, offers a prime example of the notion that even the most beautiful government girl of 1956 saw the advantages of finally getting married and becoming a housewife: "Everyone had dreams of beautiful events, and I especially want to thank you for making so many of mine come true. And now I abdicate my throne in favour of a smaller kingdom—a home."[20]

Being chosen queen of a department or queen of the civil service gave winners instant celebrity status. Their pictures and stories made headline news in *The Ottawa Journal, The Citizen,* and *Le Droit.* The public display of their victory functioned as a way to affirm and reward their beauty and femininity. They became ambassadors of the Canadian civil service and were asked to numerous social and political functions, where they met high-ranking government officials. For example, Miss RA Queen 1966, Carole Fox, met and posed with Prime Minister John Diefenbaker for the opening of the RA Stamp Exhibition.[21] Fox was described as one of the "busiest" of the civil service beauty queens, because she had travelled to seven Canadian cities in five days prior to the Tulip Festival as part of publicity for the event.[22] Miss RA Queen 1963, Suzanne Perry, shared the limelight with Premier E.C. Manning of Alberta at the opening of the 1963 Tulip Festival.[23] In a 1968 edition of the *RA NEWS*, an article listing the different functions that the queen would have to attend, including major RA events, ended with a warning that being a civil service queen "calls for lots of energy and a good sense of public relations."[24]

Of all the actual activities of the civil service beauty queen, the one function that was considered the most important and deserved serious attention was to epitomize the "feminine" image to which all woman in the civil service were to aspire. The civil service beauty contests were unique in that they were used to justify women working in a traditionally masculine domain without compromising strict codes of gender difference. Before the influx of women into the service, the definitions of the ideal civil servant were easily captured: you had to be a white male, preferably Protestant, educated, English-speaking (though French was an asset), and presumably heterosexual. The presence of women challenged this carefully scripted ideal, so that male civil servants had to renegotiate their status as "masculine" men. With these new definitions of "proper" masculine and feminine behaviour came new boundaries of gender relations and roles.

### "Mister Civil Service" and the "Ottawa Man": The Making of the Ideal Civil Servant

In March and April of 1957 the *RA NEWS* published editorials and the opinions of twelve men and women on setting up "Mister Civil Service" contests. The debate over having such a contest centred on the criteria that the judges would use in selecting the winner. Based on the discussion and editorial in the RA's newspaper, the notion of a beauty contest for male civil servants enjoyed support; of the twelve surveyed, only two people and the editor thought it was a bad idea.

The few dissenters rejected this particular variation of the beauty contest because they insisted that it would be impossible to judge "qualities" such as "personality, appearance, and intelligence." One woman could not fathom the notion of men being "gazed" at by judges in a room full of women, since the male contestants "would probably blush for shame."[25] The double standard concerning the criteria under which men and women should be judged went unnoticed by the people being surveyed. Indeed, it was assumed that "gawking" at men was inappropriate and embarrassing (the question is for whom?), whereas women were somehow immune from suffering the same "indignities." Women, moreover, were not expected to be intelligent,[26] which was not the case for Mister Civil Service. The point was that a "true" indication of the "masculine" man was primarily his intelligence; charm, poise, grooming, and his "looks," it seems, were secondary.

The advocates of the Mister Civil Service contest maintained that physique, mental alertness, cleanliness, neatness, and popularity were the features that the "typical government man" must possess.[27] At the suggestion of one man who said that Mister Civil Service should be picked the same way as "the best looking female is picked in any beauty contest," the editor reacted with disapproval. Another man suggested that the lucky man should be chosen "from the fellows with the splendid physiques." The best way to proceed, then, was to have Mister Civil Service compete in swimming trunks, "thus displaying the body beautiful," unlike the women, who competed in their office clothes.[28] Revealing the need to maintain some semblance of traditional "masculine" gender codes, one man insisted that the male contestants could not just walk on stage "like the women because it wouldn't be masculine enough." He suggested that some demonstration of strength and athletic ability was in order.[29]

The Mister Civil Service Contest never did materialize, but the plans for it reveal the interrelationship between the ideals of masculinity and femininity. Male civil servants would have to *prove* that they were "real" men by being able to display physical strength or body mass. Political savvy or intelligence was no longer the only skill and trait that the male civil servant had to possess. The presence of women meant that as men they had to distinguish themselves from "feminine" practices such as passivity and idleness. This would be difficult to do, because a job in the civil service was not considered to be physically demanding. Not surprisingly, then, one of the greatest concerns around the judging of Mister Civil Service was not just the display of the body but a demonstration of strength as proof of masculinity. Displaying only the body was perceived as insufficient, because men were not thought to be "beautiful" like women; men were supposed to be "handsome" and "manly."

*Maclean's* was also preoccupied with the idea and image of the ideal male civil servant. The image of the "Ottawa Man" was the topic of a short article written by Christina McCall Newman in 1962. According to the article, "How to Spot the Ottawa Man: A Concise Guide," male civil servants "of ambition in the nation's capital relentlessly pursue a single goal: to turn themselves into Ottawa Men."[30] The article was based on exaggerated stereotypes of ambitious and well-educated male civil servants. Its intent was to poke fun at the notion of the Ottawa Man. But like the Mister Civil Service contest, the aim of the article was to construct the image many people had of the most powerful of male civil servants. More importantly, however, the article pointed to issues around masculinity, sexuality, and class that were central to the image of the "successful" Ottawa Man.

Newman describes the Ottawa Man in terms of how he dresses, his conversations, his women, his tastes (food, drinks, interior decorating), what he does in his leisure time, and how and whom he entertains. By definition,

> the Ottawa Man is inconspicuous. He's also highly educated (very often in England as well as Canada), formal in manner, meticulous in speech. He's a snob, but a nice snob, a gentle man who does nothing common or mean (he never gossips). He is most like himself when he unavoidably fetches up—at an airport perhaps—next to Toronto Man, whom he regards as crass, vulgar, and probably in advertising.[31]

This ultimate Ottawa Man would work for External Affairs or Finance, the "elite" departments in the federal government. Indeed, Newman insists that not all male civil servants can be Ottawa Men. In fact, the majority of male civil servants could never work as the top brass in these particular departments because higher education and middle-class characteristics are considered important requirements to even be considered for these positions. General clerks, technicians, or printers could never aspire to be Ottawa Men because most of them did not come to the civil service with university degrees or from the middle to upper classes. At the least, these positions require high-school diplomas.

For male civil servants who want to emulate the Ottawa Man, Newman offers a number of instructions on speech, dress, drinking, and dating. According to the article, a well-dressed Ottawa Man always wears a navy suit (even in the summer) and gold-rimmed glasses, and carries an umbrella. He drinks sherry, wine, ale, or Scotch, and never daiquiris. His house is decorated with a "faded lithograph of the skating pond at Rideau Hall in 1872," a frayed Oriental rug, and "comfortable chairs." When he entertains he invites "important" people from abroad, or other Ottawa Men. His parties are professionally catered by caterers who only work for Ottawa Men. He only associates with people of colour, according to Newman, when he invites them over for small dinner parties, which "often feature one black, brown or yellow guest from Abroad, who comes with his Oxford accent and his wife, in a sari."[32] The Ottawa Man of the 1950s was never a person of colour himself. Indeed, very few men of colour made it to the upper echelons of the civil service.

The Ottawa Man is heterosexual and virile but not flamboyant. Like the greater part of his lifestyle, his wife and, by extension, his sexuality have to be "tastefully understated."

> He never appears with the big, built blondes in bouffants who are popular else-where; he doesn't even dream about them. His wife tries for the little-brown-hen look: shiny clean undyed hair, cashmere sweater, string of pearls, black silk dress, white kid gloves, old beaver coat—maybe a small tatty mink stole. She knows what to do at a formal dinner, she belongs to the National Gallery Association, sits on the Toy Testing Committee, and ushers at the Ottawa Choral Society.[33]

The ideal wife of the Ottawa Man is a high-class version of the "typical government girl." She is well-groomed, college- or university-educated, and from the middle to upper classes. Indeed, unlike most stenographers and secretaries working in the civil service, the Ottawa Man's wife does not have to be coached on how to "modulate" her voice or how to sit. It is the Ottawa Man's wife whom the women working in the steno pools try to imitate. Marrying a more sophisticated rendition of the typical Government Girl is as much a political move as it is socially sanctioned behaviour for the Ottawa Man. The ideal wife as Newman describes her is not sought out for her intelligence or her sex appeal; rather, she is sought out for her ability to understate her sexuality and boost her partner's masculinity.

## Conclusion: Gender and National Security

The typical Government Girl, then, was not a lone figure in the collective imagination in Cold War Ottawa. The Ottawa Man was as much a *symbol* of the ideal male bureaucrat as Miss Civil Service was a *symbol* of the model government secretary or stenographer. The Ottawa Man was an image of a career man, and Miss Civil Service an image of a "respectable" but temporary profession for women. The occupational divisions that were at the core of these very different notions of the male and female government worker demonstrate that the divisions were critical not only to the operation of the government machinery but also crucial to the social and gender organization of the Canadian bureaucracy.

The Government Girl and the Ottawa Man were security props that defined the "good bureaucratic character" that in turn exaggerated the existence of the undesirable Other such as the homosexual and the lesbian or "masculine" woman and "feminine" man. Only in the context of the Cold War and the gender anxiety that it generated did these stereotypes become clear messages of what were considered appropriate goals and aspirations for male and female civil servants. Masculinity in women and femininity in men were seen as threats to the gender and national social order. Establishing what was considered acceptable masculine and male sexual behaviour in the civil service was as much a topic of debate as defining ideals of beauty and femininity. The figure of the Ottawa Man and the anti-homosexual purges that were in full swing during the same period ensured that male civil servants were as susceptible to a system of control and regulation as women were to the advice columns on how to sit, stand, and speak. Men and women together had to *play their part* in the gender game in order to secure the safety and future of the nation. Indeed, masculine men, especially those who worked in the bureaucratic ranks with access to state secrets, had to "protect" the nation from visible and invisible "intruders." Gender practices were therefore central to the construction of the Canadian national security state.

## Notes

This article is based on research conducted for my M.A. thesis, "Searching for 'Miss Civil Service' and 'Mr. Civil Service': Gender Anxiety, Beauty Contests and Fruit Machines in the Canadian Civil Service, 1950–1973," Carleton University, Ottawa, August 1996. I would like to thank Gary Kinsman for his encouragement.

1. The idea that the Second World War was a "force that loosened moral restraints" comes from Geoff Smith, "Commentary: Security, Gender, and Historical Process," *Diplomatic History* 18 (Winter 1994), p.81. See also Geoff Smith, "National Security and Personal Isolation: Sex, Gender, and Disease in the Cold-War States," *The International History Review* 2 (May 1992), pp.307–37, for a look at a gendered and sexual analysis of the history of the Cold War in the United States and the use of "disease" analogies.

2. For more on the House Committee on Un-American Activities see W. Goodman, *The Committee: The Extraordinary Career of the House Committee on Un-American Activities* (New York: Farrar, Straus and Giroux, 1968).

3. See Gary Kinsman, *The Regulation of Desire: Homo and Hetero Sexualities*, 2nd ed. (Montreal: Black Rose Books, 1996); and his "'Character Weaknesses' and 'Fruit Machines': Towards an Analysis of the Anti-Homosexual Security Campaign in the Canadian Civil Service," *Labour/Le Travail* 35 (Spring 1995), pp.133–61 for a perspective on sexual anxiety in this period; and Mona Gleason, "Growing up to Be 'Normal': Psychology Constructs Proper Gender Roles in Post-World War II Canada, 1945–1960," in *Family Matters*, ed. Lori Chambers and Edgar Montigny (Toronto: Canadian Scholar's Press, 1998) for the toll that social and sexual anxieties took on the Canadian family.

4. David Johnson, "'Homosexual Citizens': Washington's Gay Community Confronts the Civil Service," *Washington History*, Fall/Winter 1994–95, p.46.

5. Elaine Tyler May, *Homeward Bound: American Families in the Cold War Era* (New York: Basic Books, 1988), p.94. For a discussion of the Canadian conceptualization of "family stability" and the reintegration of family values, see Annalee Gölz, "Family Matters: The Canadian Family and the State in the Postwar Period," *Left History* 1,2 (Fall 1993), pp.10–13.

6. May, *Homeward Bound*, p.94. Although the lives of these so called "deviants" were in many cases no less than living nightmares, Joanne Meyerowitz argues that some women did actively resist the domestic roles foisted on women in the Cold War era. She insists that it is historically inaccurate to depict women who lived through the 1950s as passive housewives willingly living out their lives in blissful suburbia. For more on this see Joanne Meyerowitz, ed., *Not June Cleaver: Women and Gender in Postwar America, 1945–1960* (Philadelphia: Temple University Press, 1994).

7. Gölz, "Family Matters," p.28.

8. May, *Homeward Bound*, p.102.

9. Veronica Strong-Boag, "Home Dreams: Women and the Suburban Experiment in Canada, 1945–60," *Canadian Historical Review* 72,4 (1991), p.481. This article provides a lengthy and provocative discussion on women and suburbia in Cold War Canada. See also Mary Louise Adams, *The Trouble with Normal: Postwar Youth and the Making of Heterosexuality* (Toronto: University of Toronto Press, 1998), for more on how inappropriate surveillance and care from parents were seen as causing irreparable harm to their children in this era.

10. The phrase "happy united family" is taken from Gölz, "Family Matters," p.10.

11. The construction of homosexuals as security risks has a long and multifaceted history. Homosexuals were considered "security risks" in the military and in the immigration laws before they were seen as unsuitable for employment in the public service. For more on this, see Kinsman, *Regulation of Desire*; Gary Kinsman and Patrizia Gentile, with the assistance of Heidi McDonell and Mary Mahood-Greer, "'In the Interests of the State': The Anti-Gay, Anti-Lesbian National Security Campaign in Canada," a preliminary research report, Laurentian University, Sudbury, 1998; and Philip Girard, "From Subversion to Liberation: Homosexuals and the Immigration Act, 1952–1977," *Canadian Journal of Law and Society* 2 (1987), pp.1–27.

12. Tom Coughlin, "Editorial," *RA NEWS*, May 1965, p.2.

13. Alan Philips, "The Government Girl," *Maclean's*, Jan. 15, 1953, p.25.

14. Ibid., p.25.

15. Ibid.

16. Ibid., p.38.

17. The first time I spotted the term "typical government girl" was in "Do You Know 'Miss Civil Service'?" *RA NEWS*, February 1952, p.2. I can only assume that the term was used earlier as well.

18. Beauty in this contest was defined around standards of whiteness, with two exceptions. In 1962 Betty Gittens, the only black woman to win the RA Queen title, had emigrated to Canada in 1959 from Barbados and received a job working for the government to help support two small sons and put her husband through medical school. Gisel Brown, "Princess" (runner-up) in 1967, was the only other woman of colour who made it to the finalist level.

19. Fran Jones, "How to Meet a Man," *RA NEWS*, July 1959, p.12.

20. "Time Now to Think about Miss Civil Service of 1957," *RA NEWS*, January 1957, p.3. The article also mentions that when Marie Rochon won in 1956, she chose the New York trip (her prize) as her honeymoon.

21. *RA NEWS*, January 1966, p.16.

22. D. Burton, "RA Queen's Past and Present Get Together," *RA NEWS*, August 1966, p.10.

23. Picture accompanying article, "A Million Dazzling Tulips Kick off Tourist Season," *The Citizen* (Ottawa), May 18, 1963, p.5. *The Ottawa Journal* had a picture of Miss RA Queen 1963 flanked by Premier Manning and the national leader of the Social

Credit, Robert Thompson.

24. "Between the Lines—Behind the Scenes," *RA NEWS*, October 1968, p.4.
25. A comment made by Pat Bradley, in the "RA ASKS: Should There Be a Mister Civil Service Contest?" column, *RA NEWS*, April 1957, p.20.
26. Ginnette Bonneau, a runner-up in the Miss National Archives contest, 1973, said in her interview that asking the finalist questions was a mainstay in the civil service beauty contests. However, the questions were not considered "difficult."
27. These "characteristics" were outlined in an editorial in *RA NEWS*, May 1957, p.2.
28. Editorial, *RA NEWS*, May 1957, p.2; and comments made by Raymond Gorman, in "RA ASKS: How Would You Select a Mister Civil Service?" column, *RA NEWS*, May 1957, p.20.
29. Comment made by David Lanceman, *RA NEWS*, May 1957, p.20.
30. Christina McCall Newman, "How to Spot the Ottawa Man: A Concise Guide," *Maclean's*, October 1962, p.3.
31. Ibid.
32. Ibid.
33. Ibid.

*An early gay rights demonstration in the mid-1970s, with Prime Minister Trudeau in the foreground* (from Paul-Francois Sylvestre, *Propos pour une libération (homo)sexuelle*, [Montreal: Les Editions de l'Aurore, 1976], p.135). [Kinsman, chap. 10]

GARY KINSMAN

ten ✳ ✳ ✳

# Constructing Gay Men and Lesbians as National Security Risks, 1950–70

In the 1950s and 1960s in Canada, state agencies and mass media reports defined gay men and, in a different but related way, lesbians as national, social, and sexual "dangers." A key element in this social construction of lesbians and gay men as dangerous was the national security campaigns that targeted gay men and lesbians in the public service, the military, and also more generally in Canadian society.[1]

During those years hundreds of gay men and lesbians in the public service lost their jobs or were demoted. Hundreds were purged from the military. Some were forced to inform on others, and some were followed and put under surveillance. The RCMP collected the names of thousands of suspected homosexuals. By 1967–68 its Directorate of Security and Intelligence reported having collected the names of close to nine thousand suspected and confirmed homosexuals in the Ottawa area.[2] The government even funded and sponsored research into a supposedly "scientific" means of determining sexual orientation to try to identify gay men and lesbians, a project that came to be known internally as the "fruit machine."[3]

In the context of the Cold War a particular social construction of gay men and lesbians as a "threat" emerged. Usually there was more of a public focus on the threat from gay men, but there were also depictions of the threat represented by lesbians.[4] The images of danger were organized through the concepts of gay men and lesbians crossing and defying class and gender boundaries. Initially the national security discourse and campaigns on homosexuals focused on the subjects as being subversives associated with communists, or on gay men as "fellow travellers" of communists. Sometimes the discourse presented gay men as being engaged in their sexual practices in cross-class "promiscuity," which somehow led the men to have more sympathy for people opposed to the bourgeois order.[5]

In the later 1950s and into the 1960s, the focus shifted more to gay men and lesbians as a distinct national security threat because of a purported character weakness that made them unreliable and vulnerable to blackmail from "evil" Soviet agents. The shift went from a focus on political disloyalty towards a focus on moral and character failings that led to a more general, and therefore increased, surveillance of gay men and lesbians.[6] The conceptualization of character weakness became homosexualized. Character weakness almost became a code word for homosexuality in the discourse of the Canadian national security regime.

This focus on character weakness was tied to the emergence of a new conceptualization of homosexuality in professional and ruling discourse in the 1950s and 1960s; and this new conceptualization led to a passing away (to some extent—the discourse continues to be alive and is able to be remobilized)[7] of notions of lesbians and gay men as "gender inverts" displaying characteristics of the other gender. Instead came a movement towards homosexuals being defined by a difference in sexual object choice, or what we might now call "sexual orientation."[8] What this entailed in relation to the security campaigns was not only that those who displayed the characteristics of gender inversion would be targeted as "homosexuals," but also anyone who engaged in same-gender sexual practices could then be "blackmailable," because they would have something to hide.

This shift in turn led to an intensified policing of the boundaries of heterosexuality, suggesting that even occasional participation in same-gender sex could get you into trouble, even if you had none of the markers of gender inversion. There was a shifting and a redrawing of the boundaries around proper heterosexual masculinity, and in a different way, around heterosexual femininity. Even very occasional participation in same-gender sex could get someone into trouble with the national security regime. In contrast, of course, through the same process heterosexuality in general was constructed as being safe and in some ways necessary to national security and as being in the national interest.[9]

## Moving beyond National Security Discourse

The study I am reporting on here is work in progress that draws on the methodological and theoretical insights of the work of Marxist-feminist sociologist Dorothy Smith and her alternative sociology called institutional ethnography.[10] Institutional ethnography explores how institutional relations work from the standpoints of those who have problems produced in their everyday/everynight worlds through these institutional relations. This institutional ethnographic investigation of the national security campaigns against gay men and lesbians focuses on the social organization of these campaigns—how the security campaigns were actually put together from the standpoints of those most directly affected by them.

This research is based on two sources of "data." One is interviews with those whose lives became directly implicated in the national security campaigns. To date I have interviewed twenty such gay men and four lesbians, people who were interrogated, purged, forced to inform on others, lost their jobs, or were demoted as part of the national security campaigns.[11] The knowledge I have gained from these people is the knowledge that the national security campaigns were trying to suppress and wipe out. I have also relied on other accounts and on interviews done by other researchers.

The second source of data is the "interrogation" of some of the operatives within the national security regime as well as critical textual analysis of the official documents of the national security regime from the Security Panel (an interdepartmental committee formed in 1946 to co-ordinate and oversee the national security efforts within the Canadian state) and the RCMP. The national security campaigns were mobilized and mediated through the use of concepts and policies outlined in these documents.[12] I am examining the security texts and interrogating people involved in the security regime based on the knowledge of what I have learned from talking to those most directly affected.

This approach has allowed me to move beyond the ideological[13] and conceptual organization of national security to put in question the social construction of national security risk and character weakness. This entails not taking these conceptualizations for granted and asking whose nation and which security is being defended. The national security campaigns against gay men and lesbians were not simply a mistake or caused by the homophobia of a few security officials, but were rooted in a process of social organization, state formation, and sexual regulation.[14] We need to critically examine categories of national security and character weakness to see how these campaigns were socially organized in relationship to the lives of gay men and lesbians.

Here the focus is on the areas in which these two sources of data are brought into relation with each other. What can we learn when we bring together first-hand accounts and official texts into a social-relational analysis and interrogate the security regime from the standpoints of gay men and lesbians?

## The Social Relations of Surveillance and Interrogation

The organization of the RCMP work of surveillance and interrogation involved not only the direct interrogation of suspected homosexuals, but also the collection of the names of other homosexuals and photographs of suspected homosexuals, along with the surveillance of suspected homosexual meeting spots.

As I found in talking to gay men, the interrogations had common features. Over and over again gay men reported that they were asked, "Is so and so a homosexual?" Or "Do you know of any other homosexuals who work in External Affairs [or some other department]?" They were shown photographs of particular individuals and asked to identify them as homosexuals or not.[15] Some were shown photo albums; others were shown index card files. The RCMP's technology of surveillance revolved around the collection of images, identities, and names, including photographs and the identification of these names and images tying them to particular individuals. This work was co-ordinated through broader social practices and social relations. The problem with the RCMP approach was not simply that its officers were name or identity fetishists. Their work was also part of a broader process of social organization.

For instance, Albert (a pseudonym for one of the gay men) was a civil servant whose career in the civil service ended in the late 1960s after he was identified as a suspected homosexual. Albert was approached by a member of the RCMP and asked to go to the RCMP office in Ottawa. His account of what happened there points to the importance for the RCMP of the confirmation of homosexuality by homosexual informants. Albert remembers:

> He [the RCMP officer] wanted me to co-operate with the RCMP as much as possible in helping to identify people who they already had in a file to try to determine whether or not these people were homosexuals. His terms of reference as I recall was that he didn't want any information from me unless I was absolutely certain that this person had committed a homosexual act. I think that their criteria was that they would not act on any particular file unless they had more than two or three direct indications that this person was homosexual. Of course a lot of these people were in security positions particularly in External Affairs but not exclusively in External Affairs. It was just a cardex and I was requested to go through it. . . . My understanding was that once they had two to three concrete identifications then this particular file was brought to whatever committee or agent that was dealing with this subject.[16]

Albert describes[17] how he was informed by the RCMP officer interrogating him that they actually needed to get a number of positive identifications of an individual to shift them into the confirmed homosexual category.

I also talked to Fred, who worked in the Character Weakness subdivision of the RCMP's Directorate of Security and Intelligence in Ottawa in the late 1960s. My interview with him was based on what I learned from analysis of the accounts of those like Albert whose lives were hurt by the security campaigns. In my discussions with Fred I focused on how his work day was organized and tried to avoid getting into political discussions with him. Close to 90 per cent of his work, he said, was dealing with homosexuals and almost entirely with gay men. He described lesbians as being harder to find and more suspicious of male RCMP officers. He described his work as hanging out with gay men, and making friends with them.

Basically it meant being out five nights a week trying to hang out with gay men. After making friends with them he would try to convert them into informants. His work was based on the active construction of a gay informant/RCMP relation. He would ask these gay men if they had been at a gay party or a gay event recently and whether there were any new men at these events. He would then ask whether these new men might have been civil servants. If there were such men he would try to get some identifying features of the individual. Next he would try to get a photograph taken of this individual through surveillance work. He would then take the photo back to the gay informant to get confirmation that this was indeed the person the informant had seen at the gay event.

Fred's work, then, was oriented around trying to shift someone who might be suspected of being a homosexual into the confirmed homosexual classification. In doing this work Fred was very interested in rating the reliability of his various sources.

The focus of questions in interrogation on naming other homosexuals was organized through the classifications and procedures shaping RCMP security work. The official classifications of homosexuals used by the RCMP make certain things about these relations and this work visible. The RCMP classified the people investigated into three categories: confirmed, alleged, and suspected.

The "confirmed" are those who have been interviewed and admitted being homosexuals or who have been convicted in court on a charge of sexual deviation with
another male. The "alleged" are those who have been named as homosexuals by a
source or sources whose information is considered to be reliable. The "suspected"
are those who are believed to be homosexuals by a source or sources whose information is considered to be reliable.[18]

"Confirmed homosexual" was the most privileged category, and the RCMP wanted
to move people from suspected and alleged into the confirmed classification. The
experiences of Albert and Fred reveal that the confirmed homosexual could be
produced through a series of identifications by gay informants. Here we get a
clearer sense of how the RCMP campaign was tied into the sexual policing of gay sex
in which the RCMP was also directly engaged. That policing helped to provide the
further confirmation of the homosexuality of a particular individual that was
needed to move them into the confirmed category. This ultimate goal served to
shape the work of identification and interrogation of suspected homosexuals and
homosexual informants.

The RCMP construction of the homosexual was a textual matter built upon a
number of different identifications of an individual as a homosexual. Only when
people were placed in the confirmed category did they become a textually "real"
homosexual. Once there they could then be placed into the mandated courses of
action that could lead to them being purged from their positions, transferred to
lower-level positions, or having some other form of action taken against them.
These classifications came to mediate and organize the work of the RCMP. This
practice, though, required the extension of the surveillance campaigns well outside
the confines of the civil service. The RCMP had to find informants who could
provide them with information, and officers built important informant networks
outside the civil service.

The RCMP depended on the information provided by informants, and this
RCMP/informant relation proved to be a weak link in the social organization of the
security campaigns. The tasks of constructing these networks of informants and
engaging in field investigations were expensive and time-consuming. This difficulty
was one of the pressures that led towards the "fruit machine" research, which was
supposed to provide a "scientific" and "objective" basis for determining sexual
orientation and thereby help the Force avoid field investigations and the reliance
on gay informants.

## Non-cooperation and Resistance

Our research has uncovered acts of non-cooperation with the security campaigns
and the military policies against lesbians and gay men. For instance, one lesbian I
interviewed, Sue, gave a delightful account of subversion and resistance. Sue, who
was in the military on the east coast, describes some of her activities in the militia
and at military camp in the 1950s:

And the deal was you were supposed to go out with men. So what we did was at military camp we went out with the men in the early part of the evening, and then because we were very virtuous young women we said, "Oh, we have to go home early." And the military, being very accommodating, said, "This is where the women sleep, this is where the men sleep." We said "Fine, that's cool, we'll go back with the women." Back we go with the women, and who's sleeping next to me but somebody in the Intelligence Corps—who is supposed to be watching me. . . . But let me tell ya, I ditched her. What we used to do, we dykes, we would want to go out and party. And we would take our bunk beds and we would fill them with pillows. And then we would ask the heterosexual women, and we would say to them, "We really want to meet Charlie." We would lie to them and they would cover cause they thought we were goin' out to meet men. We were goin' out to meet women. But we, we had it set up at the back of the barracks, and took over this room. We barricaded it from one side and then we had women on the other side guarding it, cause that's where we were with Charlie. But they never saw Charlie! So here we had all these straight women, guarding us and guarding our beds and making sure that the authorities never knew we were out.

Sue and other lesbians were able to subvert the military regulations. The military provided a space in which women could live somewhat autonomously from men, but at the same time it attempted to rigorously police the gender and sexual practices of women members.[19] The restrictions included dress codes for women. Sue went on:

So, we would be out with sergeants, staff sergeants, corporals, privates, lieutenants . . . no rank was untouched. . . . So we would be running all over camp. And the deal was you weren't allowed to leave the premises, so of course, we wanted wine, women, and song. So in order to get wine, women and song you had to leave the base. So you had to go out, but you weren't allowed to wear butchy clothing, you had to wear a *dress*. So what we used to do was pull our pant legs up and hide them with our skirt. And you'd go out and through the gates in your skirt right, lookin' all femmy and lovely. Well this one night we came home and we got a little too drunk, well trust me that the pants were down. And we were up on charges the next day for being in some place we weren't supposed to be, improper attire, all kinds of things. So we learned that we shouldn't drink too much.[20]

In the military, then, some people were able to resist despite difficult circumstances. Sue herself was discharged from the militia when she was identified as a lesbian. Many other women were purged from the military as lesbians during those years, and at least up until 1992, under military policies prohibiting gay men and lesbians from membership.[21]

The RCMP itself acknowledged obstacles in its investigations and non-cooperation within the civil service and from homosexual "informants." In 1962–63 the RCMP reported: "During the past fiscal year the homosexual screening program . . . was hindered by the lack of cooperation on the part of homosexuals approached as sources. Persons of this type, who had hitherto been our most consistent and productive informers, have exhibited an increasing reluctance to identify their homosexual friends and associates."[22]

Some gay men were beginning to place loyalty to their lovers and friends above loyalty to Canadian "national security" interests and the RCMP. In its 1963–64 *Annual Report* the Security Service noted: "During the year the investigation to identify homosexuals employed in or by the Federal Government resulted in initial interviews with twenty-one homosexuals, four of whom proved to be uncooperative, and re-interviews with twenty-two previously cooperative homosexuals, seven of whom declined to extend further cooperation."[23]

Here, then, is the construction of a distinction between the category of the "co-operative" and the "un-cooperative" homosexual. This was an important dividing line for RCMP work, because only homosexuals designated as "co-operative" would be helpful in producing "confirmed" homosexuals.

What provided the social basis for the non-cooperation? What was outside official security discourse, intruding into and constructing obstacles for it? Here again, as in considering the social relations of surveillance and interrogation, we must look at the relation between official security discourse and the first-hand accounts of those directly affected by the security campaigns.

What emerges from some of the first-hand accounts is the other side of this "problem" of non-cooperation: how it was socially organized in relation to the lesbian and gay networks in Ottawa. The 1960s was a period in which networks of gay men and lesbians were forming and expanding in the city. The gay community formation was becoming more extensive, including the establishment of limited social spaces, such as the basement tavern at the Lord Elgin Hotel, the gay section at the Chez Henri in Hull, the Honeydew on Rideau Street, cruising along the Rideau Canal. Mackenzie Point and Nepean Point had become important gathering places, as did house parties and other social networks.[24] In these social spaces gay talk and solidarity were developing. One form of talk that occurred in some Ottawa gay networks was what to do if the RCMP questioned you—with the conclusion often being that people should not give names to the RCMP. This practice provided a social basis for a limited form of resistance to these campaigns.

For example, a gay man named David became caught up in the national security campaigns. He was a non-civil servant in Ottawa whose name was given to the RCMP in 1964 during a sweep of a park where gay men cruised. The RCMP would round up gay men in these parks, but the officers were not so interested in charging them with sexual offences as in getting the names of other homosexuals out of them. David was interrogated by the RCMP. He was followed and his place was searched. A gay RCMP friend of his was discharged from the RCMP because of his homosexuality.

David reported that gay men who congregated in the tavern in the basement of the Lord Elgin, which had become a gay meeting spot before the early 1960s, encountered organized police surveillance. David described this situation around 1964:

> We even knew occasionally that there was somebody in some police force or some investigator who would be sitting in a bar. And you would see someone with a . . .

newspaper held right up and if you . . . looked real closely you could find him holding behind the newspaper a camera and these people were photographing everyone in the bar. As a matter of fact when my RCMP friend was about to be cashiered from the RCMP he was shown pictures that had been taken in the bar—that is, the tavern downstairs in the Lord Elgin Hotel—of everybody and you could see the vantage point at which the person had been sitting behind a newspaper and taking pictures. He said there were pictures of everybody including myself sitting there having a drink. . . . The thing is, you could even tell where the person had been sitting from the views of the walls and the people who were there and he was asked to name all the people at the various tables.[25]

This was one way the RCMP collected information on homosexuals as part of the social relations of surveillance that it organized. What is most remarkable, however, is how David described the response of the men in the bar to this surveillance.

We always said that when you saw someone with a newspaper held up in front of their face . . . that somebody would take out something like a wallet and do this sort of thing [like snapping a photo] and then of course everyone would then point over to the person you see, and of course I'm sure that the person hiding behind the newspaper knew that he had been found out. But that was the thing. You would take out a wallet or a package of matches or something like that . . . it was always sort of a joke. You would see somebody . . . and you would catch everyone's eye and you would go like this [snapping a photo]. And everyone knew watch out for this guy. . . . But the thing is that we were often quite aware that there was somebody in there that was taking pictures.

This account illustrates a form of collective non-cooperation and resistance to the security investigations, as well as making fun of the security campaign as a way of surviving it.

Michael, another non-civil servant who was interrogated by the RCMP in the 1960s, stated that the advice in the gay networks he was familiar with was to say nothing to the RCMP about people's names or identities, and "if anybody did give anything they were ostracized." There seemed to be a fairly clear ethical position of not giving names. Michael also reported that when he was left alone in the interrogation room with one RCMP officer, that officer asked:

"Is it true that you are a homosexual?" and I said "Yes!" And he looked at me and I said, "Is it true that you ride side saddle?" and he laughed and that almost ended the interview. I mean, my intent was there, don't bother me any more, because I began to get the impression that it was a witch hunt. It was a real witch hunt.[26]

Through the opening up of gay social spaces and the expansion and development of gay networks a social basis for non-cooperation was established.

## Conclusion: Texts and Resistance

I have highlighted here two aspects of my broader research into the social organization of the national security campaigns against gay men and lesbians. The first aspect is how the classifications and conceptualizations of the security campaigns, particularly categories of "suspected," "alleged," and "confirmed" homosexual, came to organize the interrelationships between the people being spied upon and interrogated and the RCMP officers. The focus was on identifying homosexuals and moving suspected and alleged homosexuals into the confirmed category so that official action could be taken against them. Security regime practices were socially organized and mediated through these classifications and texts.

Second, and contrary to what some people might think, gay men and lesbians were never simply passive and non-active in relation to the security campaigns.[27] Some lesbians and gay men, particularly those outside the public service and the military, were able to engage in acts of non-cooperation and resistance that was socially based on expanding gay and lesbian network and community formation. An important part of analysing the social organization of these national security campaigns is to recover these important stories of resistance.

This non-cooperation forced the RCMP to revise its tactics and shift its practices to put emphasis "on establishing close liaison with the morality branches of police forces, particularly in the larger centres."[28] The RCMP now had to rely more on local police forces and the policing of gay sexual practices organized through the criminal code[29] to provide them with the needed "co-operative" informants. Given that all homosexual sexual acts were illegal in Canada until 1969, relying on local police forces and morality squads was a way of getting more information and more names by "leaning" on gays who came into contact with the police and getting them to provide the names of homosexuals. This provided a clear social basis to the power/knowledge relations[30] that the security regime had organized through its operational practices and its extended network of surveillance, including local policing.

In this sense the resistance or non-cooperation of gay men and lesbians was not external to the social organization of security surveillance but also came to reshape the tactics and practices, the very grounds, of the security regime itself.

## Notes

I want to thank Patrizia Gentile, Treanor (formerly Mary) Mahood-Greer, Heidi McDonell, Dean Beeby, Patrick Barnholden, Dieter Buse, Mercedes Steedman, and especially Albert, Fred, Sue, David, and Michael. This chapter is dedicated to all the gay men and lesbians who resisted the national security campaigns. This research was funded by a Social Sciences and Humanities Research Council grant and by Laurentian University research grants.

1.   For the more general character of the national security campaigns or the general social and historical context of these campaigns, see David Kimmel and Daniel J. Robinson, "The Queer Career of Homosexual Security Vetting in Cold War Canada," in *Canadian Historical Review* 75,3 (September 1994), pp.319–45; Gary Kinsman, "'Character Weaknesses' and 'Fruit Machines': Towards an Analysis of the Anti-

Homosexual Security Campaign in the Canadian Civil Service," in *Labour/Le Travail* 35 (Spring 1995), pp.133–61; and Gary Kinsman and Patrizia Gentile, with the assistance of Heidi McDonell and Mary Mahood-Greer, "'In the Interests of the State': The Anti-Gay, Anti-Lesbian National Security Campaign in Canada," a preliminary research report, Laurentian University, Sudbury, April 1998. On the general social and historical context see Gary Kinsman, *The Regulation of Desire: Homo and Hetero Sexualities*, 2nd ed. (Montreal: Black Rose, 1996), especially pp.148–278. The emphasis on social construction throughout this chapter points to the importance of viewing all knowledge and social practices as being actively and socially created.

2.  RCMP, Directorate of Security and Intelligence (DSI), *Annual Report*, Ottawa, 1967–68.

3.  See Kinsman et al., "'In the Interests of the State,'" pp.106–16; and Kinsman, "'Character Weaknesses' and 'Fruit Machines,'" pp.153–59.

4.  On the social construction of gay men as national, social, and sexual dangers, see Kinsman, *Regulation of Desire*, pp.157–200. On the portrayal of lesbians as a threat, see Jennifer Terry, "Momism and the Making of the Treasonous Lesbian," unpublished paper, Ohio State University, Columbus, August 1995. See also Jennifer Terry, *An American Obsession: Science, Medicine, and Homosexuality in Modern Society* (Chicago and London: University of Chicago Press, 1999), pp.329–52. On the construction of lesbians as a gender, social, and sexual danger in Canada, see Becki L. Ross, "Destaining the (Tattooed) Delinquent Body: The Practices of Moral Regulation at Toronto's Street Haven, 1965–1969," *Journal of the History of Sexuality* 7,4 (April 1997), pp.561–95. On how lesbianism was depicted as a "danger" to young women in a Canadian obscenity case in the 1950s, see Mary Louise Adams, *The Trouble with Normal: Postwar Youth and the Making of Heterosexuality* (Toronto: University of Toronto Press, 1997), pp.158–64.

5.  On this see R.G. Waldeck, "The International Homosexual Conspiracy," *Human Events*, Sept. 29, 1960, reprinted in Martin Bauml Duberman, *About Time: Exploring the Gay Past* (New York: Gay Presses of New York, 1986), pp.199–202.

6.  See Kimmel and Robinson, "Queer Career of Homosexual Security Vetting," and Kinsman "'Character Weaknesses' and 'Fruit Machines.'"

7.  On the capacity of discourses formed in the past to be remobilized after they have apparently lost their cogency for the practices of ruling, see Gary Kinsman, "The Textual Practices of Sexual Rule: Sexual Policing and Gay Men," in *Knowledge, Experience, and Ruling Relations: Studies in the Social Organization of Knowledge*, ed. Marie Campbell and Ann Manicom (Toronto: University of Toronto Press, 1995), pp.80–95.

8.  On gender inversion and sexual object choice conceptualizations of homosexuality, see Kinsman, *Regulation of Desire*.

9.  On the creation of heterosexuality as the "normal" sexuality in Canada in the 1950s and 1960s, see Adams, *Trouble with Normal*; and Jonathan Ned Katz, *The Invention of Heterosexuality* (New York: Dutton, 1995).

10. On institutional ethnography, see Dorothy E. Smith, "Institutional Ethnography: A Feminist Research Strategy," in *The Everyday World as Problematic: A Feminist Sociology* (Toronto: University of Toronto Press, 1987), pp.151–79. For the specific use of it in this research on the national security regime, see Kinsman et al. "'In the Interests of the State,'" pp.52–71.

11. On the methodology used in these interviews and in the critical textual analysis involved in this research, see Kinsman et al., "'In the Interests of the State,'" especially pp.52–71. Throughout this chapter I use pseudonyms to protect the confidentiality of the people interviewed.

12. On text-mediated social organization, see Dorothy E. Smith, "Textually-Mediated Social Organization," in *Texts, Facts, and Femininity: Exploring the Relations of Ruling* (London: Routledge, 1990), pp.209–24.

13. I use ideology and ideological to refer "to all forms of knowledge that are divorced from their conditions of production (their grounds)." Roslyn Wallach Bologh,

*Dialectical Phenomenology: Marx's Method* (Boston: Routledge and Kegan Paul, 1979), p.19. See also the work of Dorothy E. Smith, including *The Conceptual Practices of Power: A Feminist Sociology of Knowledge* (Toronto: University of Toronto Press, 1990), especially pp.31–104.

14. On the limitations of the conceptualization of homophobia, which tends to psychologize and to individualize the social organization of heterosexist ideologies and practices, see Kinsman, *Regulation of Desire*, pp.33–34. On state formation, see Philip Corrigan and Derek Sayer, *The Great Arch: English State Formation as Cultural Revolution* (Oxford: Basil Blackwell, 1985).

15. On the important connections between the taking of photographs and the police work of identification, see Liza McCoy, "Activating the Photographic Text," in *Knowledge, Experience, and Ruling Relations*, ed. Campbell and Manicom, pp.181–92.

16. Interview with "Albert," Oct. 19, 1993.

17. I use "description" here and throughout this chapter to get at the explication of social organization and relations. On this, see Dorothy E. Smith, "On Sociological Description: A Method From Marx," in *Texts, Facts, and Femininity*, pp.86–119.

18. Bella to RCMP Commissioner, April 29, 1960, RCMP files, Ottawa.

19. On women and lesbians in the military, see Allan Berube and John D'Emilio, "The Military and Lesbians during the McCarthy Years," *Signs* 9,4 (1984), pp.759–75; Lisa Meyer, "Creating G.I. Jane: The Regulation of Sexuality and Sexual Behaviour in the Women's Army Corps during World War II," *Feminist Studies* 18 (1992), pp.581–601; Kinsman, *Regulation of Desire*, pp.181–83, 359–60; Cynthia Enloe, *Does Khaki Become You?* (London: Pluto, 1983); and Kinsman et al., "'In the Interests of the State.'"

20. Interview with "Sue," Feb. 23, 1996.

21. The policy of prohibiting lesbians and gay men from membership in the Canadian military was only officially changed as a result of the Michelle Douglas case in 1992. See Kinsman, *Regulation of Desire*, p.360.

22. RCMP, Directorate of Security and Intelligence, *Annual Report*, 1962–1963, p.19.

23. RCMP, Directorate of Security and Intelligence, *Annual Report*, 1963–1964, p.30.

24. Kinsman et al., "'In the Interests of the State,'" pp.123–29.

25. Interview with "David," May 1994.

26. Interview with "Michael," July 1994.

27. For instance, Kimmel and Robinson end their article with the suggestion, "For the many homosexuals affected by Ottawa's actions there was only defeat, accompanied, in all probability, by prolonged anguish." Kimmel and Robinson, "Queer Career of Homosexual Security Vetting," p.345.

28. RCMP, Directorate of Security and Intelligence, *Annual Report*, 1963–1964, p.30.

29. See George Smith, "Policing the Gay Community: An Inquiry into Textually-Mediated Social Relations," *International Journal of the Sociology of Law* 16 (1988), pp.163–83.

30. On power/knowledge relations, see the work of Michel Foucault. At the same time Foucault's insightful notion needs to be much more clearly grounded in social practices and relations. Power and knowledge are always social accomplishments produced by people. On the limitations of Foucault's power/knowledge approach, see Smith, *Conceptual Practices of Power*, pp.70, 79–80.

FRANCA IACOVETTA

eleven ✱ ✱ ✱

# Making Model Citizens: Gender, Corrupted Democracy, and Immigrant and Refugee Reception Work in Cold War Canada

> *The object in all these activities is to make Canadian citizens of those*
> *who came here as immigrants, and to make Canadian citizens of as*
> *many of the descendants of the original inhabitants of this country [as*
> *possible].*
>
> Prime Minister Louis St. Laurent, announcing the new Department of
> Citizenship and Immigration, Dec. 3, 1949

The Cold War baggage of prejudices, suspicions, and "corrupted democracy" created a highly charged context in which the process of making "New Canadians" or moulding "Model Citizens" out of Holocaust survivors, former Fascists, anti-Soviet refugees, and other immigrants became urgent moral campaigns for democratic decency and test cases for proving the greater good of Western liberal democracies. Gatekeeper intrusions into immigrant lives were cast as moral imperatives in the fight against godless communism. As social workers at the large Toronto immigrant agency, the International Institute of Metropolitan Toronto, warned, the work of reception could not stop at job placements and housing, but had to involve guidance against "loose" political thinking as well as the protection of immigrants from communists keen to recruit disaffected newcomers into their ranks.[1]

The links between the Cold War and immigrants go beyond the screening or surveillance of left-wing immigrants—an important topic that has received some serious attention.[2] The links are also manifested in the social and gender history of immigrant reception and citizenship work undertaken by government officials, professional experts, and women's and other reform groups.[3] In Canada, unlike the United States, postwar immigrants figured prominently in Cold War discourse.[4] They served both to enhance Cold War panics and surveillance and to provide Canada with opportunities for winning the moral war.

On the one hand, mass migration helped fuel contemporary elite warnings about collapsing and abnormal families, wartime casualties, and the variously defined threats to postwar security, normalcy, and moral decency. These supposed threats ranged widely—from communists, working mothers (vilified by the mainstream press and psychologists alike), and juvenile delinquents to homosexuals, loose women, and other "sex deviants"—and included, more generally, a lack of training in democratic citizenship, especially among refugees from Communist regimes, Native peoples, and Canadian youth.[5] Many critics asked: would immigrants bring a mental health problem to Canada? Would these victims of war, Nazi camps, or overcrowded and ill-equipped refugee camps be dysfunctional newcomers requiring massive, expensive support? Had years of surviving in the woods, prepared to kill attackers, steal food, forage and beg, permanently brutalized some women, men, and children, or could they be rehabilitated?[6]

The topic of the "sexual morality" of Displaced Persons (DPs, or stateless refugees) and immigrants did not receive as much public play, but some confidential caseworker notes and oral testimonies suggest concern about "untoward" sexual relations in wartime and refugee camps, about the rape of women, and the presence of "illegitimate" children. These notes and testimonies also pondered the "problem" of how to rehabilitate women who had used sex as a survival strategy: DP women from Eastern Europe who had slept with Nazi guards or collaborators who tried to avoid forced removal to German-controlled labour camps across the continent; Jewish and non-Jewish partisans pressured to take on lovers among their comrades; and so on. Indeed, front-line caseworkers had difficulty handling such cases of "situational morality," and their responses reveal a depressing combination of pity and moral disapproval that bordered on victim-blaming.[7]

On the other hand, the new immigrants gave Canadian experts plenty of opportunities for regulating and reshaping the "delinquencies" of men, women, and families according to dominant political, social, and gender norms—or, as contemporary parlance had it, "Canadian ways." I would argue, for example, that reception and citizenship activity in Cold War Canada was aimed as much at ensuring the successful adaptation of anti-Soviet refugees seeking jobs and influence in the professions and "family resettlement" as it was at undermining the old left-wing press or purging left-wing ethnic persons from unions. Seemingly disparate activities were linked through a Cold War mandate. They included, for example, efforts to bolster the presence of anti-communist DPs within their respective ethnic communities, and to transform patriarchal European families into companionate marriages more closely approximating North American middle-class models.[8] They included efforts to reshape immigrant women's cooking, shopping, and child-raising patterns (and indeed, to curtail their Old World influence on their children's education).[9] They included attempts to discredit the old-left ethnic press. The immigrant discourses and reception work indicate the interconnected nature of Cold War politics, gender ideologies, domestic and sexual containment, and varieties of surveillance.

The popular discourses of early Cold War Canada in contemporary mainstream newspapers, magazines, editorial pages, and readers' letters on immigrants do more than document the arguments of pro- and anti-immigration advocates. They provide a fascinating source of Cold War discourse. For example, the mainstream print media contain competing notions regarding the social, moral, and psychological impact of the anti-Soviet DPs on postwar Canada. There is more here than labour representatives and nativists making familiar arguments about absorptive capacities, immigrants stealing jobs, and the Canadian character. Also at play are popular and expert anxieties about dysfunctional, neurotic, and even pathologically troubled casualties of war, refugee camps, and broken families posing further threats to the fragile Canadian family and to social and moral postwar recovery. Uncompromising bigots offered particularly graphic renditions of the DP as degenerate and equated the new large-scale immigration with impending doom.

For instance, responding to a particularly grisly event—the rape and murder of two East European DP women in Toronto in 1955 by an unknown man whom the police and media dubbed "the DP Strangler"—a self-identified "United Empire Loyalist" wrote: "The folly of the Federal Government's stupid, ill-advised and ill-planned immigration policy is becoming clearly evident by the shocking increase of murders, rapes and robberies by DPs in recent months."[10] In a manner befitting the discourse of a moral panic, he continued:

> The strangler who has killed two New Canadian women and has terrorized many more is said to be a European immigrant. An Austrian DP youth of nineteen stabbed a downtown merchant in Toronto in the back in brutal fashion the other day. A rash of violent murders of passion have been committed recently by Polish, Ukrainian and Yugoslav DP's. A news story in the December 15 Telegram (page four) states that the immigration policies of the Federal Government were blamed by a lawyer for two German immigrants who were sentenced to four and five years in jail for a $25,000 bank robbery in Cooksville. The lawyer asked why the Government brings over immigrants and then fails to find jobs for them. The lawyer, Fred D. White, said "immigrants were victimized by the Immigration Department." Yet the arrogant, dictatorial Liberals continue to flood Canada with German, Italian, Ukrainian, Polish, Slavic and other non-British immigrants. Why? Are Mr. St. Laurent and Co. a party to a deliberate plot by certain interests to destroy the British Anglo-Saxon majority in Canada? It appears so, for there is no other ligitimate [sic] reason to dump tens of thousands of illiterate, diseased and mentally unfit DP's into Canada while serious unemployment exists and while there is a business recession. The voters will have to give their answer to this rotten business at the next Federal election.

The letter provoked a strong response from several ethnic organizations protesting the criminalized image of immigrants it portrayed.[11] The murder of the two "New Canadian women" cited in the letter, which received extensive coverage in the Toronto media, also served to draw attention to an increasingly popular psychiatric definition of sexual deviant: the criminal sexual psychopath.[12]

The supporters of postwar immigration were also not a homogeneous lot, though, predictably, many of them drew on economic and humanitarian arguments. *Saturday Night* writer Pauline Shapiro, for example, advised readers that "many refugees from oppressed lands are people of exceptional intelligence and integrity" who have chosen democracy over "a vicious and essentially stupid doctrine." Other writers sought to allay the fears of Canadians by assuring them that with time and guidance the refugees would recover and adjust.[13]

How were the DPs and other "Iron Curtain refugees" taken up as compelling symbols and metaphors for communist horrors and democratic decency? Journalists wrote glowingly of the anti-communist "freedom fighters," so deserving of Canadian sympathy and support, though glossing over darker issues, such as Nazi collaboration or anti-Semitism.[14] Canadians were told that the refugees' adjustment to "Canadian ways" was a moral, democratic imperative. They were told to melt the "cold blooded approach" with Canadian warmth, and "make sure the reds can't get them back."[15] When *The Financial Post*'s Michael Barkway visited an Austrian refugee camp in 1956, he offered portraits of the men, women, and children who had trekked through the frontier towns to freedom. At one point Barkway settled upon a "dark-haired" sixteen-year-old Hungarian "urchin" who breathlessly announced that "we crossed tonight too." He described the boy as "a get-up-and-go sort of youngster whom you could imagine equally well heading up a teenage-age gang or a Scout troop—depending entirely on how he is treated." Treating him right was Canada's moral obligation.[16]

An intriguing ingredient in this cause was the escape narrative. Tales of daring, narrow escapes from Communist regimes to Western freedom abound, of "freedom fighters" outwitting Communist border guards, negotiating searchlights, barbed wire, and dogs, and surviving for days in the woods until reaching a Western zone, camp, or country, and then eventually making the long, often circuitous, heroic sea voyage to Canada. A 1948 news story announced, "Happy Estonians Welcomed to Kitchener after Hazardous Atlantic Crossing in Tiny, Crowded Boat." It featured the smiling faces of the individuals and couples involved, including the "Blond Seaman," an attractive boat owner named Ludwig Tosine, "who led his countrymen and women (23 in total) to Canada via Sweden, Belgium, England, and US" by a "5,800 mile voyage" to freedom. The voyage included a "remarkable" three-month ocean trip on Tosine's forty-three-foot ketch, and then a three-month internment on Ellis Island. The party met with a rousing welcome at St. Peter's Lutheran Church.[17]

Another article, "Chose to Flee from Red Poland Rather Than Perform before Stalin," told how a "slim, blue-eyed beauty," twenty-seven-year-old Polish actress Lydia Prochinicka, escaped "red Poland" and with her theatre-producer lover, Leonidas Dudarew-Ossetynksi, ended up visiting Canada (via the United States) to perform plays celebrating Poland's pre-Soviet past. Evidently, her status as Poland's best actress meant an invitation to appear before the Soviet dictator Joseph Stalin in 1947. "I hated Stalin," she recalled, "but it was most difficult to refuse such an invitation. It was go to Moscow or escape—I chose to escape." She "made her escape from the Communist clutch" by way of France and Belgium, then Chile, and finally North America.[18]

Other stories told of Czechs riding the freedom train to the West, holding conductors at gunpoint as they smashed through Communist border points, and then the trek through frontier villages to the other side of the Iron Curtain. Both before and after their failed revolution in 1956, Hungarians fleeing their Communist homeland figured prominently in such narratives, as numerous articles detailed the careful calculations, daring escapes, close calls, and eventual freedom. In 1953 a *Maclean's* article by writer June Callwood alerted readers to the story of a family's escape with this chilling headline: "'We are escaping from bad men in the forest and if you cry, they will get us.' With these mind-scaring words this Hungarian couple silenced their child and bribed their way through the Iron Curtain to freedom in Canada." The lengthy story, conveyed to Callwood by businessman Peter Keresztes, and presented as a personal testimonial, detailed the flight from Prague to Vienna via Slovakia and France to Canada; the underground economy of money, bribery, and unreliable guards; the close calls on trains, in rivers, and in the border frontiers; police arrest in Austria and then a fortunate turn of events brought about by a policeman who turned the other cheek, and a friendly Austrian peasant woman who hid them; and finally friends in Vienna, then Paris and Toronto, and, after two and one-half years, financial success in Canada. By the time of publication, the family, we are told, had rebuilt a family enterprise in the trade business and their daughter had enrolled in the prestigious, indeed exclusive (both in class and race terms), private girls' school, Havergal. "Do we like Canada?" the story concludes. "Of course," the storyteller answers, "this is a place of freedom and peace."[19]

In exploring these tales I do not want to ignore or downplay personal tragedies but, rather, to note how such refugee discourses helped give shape to Cold War rhetoric and immigrant reception work within Canada. We need also to probe the gendered features of these stories. How do the stories of families, men, or women differ? Female escape stories highlight attractive women or madonnas with babies but gloss over, yet sometimes hint at, sexual threat. In the Hungarian tale, the teller, the husband, never refers directly to his emotions, apart from general fear, but describes his wife as tremendously cool under pressure, then an emotional wreck afterwards, subject to recurring depression and panic attacks, which he, apparently, does not suffer. It might also be useful to compare stories of political escape with other escape narratives, such as African-American ex-slave or ex-fugitive stories, or even Puritan tales of conversion and escape—in order to compare and contrast narrative structures and the treatment of such themes as escape, exodus, and transformation.

DP "freedom fighters" did not always act according to script. I have alluded to collaboration. My research reveals the gap between the "heroic" image and the "broken-down" character of many men and women who encountered Canadian social workers.[20] The alleged "immorality" of certain "freedom fighters" was also cause for frustration or embarrassment. Consider the case of a Czech man and his Romanian-born wife. Their "daring escape" from Communist border guards on "the freedom train" to West Germany was front-page news, while behind the scenes Canadian officials were trying to deport them on morality, "unemployable," and mental illness grounds. The relevant correspondence refers to their sexually promiscuous behaviour in overseas refugee camps and Canadian hostels, and their inability to find Canadian jobs. The couple ended up at the International Institute of Metropolitan Toronto, and their case file records allegations of syphilis, betrayal, wife abuse, and the husband's eventual commitment to a psychiatric hospital.[21]

Tales highlighting the escape by Jews from the Nazis also appear in the sources, though less frequently, perhaps in part because survivors for years after the Holocaust were hesitant to share their horror stories. In both cases, however, we see in the public telling of these tales an example of what might be called the folk-lorization of immigrants—serving up their tragic life stories for Canadian uses. In auditoriums across the country, for example, reception activists showcased not only New Canadian cultural talent—choirs, violinists, and singers—but also adult and child survivors and Iron Curtain refugees, who were said to "captivate" audiences with "thrilling accounts" of escape from the Soviets or Nazis.

As part of this activity, the Canadian Citizenship Branch was ostensibly created as a "new" federal agency in 1945, though it evolved out of the wartime Nationalities Branch, created to spy on and rally European immigrants and ethnics to the war cause. The few scholars who have studied the Citizenship Branch generally have treated it from a liberal perspective, seeing it largely as a stepping stone toward the more progressive multiculturalism polices of the 1970s.[22] The Branch's Cold War agenda, and how it shaped reception and citizenship work among immigrants—as well as Natives and youth—also require serious attention. The Branch's official mandate was to address a perceived social and political problem of the postwar era, namely insufficient training in democratic citizenship among three groups in par-ticular, Canadian youth, Aboriginals, and immigrant newcomers. Its work among Aboriginal people—which has not yet been subjected to critical scrutiny despite voluminous archival records—included the promotion of friendship centres intended to encourage greater cultural understanding between Native and non-native Canadians. But that work remained wrapped in a legacy of government paternalism and parsimony.[23]

The state aims for immigrant and refugee newcomers were similar. They included: promoting cultural understanding between new and old Canadians, liais-ing with immigrant and ethnic groups across the country, and encouraging new-comers to adapt to a "Canadian way of life." This way of life was glowingly described in an endless array of pamphlets, films, radio broadcasts, and other edu-cational materials.[24] A typical pamphlet told newcomers that Canada was a democ-ratic country "where you have the right to life, liberty, security of person, enjoyment of property, protection of the law without discrimination . . . where you have free-dom of speech, freedom of press, of assembly and association and . . . worship."[25]

In carrying out its official agenda, the Branch co-operated with public agencies such as the CBC and National Film Board and the vast network of publicly funded and quasi-independent social and cultural agencies ranging from the Canadian Association of Social Workers to Jewish Family Services, Children's Aid societies, and Canadian Red Cross. The Branch also worked closely with a variety of volun-tary organizations, including women's groups, adult education and literacy groups, settlement house and community homes, and patriotic and citizenship organiza-tions. It had some good ideas, including a plan to promote cultural harmony by teaching Canadians how to say "difficult-to-pronounce" European names. Other projects involved research on discrimination, including the bias against "Negroes" in North America, and removing a gender bias in the law whereby Canadian women who had married "foreigners" lost their Canadian citizenship.[26]

The "new" Branch never lost its wartime preoccupation with surveillance, and in the postwar years the political tracking of immigrant and ethnic communities remained a critical part of its hidden agenda. Witness, for example, the continuing

presence of Vladimir Kaye, professor and East European specialist, academic and
Cold Warrior, and an advisor on immigrants to the government. Kaye played a significant role in the translation of the ethnic press into English, both before and
after the war.

In the postwar years the press translation service of the Citizenship Branch,
run by a small staff of workers with multi-language skills, was undertaken not
merely to permit Ottawa to keep abreast of the country's ethnic communities.
Rather, the aims were both more ominous and self-serving: to carefully monitor
the political situation in new and old immigrant communities, find ways of curry-
ing political favour with immigrant communities across the political spectrum,
especially in heavily concentrated "voting blocs," such as Ukrainians in Western
Canadian ridings, and to offer "advice" to the foreign-language press and provide
"appropriate" materials. As Kaye himself observed during one of his many postwar
liaison trips to ethnic communities across Canada:

> The Foreign Language Press exercises great influence especially with newcomers
> because for the first two or three years it is almost the sole source of information
> for them. It is, therefore, of utmost importance to keep close touch with the edi-
> tors to advise them and supply them with the right material. . . . If left without
> attention, some of the newly arrived editors may interpret the Canadian democra-
> tic freedom in the wrong direction thus causing embarrassment to themselves and
> their readers.[27]

To meet these ends, the Branch monitored a large number of ethnic newspapers,
mostly leftist and right-wing Eastern European publications, but also moderately
liberal papers published by European groups such as the Italians, plus some Chinese,
Japanese, and other non-European newspapers.[28]

The Branch's press translation service was intended to serve another political
and ideological aim, and one fully in keeping with the corrupted democracy of the
Cold War context: to discredit the older, left-wing voices within Canada's varied
immigrant and ethnic communities while enhancing and giving a public platform
to the right-wing perspectives of the anti-communist East European refugee groups
entering Canada. In this regard Branch officials and staff carried out several related
activities. In an effort to discredit both communism and "the extreme right,"
Branch personnel regularly supplied ethnic editors with "appropriate" news and
propaganda materials, including stories celebrating immigrant successes in Canada
and detailing communist "atrocities" around the globe, and various items promoting Canadian ways. Information intended specifically for women, including both
political and cultural items, was regularly supplied on the grounds that women
wielded considerable influence over the moral and political growth of their children.

These activities reflected the anxieties and hysteria of Canada's political and
social elites. According to Kaye and other Branch officials, it was crucial that Ottawa
keep a constant vigilance on the ethnic press and continually try to influence its
offerings, because the foreign-language newspapers played so critical a role in the
lives of newly arrived immigrants and refugees desperate for news about their
homelands and prepared to read any news stories, even "lies" supplied by commu-

nists, about their former homes and the friends and families they had left behind. In their view, the pro-communist Canadian ethnic editors were not always entirely to blame. Running their newspapers on a shoestring, they often relied "too heavily" on homeland embassies or, alternatively, the Comintern for "news." In other cases, Branch staff accused leftist ethnic editors of political naiveté: Canada-born or raised editors who, having never experienced life under a Communist regime, were too quick to extol its virtues and blind to its evils.

Citizenship Branch staff also deliberately sought to enhance the presence and political impact of the new anti-communist newcomers within their respective East European ethnic community by encouraging the founding of new ethnic newspapers, especially in communities where long-standing, prewar leftist papers still operated, and then plying them with pro-Canadian, pro-democracy material. These efforts met with success. In 1950 Kaye, following a liaison trip to Toronto, happily reported that Toronto, once home to "practically the whole Communist Foreign Lang[uage] press," with the exception of Winnipeg, had witnessed "the rapid increase . . . of anti-communist publications" due to "the concentration of new immigrants in the Province of Ontario." The once thirteen-strong ethnic communist papers were now outnumbered by twenty-five new, mostly anti-communist papers, including the Ukrainian *Echo*.[29]

The Branch carried out its anti-communist and "pro-democratic" platform in other, related ways. Staff members built up a library equipped with resources designed to promote a greater understanding of newcomers, including, for instance, articles and books on Eastern Europe. A newspaper clipping and "fact sheets" service offered Branch officials and other interested parties who contacted the Branch with an endless list of documents detailing communist vices. Fact sheets, for instance, bore such titles as "Teaching the Young for Stalin," "Forced Labour in the USSR," and "Some Facts about Communists and Freedom of the Press." The ethnic press translations were organized and catalogued in part to help Branch staff handle outside enquiries related to Canada's ethnic and immigrant groups, while a repository of speeches, written by Kaye, members of the Research Division, and other "ethnic specialists," could be tapped by government officials addressing immigrant and ethnic organizations and voting constituencies. While some of these speeches focused more narrowly on themes of adjustment and Canadian laws and customs, others highlighted the communist menace.

Most of these speeches were intended as public addresses.[30] But some appear to have been secret talks shared only with trusted people. A particularly graphic illustration of the latter was a paper entitled "Methods of Marxist Propaganda among Ethnic Groups in Canada" that Kaye read at a "confidential meeting" on March 30, 1954, in Toronto. The document nicely encapsulated the various themes of the day. It began with a lengthy denunciation of communism as, among other things, "a Godless religion . . . with all the violent attributes of a militant religion" and of communists as dangerous zealots bent on world domination, people prepared to use "catchy slogans" (such as "Proletarian [*sic*] of all Countries Unite"), a "common red flag," propaganda, and other underhanded tactics designed to "arouse mass psychoses" and conversion to the creed. Then it turned to a long discussion of communist "infiltration" techniques across the world, noting, for instance, that communist strategists "are firmly convinced that gradual penetration of strategic positions by a small, well disciplined and centrally directed force can gain control of the ruling machinery in all non-communist countries, thus making war unnecessary, if they can achieve victory without employing direct military force."

After noting the presence of such Marxist "cells" in Central America and other parts of the globe, Kaye turned to Canada, explaining in detail that a strategy popular with the Kremlin and Canadian communists was to infiltrate "the ethnic groups," especially numerically large Slavic groups such as the Ukrainians, Poles, Russians, Czechs, and Yugoslavs, largely for two reasons: "because they form the bulk of unskilled labour in industry" and "because among these groups are to be found the greatest enemies of communism who either have to be converted to communism or to be neutralized, paralyzed into inactivity." Methods ranged from bombarding immigrant newcomers with pro-communist propaganda to intimidation tactics aimed at newcomers with family and kin back in communist-controlled homelands.

Turning more specifically to the pro-communist ethnic press in Canada, Kaye's address made much of the Soviet Union's role, through the All-Slav Committee, in convincing Canadian editors of the virtues of communist lands and the vulnerability of newcomers, including anti-communist refugees who fled homelands that came under Soviet control but now found themselves starved for information about their homes. These people, he said, might succumb to the lies perpetually promoted in the ethnic press:

> Correspondents of the ALL-SLAV COMMITTEE write articles to the Slavic Communist press in Canada that are intended to show the strength of the Slavs in the world, and above all, the happy life the Slavs lead in the Soviet Union. . . . The ASSOCIATION FOR CULTURAL RELATIONS ABROAD which "invites" (communist) editors and correspondents to visit the Soviet Union, fully covers also the costs of their maintenance, provides travelling facilities, rail, car and plane, hotel accommodation, theatres, recreation, etc. Soviet authorities have granted these guests permission to visit places which are hermetically sealed off and inaccessible to any other visitors from abroad. . . . In their reports there is constantly a reference to some mysterious companion who is with them. "We proceeded to Ivankivtsi . . ." or "We visited Kirov collective farm at Zastavna," etc. The reports repeat with boring monotony the stereotyped phrases which are a "must" in every Soviet article, such as "Nyzhni Stanivtsi, a one-time backward, ignorant village, changed beyond recognition under the Soviet rule. . . . In the village was opened a beautiful club; there is a library where films are shown . . ." or "Life is happier, sunnier, under the Soviet rule . . ." The reports appear regularly every week, they contain photographs of villagers, of buildings, names of those who have relatives in Canada; they bring greetings from relatives, and the invariable invitation "come and share our happy life." These articles are eagerly read by immigrants, old and new, as they often are the first news about relatives since the country was occupied by the Soviets. New immigrants, who dare not write to their relatives and friends for fear of endangering their lives, buy the papers in the hope of finding indications whether their relatives are still alive or not.

The "purpose" of these visits by special correspondents to the Soviet Union, the address continued, is "to strengthen the faith of their own followers in Canada" by offering assurances that all is well abroad; to "entice" non-communists, especially newcomers, to read the communist press; and to increase circulation. The aim of this work, according to Kaye, was twofold: to make financial gains and to spread propaganda. "The Communists calculate that if somebody reads a paper for a considerable length of time he will absorb at least something of the offered propaganda and if he does not become a convert to Communist [*sic*], he may cease to remain a supporter of the non-Communist press and its organizations. Soviet psychologists believe that if a lie is repeated often enough it will be accepted (at least by some) as truth."[31]

The interconnected character of reception, citizenship, and Cold War work is perhaps most quickly summed up by Kaye's own liaison reports. They document meetings with anti-communist editors working with new newspapers such as the Ukrainian *Echo* and the Estonian *Our Aim*; his role in developing and amassing resource materials with Slavic studies university academics; collecting updates from local unemployment, job placement, and immigration officers; setting up language classes for immigrant mothers (and then urging ethnic priests to drag them to class); and speeches.[32]

Cold War politics also went hand-in-hand with the reception and citizenship activities of the various professional and voluntary agencies.[33] While I do not want to suggest that reception activists were a homogeneous group, I shall nonetheless illustrate the interconnectedness of immigrant and Cold War work by taking up what is admittedly the easiest example: the IODE, Imperial Order of the Daughters of the Empire. And I shall do so simply by listing their priorities as defined in countless motions to parliament, meetings, and correspondence: short-term welfare supports for New Canadian mothers and their families; lobbying against obscene literature, trashy novels, and sex perverts; insisting upon English-language training for newcomers; collecting and disseminating communist atrocity stories through their fairly wide networks (including, for example, the 1948 accusations levelled at Greek communist guerrillas for burning villages and kidnapping and raping women and children); running Canadian cookbook projects and child-care classes for immigrant women, advocating obligatory citizenship classes for Canadian youth, lobbying Ottawa for more demanding citizenship exams for immigrants as well as more elaborate and impressive citizenship ceremonies, and running the Communist Alert service.

The last, blacklisting activity, of course, brought them most directly in contact with RCMP and other state surveillance forces, and the relevant sources reveal them as especially enthusiastic Cold Warriors.[34] Their publications also helped to sustain an anti-communist hysteria and solidify the link between Cold War and immigrant work. Their pamphlets decried communist degenerates from within and without, warned that "Communist revolutionaries are on the march in every country of the world"—not just in Asia and Europe but also in Canadian trade unions. Demonizing Canadian communists as "the revolutionary agents of a foreign power" blindly determined "to destroy our national life by lies, strife, and bloodshed," the IODE preached constant vigilance and advised Canadian women (and men) on "how to spot a Communist" (drawing on U.S. materials).[35] One document envisioned life in a Communist Canada in which "every surviving citizen would be subjected to a rigidly tyrannical control of every detail of his existence."

> He could not choose his job or change it. For complaining he could be ejected from his home. For lateness he could be sent to a slave labour camp in the Yukon! . . . His radio programs would be controlled as would the literature he read. Even his leisure would be confiscated for "voluntary" work on Communist projects. He could not leave Canada—an attempt at this would mean that he would be shot and his family given five years of penal servitude. In fact every phase of his life would be pried into by political police and his freedom would be taken. . . . Our Canadian way of life is perhaps the freest in human history and our scale of living second only to that of the United States. Communism would solve nothing; for to shoot one's citizens or oppress them by the million in concentration camps is no real solution for a country's economic ills. Therefore, it is our duty as citizens to further study the aims and methods of Communists so that we may draw our attention of all citizens to the threat which Communism presents.[36]

Like other highly active Cold Warriors, IODE president Marjorie Lamb and her colleagues rarely reflected on the irony of their own activities, which involved spying and blacklisting suspected communists in the name of liberal democratic rights.

Cold War politics, then, acted as a significant influence, in conjunction with other ideologies, on immigrant and refugee reception work. The very prevalence of this atmosphere of anti-communism as it permeated Cold War Canada highlights the type of society to which the immigrants were expected to conform. What remains for further study is to trace in detail the ways in which newcomers managed to negotiate this highly charged terrain.

## Notes

1. Press release, untitled, by Anne Davison, Archives of Ontario (AO), International Institute of Metropolitan Toronto (IIMT), MU 6415, file "Ethnic Press."
2. Important work on this topic includes Reg Whitaker, *Double Standard: The Secret History of Canadian Immigration Policy* (Toronto: Lester and Orpen Dennys, 1987).
3. For a preliminary effort, see Franca Iacovetta, "Remaking Their Lives: Women Immigrants, Survivors, and Refugees," in *A Diversity of Women: Ontario 1945–80*, ed. Joy Parr (Toronto: University of Toronto Press, 1995).
4. Apart from Elaine Tyler May's brief discussion of immigrant families in Cold War America, the U.S. literature does not suggest that immigrants, or practices aimed at immigrants and refugees, figured significantly at all in Cold War practices, but few have ventured to explore the theme. Valuable studies offering differing perspectives include: May, *Homeward Bound: American Families in the Cold War Era* (New York: Basic Books, 1988); Joanne Meyerowitz, "Beyond the Feminine Mystique: A Reassessment of Postwar Mass Culture, 1946–58," *Journal of American History* 79 (March 1993); John D'Emilio, *Sexual Politics, Sexual Communities: The Making of a Homosexual Minority in the United States 1940–1970* (Chicago: University of Chicago Press, 1983); Geoffrey S. Smith, "National Security and Personal Isolation: Sex, Gender, and Disease in the Cold-War United States," *International History Review*, 1994.
5. There is a growing literature on the political, social, cultural, and gender history of

Cold War Canada. See, for example: Reg Whitaker and Gary Marcuse, *Cold War Canada: The Making of a National Insecurity State, 1945–1957* (Toronto: University of Toronto Press, 1994); Gary Kinsman, *Regulation of Desire: Homo and Hetero Sexualities*, 2nd ed. (Montreal: Black Rose Books, 1996), chaps. 6–8; Mary Louise Adams, *The Trouble with Normal: Postwar Youth and the Making of Heterosexuality* (Toronto: University of Toronto Press, 1998); Mona Gleason, *Normalizing the Ideal: Psychology, Schooling, and the Family in Post-1945 Canada* (Toronto: University of Toronto Press, 1999); and Franca Iacovetta, "Parents, Daughters, and Family Court Intrusions into Working-Class Life," in *On the Case: Explorations in Social History*, ed. Franca Iacovetta and Wendy Mitchinson (Toronto: University of Toronto Press, 1998).

6. Various features of these discussions are captured in the contemporary periodical literature. See, for example: Pierre Berton, "The Long Ordeal of Mrs. Tak," *Maclean's*, June 15, 1951; B. Cahill, "Do Immigrants Bring a Mental Health Problem to Canada?" *Saturday Night*, June 22, 1957; S.M. Katz, "How Mental Illness Is Attacking Our Immigrants, *Maclean's*, Jan. 4, 1948; and Ruth Hamilton, "In a Strange Land," *Canadian Welfare*, Jan. 15, 1948.

7. These general observations are derived from my reading of thousands of confidential social work case files culled from AO, IIMT, MU 1952–65. See also Marlene Epp, *Women without Men: Mennonite Refugees of the Second World War* (Toronto: University of Toronto Press, 1999); and Marlene Epp, "The Memory of Violence: Soviet and East European Mennonite Refugees and Rape in the Second World War," *Journal of Women's History* 9,1 (Spring 1997).

8. This was the central theme of my "Making New Canadians: Women, Social Workers and Reshaping Immigrant Families," in *Gender Conflicts: New Essays in Women's History*, ed. Franca Iacovetta and Mariana Valverde (Toronto: University of Toronto Press, 1992).

9. Iacovetta, "Remaking Their Lives"; Franca Iacovetta and Valerie Konerick, "Food, Immigrant Women, and the Politics of Assimilation?" paper presented to the Gender, Race, Class and the Construction of Canada Conference, Vancouver, November 1996.

10. This and the following quotation are from press clippings, National Archives of Canada (NAC), MG 31 D69, Citizenship Branch, vol. 14, file 1955. On the case of "the DP Strangler," see Elise Chenier, "Every Parent Trembles," graduate history paper, Queen's University, Kingston, 1994, p.14; on the murders, see Chenier, "Seeing Red: Immigrant Women and Sexual Danger in Toronto's Postwar Broadsheets," *Atlantis*, special issue, "Whose Canada Is It?" ed. Tania Das Gupta and Franca Iacovetta, Spring 2000.

11. Press clippings, NAC, MG 31 D69, Citizenship Branch, vol. 14, file 1955. The file contains a copy of "An Answer on behalf of New Canadians," published in *Nasha Meta*, Feb. 26, 1955, signed by executive members of the International Lawyers Association.

12. See Kinsman, *Regulation of Desire*, chap. 6.

13. Pauline C. Shapiro, "The Better Sort of Emigrants," *Saturday Night*, May 17, 1941; Michael Barkway, "We Can Still Save Face with Our Refugee Policy," *The Financial Post*, Dec. 29, 1956, drew on his experiences interviewing prospective immigrants in an Austrian refugee camp.

14. This remains a highly contentious political issue. See, for example, the study of the 1985-86 Deschênes Commission by Harold Troper and Morton Weinfeld, *Old Wounds: Jews, Ukrainians and the Hunt for Nazi War Criminals in Canada* (Markham, Ont.: Viking, 1988), as well as the review by Ukrainian-Canadian specialist Lubomyr Luciuk and the authors' reply in *Canadian Ethnic Studies* 21,1 (1989) and 22,1 (1990).

15. J.P. Maclean, "And the Reds Can't Get Them Back," *The Financial Post*, Aug. 12, 1956; Ronald Williams, "How to Keep Red Hands off Our New Canadians," *The Financial Post*, Dec. 3, 1949.

16. Barkway, "We Can Still Save Face."

17. *The Toronto Star*, Jan. 17, 1948.

18. Pat Best, "Chose to Flee from Red Poland . . ." *The Citizen* (Ottawa), Sept. 14, 1957.

19. June Callwood, as told by Peter Keresztes, "We Are Hiding from Bad Men in the Forest," *Maclean's*, Nov. 15, 1957.

20. See, for example, Iacovetta, "Making New Canadians."

21. The newspaper clippings, correspondence between officials with the international refugee groups, and Canadian social workers are contained in AO, IIMT, confidential case file on Ladislav D. I have copied a data base of the more than one thousand case files in this collection.

22. Fred N. Dreiziger, "The Rise of a Bureaucracy for Multiculturalism: The Origins of the Nationalities Branch," in *On Guard for Thee: War, Ethnicity and the Canadian State, 1939–1945*, ed. N. Hillmer, B. Kordan, and L. Luciuk (Ottawa: Canadian Committee for the History of the Second World War, 1988); Leslie Pals, *Interests of State: The Politics of Language, Multiculturalism and Feminism in Canada* (Montreal: McGill-Queen's University Press, 1993).

23. My observations are based on a cursory look at the files in NAC, Record Group (RG) 26.

24. The Branch collection contains many documents indicating objectives and programs. See, for example, V.J. Kaye, "Historical Material on the Establishment of the Canadian Citizenship Branch," February 1961, and W.H. Agnew, Chief, Publications and Information Division, "Historical Review of the Canadian Citizenship Branch," December 1967, NAC, MG 31 D19, Citizenship Branch, vol. 11. See also Dreiziger, "Rise of a Bureaucracy for Multiculturalism."

25. Publications of the Canadian Citizenship Branch, photocopies, undated, NAC, MG 28 I17, vol. 26.

26. NAC, RG 26, is a large collection with files on these and many more organizations and activities. The work of the branch is a major theme in my forthcoming book with the working title "Making New Citizens in Cold War Canada."

27. Kaye was chief liaison officer for the Branch after the war. V.J. Kaye, Liaison Officer, Report of Trip to Toronto and Hamilton, Sept. 27, Oct. 2, 1950, NAC, MG 31 D69, Citizenship Branch, vol. 12, pp.1–2. On Kaye see also the entry on him in Dmytro M. Shtohryn, *Ukrainians in North America* (Champaign Ill., 1975), p.432. My thanks to Frances Swyripa for this reference.

28. See, for example, "List of Ethnic Group Communist Publications in Canada, Nov 1958," "List of Papers Primarily Concerned with Liberation of Their Homelands from Communism and Anti-communist Propaganda," Nov. 20, 1958, and press review, "A Review of the Press in Canada other than English and French," May 1, 1954, NAC, RG 26, vol. 11, file 1945–61.

29. V.J. Kaye, Liaison Officer, Report of Trip to Toronto and Hamilton, Sept. 27–Oct. 2, 1950, Citizenship Branch, file 1950. See also Trip to Toronto and Hamilton, March 24–25, 1950, Citizenship Branch, file 1950, and Report on Liaison Work—Dr. V.J. Kaye, vol. 11, file 1950–52, NAC, MG 31, D69, vol. 12.

30. For example, "The Role of Ethnic Organs in the Integration of Newcomers," 1957, "Address Delivered by Dr. V.J. Kaye on Sunday, April 7th, 1957, at the Masaryk Hall, Toronto (on citizenship), NAC, MG 31 D69, vol. 12.

31. "Methods of Marxist Propaganda among Ethnic Groups in Canada," paper to read at a Confidential Meeting on March 30, 1954, Toronto, NAC, MG 31 D69, vol 11, 1954.

32. For example, Reports on Trip to Toronto and Hamilton, March 24–25, 1950, June 9–13, 1950, Sept. 27–Oct. 2, 1950, and Annual Reports, Liaison Division, 1954, 1956 (including Western Canada), NAC, MG 31 D69, vol 12.

33. For more detailed examples, see Iacovetta, "Remaking their Lives."

34. This discussion draws on: IODE, *A Primer on Democracy* (n.d.), file "Anti-Communist Activities"; *Empire Study Questionnaire [on the subject of] Communism*, file "Anti-Communist Activities, 1949"; Marjorie Lamb, "Communism in Canada," February 1957; *The Alert Service*, pamphlet, June 1958; and Alert to Canadians: Developments in Communist Activity, pamphlet, Sept. 15, 1958; all in NAC, MG 28 I17, file "IODE."

35. The quotation is from *Empire Study Questionnaire* (an information sheet that fol-

lowed a question and answer format). See also IODE, *Primer on Democracy*; Lamb, "Communism in Canada"; *The Alert Service*; and *Alert to Canadians*; and the editorial and articles in the IODE's publication, *Echoes*, including, for example, "Communism and the Canadian Woman," Spring 1948, and "IODE Helps Newcomers to Become Canadians," Christmas 1953.

36. *Empire Study Questionnaire.*

# PART V

# THE MACHINERY OF STATE IN ACTION: MEANS AND CONSEQUENCES

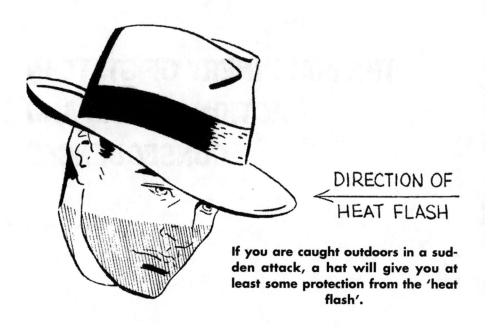

DIRECTION OF
HEAT FLASH

**If you are caught outdoors in a sudden attack, a hat will give you at least some protection from the 'heat flash'.**

*"How to Survive an Atomic Bomb," from a 1950s government-sponsored brochure.* [Smith, chap. 13]

FRANK K. CLARKE

twelve ✶ ✶ ✶

# Debilitating Divisions: The Civil Liberties Movement in Early Cold War Canada, 1946–48

In the early years of the Cold War, government actions against communism took precedence over civil liberties. In the United States the Truman administration's employee loyalty program, the inquisitional investigations of the House Committee on Un-American Activities, and the guilt-by-association charges culminating in McCarthyism were front and centre, threatening freedom of expression, freedom of association, and the rule of due process, among other basic freedoms.[1] In Canada, by contrast, the state largely succeeded in keeping its anti-communist measures out of the public spotlight.

But while Canada avoided the kind of public excesses associated with McCarthyism, recent studies challenge the view of Canada as a model of toleration and document Canada's own Cold War civil liberties abuses.[2] Indeed, the civil liberties movement was galvanized into action in the 1930s and 1940s by a series of events, including the treatment of Japanese-Canadians during the war (as well as their postwar deportation), the persecution of Jehovah's Witnesses, the Padlock law in Quebec, and the civil rights of labour. The War Measures Act, reactivated in 1939, gave the Privy Council the authority "to intern enemy aliens, fascists, Communists, Japanese Canadians, and opponents of conscription."[3]

Perhaps one of the most vivid examples of Canada's willingness to curtail individual rights in the name of national security came with what has become known as the "Gouzenko Affair" of February to March 1946.[4] The indignation over the powers the Canadian government used to override individual freedoms in that case united various civil liberties organizations that were otherwise bitterly divided during the early years of the Cold War, and the events helped lead to the emergence of new civil liberties organizations that, alongside existing organizations, began to demand greater protection for individual rights. These civil liberties organizations, though, showed pronounced divisions, especially on two key questions: whether or not the various associations should form a single national association as a more effective voice; and, most contentious of all, whether or not communists had a place within the civil liberties movement, given that many Canadians (including many civil libertarians) considered communists to be the enemies of individual freedom. Those divisions weakened the civil liberties movement by preventing

171

both the emergence of a coherent voice for individual rights and the sharing of resources necessary to sustain a credible campaign to win over public opinion. Moreover, the weakness of the civil liberties movement made it easier for the government to dismiss its members and spokespersons as a fringe element in society. As a result the federal government was not seriously challenged in its use of arbitrary power in the name of national security to the detriment of those unfortunate enough to be the targets of that power.

On February 15, 1946, Canadians learned from Prime Minister Mackenzie King about the existence of an espionage ring operating within Canada. "Information of undoubted authenticity," King said, "has reached the Canadian Government which establishes that there have been disclosures of secret and confidential information to unauthorized persons, including some members of the staff of a foreign mission in Ottawa."[5] King stated that arrests had been made that day and that a Royal Commission composed of Supreme Court justices R.L. Kellock and Robert Taschereau had been created to investigate the matter. Although King did not mention that the Soviet embassy was the foreign mission involved, press inquiries soon revealed that the Soviets were the suspected party.

The government had known of the espionage ring since September 6, 1945, when Igor Gouzenko, a cipher clerk at the Soviet embassy, defected with documents that revealed its existence. At that time the government was as surprised about the existence of Soviet spies in the country as the Canadian public would be five months later.

In its response to Gouzenko's revelations the government supplanted the traditional legal system by invoking Order-in-Council P.C. 6444 under the authority of the War Measures Act to arrest and detain the spy suspects. Although it was completely legal, the order-in-council could hardly be considered liberal, because it permitted the government to suspend such basic civil liberties as habeas corpus and access to legal counsel.[6] Only hours before King informed Canadians of the Gouzenko revelations, nine men and two women (with two additional men to follow) were arrested without formal charges and transported to specially prepared barracks at the Rockcliffe RCMP headquarters, where they were held incommunicado, inaccessible to their wives, friends, and lawyers.[7] Each detainee was isolated in a cell with windows nailed shut and overhead lights kept burning all night, and the suspects were watched over by guards day and night (according to the RCMP, to prevent suicide attempts). One of the detainees, Gordon Lunan, an army officer, also recalled flashlight arousals from sleep. Lunan was interrogated six times by the RCMP over a period of two weeks and questioned another five times by the Royal Commission before he was officially charged and allowed access to a lawyer. For other suspects, up to six weeks passed before they were charged.[8]

The King government justified its decision to invoke the War Measures Act at a Cabinet meeting on February 14, 1946, the day before the arrests. The Cabinet conclusions reveal that the government was well aware that it would be violating civil liberties if it chose to enact the War Measures Act, but it accepted the arguments of counsel to the Royal Commission that the War Measures Act should be invoked because the disclosures of espionage from the Gouzenko documents were of an "extremely serious nature." Thus, the minister of justice, Louis St. Laurent, with the agreement of cabinet, "felt justified, in the national interest in making the orders requested." In short, the security of the state, the government reasoned, justified the arbitrary means employed against the espionage suspects.[9]

The government's decision to appoint a Royal Commission to interrogate the suspects in secret was in marked contrast to the experience of the United States. In Canada the emphasis on secrecy was part of an established tradition whereby the business of government was to be conducted quietly. The cabinet and members of the senior civil service were shocked and dismayed by what they regarded as the betrayal of trust by public servants.[10] To prevent a recurrence of such a betrayal, the government would focus upon developing an internal security system by establishing a single interdepartmental body, the Security Panel, which would work in secrecy and anonymity to advise the government on appropriate internal security measures.[11]

In the days that followed the arrest of the suspects, press reports, some of them overtly sensationalist,[12] at first featured speculative stories about the identities and activities of the suspects, but as the days turned into weeks the focus turned to the treatment of the detainees. *The Toronto Daily Star* argued, "Those who value civil liberties . . . cannot but be concerned about the prolonged detention of the thirteen suspected persons 'for interrogation' . . . who are not permitted to consult their legal advisors." In the *Star*'s opinion, "Only a military emergency such as does not exist would warrant the undemocratic and, in fact, dictatorial course which such a detention involves."[13]

The press was not unanimous, however, in its view of the government's handling of the espionage suspects. The Montreal *Gazette*, for example, represented the view of Canadians who supported the government's procedures: "It is only reasonable that the hearings should be secret and that the Commissioners should take all the time necessary . . . to make the investigation as complete as possible so that steps may be taken to cut out by the very roots any 5th Column movement that is undermining the liberty and democracy of this country."[14]

At the time of the Gouzenko controversy, the civil liberties movement was little more than a collection of a few small associations scattered across the country and a few prominent individuals who lent their support. Politicians, lawyers, academics, media figures, clergymen, and some trade unionists comprised the movement. Prominent among them were Frank Scott, professor of law at McGill University, a leading constitutional expert and chairman of the national Co-operative Commonwealth Federation (CCF); B.K. Sandwell, the influential editor of *Saturday Night* magazine; Wilfred Eggleston, a high-ranking wartime federal bureaucrat and the first director of the School of Journalism at Carleton University; Alistair Stewart, the leading civil libertarian in the federal CCF caucus; John G. Diefenbaker, one of the more outspoken critics in the Progressive Conservative Party caucus of the government's actions in the Gouzenko affair; and Arthur Lower, a professor of history at United College in Winnipeg and later at Queen's University in Kingston, and known primarily for his critically acclaimed history of Canada, *Colony to Nation*, published in 1946.

Reaction from the various civil liberties organizations to press reports of the government's actions and the treatment of the detainees could best be characterized as an amalgam of anger at the disregard for due process and a desire to proceed with caution, especially because a number of the suspects did not see their cases go to court until May or June 1946. Some of the various organizations waited until most of the trials were over before taking action or commenting publicly.

The Civil Liberties Association, a Toronto-based organization led by Sandwell, represented the cautious approach in a memorandum from the association's executive council to the membership: "The Council decided . . . that it would not serve the interests of our Association to hold any sort of public meeting or demonstration until more facts are known and the trials in the courts are over."[15] Sandwell himself spoke out in the editorial pages of *Saturday Night*, expressing alarm at reports of one suspect who had pleaded guilty to engaging in espionage before the Royal Commission but withdrew the plea after attaining legal counsel. "Because of the extraordinary nature of these proceedings, some of the thirteen may be found guilty *who would not have been found guilty* by the ordinary process of law, and *who may not be guilty* at all," Sandwell wrote.[16] In the same editorial he warned his readers that the government's use of the national security argument as a justification for its actions was the ancient and unvarying excuse for every form of totalitarian destruction of individual rights.

As an indication of how disparate and decentralized the civil liberties movement was, a new organization, the Ottawa Civil Liberties Association (OCLA), emerged during the Gouzenko court trials and towards the conclusion of the last trials, unlike Sandwell's group, began a petition campaign denouncing the disregard for the suspects' civil liberties. Ironically, the first president of the OCLA, Wilfred Eggleston, had been deputy censor for the English-language press during the Second World War. Even during his tenure as a wartime censor Eggleston had showed his attachment to liberal principles by criticizing the post office's zealous interception of all mail going to the communist newspaper *The Tribune* and defending "progressive, constructive and sincere comment."[17]

On July 8, 1946, OCLA sent a resolution to all members of parliament "strongly protesting" the breaches of civil liberties during the Gouzenko affair, including prolonged detention, denial of access to legal counsel, failure to inform the suspects of the protection of the Canada Evidence Act, and publication of the commission's interim reports in a form "prejudicial" to a fair trial for the accused. OCLA called upon Parliament to take "such remedial steps as may be necessary to prevent a recurrence of such breaches."[18]

In Toronto a communist-dominated civil liberties association called the Emergency Committee for Civil Rights (ECCR) emerged as a rival to Sandwell's association. Among the more well-known members of the ECCR were C.B. Macpherson, a Marxist professor of political economy at the University of Toronto, and C.S. Jackson, the communist vice-president for the Canadian division of the United Electrical, Radio and Machine Workers. The ECCR sent a letter to Prime Minister King towards the end of the trials denouncing the government for issuing Order-in-Council P.C. 6411, which "swept aside the most sacred rights of her citizens." The ECCR also denounced the Royal Commission, which "compelled men and women to speak without aid of legal counsel and without knowing their rights," and for issuing public reports condemning the suspects before they had been charged or given a hearing in open court. The ECCR called upon King to end the activities of the commission and allow Parliament to conduct a public investigation of its actions and records, so that "the Parliament and public of Canada may know what was done to civil rights and established law."[19]

One of the more active organizations was the Winnipeg Civil Liberties Association, whose most prominent member was historian Arthur Lower. He was determined to respond to the government's actions against the espionage suspects but shared Sandwell's caution against acting hastily before all of the facts were known. After hearing a radio commentary by Blair Fraser criticizing the King government's handling of the Gouzenko affair, Lower wrote to the CBC journalist for advice: "Organizations such as ours do not wish to go off at half-cock but we would like to make a good solid statement. My own feeling is that the War Measures Act itself, must be got rid of and after that . . . Mr. King's government must be got rid of. The pattern to which it seems to be conforming more and more, is not one of liberty but, thanks to the apathy of the average Canadian, of something unpleasantly close to dictatorship."[20]

In Parliament the opposition parties demanded an explanation from the government for its illiberal measures. King sought to assure them that it was only "upon the documents which are in possession of the government now . . . that such subsequent action as was taken by myself and my colleagues was based." The prime minister referred to the second interim report of the Royal Commission, made public on March 15 (the first interim report was made public on March 2), which asserted "the existence of an organization constituting at least a threat to the safety and interests of the state." However, to ensure that individual liberties were protected, "Two justices of the Supreme Court of Canada were selected. The government did not know where in Canada it could find two persons who would be more certain to uphold justice in every particular, or who would be more zealous in protecting the freedom and liberty of the subject than would two justices of the Supreme Court of Canada."[21]

Despite his remarks, King expressed serious doubts in his diary as to whether justice was truly being upheld: "I thought it was wrong that those who are suspected should be detained indefinitely and that some way should be found to shorten the enquiry. . . . The whole proceedings are far too much like those of Russia itself."[22] King's misgivings were not misplaced, as the commissioners used the enormous powers at their disposal, including the War Measures Act, the Official Secrets Act, and the Inquiries Act, to sweep aside the civil liberties of the suspects in the conduct of the commission's proceedings. Under section 5 of the Inquiries Act, for example, the commissioners had the authority to compel the suspects to give evidence. However, the commissioners failed to inform the suspects that refusal to comply brought only the penalty of a fine.[23] Similarly, as one lawyer and civil libertarian later pointed out in *The Canadian Bar Review*, the commissioners "refrained from mentioning the protection which was available under section 5 of the Canada Evidence Act." Subsection 2 of section 5 of the Canada Evidence Act stipulated that suspects had the right to request that their answers not be used against them in a criminal trial. Thus, when invoked, the Canada Evidence Act protected suspects from self-incrimination.[24] Of the failure to inform the suspects of their rights, one of the suspects later observed, not inaccurately, that the commissioners engaged in "carefully planned entrapment—the sort of procedure the good judges would have indignantly struck down had the police in normal, lawful proceedings tried to get away with it."[25]

During their questioning of the suspects, the commissioners vehemently demanded that the suspects reveal the names of individuals who legally belonged to the Labor Progressive Party or other communist organizations. Those demands were not only unjustified but also smacked of the McCarthyism that would later poison the political process in the United States. The questioning of Dr. David Shugar and Israel Halperin provides clear examples. In response to Commissioner Kellock's question, Shugar said he was not a member of the Labor Progressive Party, but that he once belonged to a group in Montreal that studied socialism. When Kellock demanded the names of other members of the study group, Shugar asked Kellock why he was obliged to reveal names and remarked that the question did not pertain to the inquiry. Kellock's reply was blunt: "You are not the judge of that; we are the judges of that, and I have already told you that the question put to you must be answered." Halperin was even less co-operative, compelling a threat from Commissioner Taschereau: "We have the power to punish you if you do not answer."[26]

Of even greater concern, as the Winnipeg Civil Liberties Association observed months later in a newspaper article, was the disregard that the commissioners showed for the presumption of innocence: "On the basis of their inquisition the Commission published reports which had the effect of declaring each of the thirteen guilty of offences before they had been charged with any crime or had been given an open trial. Is this due process of law? Or has Magna Carta become a dead letter in our constitution?"[27] The Winnipeg Civil Liberties Association decided to back efforts in Parliament to introduce legislation designed to protect individual rights.

One such effort was an amendment to the government's Citizenship Act, which was introduced by Conservative MP Diefenbaker on May 2, 1946. The amendment was a Bill of Rights to be included in the Citizenship Act. It consisted of such rights and freedoms as freedom of religion and speech and the right to peaceable assembly. In addition, it stipulated that habeas corpus was not to be suspended except by Parliament and that no one should be required to give evidence before any tribunal or commission at any time if denied counsel or other constitutional safeguards.[28]

Diefenbaker's amendment was not the first parliamentary effort to legislate on behalf of civil liberties. That distinction went to Alistair Stewart, CCF MP for Winnipeg North, who introduced a resolution on October 10, 1945, prior to the public revelation of the Gouzenko affair but after Gouzenko's defection. Stewart's resolution was a constitutional Bill of Rights (unlike Diefenbaker's, which was merely a federal statute, a preference he showed with his own government's 1960 Bill of Rights) protecting minority rights, civil and religious liberties, freedom of speech, and freedom of assembly; establishing equal treatment before the law of all citizens irrespective of race, nationality, and religious or political beliefs; and, finally, "providing the necessary democratic powers to eliminate racial discrimination in all its forms." Stewart decided to drop his motion for a Bill of Rights in the belief that civil liberties would be discussed with the introduction of the government's Citizenship Act in the spring of 1946.[29]

The Winnipeg Civil Liberties Association supported Diefenbaker's amendment, despite its limitation as a federal statute versus a constitutional amendment, in the belief that it was better than nothing at all.[30] But after a short parliamentary debate, Diefenbaker's amendment was rejected.

While opposition politicians in Ottawa were unsuccessfully seeking greater legislative protection for human rights, members of the civil liberties movement were pondering their next moves in their efforts to see increased safeguards against arbitrary government power. In the first few months following the public disclosure of the Gouzenko revelations the reaction of the various civil liberties groups revealed how disparate and decentralized the movement was, as some groups, such as Sandwell's Civil Liberties Association, preferred the wait and see approach of the spectator, whereas the Ottawa Civil Liberties Association and especially its Winnipeg counterparts took a more proactive approach, petitioning Members of Parliament and supporting Bill of Rights legislation respectively.

Individual members of the various associations began to muse on the possibility of a national civil liberties association as a potentially more effective means of protesting civil liberties abuses and lobbying for legislation to guard against future abuses. In the April 6th edition of *Saturday Night*, Sandwell called for the creation of "some kind of a central office or clearing house for the various organizations in Canada which are devoted to the defence of civil liberties. . . . Many of their problems are entirely national in character, and a united front in regard to them is supremely desirable."[31] Lower agreed with a suggestion made by David Owen of the Winnipeg Civil Liberties Association for a dominionwide civil liberties federation, and the following month travelled to Ottawa where he met with Eric Morse (of the Ottawa Civil Liberties Association), along with Sandwell, Diefenbaker, and Senator Arthur Roebuck, who had been attorney general of Ontario in the government of Mitchell Hepburn. At the meeting Roebuck suggested that a committee for a Bill of Rights be formed to "feed" information to Diefenbaker to improve his chances of success. Sandwell was sceptical of the idea, believing that a Bill of Rights was unenforceable. Lower argued that an official declaration was better than nothing.

Before the meeting concluded, Lower offered to correspond with various key people across the country to see "whether we could not get something going" on a campaign for a Bill of Rights—an offer he acted upon shortly after his departure from Ottawa.[32]

A conference was finally arranged for the various civil liberties organizations to meet in Ottawa on December 28 and 29, 1946. The groups attending the conference included Sandwell's Toronto Civil Liberties Association (formerly the Civil Liberties Association), the Civil Rights Union (formerly the Emergency Committee for Civil Rights), the Ottawa Civil Liberties Association, and the Montreal Civil Liberties Association.[33]

The minutes of the Ottawa conference reveal a rancorous affair that exposed the deep divisions within the movement. The first issue of contention was the form and structure that a potential national association might take. Participants put forward four types of organizations for discussion: (a) no formal organization, but improved collaboration and liaison between existing civil liberties associations; (b) a national association made up of existing associations only; (c) a national association along the lines of the National Council for Civil Liberties in London, to be set up at a national conference to which all sorts of organizations would be invited, including churches, trade unions, and youth groups; and (d) a national body not based at all on the existing local associations but consisting simply of a group of about seventy-five representative members.[34] The Communist Civil Rights Union (CRU), which fought for the economic rights of labour as well as broadly based human rights, not surprisingly pushed for a Canadian equivalent of the National Council for Civil Liberties in London, which allowed for the involvement of trade unions. The minutes noted that C.S. Jackson, of the Civil Rights Union, "urged the need of a broad mass basis for civil liberties action." Frank Scott disagreed, arguing that mass pressure might be left to local associations. Others pointed out that mass pressure "would require local mass associations which did not exist and would not likely develop in some of the main cities."[35]

In offering his opinion on the form a national association should take, J.P. Erichsen-Brown of the Ottawa Civil Liberties Association raised the most divisive and controversial issue that plagued the civil liberties movement throughout the early years of the Cold War: could a communist be a legitimate civil libertarian? In rejecting Jackson's call for a national conference that would invite all organizations to participate, the minutes show Erichsen-Brown taking dead aim at the communist-dominated Civil Rights Union: "Mr. Erichsen-Brown said he objected to the whole idea of a national conference, on the ground that many people would refuse to take part in anything which had the appearance of having many Communists in it. He went on to say that Communists could not put civil liberties or democracy first and that therefore there was no place for them in a national civil liberties organization."[36] Others in the movement who considered themselves social democrats or liberals shared some degree of aversion towards communists, but for different reasons. Some, such as Eggleston, were philosophically troubled by communism and found it difficult to work with or defend those whose philosophy was the antithesis of individual liberty.

For other civil libertarians, the issue of associating with or defending communists was more complex than merely a question of philosophical difference. Lower, for example, was acutely aware of the stigma attached to communists in public opinion. While he was no admirer of communism, Lower was not a rabid anti-communist, as evidenced by his correspondence with members of the CRU. In the historian's opinion, caution was the watchword for dealing with communists, lest the integrity of the larger civil liberties movement suffer from a tainted association. Lower elaborated on his strategy of caution after attending a meeting of the CRU and one of their social functions afterward at a location for which the irony was not lost on him:

> It was rather amusing to see good communists drinking a good deal of very bourgeois whiskey afterward in a big house in Rosedale. There is no doubt, I am afraid, that the Emergency Committee contains a good many comrades. . . . I

myself think that there is room for a good deal of tactical manoeuvring in such situations. It is best to keep completely clear of them. But as second best, it may pay to work with one of their "front" organizations until just before the point at which it is due to be "ticketed." Once the label is put on an organization, its usefulness is ended, insofar as political circles, and the general public too, are concerned.[37]

Lower was accurate in his reading of both public opinion and the political circles. From the Gouzenko affair onward, public opinion hardened towards communism in general and communists in particular, especially as the West's relations with the Soviet Union steadily deteriorated.[38]

With regard to communism and the civil liberties movement, the RCMP, according to writers Reg Whitaker and Gary Marcuse, was "especially concerned" about communist infiltration of civil liberties associations. "This had the perverse effect of dismissing all civil-liberties arguments as Communist-inspired: like a rotten apple, even one Red could spoil an entire barrel."[39] It would be absurd to suggest that King regarded Sandwell, Scott, and Lower as communists, but those associated with the civil liberties movement who were tagged as communists could only have been a problem for the overall movement. For example, King falsely regarded A.R. Mosher, the president of the Canadian Congress of Labour and member of the Ottawa Civil Liberties Association, as a communist whose labour organization was "communist-inspired."[40] Knowing that it had public opinion on its side during the Gouzenko affair, the government found it easy to dismiss civil libertarians as communists or soft on communism. As a result, it was free to use extraordinary powers without fear of censure.[41]

Scott's correspondence reveals that the Ottawa conference was a bitter and disappointing experience for most if not all of those who attended. Early in the new year Scott wrote to Erichsen-Brown informing him that the Montreal association had discussed the idea of a national council but had no clear ideas as to what type of council should be established. However, "All were agreed that care must be taken to avoid control by any one group [i.e. Communists]."[42] Erichsen-Brown was in agreement with Scott, but less diplomatic in his response: "I am absolutely convinced that no civil liberty association can be organized in Canada to perform a really useful function and have any long term of life unless it has a selected membership with strong constitutional guards against communist infiltration. If at any time there was any possibility of organizing a national civil liberties union in Canada on a basis similar to that of the American Civil Liberties Union, I would be glad to participate therein."[43]

Erichsen-Brown's reference to the American Civil Liberties Union (ACLU) was telling, because the ACLU had experienced a similar strife over communist membership within its ranks. To control the influence of communists within its ranks the ACLU passed a resolution in 1940 excluding communists from its governing council. As the Cold War progressed in the late 1940s and throughout the 1950s, the ACLU took an increasingly hard line against communism.[44] Like Erichsen-Brown, Scott regarded the ACLU as a model for the Canadian civil liberties movement to emulate, and thus wrote to Roger Baldwin, the ACLU's director, to ask for advice: "I wonder if you could tell me briefly how and why it was that you came to exclude

Communist members from your Council in 1940. . . . As we are now trying to form a National Council out of our local associations, this piece of history becomes rather relevant."[45]

Scott's own anti-communism strengthened as the Cold War progressed. On observing the declining interest of the CRU in a national civil liberties organization following the rancorous Ottawa conference, Scott remarked to M.H. Fyfe, an Ottawa lawyer and member of the Ottawa Civil Liberties Association: "I imagine the reason why the Toronto Civil Rights Union is not pushing for a national council is that they recognize the sad fact that they will not be able to control it. If I am right, we shall have an opportunity to plan the organization ourselves without bickering or suspicion of motives."[46] A week later Scott was even more direct in a letter to his CCF colleague Donald MacDonald, the CCF's national treasurer: "It would be a great relief all round if the Toronto C.R.U. stays out of the picture. . . . I think we should exclude them altogether."[47] Scott's strong anti-communism was not surprising given that, as the CCF national chairman, he was at the centre of the party's efforts to disassociate itself from communists (particularly within the labour movement, the CCF's allies) to avoid being tagged a pro-communist party—tantamount to certain political extinction as the Cold War heightened. Ironically, in their efforts to exclude communists, Frank Scott and other social democrats were compromising the notion of the universality of civil liberties.

The various civil liberties associations met again in Ottawa on April 26 and 27, 1947. Absent from the spring meeting was Erichsen-Brown. The fervent anticommunist had been defeated in his re-election bid for the presidency of the Ottawa Civil Liberties Association at the group's annual meeting earlier in the winter of 1947.[48] The second Ottawa meeting proved again to be divisive, as the CRU found itself in conflict with the other associations over the issue of membership in a proposed national association. All of the associations, except the CRU, wanted to restrict membership to "general" civil liberties associations that concerned themselves with civil liberties in a broad sense. The CRU wanted membership to be open to all civil liberties organizations whether they were concerned with civil liberties in general or with a specific civil liberty, which would include groups such as the Japanese Co-operative Committee or the Quebec or Ontario Committee for the Defence of Trade Union Rights.[49]

The minutes reveal that the two positions could not be reconciled on the issue of membership, and thus the second Ottawa meeting ended with the divisions still intact. The papers of Frank Park (at the time a director of the pro-communist National Council for Canadian-Soviet friendship and managing editor of *National Affairs Monthly*), who attended both Ottawa meetings, show that only a couple of weeks after the second Ottawa meeting a national association called the Canadian Civil Liberties Council (CCLC) was created. According to the CCLC constitution, the purpose of the council was:

> (1) To defend, clarify, and guarantee by statutes those rights and liberties which are already sanctioned by justice, and by the traditions and laws of our country, and which are imposed upon us by the Charter of the United Nations

(2) To extend civil liberties by working for the recognition and establishment of such rights as are not now adequately defined or protected and such as the changing conditions of society may demand

(3) To maintain civil liberties for all by defending and extending the rights of those racial, cultural, religious, political or labour groups which, because they are minorities or for other reasons, have been, or are likely to be, deprived of them.[50]

The third purpose of the CCLC's constitution, which recognized civil liberties for specific groups of people, suggests a victory for the CRU. Perhaps the weary participants rationalized that some kind of agreement was better than nothing at all. However, the structure of the new national organization was so loosely defined as to render the new council a paper organization only with virtually no authority over the local organizations. As Frank Park observed, "I think we all agree that the new organization will be a coordinating body, a council, and that there will be no merging of the local organizations into a larger concept and that they will all retain full freedom to act by themselves."[51] In other words, the status quo of a divided, decentralized civil liberties movement prevailed.

While the various civil liberties associations were corresponding, meeting, and bickering over the winter and spring of 1947, a new development was taking place in Parliament. The government's agenda for the new session, which opened on January 30, 1947, included a promise to examine the issue of human rights. The throne speech declared: "My ministers are following with interest the activities of the United Nations with regard to the question of human rights and fundamental freedoms, and the manner in which those obligations accepted by all members of the United Nations may best be implemented. It is the intention of the government to recommend the appointment of a select committee of members of both houses to consider and report upon these matters."[52]

Although the announcement of the government's intention to create such a committee might have been a source of inspiration for advocates of a Bill of Rights, the King government never had any intention of altering the status quo with respect to civil liberties. The embarrassment of press criticism during the Gouzenko affair and the pressure from civil liberties groups and opposition MPs for civil liberties safeguards may have influenced to a certain degree the government's speech from the throne, but without question, the main reason the government decided to establish a joint parliamentary committee to look into human rights was because the government, as a signatory to the United Nations Charter of Human Rights, had an obligation to do so.[53] The government announced the creation of the joint parliamentary committee on human rights in the House of Commons on May 16, 1947, with Justice Minister J.L. Illsley to serve as the committee's chair.

The joint parliamentary committee, which met over the course of 1947–48 and reported in 1948, also revealed the divisions within the civil liberties movement. No submission came from the Canadian Civil Liberties Council, but, rather, only from separate civil liberties organizations (which mirrored how the movement protested against the civil liberties abuses during the Gouzenko affair). The CRU's submission, "Brief Submitted by the Civil Rights Union of Toronto, Showing the Need for a Bill of Rights in Canada," revealed the organization's preference for "particular" civil liberties: "It is long past time that the right to organize in a union of the workers' choice, under their freely elected officers, to bargain collectively, to strike and picket to protect jobs, should be given expression and guaranteed in a Bill of Rights."[54]

Another, and very different, submission came from the Committee for a Bill of Rights, whose two hundred signatures included those of Scott, Sandwell, Lower, and Stewart. The committee argued that the freedoms of speech, of the press and radio, of peaceable assembly, of lawful association, and religion "are all essential to the effective operation of democracy." The committee therefore urged that the Parliament of Canada "should by resolution seek an amendment to the B.N.A. Act, restraining the Parliament of Canada and provincial Legislatures from making or enforcing any laws abrogating the aforementioned liberties." As if to directly counter the CRU, the committee rejected an approach that called for specific liberties such as workers' rights: "We have excluded from our Bill of Rights references to 'economic' rights and freedoms . . . because the establishment of such rights is the function of detailed legislation and economic policy within the scope of Parliament and the provincial legislatures and indeed of international action. It is an illusion to suppose that the 'right of employment' or 'freedom from want' can be secured by the type of constitutional declaration which is envisioned in a Bill of Rights."[55]

The joint parliamentary committee's report, released on June 25, 1948, confirmed the government's desire to maintain the status quo with regard to civil liberties:

> Your Committee wishes to state its belief that Canadians enjoy a large measure of civil rights and liberties. . . . Respect for and observance of these rights and freedoms depends in the last analysis upon the convictions, character and spirit of the people. . . . There is need for more public discussion before the task of defining the rights and freedoms to be safeguarded is undertaken . . . the ultimate and effective safeguard of those rights and freedoms lies in the people themselves, and in a resolute and effective public opinion.[56]

During the Gouzenko affair, when the King government exercised enormous arbitrary powers that violated the civil liberties of the espionage suspects, a strong civil liberties movement was essential to challenge the belief that the needs of the national security state outweighed the need to respect individual rights and liberties in a democratic society. Unfortunately, the civil liberties movement remained as divided, decentralized, and incoherent as a movement two years after the Gouzenko affair as it did at the beginning of the revelations. Civil libertarians themselves allowed the Cold War tensions of growing societal anti-communism to influence their thinking as to who was a legitimate civil libertarian. The effect was to poison the debates among the associations and undermine their own hopes for a united national movement. As a result, civil libertarians spent as much or more time confronting each other as they did effectively challenging the government's Cold War civil liberties abuses.

Could the outcome have been any different for the movement, or for the state? Given the hostile environment in which civil libertarians found themselves during and after the Gouzenko affair, it is difficult to imagine anything but a divided movement. Moderate liberal and social-democratic civil libertarians such as Eggleston and Scott were determined to minimize the influence of the far left within the movement in order, as they saw it, to preserve the legitimacy of the movement. There is not as much evidence on what those on the far left of the movement thought of the position of their liberal and social-democratic counterparts, but the existing evidence suggests that they believed the principles of the civil liberties movement—to defend the civil liberties of all persons and all causes regardless of their unpopularity—were betrayed by the uncompromising anti-communism of individuals such as Sandwell, Erichsen-Brown, and Scott.

For its part, the government was not seriously challenged by a weak civil liberties movement that it chose to dismiss as being, at best, soft on communism and, at worst, dominated by communists from within. The government was greatly assisted in implementing its harsh measures against the Gouzenko espionage suspects by a favourable public opinion whipped up by the hysteria of the Gouzenko affair specifically and the early years of the Cold War in general. The government itself was also not immune to the hysteria, as rumours and suspicions bordering on paranoia were rampant as to who might or might not be a Soviet agent. David Croll, a Liberal MP at the time, recalled how especially cautious the ministers and members were around the civil service as they had no idea if there were five, fifty, or five hundred agents within.[57] The traditionally cautious Mackenzie King was no exception. Indeed, he became so paranoid that he became suspicious not only of some civil servants but also of his valet and of O.D. Skelton, a leading civil servant—who had been dead for five years.[58] Suspicion, fear, anti-communism, and tremendous state powers combined to overwhelm individual rights. Civil libertarians were well aware of the difficulties they faced without public opinion on their side, but their difficulties were exacerbated by their own internal divisions. Meanwhile, the various people who were the targets of the state's security campaigns continued for years to face the sweeping scope of the national security state's powers.

## Notes

Thanks to Ross Lambertson, whose valuable references enhanced my work. This chapter is dedicated to my parents, Jean Clarke and the late Cyril Clarke.

1.  The literature on McCarthyism and its origins is substantial. See, for example, David Caute, *The Great Fear: The Anti-Communist Purge under Truman and Eisenhower* (New York: Simon and Schuster, 1978); Richard M. Freeland, *The Truman Doctrine and the Origins of McCarthyism* (New York: Knopf, 1985); Robert Griffith, *The Politics of Fear: Joseph R. McCarthy and the Senate* (Lexington: University of Kentucky Press, 1970); Robert Griffith and Athan Theoharis, eds., *The Specter: Original Essays on the Cold War Origins of McCarthyism* (New York: New Viewpoints, 1974); and Stanley I. Kutler, *The American Inquisition: Justice and Injustice in the Cold War* (New York: Hill and Wang, 1982).
2.  J. Richard Wagner and Daniel J. O'Neal, "The Gouzenko Affair and the Civility Syndrome," *The American Review of Canadian Studies* 3,1 (Spring 1978); see also Lawrence R. Aronsen, "'Peace, Order and Good Government' during the Cold War: The Origins and Organization of Canada's Internal Security Program," *Intelligence and*

*National Security* 1,3 (September 1986). For a much different perspective, see Reg Whitaker and Gary Marcuse, *Cold War Canada: The Making of a National Insecurity State, 1945–1957* (Toronto: University of Toronto Press, 1994); and Len Scher, *The Un-Canadians: Stories of the Blacklist Era* (Toronto: Lester Publishing, 1992).

3.  Whitaker and Marcuse, *Cold War Canada*, p.58.

4.  The most comprehensive account of the Gouzenko affair appears in Whitaker and Marcuse, *Cold War Canada*. For a sympathetic interpretation of the King government's actions, see J.L. Granatstein, *A Man of Influence: Norman A. Robertson and Canadian Statecraft 1929–1968* (Ottawa: Deneau, 1981).

5.  Quoted in Robert Bothwell and J.L. Granatstein, eds., *The Gouzenko Transcripts* (Ottawa: Deneau 1982), p.12. The decision to appoint the Royal Commission to Investigate the Facts Relating to and Circumstances Surrounding the Communication by Public Officials and Others in Positions of Trust of Secret and Confidential Information to Agents of a Foreign Power was approved by the cabinet on Feb. 5, 1946; National Archives of Canada (NAC), Privy Council Office (PCO), vol. 419, Feb. 5, 1946, C294103.

6.  Under section 1 of P.C. 6444, the minister of justice could issue an order for the interrogation or detainment of an individual "if satisfied that with a view to preventing any particular person from communicating secret and confidential information to an agent of a Foreign Power or otherwise acting in any manner prejudicial to the public safety or the safety of the State." Section 2 stipulated, "Any person shall, while detained . . . under this Order, be deemed to be in legal custody." As a result, such rights as habeas corpus and access to legal counsel could be superseded by this order-in-council. NAC, Rt. Hon. J.G. Diefenbaker Papers, vol. 82, reel M-7450, undated, 1946–47, 65413.

7.  Whitaker and Marcuse, *Cold War Canada*, pp.28–29.

8.  Gordon Lunan, *The Making of a Spy: A Political Odyssey* (Toronto: Robert Davies Publishing, 1995), p.161; Whitaker and Marcuse, *Cold War Canada*, p.64; Merrily Weisbord, *The Strangest Dream: Canadian Communists, the Spy Trials, and the Cold War* (Toronto: Lester and Orpen Dennys, 1983), pp.147–48; John Sawatsky, *Gouzenko: The Untold Story* (Toronto: Macmillan of Canada, 1984), p.79.

9.  NAC, Privy Council Office Records (PCO), Cabinet Conclusions, RG 2, A5a, vol. 2637, Reel T2364, 992–3, Feb. 14, 1946; Granatstein, *Man of Influence*, pp.178–79.

10. Aronsen, "'Peace, Order and Good Government,'" pp.359, 373; Reginald Whitaker, "Origins of the Canadian Government's Internal Security System, 1946–1952," *Canadian Historical Review* 65,2 (June 1984), pp.155–56.

11. Whitaker, "Origins of the Canadian Government's Internal Security System," pp.157–58; Granatstein, *Man of Influence*, pp.181–82, 272–76.

12. U.S. columnist Drew Pearson, for example, reported from Washington that the Canadian authorities had taken in a Soviet agent who then "broke down under questioning and revealed the names of 1700 agents operating in the U.S. and Canada." Quoted in Whitaker and Marcuse, *Cold War Canada*, p.29.

13. *The Toronto Daily Star*, Feb. 26, 1946.

14. *The Gazette* (Montreal), Feb. 25, 1946.

15. "To Members of the Civil Liberties Association, Past and Present," undated, 1946, NAC, Frank and Libby Park Papers, MG 31 K9, vol. 8, file 150.

16. *Saturday Night*, March 30, 1946; emphasis in original.

17. Reg Whitaker, "Official Repression of Communism during World War II," *Labour/Le Travail* 17 (Spring 1986), p.140.

18. "Resolution of Protest by the Ottawa Civil Liberties Association," July 8, 1946, NAC, Eggleston Papers, vol. 14, file 16.

19. Margaret Spaulding [Chair of the ECCR] to King, June 28, 1946, NAC, W.L.M. King Papers, Primary Correspondence Series, MG 26 J1, vol. 416, Reel C9179, 377939-42.

20. Lower to Blair Fraser, March 9, 1946, Queen's University Archives (QUA), A.R.M. Lower Papers, box 46, file C21. In his radio commentary, Fraser criticized the government's national security argument as a justification for the extraordinary measures

taken against the suspects, saying: "We've heard this before. We heard it used to justify the procedure in the Soviet 'purge' trials of 1937. We even heard it used to defend the inquiry into the Reichstag fire." CBC broadcast script, March 2, 1946, QUA, Lower Papers, box 46, file C21.

21. Canada, *House of Commons Debates*, March 15, 1946, p.7, March 21, 1946, p.50.

22. W.L.M. King, Diary, Feb. 27, 1946, March 12, 1946, NAC, W.L.M. King Papers.

23. When one of the suspects, Dr. David Shugar, refused to co-operate with the commission, the commissioners aggressively reminded him that he could be punished but never specified that the punishment was only a fine. See Bothwell and Granatstein, *Gouzenko Transcripts*, p.273.

24. M.H. Fyfe, "Some Legal Aspects of the Report of the Royal Commission on Espionage," *The Canadian Bar Review* 24 (November 1946), p.779. Fyfe was an Ottawa lawyer and executive member of the Ottawa Civil Liberties Association. See also Weisbord, *Strangest Dream*, p.149; Whitaker and Marcuse, *Cold War Canada*, p.65.

25. Lunan, *Making of a Spy*, p.182.

26. Bothwell and Granatstein, *Gouzenko Transcripts*, pp.270–74, 312–13.

27. *The Winnipeg Free Press*, June 15, 1946. The commission's final report in June 1946 dismissed the acquittals of several of the accused, declaring that some of the suspects "gave all [the information] they had [to the Soviets] or all they could get . . . some were in positions where they would, in the future, have been able to give more and they would undoubtedly have done so." Royal Commission to Investigate the Facts, *Final Report*, p.620; cited in Whitaker and Marcuse, *Cold War Canada*, p.75.

28. Canada, *House of Commons Debates*, May 2, 1946.

29. Ibid., Oct. 10, 1945, p.900.

30. In a letter to David Owen, a colleague in the WCLA, Lower reasoned, "B[ill]s. of R[ights]. can hardly be mandatory: they are at best exhortations and statements of first principles. One cannot enforce the sermon on the Mount in a court of law, but it has not been without its influence. We might wait forever for a revision of the B.N.A. act along these lines, so lets take what we can get, if and when we can get it." Lower to David Owen, June 17, 1946, QUA, Lower Papers, box 46, file C21.

31. *Saturday Night*, April 6, 1946.

32. Lower to David Owen, June 17, 1946, QUA, Lower Papers, box 46, file C21. Lower also corresponded with officials from the communist-dominated Emergency Committee for Civil Rights (ECCR). The acting secretary of the ECCR recommended that the Winnipeg association meet with C.B. Macpherson (an executive member of the ECCR) during a stopover Macpherson was making in Winnipeg. Lower promoted Diefenbaker's Bill of Rights and suggested, "The strategic thing just now is for groups like ours to get behind him [Diefenbaker]." D. Henderson to Lower, July 20, 1946, Lower to D. Henderson, July 24, 1946, QUA, Lower Papers, box 46, file C21.

33. The Montreal association existed for a short period during the war but disbanded because it "was ruined by Communist infiltration and obstruction." Frank Scott to Lower, April 3, 1946, QUA, Lower Papers, vol. 46, file C21. The association was reconstituted in June 1946. Scott to Roger Baldwin (Director, American Civil Liberties Union), June 12, 1946, NAC, F.R. Scott Papers, vol. 10, file "Civil Liberties, Montreal Association 1945–1950," Reel H-1222.

34. Minutes of Exploratory Conference between the Montreal, Ottawa and Toronto Civil Liberties Associations and The Civil Rights Union (formerly The Emergency Committee for Civil Rights), Ottawa, December 28, 29, 1946, NAC, Frank Park Papers, MG 31 K9, vol. 9, file 156, "Canadian Civil Liberties Council, 1946–1947."

35. Ibid.

36. Ibid.

37. Lower to David Owens, Feb. 23, 1947, QUA, Lower Papers, vol. 2, file A28.

38. A public opinion poll taken on May 16, 1946, showed that 61 per cent of Canadians approved of the government's handling of the Gouzenko suspects, while only 16 per cent disapproved. A poll taken in August 1947 found 67 per cent thought communism

to be a serious threat to Canada's form of government, while 68 per cent approved the outlawing of organizations that were "largely communistic" in April 1949. Canadian Institute of Public Opinion (Gallup) polls cited in Whitaker and Marcuse, *Cold War Canada*, p.283. Whitaker and Marcuse point out that a poll was not conducted to see if the same opinions held after nearly half of the suspects were acquitted in the courts. Whitaker and Marcuse, *Cold War Canada*, pp. 72, 282.

39. Whitaker and Marcuse, *Cold War Canada*, p.212.

40. George Spence (Director of Rehabilitation, Regina, Sask., Dept. of Agriculture) to King, April 6, 1946, and King to Spence, April 8, 1946, NAC, W.L.M. King Papers, MG 26 J1, vol. 416, Reel C-9179, 377952, 377953.

41. Lower summed up the dilemma for the civil liberties movement when he wrote to a fellow civil libertarian a few months after the arrest of the Gouzenko suspects that he saw "no chance whatsoever of making any serious direct attack on [the] government's line of conduct: it knows it has the overwhelming mass of public opinion with it, in whatever it does to the 'spies,' and is not likely to agree to wear sackcloth and ashes because a few more or less eccentric people do not accept its methods." Lower to D. Henderson, July 24, 1946, QUA, Lower Papers, box 46, file C21.

42. Scott to J.P. Erichsen-Brown, Jan. 13, 1947, NAC, Scott Papers, MG 30, D211, vol. 10, file "Civil Liberties, National Council 1946–1951," Reel H-1222.

43. J.P. Erichsen-Brown to Scott, Feb. 7, 1947, NAC, Scott Papers, MG 30, D211, vol. 10, file "Civil Liberties, National Council 1946–1951," Reel H-1222.

44. William A. Donohue, *The Politics of the American Civil Liberties Union* (Oxford: Transaction Books, 1985), pp.162–75.

45. Scott to Roger Baldwin, Jan. 13, 1947, NAC, Scott Papers, MG 30, D211, vol. 10, file "Civil Liberties, National Council 1946–1951," Reel H-1222.

46. Scott to M.H. Fyfe, Feb. 14, 1947, NAC, Scott Papers, MG 30, D211, vol. 10, file "Civil Liberties, National Council 1946–1951," Reel H-1222. Scott learned of the CRU's declining interest in a national association from Fyfe in a letter only days previously in which Fyfe observed that "on the projected national Civil Liberties Association . . . so far neither Toronto body seems to have done anything." Fyfe to Scott, Feb. 11, 1947, NAC, Scott Papers, MG 30, D211, vol. 10, file "Civil Liberties, National Council 1946–1951," Reel H-1222.

47. Scott to Donald MacDonald, Feb. 21, 1947, NAC, Scott Papers, MG 30, D211, vol. 10, file "Civil Liberties, National Council 1946–1951," Reel H-1222.

48. A bitter Erichsen-Brown blamed his failed re-election bid on communist infiltration of the association: "The Commies turned out all their cohorts in town. . . . They were out to get me and had been for some time." J.P. Erichsen-Brown to Scott, Feb. 7, 1947, NAC, Scott Papers, vol. 10, Reel H-1222, file "Civil Liberties, Montreal Association 1945–1950."

49. *Memorandum on Contentious Points in Draft Constitution*, undated [April 26, 27, 1947], NAC, Frank Park Papers, MG 31 K9, vol. 9, file 156, "Canadian Civil Liberties Council, 1946–1947."

50. *Canadian Civil Liberties Council Constitution*, Ottawa, May 15, 1947, NAC, Frank Park Papers, MG 31 K9, vol. 9, file 156, "Canadian Civil Liberties Council, 1946–1947."

51. Ibid.; and *Re: Draft National Constitution*, July 24, 1947.

52. Canada, *House of Commons Debates*, Jan. 30, 1947.

53. Interview with Hon. J.W. Pickersgill, Ottawa, March 22, 1991.

54. "Brief Submitted by the Civil Rights Union of Toronto, Showing the Need for a Bill of Rights in Canada," June 6, 1948, NAC, RG 14 ACC 87-88/146, Records of The Special Joint Committee on Human Rights and Fundamental Freedoms, vol. 51, file 1947–1948 "Human Rights."

55. "Submission of Committee for a Bill of Rights in Support of Statement for a Bill of Rights to the Special Joint Committee of the Senate and the House of Commons on Human Rights and Fundamental Freedoms," June 4, 1948, NAC, Records of The Special Joint Committee on Human Rights and Fundamental Freedoms.

56. *Second and Final Report*, June 25, 1948, NAC, Records of The Special Joint Committee on Human Rights and Fundamental Freedoms.
57. Interview with Senator David Croll, Dec. 10, 1990.
58. Granatstein, *Man of Influence*, p.178.

thirteen ✴ ✴ ✴

# Interrogating Security: A Personal Memoir of the Cold War

With the end of the Cold War, scholars have begun to assess the character and nature of the national security state that emerged shortly before, during, and after the Second World War. This task resonates on several levels, especially given the opening of the Soviet archives and new debates that now rage about the seriousness of the communist threat to North America.[1] As historians work on FBI, CIA, KGB, and other U.S. and Soviet security files and records and assess the role of elite players who moulded security policies, I choose here to interrogate "security" on a more personal level—seeking to integrate some of my early life experiences as a native San Franciscan (but, since 1986, card-carrying Canadian) with my research interest in security questions since the 1930s.[2]

Several pitfalls imperil this quest. One is the subjective nature of the work, which may strike readers as self-indulgence rather than history.[3] Yet subjectivity in this case accomplishes two things. First, it recognizes that the national security state that emerged as a permanent fixture on the U.S. scene after 1947 sought to engage all Americans in its fight against communism. In a multitude of ways the state focused upon children as much as it did on adults. Few scholars have explored this aspect of security culture, while, conversely, children have found scant voice in telling their stories of the Cold War.[4] Here the child in the man acquires voice. Many men have had trouble talking about, let alone reflecting upon, their fears, anxieties, and demons.[5] But these stories are important—especially as retorts to official government, corporation, and bureaucratic "truths" that often mask, marginalize, and dismiss other narratives and their authors.[6]

The word "security" suggests many things, and it is the intersection of these meanings that counts here—especially tensions between the private and the public spheres, between the body and the state, and between early personal experiences and subsequent research and writing interests.[7] For my life accompanies chronologically the emergence of "security" as a central value of the United States and Canada of World War II and the Cold War.

Canada and the United States differ significantly in their respective historical and institutional inheritances on security definitions and questions, but outcomes in the two countries since the late 1930s have been remarkably similar. In several cases on both domestic and international fronts the two countries have marched in security lockstep—on fronts, one must note, whose distinctions blurred significantly after 1941. Whether the decisions by Washington and Ottawa to relocate their Japanese minorities in 1941 from the west coast to interior regions; the Gouzenko affair, in which a Canadian tale (no *sic*) wagged an American security elephant (and served as prime catalyst in what became known as the McCarthy era), or Ottawa's quiet complicity in the United States' ill-advised errand into the jungles of Southeast Asia in the 1960s, the two countries found much in common on security matters. When the U.S. branch-plant economy in Canada gained strength after World War II, the political economy of security was part of the transformation. Canadian leaders who questioned U.S. leadership, as John Diefenbaker did John F. Kennedy, and Lester Pearson did Lyndon B. Johnson, did not enhance themselves politically with the dominant power.[8]

In the area of national security, except for a brief hiatus of demobilizing "normalcy" in late 1945 and 1946, the Second World War lingered on for the United States. Indeed, paraphrasing Carl von Clausewitz, the final U.S. instalment of the Soviet-American Cold War that began in 1947 was in its security structures—however new their institutional expression—a continuation of the Second War (joined with traditional nativist and anti-communist themes) by other means. The terms "red fascism" and "brown bolshevism," popular in the security lexicon in the late 1940s and early 1950s, suggested how Americans casually and effectively transformed Nazis into communists. But where fascists were notable in their nationalistic posturing, communists operated through stealth, espionage, and "fifth columns."[9] Communists were doubly dangerous, because they were invisible in their day-to-day operations. Alien ideas and ideology, often analogized in such biomedical terms as "viruses" and "bacteria," now became the focal point of U.S. security concerns.[10]

My recollection of the war era is meagre; I was not politically active let alone aware during my first four years of life. Nonetheless, I recall the sacrifices our family made during the war in the name of domestic security, a paradigm given meaning by the phrase "unconditional surrender," the politico-military policy adopted by the Allies against Hitler, Mussolini, and the Japanese militarists. These sacrifices were necessary as we all pulled together to defeat the Axis powers. In San Francisco, my father (classified "4F" because he was aurally challenged—a trait he passed on to me) led local civil defence efforts in the evening; he traversed the area around our Parkside flat at night making certain that no light emanated from windows to give Japanese bombers a target. My mother, who did not say much about the war, was never an avowed hawk.[11] I remember the air raid sirens and accompanying fear; I recall being told that we were eating a certain dinner (cauliflower and broccoli) because meat and wheat were in short supply; and I recall the joy all of us felt when we learned that we had dropped the atomic bomb on Hiroshima and Nagasaki, and the war was over.[12] Here was the ultimate weapon, the guarantor of future security, indeed, the harbinger of what Time-Life publisher Henry Luce deemed the coming "American Century." But that sense of hegemony endured a scant five years. By 1950 we came face-to-face with possible annihilation by Russian nuclear bombs. What had served the Republic as "the winning weapon" in

World War II, and what promised to guarantee U.S. world leadership, now became a source of anguish.[13]

In those years national security concerns permeated North American society and culture, all the way to local levels of life. The ambience of the early 1950s, dominated by the overarching fear of communism and the desire to eradicate that evil, featured the full range of security-bureaucratic apparati. Enough demons (all communist) lurked within shadows and beneath beds to make Hollywood wealthy and Halloween redundant.[14] Americans and Canadians remained unaware of much that went on in those venues of power: human radiation experiments on unsuspecting medical guinea pigs in the United States, for example, and LSD and other mind-altering research on patients at McGill University and, later, the Kingston Prison for Women.[15] The first decade of the Cold War, as well, saw the triumph of the psychiatric establishment as the signifier of "normality," along with the prominence of consensus history, pluralism, and the notion that elites would manage the crisis. These latter assumptions emerged symbolically in a popular TV show, *Father Knows Best*. All of this reached to the San Francisco peninsula, where I resided.

My barely upper-middle class family included a Hoover-Republican, devout Catholic, and (it followed) semi-McCarthyite father; an agnostic, liberal Republican mother, who followed politics avidly, as she did "new look" fashions.[16] It included as well my mother's big brother, the ubiquitous Uncle Bob, whose front yard boasted a statue of Paul Revere and who at times in his patriotic fervour approached George Orwell's elder sibling in his interest in youthful political views. Uncle Bob resided just around the corner. My younger brother and I were both apolitical neophytes but potential anti-communist acolytes among Republican troglodytes.

The early 1950s were noteworthy in security terms on several levels. The Bomb was never far removed from consciousness, and Joseph McCarthy, the junior senator from Wisconsin, made a career (and then lost it) of ferreting communists from high places. The loyalty oaths at the University of California and other institutions created professors who either toed the dotted line signifying that they had never belonged to the Communist Party and were not engaged in attempting to overthrow the government, or found it necessary to seek other employment.

I remember well school recess in seventh grade (1954), when we students played a game called "Point of Order," patterned after Senator McCarthy's famed mantra. "Point of order, point of order, point of order, Mr. Chairman!" we would shout. Then we gleefully pointed out the transgressor of the day and, à la Arthur Miller and *The Crucible*, ordered that person's penalty of atonement. I recall my own visits to a psychiatrist during that period. My mother had noted a little too much introspection, which later became clearly identified as depression, and I remember how often the psychiatrist, Dr. Alec Skolnick, asked me about world affairs—the Russians, the Bomb, communists, and the like. Was I frightened? "We all are," he assured me.[17]

One reason for my anxiety was an article in 1954 in *The Saturday Evening Post* detailing a terrible accident at Los Alamos, New Mexico, in May 1946.[18] There, during an experiment that went awry, a young scientist, Louis Slotin, prevented a nuclear reaction at the cost of a lingering death over several terrible days. This article proved at once fascinating and horrifying. It raised serious questions even in the mind of a prepubertal adolescent about the radioactive byproducts of nuclear fission, at the same time as experts in Washington and elsewhere were reassuring us that we had little to fear. Hiroshima, one air expert pointed out, had suffered immense destruction merely because of its shoddy construction. It had been a city "of flimsy, half-rotted wooden houses and rickety brick buildings."[19] Stories in my low-brow literary domain—*Reader's Digest*, *Boy's Life*, and *My Weekly Reader*—certified that we Americans, with our well-built homes and cities, could withstand any blast. U.S. science would prevail, as the authoritative radio advertisement in the late 1940s made clear, pledging (to the point of becoming another mantra), "better living through chemistry." Pentagon civil defence consultant Richard Gerstell pointed out in his inexpensive paperback *How to Survive an Atomic Bomb* (a copy of which rested upon my parents' living-room table) that atomic radiation might in heavy doses cause "burns," but the prime "danger of radioactivity" was "mental," and with appropriate prudence people could safeguard themselves.[20] Assistant Chief of Naval Operations William S. Parsons, a member of the original Manhattan Project that had developed the atomic bomb, made the same points at elite levels, warning against the "wild 'liberal' crowd" pushing citizens towards "hysteria." Americans needed to surmount their "atomic neurosis" lest they grow "vulnerable to a war of nerves that would make the Orson Welles Mercury Theatre pale by comparison."[21]

But radiation, of course, *was* invisible, as concealed from the naked eye as germs and viruses, as evanescent as the ideology that (I had come to learn) "caused" communism, as apparently ephemeral as the secrecy that enveloped so much national security business—and much in my own mundane life. We couldn't see any of these things, and they might in fact get us. A few sceptics had already raised the possibility that atomic blasts—and after 1952 we (along with the Soviets) were conducting atmospheric tests of multi-megaton thermonuclear weapons—would produce undesirable side effects that might contaminate food and water supplies. From the viewpoint of a suggestible youth, who had poured with horrified fascination over John Hersey's agonizing recounting of the horrors that occurred under the mushroom cloud, including the radiation sickness that dogged so many Japanese after the Hiroshima and Nagasaki blasts, the question became, whom to believe?[22]

This dread of atomic radiation fused easily with the fear of communism. Both were hidden adversaries, both lethal. World events between my eighth and tenth birthdays confirmed this alarming connection. When the Soviets exploded *their* bomb, when good-guy Chiang Kai-shek fell to Mao and his red hordes, when Alger Hiss of our own State Department was convicted of lying about passing secret documents to a communist agent, when Klaus Fuchs, a physicist in the United Kingdom, admitted passing atomic secrets to the Soviets, when Julius and Ethel Rosenberg and other family members were indicted and later executed for the same offence in the United States, radio newscaster Gabriel Heatter had a field day with his signature epistle introducing his nightly Mutual broadcasts: "Bad News Tonight!!" And there was bad news—lots of it.

Strengthening youthful misgivings about government assurances that all was well and that anything could be accomplished, only given sufficient effort, popular culture also fed the scary connection between the unseen realm and the grave new world of nuclear weapons. Three science-fiction films proved especially unsettling, insofar as I still had trouble distinguishing between reality and make-believe. Cursed with an overactive imagination, I alternately thrilled to, and cowered from, *The Thing* (1951), an irradiated, walking, blood-eating vegetable that did not breathe and seemed invulnerable to U.S. air force personnel defending freedom's ramparts at the North Pole; *Godzilla* (1954), a radioactive version of King Kong, equally unstoppable and far clumsier (produced, fittingly, in Japan); and—worst of all—*Them!* (1954), featuring horrendous giant ants, spawning amidst atomic tests in the New Mexico desert and subsequently—after a quick flight westward— taking up residence in the Los Angeles sewer system.

These cinematic bogeys all came to a bad end, but not before wreaking havoc sufficient to give an idea of what post-atomic chaos might approximate.[23] They also suggested what troubled commentators and civil defence leaders already suspected: the possibility that the postwar era might in fact be another prewar era. Still, within popular culture as without, the experts prevailed. In the end the good guys won, usually with the help of an avuncular scientist, a beautiful woman, and/or a unit of the U.S. military.[24] But cinematic and comic book representations generated insatiable curiosity about communists, about Russians—who, no doubt, had to be as dreadful in reality as the grotesque caricatures encountered in popular cinematic culture. Films like *I Was a Communist for the F.B.I.*, *Invasion U.S.A.*, and *The Whip Hand* all featured barely human Red villains—and my callow imagination easily linked monstrous bugs and lizards with Moscow's fiendish slave-spies.

Youthful assumptions about "the communists" led me and a school chum to skip class for an afternoon in the late fall of 1954. I had heard that a Soviet delegation from Moscow, headed by Foreign Minister V.M. Molotov, planned to visit a United Nations meeting in San Francisco. More important, they would stay about four blocks from my school, in a walled mansion, to which our class had gone the previous spring for a swim-barbecue. That class trip provided strategic foreknowledge of the layout of the grounds. A friend and I jumped a back fence at noon, five hours before the Russian delegation's scheduled arrival, and before FBI agents appeared to secure the area. There, as it grew cooler and cooler, threatening rain, we hid behind some large bushes hard against the eastern wall bordering the property. We drank our Kool-Aid (from U.S. military-issue canteens), ate our candy bars, played cards, and read comic books. But by three o'clock the food was gone, along with the thrill, and we still had two hours left to wait. Finally, though, with the security men having failed to detect our presence, a long string of black Cadillacs rolled up the driveway. And there, then—out stepped a *real communist*— there was Molotov! I had expected him to be huge—ten feet tall, with fangs, or at least a hypodermic needle sticking from his head. Instead we regarded a hunched figure who looked a bit like U.S. secretary of state John Foster Dulles. Molotov did not look well—certainly he did not walk well—and almost immediately he was in the mansion. My school chum and I exchanged glances. These were the Russians?

Incredulity about the communist challenge grew stronger for me in the early 1950s. Yet this did not deter me from linking the Cold War security macrocosm to the microcosmic concerns about questions of psychiatric health, prepubertal sexuality, and incipient masculinity. I had visited a radiologist, because I had suffered since infancy from eczema on an anatomical private. At the radiologist's, worrying a bit about what the treatment was doing to me but assured by dominant cultural cues that the atom was our friend, I submitted to several months of therapy.[25] And ultimately, with puberty (at the ripe age of sixteen) the eczema disappeared, though scars from the radiation treatments remained. And, perhaps, those scars are not merely physical.[26] I did not speak of my feelings about any of this—the radiation treatments or my anxiety—to anyone, even at home. I could not. This was my dirty little secret.

Little inventiveness is required to see how my own requirement for "secrecy" dovetailed with the Republic's. In those days, I later learned, psychiatric cases were deemed security risks. Normality, maturity, and the stiff upper lip were goals no less for a pre-teen male in San Mateo, California, than they were for Secretary of State George C. Marshall, Navy Secretary James Forrestal (who committed suicide in 1949), Vice-President Richard Nixon, and movie star John Wayne.[27]

In November 1952, after twenty years of Democratic rule in the White House, perhaps the greatest father figure in U.S. history (after George Washington, of course) won the presidency. Dwight Eisenhower, war hero extraordinaire, buried his adversary, the intellectual (and feminized by the national security state) Adlai Stevenson.[28] My parents threw a party on election eve, a victory celebration: what better way for these two and their Republican neighbours to celebrate the nation's return to sanity after twenty years of Democratic treason. In those days California parties did not feature white wine and beer. No, scotch, bourbon, and gin consti-tuted the big three—for Republicans and Democrats alike.

About one a.m., as I slept fitfully above the madding crowd, the door sud-denly burst open. It was a neighbour, breathing heavily. Instantly he was on top of me, bouncing on the bed, breathing in my ear, and whispering through whisky-breath: "We've won, Geoffrey! We've won! Now we have a real *man* in the White House!"

The need for real men to hide their problems in security state America had actually hit home in a bizarre way two years earlier. Just as the Korean War was breaking out in June 1950, I went off alone for the first time to summer camp— for two weeks at Fern Canyon Lodge in the bucolic Santa Cruz Mountains. The first night there was horrendous—no noise whatsoever, and sleeping in a tent-cabin! Perhaps that is why I neglected to close the suitcase that my mother so care-fully packed for my fortnight away from home. With all those fresh clothes, a family of mice could not resist moving in. The next morning, when I saw a furry body scurry to the nether reaches of the suitcase, I said to myself, "I don't need that." So rather than removing the mice from the suitcase, I maintained my firm upper lip and merely wore the same clothes for two weeks. When I returned home, there was something less than joy when mother opened the suitcase. She was not "Rosie the Riveter"—she was a nice upper-middle-class lady who was my mother.[29] But how could I have told anyone—a tentmate or counsellor—that I was dense enough to allow mice into my suitcase?

All mothers suffer because of their sons, and mine has suffered more than most. But I thank her for an important insight. For she illuminated my understanding of the security state universe later that same year when she first introduced to me the name of Richard Nixon—a man she detested as much as she did her father-in-law—the only two persons she ever hated in her life. In 1950 Nixon won the U.S. Senate seat in California, defeating the Democratic incumbent, Helen Gahagan Douglas, with the type of smear campaign that became his trademark. Nixon's candidacy had gone poorly until he hit on the theme of guilt by association, a motif he had used in the Hiss perjury case. In a memorable campaign speech, in which he cribbed from her own Democratic critics, who had damned her voting record as similar to that of the detested "Red," Representative Vito Marcantonio of the American Labor Party from East Harlem, he lambasted Gahagan Douglas as "the Pink Lady . . . right down to her underwear." Here was the sort of national security state linkage—between liberated women, unchained sexuality, and communism—that Elaine Tyler May analyses so well in her fascinating study of U.S. family life after World War II.[30]

At the time I did not comprehend the pink underwear metaphor, or, certainly, the banality and anality of Richard Nixon.[31] Nor did I fathom the meaning of my mother's hatred for Nixon or, given my father's staunch anti-communism, the fact that I inhabited a household divided. I merely thought, "How strange." But the linkage became clearer to me as the school year neared its close in 1952. One of the security touchstones of our academic existence in the sixth grade (as in the fourth, fifth, seventh, and eighth grades) was the air-raid drill, in which we had been tutored to take cover from impending atomic attack. As the atom had become friendly in my radiologist's office, so too had it been tamed in the classroom, through reassurances in *My Weekly Reader* and such civil defence publicity efforts as the short documentary *Duck and Cover*.

Air-raid drills occurred at North Hillsborough School every second week, usually in late morning. (Could the Russians be this stupid, I thought to myself, not to know when we were hiding?) On this particular morning we filed quickly out from our classrooms to an inexplicably open corridor, covered only by a half-roof of ubiquitous California half shells of clay pipe. We knelt, close, very close to one another—a variation on the old game, "sardines." With hormones stirring, here was the chance I had long awaited—to kneel down cheek-by-jowl with the beautiful red-haired girl named Ginger, whom I admired but who sat across the classroom and appeared totally disinterested in me.

We knelt silently, our faces too close. I did what I had wanted to do for a long time. I kissed her. She did nothing—a commotion, of course, would alert the Russian bombers to our position. But later she told our teacher, and I was summarily dispatched to the principal's office. There, dismayed, I was informed that my behaviour was reprehensible. Most important, the principal noted, I had "endangered national security." I would have the entire afternoon to think about that.

Later that year, shortly after the execution of the Rosenbergs for atomic espionage, I received another lesson on domestic containment, with its appurtenances of rumour, gossip, and especially surveillance. Red-haired Ginger (whose real name was Prudence) had moved away to New Jersey, part of the huge demographic shift that relocated so many corporate families during the late 1940s and early 1950s.[32] This time love hit full flower, as I fell for Suzi, even shorter than I (at four-foot-ten in those days), and who, scant years later, would dye her hair platinum and become a diminutive version of Brigitte Bardot. Suzi gave me my first serious kiss—and several more—one summer night while a group of neighbourhood kids, including my eight cousins, played "kick the can" on their sprawling grounds. While all the other participants decided to get serious about kicking the can, Suzi and I stole off to a large dog house, located in a grove of bushes behind the swimming pool. There we engaged in what best may be described as earnest, though very hesitant, foreplay. Suzi, of course, stood ready to "draw the line" should that need arise.[33]

It did not. Suzi's mother and my mother were best friends. And they talked. As Suzi always did too, to her mother, usually very soon after seeing me. So my mother knew everything, often before I got home, certainly no later than the morning after any innocent assignation. Here was expert surveillance of the sort, no doubt, of which the security state only dreamed.

Sex remained a mystery, for on only two occasions prior to my fourteenth year did my parents venture into this dangerous realm for my benefit. Sure, they gave me Frances Bruce Strain's *Being Born*, for Christmas, no less. I think every kid in the neighbourhood got a copy that year. *Being Born* was a colossal bore of a book—even if it did clarify the act of reproduction. But only twice did my parents attempt to unravel these mysteries. On one occasion, while our family was on vacation in Arizona in 1953, my mother interjected into a totally unrelated conversation with me, "There's nothing wrong with masturbation." Oh, I thought, wondering what the word meant. (In retrospect I give her high marks for the intervention—this was an era of sexual silence among most parents and kids.) The second occasion, later that summer, came as my father and I stood in our backyard, watching our female German shorthaired pointer, Else, do her business. "You need to know about life," he said cryptically. "Yes," I agreed. "Look at the dog," he said. I did. And that was all he said. And that was all I did. No wonder Indiana entomologist Alfred Kinsey's path-breaking studies of male and female sexuality in 1948 and 1954 became best-sellers.

All of this learning took place before my fourteenth birthday, long before I decided to become a historian, even longer before I opted to relocate to Canada. The reasons why I became interested in issues of national security—ultimately socio/cultural constructions related to power issues concerning class, sex, and gender, and race and ethnicity—no doubt germinated during those years. I can see now that my critical interest in security and its misuse by elites, my short presence in the free-speech movement at Berkeley, my civil rights and antiwar protest during the Vietnam War years, and my professional activities with the Peace History Society owe something to these convergences.

Clearly, in at least one life the personal became political—perhaps not political enough, but nonetheless a reason for reflection about state security practices and, in several instances, action. For national security requirements during the Second World War and first decade of the Cold War profoundly influenced the trajectory of lives not only in Europe and Asia, but also in the United States and Canada. Through its myriad outlets on both elite and popular levels, the national security state told us what to fear and how to live—in short, how to be "good Americans." In the process—as historian H.W. Brands and other scholars note—the U.S. state proffered politically correct and incorrect paradigms of gender alternatives, interwoven in the nexus between national security requirements and personal insecurities, between the body and the state, embedded in what Gore Vidal calls a "climate of intimidation."[34]

We now pay for that process and that outcome. And we need to learn more about these things, at the grassroots level. Indeed, when I return to my childhood home of Hillsborough, I now see a town of locked and grated gated entrances, of signs warning that trespassers will be prosecuted to the fullest extent of the law (if not shot), and—with "no sidewalks there"—the coded message that people should not consider walking the streets, even in daylight.[35]

## Notes

1.  For a recent summary, see Ethan Bronner, "Rethinking McCarthyism, If Not McCarthy," *The New York Times*, Oct. 18, 1998, IV, pp.1,6.
2.  Pertinent publications include "Historical Perspectives on AIDS: Society, Culture and STDs," *Queen's Quarterly* 96 (Summer 1989), pp.244–63, reprinted in *Best Canadian Essays—1990*, ed. Douglas Fetherling (Saskatoon, 1990), pp.102–26; "National Security and Personal Isolation: Sex, Gender, and Disease in the Cold War United States," *International History Review* 14 (May 1992), pp.307–37; "Commentary: Security, Gender, and the Historical Process," *Diplomatic History* 18 (Winter 1994), pp.79–90; "Contagious Subversion: Cultural Constructions of Disease," *Queen's Quarterly* 103 (Summer 1996), pp.403–12.
3.  I have endeavoured to corroborate my recollections of events described here with others, especially persons involved in the events.
4.  Chris O'Brien, "'And Everything Would Be Done to Protect Us': America's Children Confront the Cold War, 1945–1963," Ph.D. dissertation, University of Kansas, May 1998. For emphasis upon the central notions of doubt and contingency during the early Cold War years, see William S. Graebner, *The Age of Doubt: American Thought and Culture in the 1940s* (Boston: Twayne Publishers, 1991), pp.20ff.
5.  E. Anthony Rotundo, *American Manhood: Transformations in Masculinity from the Revolution to the Modern Era* (New York: Basic Books, 1993). On the idea of "the enemy within," see Michael Paul Rogin, *Ronald Reagan, the Movie and Other Episodes in Political Demonology* (Berkeley: University of California Press, 1987), pp.287ff.
6.  See James William Gibson, *The Perfect War: The War We Couldn't Lose and How We Did* (New York: Vintage, 1988), pp.461–76.
7.  My dictionary (*Webster's Twentieth Century Dictionary*—unabridged, 2nd ed., p.1641) offers four relevant denotations: "(1) safety or a sense of safety; the state or feeling of being free from fear, care, danger, etc.; (2) freedom from doubt; certainty; (3) overconfidence, carelessness; (4) something that gives or assures safety; protection; safeguard. Syn—protection, shelter, safety, certainty."
8.  As, for example, on Diefenbaker and Kennedy, see Jocelyn Ghent, "Did He Fall or Was He Pushed? The Kennedy Administration and the Collapse of the Diefenbaker Government," *International History Review* 1 (1979), pp.246–70; on Pearson and Vietnam, see Victor Levant, *Quiet Complicity: Canadian Involvement in the Vietnam War* (Toronto: Between the Lines, 1986), and Douglas A. Ross, *In the Interests of Peace: Canada and Vietnam, 1954–1973* (Toronto: University of Toronto Press, 1984).
9.  The term "fifth column" originated during the Spanish Civil War, as Franco's Nationalist Army advanced in four columns on besieged Madrid. The general in charge of the offensive bragged that he had a secret "fifth column" of fascists inside the city sewing discord and defeatism, and that would "assail the Republicans from within as

his troops assaulted the city from without." See John E. Haynes, *Red Scare or Red Menace? American Communism and Anticommunism in the Cold War Era* (Chicago: Ivan R. Dee, 1996), p.18.

10. See Thomas G. Paterson, "Red Fascism: The American Image of Aggressive Totalitarianism," in Paterson, *Meeting the Communist Threat: From Truman to Reagan* (New York: Oxford University Press, 1988). On the shift of U.S. demonology from race, to class and ethnicity, and, ultimately, to ideas and ideology, see Rogin, *Ronald Reagan*, pp.44–80. On the intersection of pathology and gender in anti-communism, see Frank Costigliola, "'Unceasing Pressure for Penetration': Gender, Pathology, and Emotion in George Kennan's Formulation of the Cold War," *Journal of American History* 83 (March 1997), pp.1309–39; and Frank Costigliola, "The Nuclear Family: Tropes of Gender and Pathology in the Western Alliance," *Diplomatic History* 21 (Spring 1997), pp.163–84.

11. In this my mother was like many U.S. women before Pearl Harbor. See Rhodri Jeffreys-Jones, *Changing Differences: Women and the Shaping of American Foreign Policy, 1917–1994* (New Brunswick, N.J.: Rutgers Press, 1995), pp.97ff.

12. For a broader canvas, see William M. Tuttle, Jr., *"Daddy's Gone to War": The Second World War in the Lives of America's Children* (New York: Oxford University Press, 1993).

13. For sensitive assessments of young lives in the shadow of the ultimate weapon, see Alan Nadel, *Containment Culture: American Narratives, Postmodernism, and the Atomic Age* (Durham, N.C.: Duke University Press, 1995), pp.ix–xii; and Mark Lapin, *Pledge of Allegiance* (New York: Dutton, 1991). For the "winning weapon" and its subsequent albatross-like weight, see Gregg Herken, *The Winning Weapon: The Atomic Bomb in the Cold War* (New York: Knopf and Random House, 1980). For the ongoing cultural debate on the use of the bomb, which climaxed in the Smithsonian Institution's decision to back down from its planned exhibit to tell the *full* story of the atomic bombing of Hiroshima and Nagasaki, see *History Wars: The Enola Gay, and Other Battles for the American Past*, ed. Edward T. Linenthal and Tom Engelhardt (New York: Metropolitan Books, 1996); *Hiroshima in History and Memory*, ed. Michael J. Hogan (New York: Cambridge University Press, 1996); and Geoffrey S. Smith, "Beware the Historian! Hiroshima, the *Enola Gay*, and the Dangers of History," *Diplomatic History* 22 (Winter 1998), pp.121–30. For a marvellous deconstruction of the U.S. triumphal myth, to which I am indebted, see Tom Engelhardt, *The End of Victory Culture: Cold War America and the Disillusioning of a Generation* (New York: Basic Books, 1995).

14. For a sprightly Canadian critique of purported "un-Americanism" in the 1950s United States, especially in arts and letters, see Robert Fulford, "American Demons of the 1950s," *Queen's Quarterly* 102 (Fall 1995), pp.525–45. On Hollywood, see Rogin, *Ronald Reagan*, pp.236–71; Victor Navasky, *Naming Names* (New York: Viking Press, 1980), and Nora Sayre, *Running Time: Films of the Cold War* (New York: Dial Press, 1982). On cultural representations of anti-communism, see Michael Barson, *"Better Dead Than Red!"* (New York: Hyperion, 1992).

15. On radiation experiments and coverups, see Clifford Honicker, "The Hidden Files," *The New York Times Magazine*, Nov. 18, 1989, pp.39ff. For the "mind" experiments, undertaken in the name of national security, and the fallout, see Anne Collins, *In the Sleep Room: The Story of the CIA Brainwashing Experiments in Canada* (Toronto: Lester and Orpen Dennys, 1988); and Mike Blanchfield, "The Case for Prison's LSD Tests," *The Citizen* (Ottawa), March 1, 1998, pp.1,4.

16. On the "new look," see Karal Ann Marling, *As Seen on TV: The Visual Culture of Everyday Life in the 1950s* (Cambridge Mass.: Harvard University Press, 1994), pp.8–49.

17. Skolnick subsequently sent my mother an autographed offprint of an article he had written, which argued that Soviet schoolchildren, lacking the educational infrastructure of the land of the free and home of the brave, were more maladjusted and less independent than their U.S. counterparts. See Alec Skolnick, "Some Psychiatric Aspects of the

'New Soviet Child,'" *Bulletin of the Menninger Clinic* 28 (May 1964), pp.120–44.

18. Stuart Alsop and Ralph E. Lapp, "The Strange Death of Louis Slotin," *The Saturday Evening Post* 226 (March 6, 1954), pp.25ff. See also R.N. Schwartz, "Martyr to the Atom," *Coronet* 30 (September 1951), pp.53–55.

19. Major Alexander P. Deseversky, "Atom Bomb Hysteria," *Reader's Digest*, May 1946, pp.121–26.

20. Richard Gerstell, Ph.D., *How to Survive an Atomic Bomb* (Washington, D.C.: Combat Forces Press, 1950). See also Gerstell, "How You Can Survive an A-Bomb Blast," *The Saturday Evening Post*, Jan. 7, 1950, pp.23ff.

21. Parsons quoted in Paul Boyer, *By the Bomb's Early Light: American Thought and Culture at the Dawn of the Atomic Age* (New York: Pantheon Books, 1985), pp.316–17.

22. John Hersey, *Hiroshima* (New York, 1946). When I read this book, at age ten, I could not believe what I read.

23. David J. Skal, *The Monster Show: A Cultural History of Horror* (New York: Norton, 1993), p.248; Michael J. Strada, "The Cinematic Bogy Man Comes Home: American Popular Perceptions of External Threat," *Midwest Quarterly* 28 (Winter 1987), pp.248–70.

24. For an overview see *Nuclear War Films*, ed. Jack G. Shaheen (Carbondale, Il.: Southern Illinois University Press, 1978).

25. On the promise of the atom, see Boyer, *Bomb's Early light*, pp.294–98. For darker aspects of the nuclear ambience, see Spencer Weart, *Nuclear Fear: A History of Images* (Cambridge, Mass.: Harvard University Press, 1988); and Michael S. Sherry, *In the Shadow of War: The United States since the 1930s* (New Haven, Conn.: Yale University Press, 1995), esp. pp.118–22.

26. Compare with the individuals in Michael D'Antonio, "Atomic Guinea Pigs," *The New York Times Magazine*, Aug. 31, 1997, pp.38–43.

27. On John Wayne and early Cold War masculinity, see especially Garry Wills, *John Wayne's America: The Politics of Celebrity* (New York: Simon and Schuster, 1997), pp.16–27 and passim.

28. On the FBI's attempt to prove Stevenson's "homosexuality," an allegation based on a rumour picked up by a field agent from an inebriated Bradley University basketball player at a bar in Peoria, see *From the Secret Files of J. Edgar Hoover*, ed. Athan Theoharis (Chicago: Ivan R. Dee, 1991), pp.282–91.

29. As a homemaker, my mother was a "good" American female. Soviet women, of course, "worked in masculine jobs and had their kids raised outside the home in state-run child care centers that brainwashed kids to become good little comrades." As Susan J. Douglas writes, "Therefore, our kids had to be raised at home by their moms if they were going to remain democratic and free." See Douglas, *Where the Girls Are: Growing up Female with the Mass Media* (New York: Times Books, 1995), p.47.

30. Elaine Tyler May, *Homeward Bound: American Families in the Cold War Era* (New York: Basic Books, 1988). The use of metaphor to imply guilt by association reached absurd proportions in the Florida Democratic primary in 1950. There, liberal Claude Pepper was bombarded with innuendo by his opponent, George Smathers. Among other things, in exposing his opponent's "secret vices," Smathers charged "The Red Pepper" with being "a known extravert," his sister a "thespian," and his brother "a practicing homo sapiens." When Pepper attended college, moreover, he actually "matriculated," and—worst—he "practiced celibacy" before marriage. These charges helped Smathers defeat Pepper in rural Florida and contributed to his primary victory. See Irving Wallace et al., *The People's Almanac Book of Lists #2* (New York: Morrow, 1980), pp.36–37.

31. Two recent works that stress Nixon's paranoia, mendacity, and pettiness are Greg Mitchell, *Tricky Dick and the Pink Lady: Richard Nixon vs Helen Gahagan Douglas— Sexual Politics and the Red Scare, 1950* (New York: Random House, 1998); and Vamik D. Volkan, Norman Itzkowitz, and Andrew W. Dod, *Richard Nixon: A Psychobiography* (New York: Columbia University Press, 1998). See also Ingrid Winther Scobie's fine

biography of Gahagan Douglas, *Center Stage: Helen Gahagan Douglas, A Life* (New York: Oxford University Press, 1992).

32. For the corporation as a male "safe haven," and the notion that mom in postwar America was often married to the corporation, see Barbara Ehrenreich, *The Hearts of Men: American Dreams and the Flight from Commitment* (Garden City, N.Y.: Anchor Press/Doubleday, 1983), pp.14–41; and May, *Homeward Bound*, pp.77–91.

33. May, *Homeward Bound*, pp.114–34.

34. H.W. Brands, *The Devil We Knew: Americans and the Cold War* (New York: Oxford University Press, 1993); Gore Vidal, "America, The Last Empire," *Vanity Fair*, November 1997, p.255.

35. For similar views of how Cold War security concerns came to dominate our domestic lives, see Ann Markusen, Peter Hall, Scott Campbell, and Sabina Deitrick, *The Rise of the Gunbelt: The Military Remapping of Industrial America* (New York: Oxford University Press, 1992); Edward Pessen, *Losing Our Souls: The American Experience in the Cold War* (Chicago: Ivan R. Dee, 1993); Roger W. Lotchin, *Fortress California, 1910–1961: From Warfare to Welfare* (New York: Oxford University Press, 1992); Mike Davis, *City of Quartz: Excavating the Future in Los Angeles* (New York: Verso/Vintage, 1992), esp. pp.228–60; and Edward J. Blakely and Mary Gail Snyder, *Fortress America: Gated Communities in the United States* (Washington, D.C.: Brookings Institute Press, 1997). For Hillsborough, California, see Michael Svanevik and Shirley Burgett, *No Sidewalks Here: A Pictorial History of Hillsborough* (Hillsborough, Cal., 1992).

**Top Left:** *"It really understands women."* From an advertisement for lie detectors in *Look*, January 4, 1938. **Top Right:** *"Dedicated to Truth."* The APA uses both the scales of justice and a polygraph scroll in its logo. **Bottom:** *"The polygraph of your dreams."* [Bunn, chap. 14]

GEOFFREY C. BUNN

fourteen ✶ ✶ ✶

# Euphoric Security: The Lie Detector and Popular Culture

On August 28, 1996, *The Globe and Mail* reported that Canada's highest-ranking military officer, Chief of Defence Staff Jean Boyle, had "passed [a] lie-detector test." General Boyle had been front-page news ever since he had been called to testify at the inquiry into allegations of military misconduct in Somalia. "It's a good indicator of truthfulness," said the former senior polygraph examiner for the Department of National Defence. "Not 100 per cent but [it] falls in the range of about 90 per cent." Accurate or not, the lie detector failed to rescue the general's credibility; on October 8 he resigned from office.[1]

"Polygraph clears McLean," *The Globe and Mail* headlined on September 10, 1996. One of his former employees had recently charged the Speaker of the Ontario House of Commons, Allan McLean, with sexual harassment. In a desperate bid to extricate his client from the scandal, his lawyer arranged for the Speaker to take a lie detector test. Although the attorney maintained that the polygraph exonerated his client of "allegations that he sexually harassed a subordinate," it was a futile gesture; McLean resigned from office on September 19.[2]

September 1996 was also the month in which the fast-food restaurant chain Harvey's began broadcasting a television commercial featuring a white-coat-wearing scientist giving a lie detector test to one of its hamburgers. "You're delicious," said the scientist, to which the lie detector responded with a "ting" of approval. "You've never inhaled": "ting." "You're beautiful": "ting, ting." The test established the hamburger's credibility and integrity, that is, its nutritional content and its value for money. "Harvey's Ultra," the scientist concluded, clipboard in hand, "It's an honest new hamburger."

In October *The Glimmer Man* opened across North America. Starring Steven Seagal, the movie told the story of an eccentric detective who renounces his pacifism to solve a serial murder case. Suspected of involvement in one of the ritual slayings, Detective Cole is asked to take a lie detector test. His Buddhist background enables Cole to control his physiological responses exactly, and he beats the machine easily. "Everything reads true," says the astonished polygraphist, "You have total control over your emotions. I've never seen anything like it." Cole does lose control, however, when the questioner begins to ask irrelevant questions about

201

his shady past. He rips off the polygraphic apparatus, throws in his police badge, and storms out of the room, determined to prove his innocence his way. The test plays an important role in the film because it provides the justification for Cole to "go it alone," renounce his pacifism, and seek revenge.

Here, then, are four lie detector tests: two are real and involve government officials, two are fictional, involving a Hollywood cop and a "$1.88 Harvey's Ultra." Although all four suspects successfully "passed the lie detector test," only the hamburger kept its job, going on to star in a number of similar commercials with its scientist sidekick. I would suggest that such anecdotes, images, and narratives do not merely represent the lie detector, but that they play a constitutive role for the science of polygraphy by rendering the instrument authentic, credible, and effective.

Doubtless inspired by such publicity, a *Toronto Star* writer wondered, "How and why does a lie detector machine work?" He noted, "While police use polygraphs as an investigative tool—if a suspect is willing," and added that "this evidence is inadmissible in criminal trials in Canada" as a result of a 1987 Supreme Court ruling. "The jury ultimately has to make a final determination of credibility," a criminal law expert pointed out, and the justices "don't want the jury overwhelmed by our love affair with machinery." *The Globe and Mail* concurred: "Lie-detector tests seen as inaccurate."[3] In 1987 (the year in which the U.S. government banned the use of polygraphs in all but government organizations), the Canadian Supreme Court thwarted one more attempt to advance the cause of justice through science.

Popular culture and the mass media, then, have played a pivotal role throughout the lie detector's history, and this role must be kept in mind when we consider the extent to which the instrument has been implicated in national security issues.[4] Despite the Canadian parliamentary oversight committee's rejection of lie detector tests, CSIS continues to employ this technology. *The Globe and Mail* reported on March 20, 2000, that in the case of an operative accused of improper conduct, CSIS management insisted that the agent take a polygraph test. In the 1980s, Canadian military security also used a lie-detector in their interrogations of Michelle Douglas. Douglas was grilled about her sexual activities before she was forced out of the military as a lesbian. Her legal challenge to this exclusionary policy led to it being overturned in 1992. Indeed, the lie detector's contributions to the maintenance of national security have been far from straightforward. Although the instrument has certainly been occasionally deployed in national security campaigns on behalf of governmental agencies, the lie detector's indebtedness to the domain of its emergence necessitates an expansion of the understanding of national security to include popular culture.

## "Lie Detector Tells All"

In many ways—and particularly in popular registers—the lie detector embodies the very ideal of "scientific justice" and has done so throughout its short and ignoble history. "Electric Machine to Tell Guilt of Criminals" headlined *The New York Times* in 1911. "If it is perfected so as to be infallible it will make expert testimony unnecessary and may eliminate juries in trials." The piece predicted, "There will be no . . . horde of detectives and witnesses, no charges and countercharges, and no attorney for the defense."

> These impedimenta of our courts will be unnecessary. The State will merely submit all suspects in a case to the tests of scientific instruments, and as these instruments cannot be made to make mistakes nor tell lies, their evidence will be conclusive of guilt or innocence, and the court will deliver sentence accordingly.[5]

Some ninety years later the polygraph profession continues to claim powers of scientific accuracy, truth, and justice for its sacred instrument. The logo of the American Polygraph Association is particularly telling. The classically robed central figure is blindfolded and carries the scales of justice in one hand and a polygraph scroll in the other. The motto "Dedicated to Truth" completes the image, the totality of which is captured within an officious circular seal.

Although "Dedicated to Truth," the image contains a troubling falsity: a blindfolded operator would not be able to interpret the complex hieroglyphics on the polygraph chart. The contradiction is established by the portrayal of polygraphy as "blind justice" on the one hand and its depiction as an "automatic" science needless of expertise on the other. The flowing robes also suggest a religious motif. The scroll is indeed a curled parchment upon which is inscribed The Truth.

The rhetorical power of the chart is considerable. A seemingly endless roll, the image symbolizes the total calculability of the body and the ease with which its hidden truths can be rendered visible. Three primary corporal systems are constantly monitored by the polygraph: the lungs, the heart, and the skin. Phenomenologically, there appears to be no escape from the grid of intelligibility that is the graph paper and its sine wave curves whose amplitudes and resonances may be computed to produce a general calculus of guilt. The chart itself has magical prowess by virtue of its immediate access to the body. "My charts don't lie," says the polygraphist in the 1993 movie *Fire in the Sky*. "If you ask me, those boys are telling the truth."

If the sacred scroll contains esoteric writings, the polygraphist must be a mystic, a knower of ancient corporal verities. The polygraphist is certainly a magician, as illustrated by the notorious "stim test." Asked to "pick a card," the subject of the polygraph exam is told to lie when asked about the card's value. The polygraph detects the lie and the subject is consequently impressed with the instrument's abilities.[6] The 1995 TV movie *Nothing but the Truth*, for example, opens with a polygraphist impressing her class with the abilities of her magic machine. The "stim test" is also featured in the 1947 movie *Call Northside 777*. So crucial is this little piece of theatre for establishing the instrument's credibility that polygraph handbooks advise operators to fake the results in order to avoid the potential embarrassment of failure.[7]

Despite its rhetorical potency and magical ability, the chart exists at a problematic junction. Although it claims merely to depict the body's forces in a straightforward, transparent manner ("see for yourself"), its interpretation does require expertise. The polygraphist must mobilize scientific credentials yet simultaneously belittle esoteric knowledge and defer to the machine's astonishing truth-telling abilities. This dilemma of expertise is resolved by transferring agency from the human operator to the instrument. Polygraph examinations invariably begin with an explanation of the functions of the various gadgets and attachments.[8] By so focusing attention on the instrument and its abilities, the operator is rendered invisible.

Although the pre-test interview is ostensibly a "dissection" of the lie detector—an apparently frank revelation of its constituent parts and inner workings—the procedure serves to mystify the examination by emphasizing the machine's competencies at the expense of the operator's. The "lie box" is a "black box," a mysterious and intimidating piece of technology. By pretending to "open the black box," the polygraphist actually closes it by rendering his own activities irrelevant. The operator thus becomes an "invisible technician" whose actions are merely those of the lowly tinkerer.[9] The arbitration of truth is a task delegated up the chain of command to the senior humanized polygraph machine.

Sentience and agency are a staple feature of advertisements and popular representations of the instrument. A 1938 *Life* magazine advertisement for Gillette razor blades is headlined "Lie detector tells all, reveals startling facts about razor blades."[10] A 1990s TV commercial for Pepsi Cola gives the lie detector a sense of humour. Having been shown to be speaking the truth about the soft drink, an actor waxes lyrical about his thespian future, forgetting that he is still attached to the machine. The familiar buzz and flashing red light signal "lie" when the actor predicts a bright future for himself. The lie detector's persistent omniscience is wickedly parodied in an episode of *The Simpsons*, when bartender Moe is forced by the polygraph to admit that his "hot date" alibi is nothing more than a fabrication designed to hide the fact that tonight he is staying home with his mother.

The instrument's agency reaches an apotheosis in the 1967 *Star Trek* episode "Wolf in the Fold." Scotty has been accused of a series of murders and is obliged to take a lie detector test administered by *The Enterprise*'s on-board computer. Kirk asks the questions, but Scotty's physiological responses are recorded, interpreted, and reported by the speaking computer: "Subject relaying accurate information. No physiological changes." The "lie box" then, is the only labourer in the testing situation, a feature emphasized by popular depictions and polygraph handbooks alike.

### "It Really Understands Women"

Subjects of lie detector examinations must have particular characteristics too. In 1938 *Look* magazine illustrated a report on "a machine to measure lies" with a photograph of a woman attached to the instrument by a headband and palm galvanometers. "Dr. Orlando F. Scott, the inventor of the machine, says that women respond with so much electrical energy that their lies are easier to detect than those of men." A 1938 newspaper photograph of the "Darrow photopolygraph" is captioned, "It really understands women."[11] Women possess the ideal subject characteristics of emotionality, verbosity, and deceptive tendencies; they are, it appears, inherently suspect. The polygraphist, however, is composed and taciturn, the very embodiment of scientific rationality. This gender dimorphism has been a consistent theme of lie detection in, again, both polygraph manuals and movies, magazines, and newspapers.

As Ludmilla Jordanova demonstrates, the notion of nature as a woman unveiled by science has a long history.[12] Science is a gendered enterprise in which masculine power is wielded over feminine "nature." In pictures of lie detector tests, examiners are invariably clothed in the vestments of authority, such as the police uniform, the scientific white coat, or the business suit. Female suspects, in contrast, are usually casually attired. In some photographs the tight-fitting pneumographic tube accentuates the suspects' breasts. The erotic meaning inherent in the scientific "lifting of the veil" is therefore echoed by the ideal polygraph examination scene. Male examiners are invariably shown gazing intensely at their female suspects, ostensibly seeking "behaviour symptoms" of deception. Furthermore, examination rooms are designed to provide numerous opportunities for voyeuristic surveillance via two-way mirrors and concealed microphones.[13]

Ideally, then, the polygraphist should be male. The symbols of his office are, appropriately, The Briefcase, The Desk, and The Secretary. Manuals advise examiners to have their secretaries observe the demeanour and poise of the waiting subject, prior to the examination proper. Throughout the test the subject's mannerisms, movements, and actions are all recorded by direct observation, two-way mirror, and other forms of instrumentation. The resultant information is gathered together to allow the polygraphist to compose a final diagnosis of guilt. Thus, far from being a form of "blind justice," lie detection establishes its claims through visible means. It is an ocular surveillance technology.

A 1996 in-flight *USAir Magazine* advertisement for "Counter Spy Shop of Mayfair London" neatly encapsulates some of these themes. "Night Vision Systems," "Custom Hidden Video Systems," and "Phone Taps and Room Bugging Devices" are only some of the products that the private security company can offer to help maintain corporate or individual security. The claim to "Know If Your Caller Is Lying with the Truth Phone(tm)" is illustrated with a photograph of a sexy blonde seated on a white box. Her free-standing male partner is surrounded by surveillance apparatuses and equipment in various black briefcases. The talkative seated woman is speaking into the Truth Phone. Technology is "black-boxed" and thus allows knowledge to flow smoothly and without problems through conduits free of corrupting human agency.[14] The scene is glamorous and intimidating, reminiscent of James Bond's sophisticated high-tech, high-society escapades.

Unlike the semiotic discourse of lie detection from which this image is taken, one feature of the scene is only minimally emphasized: The Chair. Subjects of lie detector tests must not merely be seated, they must be tied to the chair itself. (A technology of liberating truth is thus rendered operable by coercion.) A widespread awareness of the effective techniques for "beating the lie detector" has led to the development of counter-countermeasures by the polygraphy profession. But although muscle-clenching detectors have recently rendered the chair an even more important facet of the examination, The Chair draws its intimidatory power from its resemblance to at least two other "seats of justice."

Seated in a witness box, a portable dock, the suspect of a lie detector exam is "on trial." But the chair is also an "electric chair." ("Can these attachments give me an electric shock?" is a question commonly asked by fearful suspects.) The lie detector thus embodies the dream of automatic justice. Once the lie is detected, the direction of the flow of electricity can be reversed to immediately dispatch the convicted.

To speak of the lie detector "in the courts" or to study the "legal admissibility of polygraph evidence" is therefore to miss a crucial but obvious feature of the examination. A lie detector test is itself a mini-trial, because it promises both the discovery of the truth and immediate punishment. Its primary use has always been to intimidate suspects into confessing, a feature that renders the ordeal uncomfortably similar to that which it was designed to replace—the "third degree." The lie detector is not "of the courts," then, because it operates within an extralegal ecology. The Oklahoma City bombers took lie detector tests. The Atlanta Olympics bombing suspect took a lie detector test. O.J. Simpson took one, as did the Speaker of the Ontario House of Commons. The Harvey's Ultra took a lie detector test. In the circulation of pre-trial gossip, "passing a lie detector test" is a powerful rhetorical resource, a fact recognized by General Boyle's astute military police advisor, who told the chief of defence staff to take the test "to help counter negative media coverage."[15] Yet in each case of "passing the lie detector test," almost as an aside, it is invariably mentioned that, regrettably, "The lie detector is inadmissible in a court of law."

## The Lie Detector Era

The polygraph industry was professionalized during the Cold War. The International Society for the Detection of Deception was founded in 1947, and the CIA established its own lie detection program the following year.[16] The U.S. army first bought a polygraph for its Chicago Counter-Intelligence Corps School in 1945. Its head, Col. Ralph W. Pierce, had been greatly impressed with the work of Leonarde Keeler, the polygraph pioneer who had been running a successful lie detection business in the city since the late 1930s.[17] The first systematic use of the instrument by a U.S. federal government agency took place in August 1945 at Fort Getty, Rhode Island, where several hundred German prisoners were given lie detector examinations prior to being sent to work with the occupation forces in Europe.[18]

The most important opportunity for the nascent profession occurred in February 1946, when a group of polygraphers established an experimental screening program for employees of the Oak Ridge atomic-bomb manufacturing plant in Tennessee.[19] Security was at a premium in the plant, and because the operation employed eighteen thousand people, the personnel screening program was vast. Over a period of seven years, eleven full-time polygraphers examined up to one hundred employees a day. They asked questions like "Have you removed any uranium or classified products from the plant without authorization?" and "Have you ever been arrested for a criminal offence?" and "Are you in sympathy with Communism or the Communistic form of government?" Explained American Polygraph Association member John G. Linehan, "It is of paramount importance that persons selected and retained on jobs where revealing national secrets and/or endangering sensitive products can critically harm one's country have integrity, be dependable, and of honorable intent."[20]

Costing some $361,000, the Oak Ridge polygraph program was apparently a most impressive contribution to the maintenance of national security. Nevertheless, in April 1953 the Atomic Energy Commission terminated it on the grounds that "the machine's techniques offer only indeterminate marginal increase in security beyond that afforded by established . . . security measures." The AEC report concluded:

> The substantial cost of the Oak Ridge polygraph program in dollars, plus the intangible cost in employee morale, personnel recruitment and labor relations which might accrue from use of the machine substantially outweighed the limited advantage of polygraph use. The study showed there is little data available indicating that the polygraph has any value in detection of intent to commit sabotage or espionage, or sympathy with subversive movements or ideologies.[21]

Although the machine was thus deemed unacceptable by a major federal agency, the profession continued to grow during the 1950s. Not surprisingly, one of the instrument's most vocal advocates was Senator Joseph R. McCarthy. In May 1949 he requested lie detector tests for U.S. army investigators accused of brutalizing indicted Nazi war criminals.[22] By the fall of 1950—after McCarthy had accused it of employing homosexuals—the State Department was using the instrument to investigate cases of "Miscellaneous Morals." In December 1951, the Republican Senator asserted that all government officials and employees in sensitive positions should be required to submit to lie detector tests. He later demanded that Charles Bohlen, appointed ambassador to Soviet Russia by President Eisenhower, should also take a lie test.[23]

But for every advocate there was an equally vehement opponent. At a meeting of the Senate Armed Services Committee in January 1952, Senator Wayne Morse rose "in righteous anger against the lie detector."[24] His accusation that the instrument violated "the basic guarantees of personal liberty and freedom set forth in the constitution" resulted in the Department of Defense banning its use in testing job applicants.[25]

The polygraph profession's ambitions to have its instrument assist in the administration of national security were ultimately thwarted. The technology of lie detection was too equivocal to be accepted by the authorities of state. Instead, the instrument found a permanent home in a domain that was tolerant of both ambiguity and controversy: popular culture. As the 1950s progressed, a wide variety of mass circulation magazines featured articles about the lie detector.[26] While *The Nation* was wondering "Do Lie-Detectors Lie?" *Reader's Digest* was asserting that the instrument "speeds justice, reduces court costs and protects the innocent."

*Radio & Television News* even showed enthusiasts how they could make their own lie box. No wonder *The Reporter* labelled the period "The Lie Detector Era."[27] By 1961 the machine was sufficiently famous to inspire the creation of an eponymous TV show.[28] The task of providing an appropriate domicile for the instrument thus fell not to the U.S. government but rather to KTTV of Hollywood.

## Conclusion

The instrument's attempts to insert itself into the orthodox institutions of state security—the police, government, judiciary—have been perpetually frustrated. In this sense, the lie detector has failed. But in a different public sphere—those apparently illegitimate realms of popular culture and the mass media—the instrument has enjoyed phenomenal success. Newspapers, magazines, comic books, movies, TV shows, toys, advertisements: these are the domains in which the machine has flourished.

The lie detector test is a court unto itself. It is a trial that plays no part in trials and a machine with human agency. A form of "blind justice," it operates according to scopophilia. It is a scientific fetish, a neutral and reliable science that depends upon stereotypical knowledge of gender differences to function. A mysterious black box whose innards are continually on display, it is a modernist technology of individual emotion that operates according to a premodern system of communal justice whose pre-eminent tactic was public humiliation and shame. It measures not the "honest body" but rather assesses the "dishonest face." Lie detection is a technology of physiognomic surfaces, not physiological depths.

The Black Box, The Chair, The Chart, Passing the Test, Beating the Test: these are all components of the "regime of signs" that make up the lie detector. A form of semio technique, it thrives off ambivalence and controversy.[29] Its mythic status is guaranteed by popular culture. As Roland Barthes observed, myths are unconcerned with contradiction so long as they establish "euphoric security."[30] This is the task that the lie detector has successfully devoted itself to throughout its lengthy quest for justice.

## Notes

1. Paul Koring, "Investigators Advised Boyle to Take Polygraph Test," *The Globe and Mail*, Aug. 23, 1996, p.3; Paul Koring, "Boyle Passed Lie-detector Test," *The Globe and Mail*, Aug. 28, 1996, pp.1,7; Jeff Sallot, "Boyle Leaves Defence Post," *The Globe and Mail*, Oct. 9, 1996, p.1.

2. Martin Mittlestaedt, "Polygraph Clears McLean, Lawyer Says," *The Globe and Mail*, Sept. 10, 1996, p.3; James Rusk, "Speaker Steps Aside Because of Health," *The Globe and Mail*, Sept. 19, 1996, p.3.

3. Walter Stefaniuk, "You Asked Us," *The Toronto Star*, Oct. 1, 1996, p.A7; Jane Gadd, "Lie-detector Tests Seen as Inaccurate," *The Globe and Mail*, Sept. 11, 1996, p.A6.

4. See Geoffrey C. Bunn, "The Hazards of the Will to Truth: A History of the Lie Detector," unpublished Ph.D. dissertation, York University, Toronto, 1998.

5. "Electric Machine to Tell Guilt of Criminals," *The New York Times*, Sept. 10, 1911, p.V6.

6. For example, see Thomas H. Jaycox, "Scientific Detection of Lies," *Scientific American* 156 (June 1927), p.372.

7. John E. Reid and Fred E. Inbau, *Truth and Deception: The Polygraph ("Lie Detection") Technique* (Baltimore: Willi, 1977).

8. Ibid.

9. Steven Shapin, "The Invisible Technician," *American Scientist* 77, pp.554–63.

10. "Lie Detector 'Tells All,'" *Life*, Nov. 21, 1938, p.65.

11. "A Machine to Measure Lies," *Look*, Jan. 4, 1938, p.29; "Psychological Museum Bares One's Innermost Feelings," *Herald and Examiner* (Chicago), May 8, 1938.

12. "The metaphorical associations of (un)veiling are rich and diverse, going far beyond their direct connections with scientific knowledge, encompassing religion (nuns, ideas of revelation, the cover of a chalice), clothing, crime, mystery, horror and deceit of all kinds." Ludmilla Jordanova, "Nature Unveiling before Science," in *Sexual Visions: Images of Gender in Science and Medicine between the Eighteenth and Twentieth Centuries* (New York: Harvester Wheatsheaf, 1989), p.91.

13. Reid and Inbau, *Truth and Deception*, pp.7, 152; Jordanova, *Sexual Visions*, p.90; and James Allan Matté, *The Art and Science of the Polygraph Test* (Springfield, Ill.: Thomas, 1980), p.133. See also Matté, *Art and Science*, Figure 67, p.132; and Reid and Inbau, *Truth and Deception*, Figure 1, p.5. Reid and Inbau also discuss some of the potential hazards of attaching the pneumographic tube to women (p.22, n.28).

14. For an analysis of black boxes, see Bruno Latour, *Science in Action: How to Follow Scientists and Engineers through Society* (Cambridge, Mass.: Harvard University Press, 1987).

15. Koring, "Investigators Advised Boyle."

16. Dwight MacDonald, "The Lie-Detector Era, II," *The Reporter* 10 (June 22, 1954), pp.22–29.

17. J.P. McEvoy, "The Lie Detector Goes into Business," *Reader's Digest* (U.S. edition) 38 (February 1941), pp.69–72.

18. Dwight MacDonald, "The Lie-Detector Era, I," *The Reporter* 10 (June 8, 1954), pp.10–18.

19. "Lie Detector Tested in Atom Bomb Plant," *The New York Times*, March 14 1946, p.12.

20. John G. Linehan, "The Oak Ridge Polygraph Program 1946–1953," *Polygraph* 19,2 (1990), pp.131–37, 133.

21. MacDonald, "Lie-Detector Era, I," p.17.

22. "Reprieves Continued for 6 Malmedy Nazis; McCarthy Walks out of Senate Investigation," *The New York Times*, May 21, 1949, p.3.

23. MacDonald, "Lie-Detector Era, II," p.26; "Lie Detector Tests Urged by McCarthy," *The New York Times*, Dec. 22, 1951, p.5; MacDonald, "Lie Detector Era, I," p.16.

24. Anthony Leviero, "Truth about the Lie Detector," *Science Digest* 31 (May 1952), pp.6–8.

25. MacDonald, "Lie Detector Era, I," p.18.

26. "Lie Detector Tests on Workers," *Business Week*, April 28, 1951, p.24; "Lie Detector vs. Civil Rights," *Senior Scholastic Teacher Edition* (Dayton) 59 (January 23, 1952), pp.5–7; "Justice by Gadget," *The Reporter* 8 (1953), pp.1–2; "Lie Gadgets," *Scientific American* 188 (June 1953), pp.46–47; "Lie-Detector Indian," *Newsweek*, June 8, 1953, p.30; William Leonard, "How the Lie Detector Works," *Science Digest* 46 (July 1959), pp.1–5.

27. Jules H. Masserman and Mary Grier Jacques, "Do Lie-Detectors Lie?" *The Nation*, 174 (April 19, 1952), pp.368–69; Karl Detzer, "Don't Underestimate the Lie Detector," *Reader's Digest* (Canadian edition) 63 (November 1953), pp.95–99; Edwin Bohr, "Lie Detector," *Radio & Television News* 49 (June 1953), pp.56–57, 124; Macdonald, "Lie Detector Era, I," and "Lie Detector Era, II,"

28. Helm, "Lie Detector," in *Variety Television Reviews*, 1960–62, vol. 7 (New York: Garland Publishing, 1989).

29. For the semio-technique see Michel Foucault, *Discipline and Punish: The Birth of the Prison* (New York: Vintage, 1979), pp.73–103.

30. "Myth . . . could not care less about contradictions so long as it establishes a euphoric security." Roland Barthes, "Einstein's Brain," in *Mythologies* (London: Jonathan Cape, 1985), p.77.

# PART VI

# FINDING SECURITY
# IN THE ARCHIVES

# ❦Motion Regarding ATIP Recommendation❦

The participants at the "Whose National Security?" conference held at Laurentian University, Sudbury, November 22 to 24, 1996, represent many organizations involving scholars and community-based researchers with extensive experience using the ATIP (Access to Information and Privacy Act) legislation. As experienced ATIP users, we have encountered numerous frustrations with unnecessary barriers to Canadians' right to know. We therefore resolve that participants in the "Whose National Security?" conference recommend that the Minister of Justice follow through on his commitment to implement a consultation process with the Canadian people on the amendments to the Access to Information and Privacy Acts. An appropriate starting point for such consultations is the unanimous all-party recommendations of the five-year parliamentary review of the ATIP legislation, entitled "Open and Shut." An amended act should be guided by the principal of openness and provide the most extensive access to information for all Canadian citizens.

LARRY HANNANT

fifteen ✷ ✷ ✷

# What's in My File? Reflections of a "Security Threat"

Years ago I was an activist with the Communist Party of Canada (Marxist-Leninist). I was always a rather imperfect communist. Although I tried hard, I always seemed to be crossing sickles with party leaders, and I never became a member of the party. But that didn't matter. Marching on the front lines at demonstrations, being notorious as the communist editor of the university student newspaper in a small Ontario city, and owning the local communist bookstore, I was fairly high profile. So I had a good idea that the Royal Canadian Mounted Police kept a file on me, perhaps containing reams of paper and more photos than even my parents had.

Years after I became a former communist, the Access to Information and Privacy Act came into effect. In 1987, curious to see if I could manage to pry anything from the Canadian Security Intelligence Service (CSIS), I made a request for my records. By that time I had been out of communist politics for seven years. I thought that might be time enough to allow CSIS to judge me to be safe and release my file. As it turned out, CSIS did not share my idea that I was now a respectable, trustworthy citizen, and its response to my request was negative. Putting aside the bureaucratic jargon, CSIS refused to confirm or deny the existence of a file in my name.

In 1988 I appealed to the federal privacy commissioner, and asked in addition about news reports that CSIS was destroying a number of security-related files. If there was a file on me, I wanted to be assured that it would not be destroyed. In response Julien Delisle, an investigator in the privacy commissioner's office, repeated what CSIS had said, and added, "The Privacy Act does not permit me to confirm or deny the existence of personal information. You should note, however, that the destruction of security files is not an issue in this matter."[1] How ironic his comment was I would learn only years later.

In 1996 I was speaking with a friend who knew someone whose partner was an employee of CSIS. (This sounds convoluted, but the details have to remain clouded to protect the innocent—and the guilty.) I learned that CSIS certainly had not forgiven my past; it still had an active file on me. What I heard was that after my request, as a test, my name had been punched into the CSIS database of "threats

213

to the security of Canada." That had apparently set the bells ringing and the red lights flashing.

I found out that CSIS files recorded that I had hosted an Irish terrorist in my home at just about the same time as Julien Delisle in the privacy commissioner's office was assuring me that destruction of my file was not an issue. Delisle had certainly not misled me when he wrote that there was no prospect of my file being shredded. With the comic absurdity that perhaps only the murky security intelligence world can produce, I was now considered to be a threat to Canada's security because of aiding and abetting terrorism.

When I heard this, I cast my mind back to possible guests at my home in the years 1985 to 1988. Which was the terrorist? I thought I could safely rule out my in-laws, who had visited on several occasions. Just one possibility came to mind. In those years I had been a member of an Irish support group whose main purpose was to expose the duplicity and brutality of the Thatcher government's policy and practice in Northern Ireland. Our main activity was to try to change people's ideas about the situation in Ireland by holding public meetings and writing letters and articles on the issue. From time to time, as our meagre resources allowed, we brought speakers from Ireland to offer an insider's perspective on the conflict. One was Father Des Wilson, an activist priest from Belfast who for many decades had been devoting himself to building self-help enterprises among the city's unemployed. Father Des had been a guest in my house. Only by the most perverted thinking could he be considered a terrorist.

Late in 1996 I again asked CSIS for my file and received the standard bureaucratic brush-off. The service refused to say if it had a file on me. Translation: "We're still watching you." To paraphrase Gilbert and Sullivan, "Stick close to your desk and never plant a bomb, and you, too, may be classified as a terrorist threat to the Canadian state."

This personal experience and a decade of academic study of issues such as the development of the Canadian security screening system have led me to be inordinately curious about security intelligence issues. I like to imagine that being inquisitive and occasionally politically active has not harmed my health, my career (such as it is), my friends, my family, my future. But in idle moments, I wonder. And I am troubled by some bigger questions. Who gets defined as a security threat? By whom? What are the consequences of being defined as a security threat for the individual? What are the consequences for society of defining some individuals as security threats?

Who gets defined as a security threat? Perhaps we should ask an important preliminary question: who gets *passed* through the procedure by which security threats are identified? The short answer is everyone. Our society is commonly spoken of as a surveillance society. The very process of living a perfectly normal life today requires leaving behind a paper or, increasingly, computer trail. Once the information is deposited, it is very simple for the state to accumulate it. Indeed, it is virtually inevitable that at least some of the information will be accumulated. Sometimes the state lets people know that it is collecting information and matching it with data obtained from other sources. In the late 1990s the British Columbia government, for instance, publicly announced that social assistance recipients would have to agree to allow the provincial government to compare its data with information from many other sources. This comparison would include federal human resources databases such as the Canada Pension Plan and the Department of Citizenship and Immigration and foreign government databases. More than that, the social assistance recipient must also formally give consent to the government to contact and obtain information from a host of provincial data-bases—such as the motor vehicle branch and the registrar of companies—and information from other sources such as banks, landlords and former landlords, and past, present, or future employers of the recipient or the recipient's family members. As one person on social assistance observed, "at least in an honest police state they wouldn't humiliate me by asking for my permission" for the surveillance.[2] But humiliation is, indeed, part of the very process of enforcing compliance.

Since 1984 CSIS has had access to all those computer databases, and more. It can get confidential health records, income tax returns, passport information, employment insurance and social assistance files, details of child support arrangements and payments, business failures, and a number of other types of files. One of its few formal limitations is that to place telephone wiretaps it must first obtain the permission of the federal solicitor general and a federal court judge.[3]

In most cases the state collects information with the absolute minimum of public awareness, and it does so with remarkable success. By the 1920s, just a few years after the RCMP was founded, the force was already building its files with astonishing zeal. Greg Kealey has shown that by the mid-1920s RCMP files on left-ists numbered in the millions of pages. This push for information advanced in the 1930s, with the RCMP adding new weapons such as telephone wiretaps to its intru-sive arsenal. The Second World War offered the RCMP an invaluable opportunity to extend its surveillance even further. By 1945 the RCMP had subjected over two million Canadians—about one person in five—to some rudimentary security screening.[4] The inquiry proceeded apace during the Cold War and after, so that by 1981, when the McDonald Commission issued a summary of its investigation of the RCMP's criminal acts in the 1970s, the force had files on some eight hundred thousand Canadians deemed to be subversives.

Officially, many of those subversive files have since been destroyed, but there is little reason to suppose that the system has learned to tolerate "subversion." The security intelligence industry has apparently not been cured of its single-minded pursuit of every iota of data on any perceived danger to the "security" of Canada or its allied countries. In this social system, economic classes continue not only to exist but also to clash. Even the rich seem to have acknowledged this. An article in no less an establishment publication than *The New Yorker* in October 1997 quoted a Wall Street investment banker as saying, "The longer I spend on Wall Street, the more convinced I am that Marx was right."[5] So I'm not really surprised to learn that CSIS still maintains a file on me. The existence of that file indicates that CSIS has not abandoned the now eight-decade-old struggle to monitor and, by exten-sion, stifle all serious opposition to the status quo.

In sum, who is under scrutiny or potential scrutiny by the security intelligence system? All of us.

But once people are processed by the system, how do the authorities decide who is a serious opponent and who is not? Who is defined as a security threat? The definition of a security threat is frustratingly vague for the people who are potentially labelled as threats. Indeed, the vagueness of the definition is an integral part of the terror of the process. We simply cannot be sure whether we are a target or in line to be labelled a threat. Moreover, the state takes efforts to ensure that we cannot easily get that knowledge. Those who enquire are invariably met with the Kafkaesque reply, "We can neither confirm nor deny that there is a file on you." In such a circumstance, everyone who even suspects that they've been defined as a security threat must assume the answer to be yes. This is a form of psychological coercion.

Going further, who has the right to define some Canadians as security threats? In the great Western bureaucratic tradition, we have consigned that task to security "professionals." The expectation is that these professionals will remain above partisan politics. In general that has been true, and we have some reason to be thankful for that. Until 1984 the RCMP zealously guarded its primary role in and control over security intelligence. Citizens who wanted to become freelance sleuths were vigorously put in their place. No less important, various Canadian governments have studiously avoided involving themselves in security intelligence or taking a direct hand in overseeing the RCMP's security intelligence operations.[6] Well might talented Second World War bureaucrats such as Norman Robertson of External Affairs and Jack Pickersgill in the Prime Minister's Office ridicule the RCMP's amateurishness and yearn to have a more direct political hand in security intelligence affairs. But they knew well that their prime minister, William Lyon Mackenzie King, had not the least interest in maintaining close control over the RCMP. There were times in the turbulent twentieth century when politicians were more interventionist with regard to security intelligence—the government of Pierre Trudeau in the early 1970s, for example, when faced with the upsurge of Quebec nationalism. But that experience shows that politicians can be as inept as "professionals" at security intelligence. Thus Canada's standard practice has been to keep partisan politics out of security intelligence. This trend has been reinforced since 1984, when a multiparty oversight agency, the Security Intelligence Review Committee (SIRC), and greater court supervision were introduced as further guarantees that security intelligence would not be marked by political partisanship. And looking at countries in which the security intelligence force and/or military and police are in the pockets of the politicians, we have cause to breathe slightly more easily for it.

Yet while Canada's security intelligence service has mostly been above partisan politics, it has not, of course, been above politics. The very process is implicitly and explicitly political. The security intelligence agencies exist to maintain and protect a political system.

We should note, too, that what they protect is an international system. This is important because it means that it is not just Canadians who define what constitutes a security threat. Security intelligence is far from a made-in-Canada product. Already at the founding of the RCMP, British security services and their assessments of risk were influential here. Beginning in the Great Depression, U.S. views also began to shape Canadian assessments and outlooks. With regard to this international involvement in Canadian security intelligence, we know much more about the period before 1945 (and even then not a lot) than we do about the more recent era. This post-Second World War security intelligence liaison is a regrettable blind spot among security intelligence researchers. Granted, it is a relationship that is very hard to investigate. The Access to Information Act—which has aided research on domestic security intelligence—exempts information obtained by Canada from foreign governments.

The way in which security threats are established and assessed is also important. In 1969 the Mackenzie Commission set out two aspects to assessing loyalty. The first was acquiring data about a person's history. The second was using that information to forecast the person's future performance or reliability. The second aspect is clearly the more difficult. The Mackenzie Commission lamented: "It would be an ideal situation if it were possible to process an individual through a series of more or less mechanistic tests and arrive at an objective judgment of the subject's future loyalty. . . . Unfortunately . . . this is not possible, nor likely to be possible in the foreseeable future."[7]

What is "ideal" is obviously in the eye of the beholder. Many people would strongly disagree with the Mackenzie Commission's view that a simple "mechanistic" test for reliability would be a marvellous addition to our society. But the commission was at least correct in its assessment that the likelihood of inventing such a device was slim. The dim prospect of creating such a device, however, has not prevented the state from seeking some foolproof loyalty-testing mechanism. This is the search for what I call the infernal machine. From the fingerprinting that began in the 1920s, the exploration into hypnosis during the Second World War, and on to the "fruit machine" tests to seek out homosexuals in the 1950s, the RCMP has regularly tried different methods of ascertaining loyalty.

Sometimes the Force has been convinced that it has discovered the answer. Then the inevitable disappointment occurred, and the state found that a perfect mechanism for establishing trust did not exist. So it had to resort to an imperfect means—human judgement. Human judgement is notoriously flawed, and gave us such fiascos as the RCMP crimes of the 1970s, when members of the Force planted bombs, stole computer records, kidnapped activists, and committed arson in their campaign against the nationalist left in Quebec. Judgement can also be influenced by the particular state of struggle and contention within society. The RCMP officers who, in the 1930s and 1940s, endlessly harped on the theme of the communist threat to Canadian society were not simply guilty of faulty judgement. They spoke for a sector of society—primarily one class—that feared the threat of social upheaval represented by communists. Today communists do not represent a real menace to the status quo in this country (if they ever did), but the economic, political, and social disparities that gave birth to the Communist Party in 1921 have not been eradicated. So biased human judgement within the security intelligence system is just as important—and just as fraught with problems—as it has always been.

Being labelled a security threat has its heavy consequences, both to the individual and to society. Much of the security intelligence process is hidden, uncharted, and intangible, so the direct costs to individuals are rarely known publicly. This is especially true in Canada, where surveillance, screening, and identification have been much more covert than they have been in the United States. During the Cold War in particular, many Americans lost jobs and suffered damage to their careers and their basic rights because they fell afoul of the security intelligence agencies. But the relatively scanty evidence of such persecution in Canada does not mean that the security regime has had no effect on individuals here. The toll here has been emotional and psychological. The tension of believing that one is under surveillance and the pressure this puts on people and their relationships have not been extensively examined, but they are very real.

The consequences to the individual must also include the pressure to scale back or abandon controversial public activity. People who fear that they are being labelled as security risks must constantly ask themselves whether the benefit of their action is worth the cost. You might call this "identification chill," like the "libel chill" that afflicts journalists. This is particularly important in a society such as ours, where the focus is on individual achievement, success, and welfare. The benefits of social activism are rarely individual. One does not get rich or advance one's career by being a militant shop stewart, a dedicated student activist, a defender of those on social assistance, or a supporter of a reviled liberation movement abroad. The beneficiaries of this type of work are the community and intangible concepts such as social justice and human rights.

If activists are made aware constantly not only that they are not advancing themselves by their efforts but also that they may very well be hurting their chances for monetary and career success, the outcome is apparent. They often get worn down and opt to pursue a less active life.

Some people have not been cowed by this prospect. Recently I interviewed a number of U.S. exiles from the Cold War era. Several of them were jailed in the United States, had their careers ruined, and were forced to leave their homes and families and move to Canada. Yet they had few complaints about their treatment. Their attitude went something like this: "That was an unjust system and I opposed it. Should I be surprised that it kept me under surveillance and persecuted me?" Their response was just to keep on working on whatever cause they regarded as important.

One of the consequences for society as a whole of defining some people as security threats is the creation of an environment in which petty vindictiveness assumes considerable power because it can be allied with the state's political campaign. Sometimes informers are motivated by money. Sometimes pressure from the security intelligence apparatus, applied at sensitive points, can force people to inform. For instance, Leonard Peltier, an American Indian Movement activist from South Dakota, was extradited from Canada in 1976 on the basis of two sworn affidavits from Myrtle Poor Bear, who claimed she was Peltier's girlfriend and had witnessed him killing two FBI special agents in 1975. After the extradition hearing, but before Peltier's extradition, the affidavits were discovered to be false. Poor Bear had never known Peltier and had not been present at the time of the agents' deaths. Poor Bear had been pressured to lie by the FBI, who threatened to seize her children and intimated that she would suffer a fate similar to that of AIM activist Anna Mae Aquash—a mysterious, never-solved death.[8] (Canada nonetheless extradited Peltier.) Security intelligence forces clearly use that kind of intimidation to gain information.

No less often, in Western countries, ideological motives support intelligence accumulation, and "public-spirited vigilance" might be the most important source of intelligence. But what lies behind this co-operation with the security intelligence agencies is often petty jealousy masquerading as national loyalty. In his memoirs John Kenneth Galbraith described it well. During the Second World War he worked as a U.S. government regulator of steel prices. Whenever he turned down some steel manufacturer's request for a price hike, he invariably found that he was reported to the FBI as a communist. This type of response became particularly powerful as a vindictive weapon during the Cold War, when the public atmosphere of the day condoned ratting on your neighbour as a patriotic duty.

But that poisoned environment was not restricted to the Cold War. For instance, in May-June 1940, at the height of the fifth-column crisis in the first year of the Second World War, some public-spirited citizens in Lindsay, Ontario, informed the RCMP about the doings of Jean Watts, who was closely involved with the Communist Party of Canada and would shortly join the Canadian Women's Army Corps.[9] In such an atmosphere more than just political criteria come to be regarded as grist for the intelligence mill. That lesson impressed itself on Ruth Budd, a bassist with the Toronto Symphony Orchestra who was barred from the United States and fired from the orchestra in 1951 because of her politics. She remembers overhearing one of her fellow musicians saying, "Well, she must be a Communist, she reads a lot!"[10] The social deviance of reading too much was enough to get someone on the blacklist.

Timothy Garton Ash has a made an intriguing excursion into the question of the social consequences of the security intelligence system in *The File: A Personal Story*.[11] Much of the book is an exploration of the issues surrounding the extraordinary opportunity to study security intelligence presented by the collapse of the East European regimes in 1989. In East Germany, just as people were beginning to smash down the Berlin Wall, the Ministry of State Security, the Stasi, had some ninety thousand employees and more than one hundred and seventy thousand "unofficial collaborators," freelance informers. About one in every fifty adult East Germans had a direct connection with the secret police. After the regime fell, anyone could apply to see his or her Stasi file. More than one million people did so in the following years. Garton Ash, who in the early 1980s was a British graduate student who lived in East Europe and studied society and politics there, applied for and received his file. Then he set to tracking down the people who had created and updated the file and who provided details to the Stasi for it. The result, *The File*, offers a unique vision into the heart of a repressive bureaucracy.

To his credit, Garton Ash took the matter further. Back in Britain, curious about what goes on in his own country, Garton Ash sought information about the security intelligence system. He talked with the spy novelist John le Carré, other former intelligence officers, and even people in the British secret service. The inquiry took him to the offices of MI5, Britain's domestic security service. Interviewing a senior MI5 officer, Garton Ash asked, "Do you have a file on me?" The answer: "Yes, since you ask, we do. We have what's called a white card file on you." A "white-card file" is a non-adversarial file, probably related to MI5's interest in recruiting Garton Ash earlier on. Could he read the file? No.

Garton Ash asked the logical next question. What stops MI5 from subjecting Britons to a surveillance system as extensive as the Stasi had on East Germans? What prevents the secret service from going over the top? But the answer he got, and what he made of it, are unfortunately inadequate to the real problem he poses. The MI5 officer replied that Britons were protected by "the whole ethos of the service . . . our attitudes . . . the kind of people we are." And, too, MI5 is "closely supervised by the Home Office. . . . The Home Office was no pushover, you can be sure." Garton Ash correctly observed that this is a "pretty slender thread, even if drawn from the best British worsted."[12] But to answer his own queries, Garton Ash could offer only this enigmatic solace: "The domestic spies in a free country live this professional paradox: they infringe our liberties in order to protect them. But we have another paradox: we support the system by questioning it. That's where I stand."[13]

This is a thin gruel indeed. In Canada, no one whom the state regards as in any way dissident gets the kind of clubby privileged access to the inside that Garton Ash was able to obtain. No CSIS officer sits down with the subject of security intelligence reports and confirms that a file exists on her or him and attempts to rationalize that the personal privacy of Canadians is safe, despite the secrecy of the intelligence service. We know so little about the contemporary Canadian security intelligence system that we cannot possibly offer any informed view on whether or not it merits the slightest iota of support from citizens.

Still, more formal safeguards and checks are supposedly available to us. Garton Ash's MI5 officer mentioned the Home Office. In Canada the CSIS Act imposes legal restrictions on surveillance by the Intelligence Service. The act stipulates restrictions that are supposed to prevent the wholesale abuse of the surveillance capacity that had occurred under the old RCMP Security Service; and the act also provides for a new oversight committee, SIRC. But social and political activists who contemplate the CSIS Act see little to reassure them on that score.

Just the open sources we do have, such as news reports, indicate reason to doubt the effectiveness of such oversight. For instance, in October 1997 a rare public conflict between the courts and CSIS showed that CSIS had been routinely bypassing supposed safeguards, with the approval of the Federal Court of Canada. In that case, a Federal Court judge rejected a CSIS application for a special warrant that would allow it to conduct extensive wiretaps without going through a judge. But a CSIS spokeswoman remarked that similar applications had been granted "numerous times" in the past, including by the very judge, Madame Justice Donna McGillis, who rejected that particular special warrant.[14] In short, the careful supervision of CSIS by oversight agency and judicial process might be chimerical.

The Access to Information and Privacy Act was supposed to open up the government vaults to scrutiny from citizens. Although the Act has been invaluable for historians—I'm the first to acknowledge that without it I could not have hoped to have written some of the history I have managed to do—it has proved mostly to have been an ineffective means of monitoring the surveillance state. The Act has been a cruel deception for the two or three generations of activists who have been in the forefront of popular politics since the late 1960s. Of all those people, perhaps only a few have been able to use the act to obtain their files. A few high-profile activists, such as June Callwood, have tried to obtain files dating from the years after 1968, and their efforts have come to naught. The astronomical cost of fighting a court challenge deterred Callwood from pursuing her case.[15] The success of the Canadian Union of Postal Workers in obtaining RCMP files on its activities, mostly from the 1970s, is one of the notable exceptions to this general rule.

I'm puzzled by Garton Ash's observation that "we support the system by questioning it." Beyond questions we have no effective means of either ascertaining even rudimentary details about this infernal machine or exercising the slightest discipline over it. And I doubt that CSIS interprets such questions as evidence of us supporting it.

So, if questions do constitute the sole weapon in our arsenal, let me return to the one I have been asking now for almost a decade and a half: what's in my file? I continue to seek a response. In a self-respecting democracy, the government should not have to fall—as the East German government did—in order for me to get the answer.

## Notes

1. Julien Delisle to author, Feb. 1, 1988.
2. *Times Colonist* (Victoria), Jan. 28, 1998.
3. Richard Cleroux, *Official Secrets: The Inside Story of the Canadian Security Intelligence Service* (Toronto: McClelland and Stewart, 1991), pp.71–72.
4. Gregory S. Kealey, "The Early Years of State Surveillance of Labour and the Left in Canada: The Institutional Framework of the Royal Canadian Mounted Police Security and Intelligence Apparatus, 1918–1926," *Intelligence and National Security* 8,3 (July 1993), p.134; Carl Betke and Stan Horrall, *Canada's Security Service: An Historical Outline, 1864–1966* (Ottawa: RCMP Historical Section, 1978), obtained through Access to Information Act; Larry Hannant, *The Infernal Machine: Investigating the Loyalty of Canada's Citizens* (Toronto: University of Toronto Press, 1995), p.84.
5. John Cassidy, "The Return of Karl Marx," *The New Yorker*, Oct. 20–27, 1997, p.248.
6. See the discussion of this issue in Betke and Horrall, "Canada's Security Service," pp.xvi–xvii, 426; for my commentary on it, see Larry Hannant, "Access to the Inside: An Assessment of 'Canada's Security Service,'" *Intelligence and National Security* 8,3 (July 1993).
7. Canada, *Report of the Royal Commission on Security* [Mackenzie Commission] (Ottawa: Queen's Printer, 1969), p.30.
8. Peter Matthiessen, *In the Spirit of Crazy Horse* (New York: Viking, 1991), p.342; on the extradition of Peltier from Canada, see also John Privitera, "Toward a Remedy for International Extradition by Fraud: The Case of Leonard Peltier," *Yale Law and Policy Review* 2,49 (1983).
9. Letters (correspondents' names deleted) to RCMP Commissioner, May 16, June 3, 1940, CSIS Access 117–95.
10. Len Scher, *The Un-Canadians: True Stories of the Blacklist Era* (Toronto: Lester, 1992), p.29.
11. Timothy Garton Ash, *The File: A Personal History* (New York: Random House, 1997).
12. Ibid., pp.241–42.
13. Ibid., p.248.
14. *The Globe and Mail*, Oct. 1, 1997, p.A5.

15. Michael Valpy, "Spying by Police a Frightening Thing," *The Globe and Mail*, Nov. 22, 1989; Michael Valpy, "How the Mounties Get Their BLANKS," *The Globe and Mail*, Nov. 23, 1989; and June Callwood to the author, Dec. 6, 1989 and telephone conversation, Feb. 9, 1998.

KERRY BADGLEY

sixteen ✳ ✳ ✳

# Researchers and Canada's Public Archives: Gaining Access to the Security Collections

Among the many, many kinds of government documents relating to national security and intelligence available at the National Archives of Canada, the records of the Canadian Security and Intelligence Service (CSIS) are, not surprisingly, one of the more popular sources of information; and, as authors such as Greg Kealey and Reg Whitaker have shown, researchers have barely begun to scratch the surface of these records. Information on individuals, political parties, student groups, unions, peace organizations, and feminist groups, among many others: all of this can be found in what is classified as Record Group (RG) 146.[1] Obviously, then, it is paramount that researchers working in this rich field know how to gain access to these files.[2]

Indeed, the CSIS files, RG 146—which also contain most of the surviving files of its predecessor, the RCMP Security Service—are a treasure-trove of information on security and intelligence. Although this is especially true for researchers undertaking historical research, these documents are of considerable use for those in other disciplines as well. They are also distinct from other record groups in that there are special conditions governing their disclosure and use. For one thing, a formal Access to Information request is necessary to attempt to gain access to CSIS records. In the case of other government records, the researcher can make use of either formal or informal procedures.

Many researchers make use of the informal process because it often gets them the records they require, and with minimal delay. In the case of informal requests, all a researcher needs to do is fill out a standard request form and submit it at the Circulation Desk in the Archives' Reading Room. If the material was previously reviewed by Access review analysts at the Archives and is now open, the researcher may obtain these records as early as the next day.[3] If the material was not previously reviewed, its accessibility is assessed by Archives' review analysts. During the review, the file might be opened in its entirety, partially disclosed (that is, some information removed pursuant to the legislation), or completely closed to the researcher. If material is removed or the file closed, researchers can consider filing formally to try to gain access to the material that they did not see.

A formal request takes considerably more time. First of all, researchers are required to submit a formal access request form (copies of which are available at the National Archives and every other federal government institution covered by the legislation), accompanied by a five-dollar fee, as required under the Act.[4] The fee entitles the applicant to five "free" hours of search and preparation time.

In general, the nature of the formal request determines whether or not the Archives will consult with the creator department regarding the accessibility of the requested records. RG 146 records, however, are a different matter. Given that RG 146 files are almost exclusively concerned with national security and intelligence issues, and since many of the records are quite sensitive, the National Archives always consults with CSIS before determining the accessibility of the records. In other words, CSIS is asked to provide advice on the accessibility of the records that the Archives identifies as relevant to the request.

Under the legislation, the department to which a formal request is submitted is required to respond to the applicant within thirty days of receipt of the request. When consultation is required, though, researchers may receive the initial response in the form of a letter, informing them that an extension is required to process the request. This almost invariably happens with RG 146 records, since consultation with CSIS is always undertaken. The National Archives, as with all government departments, has the right to take an extension, but the researcher, in turn, has the right to complain to the information commissioner about the extension, and to lodge a complaint.

Given that these extensions can be quite lengthy if they involve hundreds or thousands of pages, researchers are advised to do two things before even making the request. First, researchers should consult with the archivist responsible for RG 146 records to determine whether there is information pertaining to the topic. If there is, then the researcher will be directed to search through the relevant finding aids.[5] A search through the finding aids should give the researcher an idea of the extent of the records.

Second, researchers should try to be as specific as possible when making their requests. Although there is a strong temptation to cast very broad nets when conducting research, this does not always work when it comes to CSIS records. Researchers who ask for RG 146 records "pertaining to the Communist Party of Canada," for instance, will receive phone calls from one of the Archives' access review analysts, asking them to narrow down the scope of the request. Consequently, a researcher interested in the activities of the Workers' Unity League (WUL) in Brandon, Manitoba, should not request all records relating to the WUL. Conversely, if a researcher is interested only in a specific date range, then the outside dates (that is, the "from and to" dates) should be mentioned in the request. Generally speaking, a good rule to follow when requesting RG 146 records is to make a specific request first and, if the documents point to another potential source of information within RG 146, to then file subsequent requests.

Some researchers stagger their requests out over a long period of time so that they are ensured of a steady stream of documents to work from, rather than being inundated with hundreds or thousands of pages at one time. There is another bonus to be had from taking this approach: by filing several small requests, fees for search and preparation time can be kept to a minimum or, in many cases, completely eliminated. In addition, some researchers, when dealing with a potentially large set of records, submit separate requests for each month of the years that pertain to the subject. I have seen researchers submit requests for information about the Front de Libération du Québec, for example, on a month-by-month basis for the years 1970–71.

If at all possible, researchers should leave an adequate amount of time for the Archives to process the request, so that a lengthy consultation or unanticipated delays will not cause missed deadlines. At times review analysts have had to process requests involving thousands of pages—I have handled several such requests myself. Understandably, these requests cannot be completed overnight, and researchers in a rush can be disappointed when the documents do not arrive as early as expected. It is best to be pessimistic and assume a long consultation period. That way, the chances of being disappointed will be minimized.

In addition, researchers are encouraged to consult the "public-use copies" available at the National Archives. These documents are photocopies of documents from all RG 146 access to information requests that the National Archives has processed and made available for consultation.[6] At present, over forty boxes are available, containing thousands of pages of publicly available records dealing with subjects as diverse as the Winnipeg General Strike, the Communist Party of Canada, unions, surveillance of university campuses, civil liberty associations, fascist organizations, the FLQ, and ethno-cultural groups.

Some public-use copies relate to individuals who, for one reason or another, were under Security Service surveillance. In most cases, one can obtain records pertaining to individuals provided that the person to whom the information relates has been dead for twenty years or more. For example, researchers can consult an extensive declassified file on François Mario Bachand, an FLQ terrorist who was assassinated in France in 1971, because another researcher requested these files a few years ago.

When researchers request files pertaining to individuals, they should be sure to include all possible pseudonyms or different spellings of the name in the request. In some cases, if the search under the name specified in the request does not produce any results, the researcher might be told that no records exist, even though they might be in the collection under another name.[7]

Something that almost always occurs in the case of a CSIS request is that material is exempted (that is, removed) under the Access to Information Act. In these instances, the researcher will notice a stamp near the exemption, which merely states that information has been removed pursuant to Access to Information and Privacy legislation. If material is exempted from other RGs, a researcher is informed under what section or sections of the legislation the material has been removed. CSIS records, yet again, are a different story. Rather than listing under what section(s) of the Act the information was removed, the researcher is informed in a letter of the section(s) of the legislation that have been invoked in removing information from the files. In fact, there was even a court case in which researchers attempted to have CSIS put the reason for the exemption directly beside the blacked-out material. CSIS won the case, and the Archives adheres to this ruling when exempting material from CSIS records.

All of this must sound somewhat discouraging: automatic consultation with CSIS, almost guaranteed exemptions, not being told the reason for the exemption, and so on. Taken together, it seems as though the odds are stacked against researchers in favour of those of us on the other side of the Act. There are some elements in the process, though, that work to the benefit of researchers.

For one thing, there are bright sides to mandatory consultations. There are times, for example, when CSIS officials inform Archives' staff that certain information is no longer considered to be as sensitive as it once was. Hence, CSIS might actually recommend releasing the information that another department, lacking specialized expertise, might consider closing. Thus, in some cases the consultation process probably nets researchers more information than they would have received without it.

Moreover, because RG 146 requests are formal requests, the applicant has the right to lodge a complaint with the Office of the Information Commissioner. Researchers can complain about the exemptions, the length of time to process the request, and the fees that were levied, among other things. Thus, another advantage to working with RG 146 records is that researchers have the automatic right to appeal the outcome of the request to the Office of the Information Commissioner.

A complaint might yield the researcher some additional information, but that is not always the case. If applicants are unhappy with the information commissioner's decision, then they can appeal to the Federal Court. Although this procedure can be quite time-consuming and potentially costly, the decisions rendered in these court cases sometimes lead to greater openness on the part of government departments and agencies. In some instances the information commissioner has taken government departments to court in an attempt to have additional information released.

In addition, people have the right to see what a government department or agency has collected regarding themselves. Moreover, if you are working on a fairly recent subject, and are in contact with individuals who were part of the movement, group, or event under surveillance, then you might consider having these people file requests under the Privacy Act to obtain their files. One of the advantages of using the Privacy Act to obtain information is that it does not cost researchers a cent to do so. The Privacy Act is predicated on the principle that a person should not have to pay in order to obtain information that the government has gathered. This means there are no photocopying costs (something for which fees can be levied under the Access to Information Act). As is the case with access to information requests, a person who believes that a request was not responded to in a timely manner, or that the exemptions are questionable or excessive, has the right to complain.

Researchers can also find security and intelligence records in sources other than RG 146. Some of the records contained in RG 2 (Privy Council), RG 18 (Royal Canadian Mounted Police), RG 26 (Citizenship and Immigration), RG 24 (National Defence), RG 25 (External Affairs), RG 73 (Solicitor General), and RG 76 (Immigration) touch upon national security, and they might, if nothing else, provide context or, perhaps, reasons for policy decisions made in national security and intelligence areas.

As well, there are several other, lesser-known departments and agencies that can assist researchers exploring national security themes. There are files in RG 19 (Finance), RG 20 (Trade and Commerce), RG 55 (Treasury Board), or RG 60 (Defence Production) that might be of assistance to researchers. Even something as seemingly innocuous as the Canada Unity Information Office (RG 137), established in 1977 largely to counteract the "subversive propaganda" of the Parti Québécois government, could shed light on the nature and extent of security and intelligence operations in Canada, and the goals of these activities.

In addition, the records of certain royal commissions might be of assistance for those interested in national security records. The Royal Commission on War Criminals (RG 33/144), the Royal Commission on Espionage in Government Service (Gouzenko Affair) (RG 33/62), the Inquiry into the Case of Gerda Munsinger (RG 33/96), and the Commission of Inquiry Concerning Certain Activities of the Royal Canadian Mounted Police (RG 33/128—better known as the McDonald Commission) are now under the control of the National Archives. A large percentage of these records are open for consultation. There are good general inventories and finding aids for all these RGs, and I advise researchers to consult with the relevant archivists before making a trip to Ottawa.

Finally, at least one other important source of information exists: records held in the National Archives' Manuscript Division. Unlike government records, which are subject to access to information and privacy legislation, the only restrictions placed upon private papers are those imposed by the donors. The Manuscript Division holds records of former prime ministers, prominent cabinet ministers, high-ranking bureaucrats, and other political figures. Again, these records are backed by good finding aids, and researchers can contact the relevant archivists in the Manuscript Division for additional information.

Access review analysts at the National Archives take considerable pride in being as helpful as possible to researchers. Rather than search for ways of keeping government records out of the hands of researchers, we strive to provide as much information as possible to applicants for information. Although it is a federal institution, the National Archives of Canada is, at the same time, a research institution. As such, analysts believe that openness and making as much information available as possible to researchers should be the guiding principles of the operation.

## Notes

The views expressed here are those of the author and not of the National Archives. The author wants to thank the editors, and the organizers of the Whose National Security Conference, for the opportunity to present the material and to participate in an exchange on archival usage.

1.  Federal government documents are currently arranged in Record Groups (RGs). By way of definition, a record group is a collection of records, organized on the basis of a government department, agency, or branch that exhibited administrative continuity over a

      period of time.

2.    I will forego describing relatively routine matters, such as how to register, hours of service, and photocopying regulations. For the uninitiated, I suggest you consult the National Archives' web-site (www.archives.ca), or telephone the Archives before making your research trip.

3.    An official form is not necessary. The National Archives of Canada considers any written request that refers to the Act and is accompanied by five dollars as a formal access request.

3.    Most of the government records are now stored off-site in the new Gatineau facilities, and can take between twenty-four and forty-eight hours to be transferred to the Reading Room.

4.    A finding aid is a list of the files held in a particular records group. Thanks to the efforts of some security and intelligence researchers, CSIS has released fairly extensive finding aids for its archival collection.

5.    A separate list, which describes the declassified records open for consultation in the CSIS reading room, is also on file at the National Archives.

6.    Researchers should also use as many alternative names or titles as possible when requesting information on groups and organizations. Researchers requesting information pertaining to the Communist Party for certain periods, for example, can play it safe and mention the Labor Progressive Party in the request as well.

HEIDI MCDONELL

seventeen ✳ ✳ ✳

# The Experiences of a Researcher in the Maze

In the course of searching for archival sources for a research report on the national security campaigns against gay men and lesbians in Canada, a group of us have encountered a number of difficulties and obstacles.[1] These obstacles in turn provided us with a sense of how these "security" documents are organized or, more to the point, scattered and unorganized. As the main archival researcher, I found it very interesting to be an out lesbian in 1995–96 going into offices in which I knew people had been interrogated. This knowledge of past activities was especially strong when I visited the CSIS visiting room.

When you arrive at CSIS you are given a pass that you must use to go through doors from one room to another. As I was led to one office labelled "Interview Room," I thought, "Well, I'm glad it's 1995 and not 1962." Although the historical context had changed since the height of the country's anti-homosexual national security campaigns, the lingering political and social controversies concerning homosexuality continued to plague our successes around gaining access to pertinent information.

Perhaps the most significant difficulty we encountered concerned the Security Panel, the interdepartmental bureau that co-ordinated national security work within the Canadian state in the 1950s and 1960s. (See "Introduction," pp.1–2.) Although the Security Panel created documentation like a governmental department, in the Archives it does not have a finding aid of its own that we could search and therefore use to locate documents necessary to our research. The Security Panel was basically made up of many different departments, so it had a sort of early interdisciplinary approach to queer (lesbian/gay) studies. The departments involved at various times in its affairs included not just External Affairs, the Privy Council, and the RCMP, but also the Department of Justice, Health and Welfare, Defence Production, Citizenship and Immigration, and the Civil Service Commission. We concentrated our efforts on the record groups and finding aids of the departments that were part of the Security Panel. Another important tool, aside from the finding aids, are the ATIP (Access to Information Program) lists or access lists that every department produces as a record of all access to information requests made by individuals. Most of the informal and formal requests that I made were from information provided by the finding aids and these ATIP lists.

As I worked I began to notice that the departments in question released the same documents to us regardless of the access request we submitted. In other words, we would receive a new batch of documents from, say, the Department of National Defence that were identical to the documents we had received from the Privy Council Office (PCO) a week before. This poses a problem for researchers in terms of access to information request numbers, because every request is issued a different number and it is difficult to figure out what has already been released. As well, not all access offices are created equal. In some access offices (each department has an access co-ordinator and access office) you can walk right in and get served with a smile; in others you are treated in a distinctly cool manner. For example, the PCO was in general a pleasant experience. The access officers at the PCO are used to dealing with people because reporters are constantly requesting information on the prime minister and how and where he spends public funds. On the other hand, the External Affairs access officers were not as co-operative. I was told that in order to look at their ATIP list I would have to pay a fee, which takes about a week to generate. I was informed that the access office at External Affairs had established this internal policy.

One particularly puzzling yet interesting aspect of this process is that there exists no connection or communication between what had been released through access requests by the departments and what had been released through the public archives. I once asked an archivist at the National Archives if I could look at some of the submissions made to the Royal Commission on Security and was promptly told that I had to fill out a new access to information request. I found this odd so I pulled out a copy of the documents I had already obtained through a request from CSIS, where I had been given the first two hundred pages of documents photocopied free. Needless to say, this was an enlightening moment for me as a researcher. I suggest that if you are doing research in the area of national security you make a list of the documents that you have received through access to information requests and share the information with the archivists at the National Archives so that they can then release their own copies of these documents.

Our research points to two elusive sets of documents that we think exist but have proven difficult to locate. The first relates to the infamous "fruit machine," which was designed to detect homosexuals.[2] We know from the documents we have gained access to that this research was funded by the government and was built and tested on pilot groups, but documentation of this technology and many of the reports on it are nowhere to be found. The other "holy grail" is what we have named the "tripartite agreement." This agreement between Britain, Canada, and the United States supposedly has specific references to how these countries would deal with homosexuals found in government employment. My search for this agreement began with the access lists from External Affairs (once I was finally allowed to look at those lists), where I found some access requests made by other individuals that I thought would prove fruitful in my endeavours. Since these requests were already assigned numbers, I transcribed them to the access to information form, and waited for a response. Within the next thirty days I received a letter saying that the first thirty-day period for the search was up so they would now give me another 120-day period free of charge to process my request. When this period came to an end I received a letter that told me the information I requested could not be released to me due to subsections 13-1A, 13-1B, and 15-1 of the Access to Information Act. According to that letter, External Affairs had consulted with other government institutions, and all documents I requested were being withheld in their entirety under the above-mentioned subsections of the Access Act.

These and other subsections of the Access to Information Act we have encountered during the course of this research reveal much about how certain state documents are constructed as "sensitive" and therefore classified. Subsection 15-1 is the subsection cited most often in the documents we have requested. Entire pages are "whited-out" or "blackened" with the numbers "15-1" penned in the margins by an access officer. This subsection stipulates:

> The head of a government institution may refuse to disclose any information requested under this Act that contains information the disclosure of which could reasonably be expected to be injurious to the conduct of international affairs, the defence of Canada or any state allied or associated with Canada or the detection, prevention or suppression of subversive or hostile activities, including, without restricting the generality of the foregoing, any such information.[3]

In effect, subsection 15-1 states that the information is withheld, ironically, on the grounds of national and international security. Subsections 13-1A and 13-1B stipulate that the "head of a government institution" will not disclose information requested that was obtained in confidence from the government of a foreign state or an institution or an international organization of states or an institution.

Subsection 21 of the Access Act is also often cited. This subsection entitles the government to withhold information requested that contains:

> (a) advice or recommendations developed by or for a government institution or a Minister of the Crown,
> (b) an account of consultations or deliberations involving officials or employees of a government institution, a Minister of the Crown or the staff of a Minister of the Crown,
> (c) positions or plans developed for the purpose of negotiations carried on or to be carried on by or on behalf of the Government of Canada and considerations relating thereto, or
> (d) plans relating to the management of personnel or the administration of a government institution that have not yet been put into operation, if the record came into existence less than twenty years prior to the request.[4]

The combination of these subsections is clearly meant to protect the government and create impenetrable obstacles for researchers who want to uncover information on security issues. Indeed, these subsections are so vague and broad-ranging that almost any document we request through the Access Act can be prohibited as a threat to national security.

Still, if there is one thing we have learned from the people interviewed for this project, it is that possibilities for resistance, subversion, and non-cooperation are everywhere. Sometimes those sites of resistance come in the form of a person. One access officer I worked very closely with helped me sort through some of the red tape I encountered. He would often read the information that I had requested informally and tell me whether it was useful for the research I was conducting. He was, in a sense, a much-needed insider who helped me sift through stacks and stacks of useless information. Based on my experience, if the information makes it to the Archives from the departments, it is considered more readily "public" and thus easier to access.

I have come to the conclusion that because the Security Panel was quite nebulous in terms of its bureaucratic organization, being neither a department nor government office and because it advised the prime minister and his cabinet on highly classified issues, it may have had a completely separate system of storing and archiving the information that it generated. There is the possibility that some of this security information may be in the records of the PCO. Unfortunately, as I discovered, there is what is called a "cooling out" period of two years on documents sent from the PCO to the National Archives warehouse. Access requests, however, might play an important role in hurrying along the process of obtaining these documents from the warehouse.

The Access to Information Act has proven to be a double-edged sword: while it has allowed us to obtain documents that have revealed a sad chapter in gay and lesbian history, it was created ultimately to *protect* the very same state institutions that initiated the anti-homosexual national security campaigns.

## Notes

1. The research was for Gary Kinsman and Patrizia Gentile, with the assistance of Heidi McDonell and Mary Mahood-Greer, "'In the Interests of the State': The Anti-Gay, Anti-Lesbian National Security Campaign in Canada," a preliminary research report, Laurentian University, Sudbury, 1998.
2. On the "fruit machine," see Kinsman et al., 'In the Interests of the State,'" pp.106–16; and Gary Kinsman, "'Character Weaknesses' and 'Fruit Machines': Towards an Analysis of the Anti-Homosexual Security Campaign in the Canadian Civil Service," *Labour/Le Travail* 35 (Spring 1995), pp.153–59.
3. Access to Information Act, R.S.C. 1985, CA-1.
4. Ibid.

# PART VII

# OLD METHODS AND RECENT TRENDS

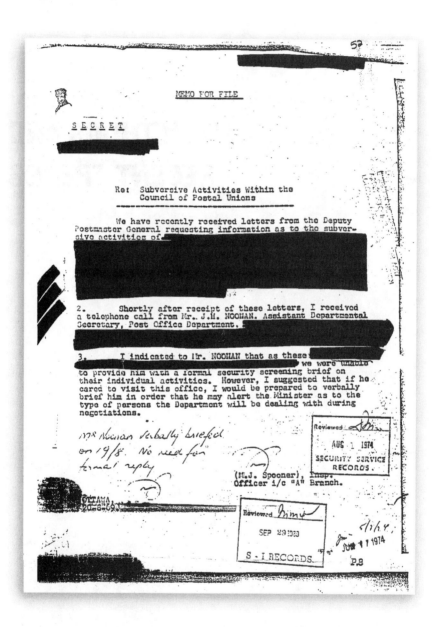

MEMO FOR FILE

S E C R E T

Re: Subversive Activities Within the
Council of Postal Unions

We have recently received letters from the Deputy
Postmaster General requesting information as to the subversive activities of ████████████████████

2.        Shortly after receipt of these letters, I received
a telephone call from Mr. J.H. NOONAN, Assistant Departmental
Secretary, Post Office Department.

3.        I indicated to Mr. NOONAN that as these ████████
████████████████████ we were unable
to provide him with a formal security screening brief on
their individual activities. However, I suggested that if he
cared to visit this office, I would be prepared to verbally
brief him in order that he may alert the Minister as to the
type of persons the Department will be dealing with during
negotiations.

*Mr Noonan verbally briefed
on 19/8. No need for
formal reply*

(M.J. Spooner), Insp.
Officer i/c "A" Branch.

Reviewed ████
AUG 1 1974
SECURITY SERVICE
RECORDS

OTTAWA

Reviewed ████
SEP 29 1983
S - I RECORDS

JUN 11 1974
P.8

An RCMP surveillance report on the Council of Postal Workers, with information blacked out
by Access to Information Officers for reasons of "national security." [Hoogers, chap. 19]

eighteen ✷ ✷ ✷

# Remembering Federal Police Surveillance in Quebec, 1940s–70s

I first became aware of federal police surveillance when I was in the student movement in Quebec. In autumn 1937 a group of mostly non-fraternity McGill students joined with similar groups in numerous other English-Canadian campuses in the founding of the Canadian Student Assembly (CSA). Our sole demand was that the federal government establish five hundred scholarships for men and women students unable to afford university tuition fees. Applicants would be chosen on the basis of their academic standing.

From McGill we also contacted students at the "Hautes études commerciales" of the Université de Montréal; we were also joined by Université Laval students at the Département des sciences sociales, founded by Georges-Henri Lévesque, a Dominican priest whose modern ideas differed with the Jesuit teachings that had prevailed in Quebec classical colleges.

At McGill the Canadian Student Assembly was tolerated with reluctance. At the time CPR president Sir Edward Beatty was the university's chancellor, and the Board of Governors consisted of Sir Charles Gordon, president of the Dominion Textile Company, and other worthy gentlemen who were not well-disposed to taxpayers' money going to the poor.

After war was declared in 1939 the CSA encountered open hostility, not only at McGill but also on several other English-speaking campuses. We were given to understand that the duty of male students was to join the armed forces while women were expected to serve the country in the armed forces or in other appropriate ways. It was not a time to be asking for money from the government. Since the CSA was under attack and the graduation of several of the activists came up around the same time, the student organization ceased around 1940. Still, a seed had been planted and at the end of World War II university doors were opened, courtesy of the federal government, to veterans who chose higher education.

During the Christmas-New Year's break of 1939–40 the CSA held a Canada-wide conference in Ste-Anne-de-Bellevue outside Montreal, at Macdonald College, affiliated with McGill. Most delegates were billeted at the college dormitory. Early on the first morning I ran into a stranger in the women's washroom. She told me she was a delegate from Sacred Heart College in Montreal. I knew her story could

235

not be true—I had been involved in the conference preparations and knew that she did not have credentials from the conference committee—and I realized that someone in authority at Macdonald College must have provided her with a room. Instead of challenging her, I decided to remain silent and observe what she was doing. I noticed that by the end of the opening session she had gone to sit near a Western delegate, the most outspoken radical on the floor. She stuck close to him for the duration, applauding his speeches, spending free time with him, and getting to know his entourage. Later I found out she was trying to seduce him, apparently hoping it would result in some continuity by correspondence, but after learning that his new conquest from Quebec was not what she appeared to be, the young radical cut her off.

After exams, in the spring of 1940, I did volunteer work in Montreal for the Canadian Youth Congress (CYC), an organization looking out primarily for the economic needs of Canadian youth. Early one evening, when I was at the CYC office with a fifteen-year-old girl who had come to do volunteer work for the first time, we were visited by three men from the RCMP. They searched through the files, placed records in boxes, and took us and the boxes to RCMP headquarters in old Montreal. We were held there for about five hours, mostly under the supervision of a fourth officer who refused to give us any information or to allow us a phone call to our mothers or to anyone else.

In the end we were taken to another room to appear before a man who seemed to be in command, although he was in civilian clothes. It was in the late evening, and it appeared that he had rushed to the office from home. He harangued us, sometimes wildly, always refusing to say whether we were to be arrested, charged, detained, or incarcerated under the War Measures Act or just allowed a phone call. Finally, he signalled to the officers who had brought us to headquarters to take us away. Once out of the building, they told us they were to take us home, but we had them let us off well before we reached our destinations. The CYC closed its Montreal office immediately after the raid. We reasoned that if young men had been found in the office instead of two female students, the men might have been carried off to the prisoner of war camp in Petawawa. With the issue of conscription legislation heating up—a national plebiscite in 1942 would show 85 per cent of Quebec francophones opposed to conscription—the federal government was determined to pre-empt all youth protests, especially in Quebec.

Prior to the raid, a man had been dropping by the CYC office two or three times a week during the time when young people came around after a day's work to report, pick up leaflets, or attend a committee meeting. The man had no obvious reason for being there. He would greet people as though they were friends. He had an easy smile and flirty eyes, anything to appear relaxed and friendly. Once during a public meeting, when there was tension in the air, he made a wild, provocative speech designed to encourage young innocents to follow suit. Immediately after, an experienced CYC activist spoke about the dangers of making irresponsible statements in wartime, analysed the current situation, and suggested guarded action. It cleared the air. Later, somebody obtained proof that the "relaxed" visitor and emotional speaker at the CYC was an RCMP informer. One could conclude that he was also an *agent provocateur*.

Later I learned that the uninvited student delegate to the CSA's 1939–40 Christmas conference was the daughter of the RCMP officer who had vented his spleen on me at the headquarters in the spring of 1940. His daughter eventually joined the Canadian women's armed forces.

## Unions

During 1943–44, when I was a union organizer for the United Textile Workers of America (AFL) amongst the cotton-mill workers in Montreal and Valleyfield, our union occasionally reserved paid broadcasting time on Montreal radio station CKAC, owned by the Berthiaume-Du Tremblay family, who also owned *La Presse*, the main French-language daily newspaper. I would submit my text in advance to M. Claude Bourgeois, the official government censor at the station under wartime regulations. He would read and initial two copies of the text. One copy went to the radio station's files, and I retained the other one to read on the air on the night of the broadcast. Once when I finished the broadcast, my chair was immediately taken by the personnel manager of the Dominion Textile Company, who read a point-by-point corporate reply to the union's arguments.

I went to see M. Bourgeois the following day. He explained that the RCMP had walked into the radio station unannounced and ordered staff to hand over the station's copy of my text. The police took it away and obviously gave it to the Dominion Textile Company, which had no trouble reserving the next time-slot on the radio. The next time we had a slot arranged on the radio I took my text before-hand to M. Bourgeois's home, where he checked and initialled it, and gave it back to me without retaining a copy for CKAC. When I delivered my text over the air, I left the copy with the radio station. This was M. Bourgeois's way of coping with an RCMP "dirty trick."

Other "dirty tricks" were not so easy to counter. For example, in 1942, when Kent Rowley was beginning to have some success in recruiting workers at the Montreal Cottons plant (3,300 employees) in Valleyfield, an anonymous, spurious leaflet about him was circulated around town. The leaflet was inspired by an RCMP record that was a tissue of lies combined with just enough facts to give the document credibility.

The unsigned leaflet stated that Rowley had been interned, which he had been, for over two years. But the leaflet did not indicate that he had volunteered for the army in 1939 and was honourably discharged along with others when his regiment's ranks were thinned out just before going overseas. Nor did the leaflet state that he was arrested and interned in Petawawa in 1940 after he denounced Prime Minister Mackenzie King and his chief Quebec minister before the Montreal Trades and Labour Council for reneging on their promise to the French-Canadian people that their sons would never again be conscripted for overseas wars. In Quebec internment for that cause was deserving of a badge of honour. He was joined at Petawawa by Montreal mayor Camillien Houde, who had made a similar statement—and who was promptly re-elected mayor on his liberation. Under the War Measures Act no formal accusation was made, nor was Rowley ever put on trial.

When the injurious leaflet came out, strong union members tried to explain to others that it was evidence of the company's determination to destroy the union, as it had always done in its long history. But false propaganda is difficult to counter, especially when it originates from a seat of power.

In 1944 I was living in Valleyfield, reorganizing union forces there. The federal government had certified our union, but the certification was ineffective in the face of management's refusal to negotiate during a period when strikes were illegal due to the war. Malicious company attacks were whispered about me in town and carried by prominent representatives of the church as well. Among several rumours spread at the time, one story said I was a Russian agent, dropped off by a Soviet submarine along the Gaspé coast. The story caused a lot of discussion, and it even went around the Welland cotton mill after the war, among new immigrant workers from Southern Italy and Eastern Europe.

In 1944, early one evening in Valleyfield, a large band of Catholic youth marched out of the Cathedral basement over to our union hall, vandalized it, and then went on to surround city hall, where we were holding a union meeting. They threatened to run Kent Rowley and me out of town. The provincial police were called, but they came only to the outskirts of town, where they waited until the riot spent itself. In the end, it was parents who went about the streets after midnight, looking for their sons. They found them around city hall and took them home, putting a damper on the party.

The RCMP also circulated its own "confidential record" of Rowley and Parent among certain employers and at least one journalist from *The Hamilton Spectator*, in addition to certain politicians, doubtless among them Quebec Premier Maurice Duplessis. The record also went to Washington, to the secret services, as Rowley was informed by the union's international president, Tony Valente. From what we were able to guess, the "record" described us as dangerous characters. One U.S. employer, testifying against the union in a case before a labour disputes commission, blurted out the information one day. He was quickly checked by the sitting magistrate and apologized, admitting he had been warned not to talk about the subject.

On two separate occasions, once in 1947 and again in 1971, while preparing Kent Rowley's defence in trials involving strikes, our lawyers were allowed individually a quick look at RCMP records concerning us. It was only in 1971 that we learned from our lawyer that the record contained a complete fabrication to the effect that Rowley was supposed to have had psychiatric troubles, causing him to be violent in the prisoner-of-war camp. This lie had gone the rounds for years amongst corporate executives, politicians, and police without our knowing about it.

Meanwhile, Quebec provincial police officer Paul Benoit, known to various unions as the most notorious strikebreaker in the force, tried his best to knock out Rowley's brains when he ran into him on picket lines in 1946, 1947, and 1952.

## Wire-Tapping, Informers, and *Agents Provocateurs*

One day during a strike in 1952 I had a telephone conversation with a colleague from another union who told me he had been advised to stop meeting with us for fear of damaging his union's relations with higher-ups. When I sent two highly trusted union officers to see him at his union hall, he asked if I had spoken to anyone, other than those two, about that phone call. He said the bishop had repeated word for word to his superior union officer everything he had said to me. Obviously, the police had turned the tapped conversation over to the bishop, all in the interests of trying to isolate our striking members.

The most active police agent we ever had in our ranks was a young woman hired into one of the Montreal mills of the Dominion Textile Company immediately after we had won our first collective agreements in the 1946 strike. The company hired her to work in the department and on the shift, where the only known Communist Party member in the mills had a job. She went to live with him, attended union meetings with him, and, it appears, had him recruit her into the Communist Party. She conformed to the stereotyped picture of the "militant" and provoked clashes between one set of young workers impatient for quick action and experienced union activists, who were disciplined in working out and executing union strategies. One night, she travelled through all departments of the plant, apparently unobserved by the foremen, and pulled the entire shift out on the street under false pretences. It happened to be a critical time in union relations with the company and the government. Her objective was to have the striking shift pull out the other shifts as they arrived for work, causing a snowball effect, then to go to the other mills and spread the walkout before a membership meeting could be called for discussion and decision. The strike would have been illegal and a disaster. The vigilance and understanding of experienced members saved us from a spreading strike without benefit of a democratic decision-making process.

When, in 1952, our union members were betrayed by the corrupt Washington leadership of the United Textile Workers of America (AFL), the company no longer needed the *agent provocateur*. She left the mill and eventually married a man connected with the military. As for the AFL union leadership that had betrayed us, they were finally exposed for union corruption by the U.S. Senate Committee on Racketeering in Unions, under the Kennedys.

## The Textile Worker Who Said "No"

A union man from the Valleyfield cotton mill had been in the strikes of 1946 and 1952 and was involved in other protests. He had been elected chief steward on the night shift, was fired over a union demonstration, and went to work for the union. But the union came on hard times and he was out of a job again. One day two RCMP officers went to visit him and offered him a job. But to get it he would have to make a public denunciation of his union friends. He listened silently. When they asked for his answer he replied, "Do you mean, Mister, that every morning when I look in the mirror to shave, I'll be asking myself, 'What kind of a dog are you?'" The RCMP officers rose and went out the door.

In the lengthy Quebec textile strikes of 1946, 1947, and 1952, police arrests were timed and calculated to disorganize and discourage the workers and persuade them that it was useless to carry on in the face of the overwhelming power of government, police, and the courts, let alone a company that often threatened to close its doors for good. Police frequently arrested strikers on picket lines, and while in detention some strikers were taken into a separate room for questioning and police intimidation. Police made promises to them, if they would denounce strike leaders.

When a trial was due, Premier Duplessis, as attorney general, acted to influence the choice of the sitting judge. In most cases, he succeeded. On rare occasions when he failed to choose the judge, we won our case. In the Court of Appeals, where three or more judges sat on a case, the manipulation did not work, although evidence was limited to whatever proof had been allowed in the original trial. Provincial police officers were frequently the most important witnesses. There was one known instance of manipulation of the jury.

## Ottawa, 1947

In 1947, Pat Sullivan, former president of the Canadian Seamen's Union (CSU) and at the time secretary-treasurer of the Trades and Labour Congress of Canada (TLC), publicly denounced the CSU as "communist-dominated." It was a time when Canadian seamen were in a battle for their jobs and the survival of Canada's deep-sea merchant fleet, which had been rapidly built up during World War II to carry troops, munitions, and other supplies to Great Britain. Crossing the North Atlantic waters had been highly dangerous due to Nazi U-boats. After the war the Great Lakes Shipping companies and the federal government were determined to scuttle the publicly owned deep-sea merchant fleet.

In the spirit of U.S. Senator McCarthy's tirades against anyone remotely progressive, Sullivan's attack on the Canadian Seamen was loudly featured throughout the big press and radio, and Sullivan knew he had to resign as secretary-treasurer of the Trades and Labour Congress. Kent Rowley was in Ottawa on the morning when the news of Sullivan's resignation broke, and he went to the Trades and Labour Congress office at 9 a.m. President Percy Bengough sat alone at his desk. A bemused Bengough was thoughtful and may have been relieved to see a friend. He pointed to a filing cabinet drawer which he said contained RCMP records he had received from the Force. There were copies of reports to police from two well-known union leaders in Quebec about identical meetings they had attended. Neither one knew the other as an agent, which meant the RCMP had a cross-check on both informers.

## The Informer Who Was Paid $50 a Month

In 1947 Kent Rowley was serving a six-month sentence in Montreal's Bordeaux jail on a charge related to the successful 1946 Valleyfield strike. At the 1947 convention, Trades and Labour Congress delegates voted to protest the jailing and asked for Rowley's release. But when the textile union appealed for similar support from the Canadian Congress of Labour (CCL) Convention, it was refused. The reason given was that I had personally led a raid against a CCL organizing campaign in a Quebec City tobacco plant. The truth was that the AFL tobacco workers' union had won over the workers at the Quebec City plant, but I had nothing to do with the operation.

It was CCL organizer Pat Walsh who told the story, a total fabrication. It had served the purpose of turning down our request for solidarity. At the time, the same Pat Walsh was also head of an obscure "Anti-Communist League." He made further news by attacking Mine Mill when it was defending itself against the U.S.-inspired witch-hunt of militant unions.

Eventually, MPs in the House of Commons asked Prime Minister Louis St. Laurent questions as to whether the same Pat Walsh was an RCMP agent. St. Laurent denied it but the questioning persisted. One day in exasperation, the prime minister stated in the House that Walsh was *not* an RCMP officer—he only received $50 a month.[1]

## Sam Baron and the U.S. Secret Service in Canadian Unions

Around 1945 or earlier, when it looked as though our union's persistent campaign to win first collective agreements in the Montreal and Valleyfield cotton mills might succeed, a new rival textile union arrived on the scene: the Textile Workers' Union of America (CIO). Its chief officer in Canada was Sam Baron, former head of the CIO textile union in the New England states, from which base he repeatedly attacked the somewhat more progressive leadership of President Emil Rieve of that union.

Baron quickly acquired a new Canadian base among Cornwall, Ontario, textile workers, who had conducted a militant strike in 1937 but had later fallen into the hands of leadership more acceptable to the employers. From Cornwall, Baron contacted other employers and obstructed the organizing efforts of our union wherever working people invited us in. Baron also launched raids on us in several plants where we had collective agreements. The longest and most hard-fought raids were against our three thousand members in the Montreal area and in Yarmouth, Nova Scotia. In these contests, Baron was repudiated by the workers but seeds of division remained to injure us in future rounds with companies and governments. Baron, as CIO textile union leader, was the main spokesperson in the Cold War campaign to expel the Mine-Mill and United Electrical Workers unions from the Canadian Congress of Labour.

In 1952, eight weeks after six thousand Quebec cotton mill workers had gone on strike in Montreal and Valleyfield, Tony Valente, the United Textile Workers' international president, personally fired Kent Rowley and the entire Canadian staff and appointed Baron as head of the union. Baron went on to sign collective agreements on company terms. The strikers were so reluctant to return to the job under those conditions that it had taken an additional six weeks, with company, police, and government help, to break the strike.

Some considerable time after that, when the company felt sure the workers' resistance was broken, Baron returned to the United States. According to a journalist friend of his in Montreal, the Canadian government had paid all the hospital expenses for his wife's long illness, in recognition of Sam's valuable services to this country. Baron was an old pro when it came to U.S. secret service work. As a journalist he had gone to Spain during the Civil War. On his return to the United States he testified before the Dies Committee of Congress, which was looking for communists everywhere. The burden of Baron's testimony was that while the slaughter of the Spanish people was most unfortunate, any help the U.S. government sent to the Spanish government for its defence against General Franco's fascist forces would only in the end help the Soviet Union take over Spain.

## Quebec: The FLQ and Federal Strategy

In October 1970 the Trudeau government enacted the War Measures Act. The Canadian Armed Forces, by land and by air, swarmed over greater Montreal and other less-populated areas of Quebec. Close to five hundred people were taken from their homes and driven off to the Fullum Street jail in Montreal. Women were later removed to a separate jail. Well over a thousand homes were raided. Kent Rowley and I were working in Ontario at the time; we were fortunate that a neighbour had keys to our house in Montreal. She was able to run over and open our door to the police before they could break it down.

It was an unforgettable October in Quebec. The crisis followed upon the kidnapping of British diplomat James Cross and of Pierre Laporte, a Quebec government minister, by two cells of a fairly small group called Front de Libération du Québec (FLQ). The group consisted of a few clandestinely operating separate cells. Its members sought to bring about Quebec independence by a series of exploits, violent if necessary. They hoped their actions would motivate people to take their destiny into their own hands. Pierre Vallières, the author of *White Niggers of America*, was considered by many to be a guru of the FLQ at that time. It would appear that the "secret" operations of these cells were a secret to all but the RCMP, who had infiltrated nearly every cell, often with agents who, as volunteers, did typing, mimeographing, and ran to and fro for members of the cells, managing to acquire some considerable information on their operations.

The government decided it had to secure the safety of Cross, and for this it allowed the flight to Cuba of members of the cell involved. Defence lawyer Bernard Mergler, a devoted defender of union and civil rights, was called in and managed that operation brilliantly, having, for once in his career, the co-operation of police forces. However, the same governments refused all requests to negotiate the release of Pierre Laporte, the Quebec minister in captivity. Having understood this in watching a television report on the Quebec government's reaction to his personal appeal to Premier Robert Bourassa, the unfortunate Laporte tried to escape and only succeeded in cutting himself and breaking a window. His captors panicked, and Laporte was found dead in the back trunk of an automobile left at the military airport in St-Hubert.

The kidnapping triggered the adoption of the War Measures Act, the military occupation of Quebec, mainly in Montreal, and massive arrests and intimidation of the population. During that occupation, not a single union went on strike in Quebec and several labour disputes were settled quietly, without great resistance, a most unusual state of affairs for the times.

## RCMP "Dirty Tricks"

In the years before and after the events of 1970, the RCMP engaged in a number of "dirty tricks" intended to be blamed on the FLQ. The Keable Commission on the investigation of dirty tricks by the police in Quebec tells the story of the police interference aimed at putting the blame on the FLQ. The news about RCMP "tricks" started to come out after the arrest of an RCMP officer by the name of Samson. He was caught laying a bomb in front of the house of Sam Steinberg's daughter. The Steinberg family ran one of the large food chains in Quebec. The officer was caught because he wounded himself in the operation and had to be hospitalized. He was put on trial, and during his trial he warned the RCMP that if they pushed him to the wall, he would talk. They did push him to the wall, and he talked. He spoke about how one of the RCMP dirty tricks was made out to be a dirty trick of the FLQ. Partly as a result of this incident, René Lévesque appointed the Keable Commission to look into all of these matters. The commission made a thorough investigation but it was constantly being hindered and obstructed in its investigation by the RCMP and the federal government. They took the Keable Commission to court many times, and each time delays froze the proceedings until the court agreed or made some decision as to whether Keable could continue or not. Some of the dirty tricks that emerged out of the commission's report were very interesting.

There was the RCMP's Quebec Watergate. There had been a break-in at a press agency tied to the Parti Québécois (PQ). No one could find out, though a lot of people had suspicions, who was responsible for the break-in. The thieves stole the lists of subscribers to the news agency. The people on the lists could be assumed to be sympathizers or members of the PQ. The lists contained the cream of the intellectuals, those who studied theoretical matters and questions concerning the political climate in Quebec. They included a lot of young people's names, politically active people. It was Samson who revealed that the RCMP was a party to the theft. Indeed, the Force did it in collaboration with the Montreal city police. The RCMP would not do a break-in without telling the local police. There had to be collaboration or the job could be messed up.

Other dirty tricks that the Keable Commission reported included the case of a barn burning. The incident was presumed by a lot of people to have been instigated by the FLQ, but it was carried out by some RCMP agents. And dynamite was stolen from a construction site by RCMP agents. Also, some FLQ leaflets were written and distributed—but they were not composed by FLQ members, but by the police, who also bought off the man who had the FLQ letterheads, which meant they were able to issue the leaflets on FLQ stationery. Those leaflets were widely publicized. They were provocative, making the FLQ appear to be much worse than it actually was. It would appear that the RCMP wormed its way into each of the few FLQ cells. Sometimes the RCMP just had individuals who made themselves useful by running errands and performing small services for FLQ members, meanwhile gathering information.

There was also a police operation called "Poupette," which is an uncomplimentary vernacular word for a woman signifying "doll." The code name was used to identify the operations of Carole De Veault, who infiltrated the FLQ and also got involved with a prominent supporter of the Parti Québécois. Later De Veault wrote about her exploits in a book co-authored with journalist William Johnson, later president of Alliance Quebec. De Veault managed to be a liaison between a couple of cells, and it appears that she saw most of the publications of one of the most active cells, the one that kidnapped Cross. One might suspect that she influenced the tone of some of the publications, their use of adjectives, and their exaggerations, because she was one of the most trusted people, very active, always available to do anything they asked. Another agent, who went by the name of Nigel Hamer, was connected with two FLQ cells, including the Cross cell. He appears to have been one of those people who also drove people around. One can only wonder what he knew about the kidnapping of Cross. Hamer was kept out of the picture when the FLQ people were arrested. It was only years later, around the time of the Keable Commission, when it was clear that the researchers were getting close to Hamer, that he was charged. He went to court and pleaded guilty, and the judge decided that he was a good teacher, a good husband, a good father, so he was let off. But it is pretty clear to me that he was an agent and he had managed to be spared when the others were picked up.

The Keable Commission report makes for interesting reading, full of facts and details. The evidence shows the effort and the expense that the RCMP put into these operations. Just to make sure that they did their work, each informer had a handler. The handlers in turn consulted with higher RCMP officers and must have taken orders as to how they should instruct their informers. In one other example of RCMP actions, the police convinced one of the FLQ cells to steal a Brink's truck. It didn't work out, but the commission's evidence shows how costly the adventure was. It involved RCMP informants, the working out of influence on the FLQ, the handlers, and everybody else down the line, including sixty-five police; the thing fell through. Now think of the RCMP operations that did succeed and how much time, people, and expense went into them.

Trudeau's government appeared determined to connect the FLQ and the PQ, through the adventures of Carole De Veault, who worked in both camps, for once. The operations served their purpose, for in much of the English-speaking media news about the FLQ and the Parti Québécois was doctored to give the impression that the FLQ was an arm of the PQ. But while the FLQ was operating, René Lévesque, as the Parti Québécois leader, was deeply alarmed. Lévesque argued that the FLQ approach was in error, and he managed to convince most of the Quebec public of that. But outside Quebec, the myth remained.

I believe that for many years the federal strategy was to have the Canadian public confuse the FLQ with the PQ. The PQ, a mildly social-democratic party, stood for sovereignty association. The proof that the RCMP strategy did not succeed in Quebec was the election to power of René Lévesque's PQ in 1976.

## A Mole in the Quebec Government

Notable among federal police operations was the recruiting of Claude Morin. After Lévesque assumed power in 1976, one of his first cabinet members was Claude Morin, who became the minister of intergovernmental affairs. As such, Morin was appointed to go with Lévesque to the constitutional talks in Ottawa in 1982. What Lévesque didn't know until after those talks was that his right-hand man, his senior advisor, "expert" on the Canadian constitution, was working with the RCMP. He had worked for the RCMP at least since 1969.

To this day, this divisive strategy has caused a lot of misunderstanding, especially given the "Two Solitudes"—an attitude that lingers on even in the labour movement. When has it been possible to organize massive labour protest demonstrations on Parliament Hill—like the ones we had at the end of World War II—with large representation from Quebec unions alongside those of the rest of Canada?

When people in Ontario and the rest of Canada think of the situation in Quebec, and think of the relationship with us in Quebec, they should be sensitive to the fact that the big news propaganda is always anti-Quebec, trying to paint us in as bad a light as is possible. When the government of Quebec asks for talks towards a partnership with Canada, should Quebec become sovereign, the response from Ottawa is always, a loud "No! You are separatists and we'll have nothing to do with you." Unfortunately, a lot of the Canadian public do not have access to solid information on Quebec. They demonize the Quebec government and the people of Quebec. Quebecers are seen as the people that you don't talk with, and therefore it becomes more difficult to have decent negotiations and discussion about how we are going to live side by side, one way or the other.

This is not to excuse the Quebec government for its failure to enact equitable economic and social policies. With minor differences, its conduct has been no worse than that of other provincial governments and of the federal government. There must be earnest and patient dialogue if our peoples are to build a system where justice will stand a better chance.

## Note

1.   See Canada, *House of Commons Debates*, June 25, 1959.

nineteen ★ ★ ★

# In Whose Public Interest? The Canadian Union of Postal Workers and National Security

Of all the social movements in Canada, few, if any, have been more spied upon, infiltrated, and harassed by national security agencies than the labour movement. Labour's response to this consistent targeting has been uneven at best. Although unions may have enjoyed a modicum of success in dealing with the "goons and the ginks and the company finks," they have not been very effective with "spooks." Unions simply have not dealt with "national security" as a priority.

Though the facts are difficult to verify, it seems that the Canadian Security and Intelligence Service (CSIS) surveillance of trade unions is now not as extensive as the blanket surveillance formerly practised by the RCMP Security Service. Yet some labour activists are nervous about recent revelations suggesting that CSIS may not have backed away from the bad old days. There was the case of Marc-André Boivin, a long-time RCMP and CSIS *agent provocateur* and bomber in Quebec's Confederation of National Trade Unions (CNTU). After ten years as an employee with the unions, Boivin pleaded guilty in 1987 to a conspiracy to bomb hotels that union members were striking, and admitted to having secretly worked for CSIS and its predecessor, the RCMP Security Service.

In 1987 NDP MP Svend Robinson revealed that CSIS had infiltrated the Canadian Auto Workers union, the Canadian Union of Public Employees, the British Columbia Federation of Labour, and the Centrale de l'enseignement du Québec (CEQ). These revelations elicited a coy response from Solicitor General James Kelleher. He stated that the law prohibited CSIS from targeting unions, but that, of course, it could still investigate individual members of unions. Then there was the CSIS agent who, in 1985 union elections, worked closely with an opposition slate to replace the progressive leadership in the B.C. Carpenters Union Provincial Council.

There is verified evidence that during a 1987 strike, the national headquarters of the Canadian Union of Postal Workers (CUPW) was under surveillance by "a high level law enforcement agency . . . probably done with a court order." The surveillance was by both "visual and electronic" means.[1] CSIS was on the union's short short list of culprits. A public statement made by CSIS in 1995 that CUPW was not a "target of investigation" was cold comfort. There was a reason for the union's lack of confidence in CSIS's statement. During the particularly difficult first round of negotiations for the newly merged CUPW and Letter Carriers Union of Canada (LCUC) membership, CBC-TV discovered that CSIS's star *provocateur*, Grant Bristow, was employed at Canada's largest postal plant.

CUPW's concern with security police surveillance of trade unions predated the birth of CSIS. In 1979 the union exposed an ex-Canada Post Security and Investigation (S&I) officer who admitted that the RCMP and S&I worked together on illegal mail openings and surveillance of union activists. Because of these disclosures, in 1981 National CUPW publications sounded alarm bells over the McDonald Commission report on RCMP interference in unions. The matter, however, was less than obsessional. The union, for example, did not publicize the 1987 bugging of its national strike headquarters. Later, when the media discovered the story, reporters asked the union why and noted its answer:

> Union officials did not make it public because the strike was a hectic time and they simply assume they were under surveillance. "People will just think you are paranoid (if you talk about wire taps)," said Deborah Bourque of the union's National Executive Board in Ottawa. "It (surveillance) becomes part of your everyday life. If there is static on the line, we will say, "There is the RCMP.""[2]

## The CUPW Files

Nevertheless, when the Ottawa and District Labour Council suggested in 1990 that unions ought to apply for their security files under the Access to Information Act, these past experiences led us to agree with their proposal. Following our application, and a mostly fruitless complaint about the lack of results to the information commissioner, CUPW received 1,667 of 4,020 pages of RCMP Security Service material on CUPW National and its Vancouver local. The authorities completely severed a total of 2,353 pages covering the period from 1965, when CUPW first emerged, to 1984, the point at which CSIS did likewise. No archival material purportedly exists for the period after 1984, when CSIS replaced the RCMP Security Service. The 1,667 pages may seem like a lot, but unfortunately most of it turned out to be news clippings and old union bulletins. The package included only 275 or so heavily censored pages of police reports, memos, and correspondence.

CUPW tried to obtain the remaining documents through a legal challenge against the federal government, and during that suit we learned that the lion's share of "severed" and "exempted" material was kept from us under section 15-1 of the Access to Information Act. That section relates to the right of the government to refuse disclosure of records harmful to "the defence of Canada . . . or the detection, prevention or suppression of subversive or hostile activities." The government denied us access to a smaller portion of the CUPW material under three other sections of the Act. These included section 16-1, which deals with "lawful investigations" of any law of Canada or threats to Canada's security "within the meaning of the Canadian Security Intelligence Service Act." It is impossible to decide which exempted or severed portion was denied under which section.

Still, we learned a lot from the material we did receive. Reading between the blacked-out lines in the Vancouver files, we found out that the local was under constant surveillance from 1965 to 1984. The security cops' curiosity occurred not only during strikes, but also during regular local activities such as elections and shop-floor organizing campaigns. The RCMP operated under the assumption that "radical factions," "communist elements," and "revolutionary elements" dominated all union affairs. At any given moment, "subversives" and "counsellors of violence" might be poised to hijack union activities. Unstated, but evident in the severed material, is the RCMP's belief that union members didn't have the brains to come to their own conclusions about how they wanted their local and union to function. The RCMP code description for this sad state of affairs was "membership apathy."

On one level such rantings may seem merely ridiculous, but on another level they appear to be not so harmless and perhaps even dangerous. Take, for example, the evidence in the "secret" security intelligence files during the 1975 national strike. In November 1975 RCMP spies concluded that "violence, such as destructive occupation of the post office [in Vancouver] is now a possibility" and that "[names deleted] will counsel violence in the 'showdown' situation developing in Vancouver."[3] I'm sure we will never know how close RCMP officers came to acting on these conclusions, but the secret report could have easily served as justification for the most severe of repressive measures, including mass arrests and police violence. Those of us in the local leadership during the 1975 strike know that the RCMP "intelligence" reports were utter fantasy—but it was a fantasy that could have resulted in ugly consequences.

The files on the National CUPW contain a similar assessment of "communist subversives" versus apathetic members, except in Quebec, where the communist subversive theory was replaced with "separatist subversion." The RCMP security chiefs' focus was on the Montreal local, where they believed the Post Office Department, as a creature of the federal government, was a natural target for separatists. "Goons" in Montreal carried out "subversive" activities, but in Quebec the common ethnic composition of the membership supposedly invited greater unity between the "subversive separatist goons" and the general membership—contrary to their counterparts in English Canada, the vast majority of whom the RCMP saw as apathetic or ineffectual.

One report shaken loose from the CSIS censors by the information commissioner verifies that as early as 1969 RCMP security officers had briefed Post Office management at the Deputy Postmaster General level on the "type of persons" making up the then-Council of Postal Unions negotiating team (a joint committee of the CUPW and the Letter Carriers Union of Canada). The heading of the Report is "Re: Subversive Activities Within the Council of Postal Unions."

The most surprising document to escape almost intact from the censor tells the story of a major disagreement between the Post Office Department at its highest levels and the RCMP security squad. On January 15, 1979, Deputy Postmaster General James Corkery wrote a long letter to his "friend" Robin Bourne (Assistant Deputy Solicitor General, Police and Security), to grumble about how the RCMP's spying at Canada Post was not going far enough. Corkery apparently knew everything the RCMP was doing and everything the RCMP was finding out. He demanded that the RCMP monitor not only known communists and "subversive leaning" individuals but also people who were "labour-oriented." He argued that this "plethora of zealots bent on self-destruction," who directed so many locals in CUPW, were responsible for the "disruptive situation" in the Post Office. From what we can tell, the RCMP told Corkery to calm down, saying his was an "extreme management position," and calling it "misleading." In a meeting RCMP representatives told Corkery and Canada Post's then-head spook, Security and Investigations Director Paul Boisvert, that the RCMP had "no mandate to look at zealots." Nevertheless, Corkery made many waves with his efforts to expand RCMP surveillance of postal workers. The RCMP produced an updated paper on "subversive elements within CUPW."

Because they have suppressed so much information surrounding these events, we cannot be sure how far Corkery got. Subsequently, Robin Bourne was also the executive director of the 1980 Marin Royal Commission on Post Office Security— despite being close friends with Corkery (a principal mover and shaker in establishing the Commission) and despite being involved in the furious debate over how extensive the surveillance and investigation of postal workers should be. Moreover, in testimony before the commission, whose mandate included investigation of all aspects of security of the mail and all personnel security issues, Corkery baldly asserted that he had given directions to postal security and investigations officers to "stay well away from" any involvement "in the raucous of relationship with some of our unions."[4] The CSIS files reveal that the conflict between his public assertions and what really happened behind the scenes could scarcely be more blatant.

The released files on CUPW reveal several other RCMP obsessions, but nothing stands out in such stark relief as the amazingly close working relationship between the security officers and the upper-level management of Canada Post.

## CUPW and the Access to Information Act

In 1995 Justice Minister Allan Rock informed Parliament that he "fully intend[ed] to consult with Canadians to develop more comprehensive and up-to-date access to information legislation."[5] That was good news. Although section 2 of the Access to Information Act boldly states its purpose as providing "a right of access to information in records . . . in accordance with the principle that government information should be available to the public," CUPW's experience suggested that the government should gear the Act, with respect to security matters, to establishing clear regulations on the release of information.

Sadly, our joy was short-lived. Upon writing the minister in April 1995, inquiring as to when the consultations would begin, and what form they would assume, I received a reply referring to a "lack of resources and lack of time on the legislative calendar." Rock noted that his department had established no process, and I was led to understand that, with the department's commitment to other social justice projects, and the minister's concern about "proceeding with too many major initiatives at any one time," we would just have to wait in line. Nonetheless, the union decided that if we were ever going to be able to bring to light the inadequacies of and roadblocks to access in the Access to Information Act, the matter would require a court test, if only to illustrate its unworkability. Incredibly, since the Act was established in 1983 no one had ever taken a case to court involving the sections invoked to restrict our files.

We began our case by requesting access (through the union's lawyers) to the severed and exempted material. Our petition, addressed to the Federal Court of Canada, was based on the commitment of CUPW counsel to undergo security screening and to forego revealing any of the material to anyone, including the union. This approach seemed eminently logical. It is a profoundly difficult chore, even for lawyers, to argue that certain material ought to have been released without having any idea what is contained therein. The situation is reminiscent of scenes from Franz Kafka's *The Trial.* Since counsel is not even privy to information on which section of the Access to Information Act has been invoked to cover which exempted page, and faces exclusion during *ex parte* hearings, the lack of access necessitates making legal arguments from within a void.

## CSIS Affidavit

The first obstacle in our legal case was to find a Federal Court judge with clearance to hear the petition. Judges assigned to such cases must themselves have undergone high-level security screening, and apparently only a handful of judges have the pristine credentials that satisfy the high standards of the national security establishment. Eventually a judge was found and the case scheduled. We then received a remarkable affidavit from CSIS. Under the signature of a desk head from the antiterrorism branch, the affidavit expressed alarm and opposition to the CUPW request for access to RCMP documents requested by our legal counsel.

The CSIS affidavit maintains that the material in CUPW files is far too sensitive to ever be seen, even by counsel. In the first place, counsel may be untrustworthy ("in breach of his undertaking") and may deliberately leak secret information to the client. Alternatively, counsel may be an idiot and "inadvertently" disclose the undisclosable. Either way, "there would be no remedy available to CSIS," thereby leaving it "no choice but to change some or all of its methods to ensure they were secure.." The effect would be to "impair the ability of CSIS to provide timely advice to the Government of Canada on threats to National Security."[6]

The affidavit casts CSIS in the role of inheritor of RCMP Security Service information: "In respect of groups or individuals who presented immediate or potential threats to the security of the country because they were engaged in 'subversive or hostile activities.'" The RCMP "maintained information in a manner which allowed it to be subjected to extensive cross-referencing . . . between groups and individuals," as did its successor.[7] The argument of "interconnectedness" arises regularly throughout the CSIS affidavit and factum. The union may not be given the information, it transpires, because it involves investigation into individuals. Since individuals were often investigated in their capacities as union officers as well as members of a social movement (referred to as "terrorist or subversive groups"), the principle of a security agency collecting information on "groups and individuals and also on the groups and individuals with whom they established contact" would be horribly compromised.[8]

This is chilly, Cold War terrain, and the permafrost is not likely to experience any melting away as the result of the sunlight of scrutiny. The affidavit states:

> One of the ways in which foreign influenced subversive organizations operated in Canada during the period in question, *and now*, was by attempting to exploit volatile issues. Their tactics included penetration of organizations as well as the manipulation of such organizations and unsuspecting individuals, with a view to furthering their own causes. These organizations through manipulation, would be used to confuse public perceptions, sway opinions, and generate pressure on the Government from the general public by focusing public attention on specific issues.[9]

Anything remotely resembling accountability or due process cannot apply to this case, because:

> Identifying "subversive or hostile activities" in legitimate broad based political movements requires discriminating evaluation of the activities of such movements and the individuals involved. Such an evaluation can only be effective if a security agency is able to analyze interconnecting relationships on an ongoing basis. It is also necessary to keep informed of political, social and economic conditions in order to detect exploitation and anticipate potential threats to security. Accordingly, the RCMP Security Service maintained files during the period in question by cross-referencing to the file of a group or individual all reports, public information or assessments relating to that group or individual or to that group or individual's activities. CSIS continues to follow that practice.
>
> ... It is for these reasons that the information contained in the file relating to the Applicant's request relates not only to the Canadian Union of Postal Workers, but also to other groups and individuals. The information about CUPW is inseparable from the larger context necessary to provide an accurate assessment of its involvement in any given situation.[10]

The broad sweep of the CSIS claim is impressive. The insinuation made by CSIS— that the Vancouver local and CUPW have generally been compromised by subversive penetration and that CUPW's focus on its membership's education and public campaigns were furthering acts of subversion—is an untenable accusation that has no public credibility.

There is a great deal more argument in this vein in the affidavit. Lengthy sections are devoted to the need for CSIS, as the successor of the RCMP Security Service, to protect human sources, third-party information, and methods of operation lest the credibility of CSIS itself be destroyed. Moreover, there looms the ever-present danger of the dreaded "Mosaic effect."

> A person without experience in the field of security intelligence can easily without knowing it make a statement which discloses sensitive information. This is because one piece of information in isolation may not appear sensitive but to an

informed individual that piece of information can be used with other information to develop a more comprehensive picture. This process of piecing together information is known as the Mosaic effect.[11]

The Berlin Wall may have crumbled, but a solid, more resilient, if invisible, wall is apparently still in place around the CSIS building on Ottawa's Bank Street.

## The Interim Hearings

The CSIS affidavit defence of censorship raises questions about the union's right to know items of importance to its own well-being. We are not terribly interested in CSIS or RCMP techniques, the ins-and-outs of "enciphered communications," or other elements of advanced "jiggery-spookery." We are not interested in who in the union was phoned by an RCMP/CSIS agent in order to ascertain what went on at yesterday's executive meeting. But we are interested in the suppression of important information in perpetuity. This is not acceptable.

From the 1960s through to the 1980s, the RCMP Security Service and our employer were thick as thieves. The celebrated cases of CSIS operatives Marc-André Boivin and Grant Bristow prove conclusively that CSIS "methods of operation" included the planting of *agents provocateurs* inside unions. Access legislation should not exempt security agencies from public scrutiny. We should have the right to gain access to information in government records, and, accordingly, CUPW counsel argued that CUPW had the right to know if this "method of operation" was used by the RCMP security police. It is not only CSIS's reputation and credibility that are at stake here, but also the union's. As an organization involved in lawful activity, CUPW should have the right to know if and when CUPW's members and their activities have been compromised by leaders whose real employer was the RCMP Security Service. For the same reason, obviously, it is important to know if "subversives and terrorists" really were ruling the union's roost.

CUPW characterizes these RCMP files as part of its hidden history; it deserves exposure to the light of day. In the summer of 1996 a Federal Court judge heard the union's petition. While Judge Marshall Rothstein avoided reference to the Cold War rumblings of the CSIS affidavit and factum, he nonetheless ruled against us. Commenting on his personal discomfort with the rules of law that dictated his decision, the judge noted, "Disclosure cases are difficult since the respondent will always have more information than the applicant."[12] Although this imbalance could be lessened if counsel for the applicant had access to the RCMP files, Judge Rothstein argued that no legal basis for disclosure to counsel existed in our case. He concluded, "Counsel for the applicant will be required to make his arguments on the merits without access to the undisclosed documents."[13]

While CUPW planned to continue with this court challenge, we were no longer astonished by the revelation that no one had mounted such a court challenge before this one. First, the costs are astronomical and the legal process seems never-ending. Second, the information commissioner has no power to order disclosure, and although technically the information commissioner has the option of taking legal action should she/he believe exempted information ought to be revealed, the reality is that the commissioner will not litigate in the murky waters of the secrecy provisions in the Access to Information Act. Section 52 of the Act provides that applications for review in Federal Court must be heard *in camera* and *ex parte*. Judge Rothstein confirmed that this section prohibits the counsel for the requesting party from having access to exempted material in all section 1-3 and 1-5 cases. In addition, *ex parte* provisions can be invoked with regard to other exemption sections of the Act at the discretion of the judge. We are left with the absurdity of the judge, having heard only one side of the argument, reading the exempted and severed documents, listening to the blandishments of CSIS, and deciding on the case.

The drawbridge over the moat of official secrecy is fundamentally imaginary. As a result, CUPW may seem a little perverse for suggesting to other unions and social justice groups that they should enter CSIS's fortified castle. But it is precisely the unworkable nature of the process that has led us to suggest to others that they request their security files. The case for major revisions of the Act would be strengthened through other unions' efforts to bridge the CSIS moat. If Canadians are to awaken from the "nightmare" of CSIS secrecy, "The first step," as writer George Martin Manz puts it, "is to pull back the veil of secrecy and to arm ourselves with this knowledge."[14]

## CSIS and the CLC

Manz has also proposed a second step: "to organize enough people to force the dream to end." It is in keeping with this second step that CUPW has challenged the function of national security in general and, at the level of the Canadian Labour Congress (CLC), of CSIS in particular. As a result, at the 1996 Vancouver CLC convention, CUPW put forth a resolution that had already received a recommendation of concurrence from the CLC's Human Rights Committee and the active support of several labour councils and other unions:

> **Resolution No. HR-12**
> WHEREAS the cold war is over; and
> WHEREAS the Canadian Security and Intelligence Service continues to infiltrate, disrupt and keep under close observation peace groups, unions and other working class institutions: and
> WHEREAS Grant Bristow, as an agent of the security services, used taxpayers' money to establish the Heritage Front which is a right-wing terrorist organization;
> THEREFORE BE IT RESOLVED that the Canadian Labour Congress demand that CSIS be disbanded with all unionized CSIS workers being reassigned to other government departments and agencies; and
> BE IT FURTHER RESOLVED that the federal government redirect the financial savings gained from disbanding CSIS towards investigating the income tax returns of corporations.

As with most resolutions, this one did not reach the convention floor. But, significantly, following the convention it was subsequently adopted by the CLC Executive

Council during its review of undebated resolutions. The resolution thus became the CLC policy on CSIS.

I would be the first to admit that this resolution does not constitute the final word on CSIS by CUPW or by the CLC. Nonetheless, it represents an enormous step towards elevating the institutional practice of national security onto the political agenda. Its passage reflects a profound change in the labour leadership's attitude towards the role of spying. Espionage is no longer seen, even within unions themselves, as a normal part of the state's functions.

A scant fifteen years ago numerous union leaders were priding themselves on keeping their unions free of communists. Some unions insisted that potential staff members undergo security clearance checks before being hired. It is safe to say that some union members, if they weren't themselves informers, welcomed a close relationship with the RCMP Security Police. RCMP security surveillance has now been well documented, and it is clear that some union leaders encouraged, and even engaged in, security work.[15] Many of those spied upon did not experience the satisfaction that Gil Levine, former research director of the Canadian Union of Public Employees, found when, in a bizarre twist of events, he was able to confront the former Security Service agent assigned to spy on him.[16] Levine and other union researchers know that this surveillance was often inspired by the union leaders themselves. This complicity forced many effective organizers and committed left-wing militants right out of the unions. More importantly, it resulted in red-baiting and paranoia and led to conflict, division, and weakness within the unions and to the weakening of the labour movement in general.

The implications of the CLC's decision to support the CUPW resolution calling for the disbanding of CSIS are significant. The support means a recognition that the Cold War excuses for maintaining a "national security-based culture" no longer find resonance within the CLC leadership. It means a recognition of the profoundly antidemocratic nature of "secret" state security projects. It means a recognition of the ways in which such "secret" state security projects cast suspicion upon and marginalize organizations, groups, and individuals who do not fit their definition of "normal" or who challenge the status quo culturally, socially, and politically. It means a recognition that the focus of national security campaigns is characteristically on those without power and influence, and it directs public attention away from the activities of corporate and state power. It means a recognition that the culture of a secret information society provides a weapon to law-enforcement agencies, preventing workers, immigrants, Aboriginal peoples, gay men and lesbians, people of colour, women, youth, peace activists, artists, intellectuals—all those who have been the object of these campaigns—from assuming an equitable and honoured place in our society.

And it means, at long last, that the labour movement is beginning to assume a role it has long avoided—to champion the struggle against the secret information society, to support the victims of those security campaigns, and to fight for an alternative to the resultant squandering of human and financial resources in the interests of the rich and powerful. It is our hope in CUPW that we can build upon this first step, to ensure that the labour movement acts upon this resolution in a way that will make national security a real matter of public debate in this country.

# Notes

1. "Security Report," commissioned by Perley-Robinson, Panet, Hill and McDougall, a law firm acting for CUPW, Ottawa, 1987.
2. Peter Edwards, "Postal Unions Likely Spied upon, Secret Report Says," *The Toronto Star*, June 19, 1991, p.A16.
3. CSIS files on CUPW, Vancouver Local, November 1975, National Archives of Canada (NAC), RG 146, p.62.
4. Canada, *Commission of Inquiry into Post Office Security*, Judge René J. Marin, Commissioner, *Verbatim* (James C. Corkery, Deputy Postmaster General), Oct. 10, 1980, p.2627.
5. Canada, *House of Commons Debates*, March 22, 1995, p.10851.
6. Public Affidavit of David Leigh Stewart, "In the Matter of an Application Pursuant to Section 41 of the Access to Information Act, R.S.C. 1985, C A-1; ...", between Evert Hoogers, Applicant and Minister of Canadian Heritage, Respondent, Ottawa, p.8.
7. Ibid., p.4.
8. Ibid.
9. Ibid.; emphasis added.
10. Ibid., p.5.
11. Ibid., pp.10–11.
12. Judge Rothstein, "Reasons for Order in an Application pursuant to Section 41 of the Access to Information Act, R.S.C. 1985, C A-17 ..." Federal Court of Canada, Trial Division, May 29, 1996, p.9.
13. Ibid.
14. George Martin Manz, "Spies in Our Midst," *Briarpatch*, October 1991, p.29.
15. See, for example, Bruce Livesay, "Mounties in the Movement," *Our Times*, August/September 1995.
16. Ibid., p.33.

ZUHAIR KASHMERI

twenty ✷ ✷ ✷

# When CSIS Calls: Canadian Arabs, Racism, and the Gulf War

*The national security campaigns were reactivated against the "enemy within"—this time Arab Canadians and Muslims—in the context of the Canadian government's participation in the 1991 Gulf War. CSIS and the RCMP organized the surveillance and harassment of many Canadian citizens and residents. Zuhair Kashmeri, in this excerpt from his book* The Gulf Within: Canadian Arabs, Racism and the Gulf War *(1991), reports on the many human rights violations that occurred as a result and that continue in the national security construction of Arabs and Muslims as a "national security" threat to Canada.*

A national security operation of the kind launched by the RCMP and CSIS during the Gulf War requires three prerequisites to ensure success: a co-operative media, political backing, and unsophisticated targets. The two agencies were blessed with all three. Perhaps the easiest of the three was the media, one police officer said in a candid conversation. The media had new technology to write about, new buzz-words to explain, the villains and convoluted politics of the Middle East to discuss. . . . Politicians could have reined in the Mounties and CSIS, but they wouldn't when bureaucrats quietly informed them that they would have to face the people if, in fact, something did happen. And the targets? They were mostly new Canadians; they were hardly likely to protest and lobby.

During the operation, the public front put forward by the agencies was one of calm and composure. CSIS, for instance, would point out that its agents were behaving like reporters—simply knocking on doors and holding polite conversations. Yet another agency, Canada Customs, which does the initial immigration checks at points of entry, had perhaps the best excuse for some of its excesses. It minded the doors Arab terrorists could sneak in, and hence it had to be even more vigilant.

However, when one breaks down the security operation into its components and examines each aspect separately, the scenario is frightening—and ought to make Canadians sit up and rethink whether Canada's involvement in the war was worth the human costs.

CSIS had a dual role. On the one hand, it was to provide a risk assessment to the government, based on its interviews with Arab, mostly Iraqi, Canadians. In its other role, it was to target suspects. But in a majority of its public statements it stressed assessment, painting a picture of benign agents telephoning in advance like encyclopedia salespeople and offering multiple choices of times and venues or visiting homes after supper during the quiet hour and politely requesting information to help Canada. Based on these interviews and on information its own people were sending from the Middle East embassies where they are stationed, it provided regular assessments to the government.

Arabs were nevertheless angry at these interviews, even though CSIS spokesman Gerry Cummings defended the method, turning the table on the Arabs. "Are they Canadians?" he asked. "They have said that they owe their allegiance to Canada. They've been here for a long time. It is a possibility that they can help this country in a time of stress, and a very open, legal, legitimate representative of the government of Canada comes and asks you some questions about violence within this country. Is that oppression? Is that intimidating?"

In fact, the interviews were not as benign as Cummings and CSIS Director Reid Morden made them out to be. If all CSIS wanted to know was whether the respondents believed something would happen in Canada, it could have commissioned Gallup to do a weekly survey. But CSIS was after more than just this information. It had targeted Arabs and Muslims, and it wanted to know about their political beliefs. It wanted to fathom the amount of support for the Gulf War, not among the people at large, but among a distinct racial and religious group—Arabs and Muslims. Canada's constitution guarantees citizens and residents the freedom of expression and belief, so the RCMP and CSIS interviews did not violate any law. When a police officer arrests a person, the law is very clear. The officer must have "reasonable and probable grounds," or what the Americans call "just cause," to do so. The officer cannot arrest someone on the basis of a vague suspicion. But there is no law controlling when and under what circumstances officers can show up at someone's doorstep to talk to him or her. The law gives individuals the right to refuse to talk, but experience shows that the authority surrounding police officers overwhelms even the bravest. Arabs subjected to RCMP or CSIS questioning often stated, "I agreed to talk because I didn't want the police to think that I was guilty of something." For Canadians of Third World origin, the presence of a police officer or security agent is intimidating. And discussing politics with Mounties or CSIS agents—even though the latter are not police officers and have no power to arrest—is not like discussing politics with a group of friends. One officer asks questions, and the other makes notes. Those who experienced this questioning during the war found it unnerving. Consider the interview of an Iraqi-born research technologist who lives in Vancouver. He is a Canadian citizen and has been in the country for seven years. . . .

Two CSIS agents showed up at his home one Friday evening, unannounced. They were curt and rude, he said. "They showed me their badges and asked me if I was of Iraqi origin. When I said yes, they wanted to come in and talk to me. I said, 'No, you don't have a warrant to come in.' They insisted. . . . I said, 'Give me your cards, and I'll call you on Monday.' They refused, and I said, 'Okay, in which case I can't call you.' Finally, they gave me their cards, and then one of them warned me, 'If you don't call us on Monday, we'll be here at your house on Tuesday evening.' That was threatening, it wasn't a request."

The physicist set up an interview at work. When CSIS arrived, his boss was in the room along with the head of the company's security. The physicist taped the interview and provided this author with a copy of the tape.

The agents began by asking whether he was a Shia or a Sunni Muslim, and when he said he was just a Muslim, they insisted on knowing which denomination.

Here are some of the other questions:

> Since we have a war going on in the Gulf, I would like to solicit your general view of the war and Canada's involvement and the United States' involvement.
>
> Do you support the government of Saddam Hussein?
>
> How do you feel about Canada's role in participating? In that it is your homeland and the place of your birth? Do you think that Canada should have avoided playing a role in the war?
>
> Part of our responsibilities and duties is to do with terrorism and prevention of terrorism. So when we are at war with another country, we solicit the views of communities and people who are born or related to the general area of the Middle East. It is an ongoing thing as well, but it is particularly heightened at this particular junction in time. Because of that, I ask you about your feelings in regard to the war. And when you were in Iraq, did you ever belong to a political party? Were you a member of the Ba'ath Party [of Saddam Hussein] at any time?
>
> Did you ever involve yourself in any activities, or were you ever a member of any group opposing the government of the Ba'ath party? Or the Al Dawa party [a Shia opposition group in Iraq]? Are you familiar with that organization? What does that organization mean to you?
>
> Did you ever travel to Iran?
>
> Do you practise your faith? So you worship . . . I don't mean practice as just believe . . . you practise and you attend prayers? You do attend services? . . .

The interview was unconscionable. It was tantamount to intimidation, invasion of privacy, and a violation of the man's rights under the Canadian Constitution. Right at the outset, for instance, the two agents are heard on the tape announcing that they had offered to interview the Iraqi in private but that he chose to have the other two in the room. Is it agreed, one of the agents says, that if at any time Mr. J chooses to reply in private that the other two will leave the room? They clearly imply that at any time their interview might lead to some sinister topic such as terrorism.

On the aspect of terrorism, question four is very cleverly worded. If we strip away the garnish surrounding the question, we are left with: "Part of our responsibilities and duties is to do with terrorism and prevention of terrorism. . . . *Because of that*, I ask you about your feelings in regard to the war." The implication is clearly that CSIS does suspect the Iraqi of being a potential terrorist.

For the state to inquire into and record the political and religious beliefs of one of its citizens is itself an Orwellian horror. These two agents were doing the very thing that Canadians have condemned in the past when discussing totalitarian regimes. While the physicist was not overtly threatened during the interview, he was nevertheless unnerved by it. When a security organization evinces a particular interest in the beliefs of a citizen, the effect is inevitably intimidating.

And what was it that this person was involved in? He was not part of any Iraqi political movement in Canada. . . . He was part of an Islamic study group in Vancouver, which discussed religious issues to bridge the gap between the different Islamic sects. . . . CSIS must have interviewed the handful of other people in the study circle, which quickly broke up once the war started.

And what was the reason for the invasion of this Canadian's privacy? The agents said that their security concern was aroused by the fact that the company was a defence contractor for Ottawa. When the boss remarked that the company had long since been sold to a Japanese firm and was not involved in defence contracting, the agents quickly suggested other reasons for the interrogation—among them, that they wanted to know the physicist's personal views about the war. His reply was very noncommittal—to ensure that he was not persecuted because of his views.

The agents said they might want to come again. The technologist did not want them to return and told them that the reason he had spoken to them was that he had nothing to hide. He had been afraid that if he did not submit to the interview, he might lose his job. CSIS was at an advantage here, and it knew it. Had he refused to be interviewed, they could have interviewed his boss about him, in the process leaving the impression that there was some security concern about the man.

Perhaps the most questionable statement from the agents came after the technologist told them that the next time they should phone ahead of time and "bring a warrant or something, I haven't done anything and why should I be investigated?" One of the two replied: "In a democracy . . . we have the right to come and ask you [questions] and talk to you."

But was there a real and tangible threat of terrorism? Strangely enough, the assessments that CSIS did from September to the end of the war on February 28 all indicated little or no threat. This low-risk assessment continued even after Saddam Hussein was quoted in the media asking Muslims the world over to strike at coalition targets. The assessments were also distributed to the RCMP, local police forces, and Customs and Immigration.

This raises several questions. Why were these assessments not made public boldly and only referred to as asides in the debates of the Commons' External Affairs committee? Why was the media not requested to stop their search for terrorists in view of this low-risk assessment? Why was the RCMP unleashed with full force, utilizing its National Emergency Security Plan, which had never been used to this extent before? Why did prominent leaders, such as the prime minister and the solicitor general, speak from both sides of their mouths—there is a threat, but there is no imminent threat, but Canadians should be vigilant—creating a public paranoia that only fed the security apparatus? And more importantly, if there was no threat, why did CSIS itself continue to target people?

CSIS launched what Arabs like Rashad Saleh, former head of the Canadian Arab Federation (CAF), believe was one of the most pervasive and intensive security sweeps ever launched in Canada. "We've been going through many wars, in 1967, 1973, 1982 in Lebanon, but we never went through this kind of treatment," he said. "I've got feedback from Iraqis, Palestinians, Egyptians, Jordanians, you name it. We had at one point some thirty complaints, including from cities like Burlington, Oakville, and Ajax. Those are cases known to us. In each case those people were asked about three to five others by the security forces, so you can imagine the number."

It reached a point where James Kafieh, the president of CAF, published hundreds of brochures titled *When CSIS Calls*. The brochures listed the rights of Arab Canadians, including the right to refuse to talk to CSIS. They informed Arabs that they could in addition choose the place of meeting, have other people or lawyers with them, or ask CAF for assistance. Local Arab groups were given this brochure, and they reproduced it in the hundreds.

The secrecy of the security operation blinded both the media and ordinary Canadians and got the full backing of Ottawa. It was done so quietly, and so swiftly, and left such a chilling effect that although hundreds of Arab Canadians were interrogated in their homes and offices, just a fraction called CAF to complain—and few of those complaints were of a nature that could be explained to the media in a way that would elicit a news story. In fact, most were either ignored by the media—they would require too much effort to dig out—or written up like the protestations and claims of a criminal being given his day in print.

CSIS Director Reid Morden, who refused to be interviewed for this book, acknowledged before the External Affairs committee of Parliament that the feeling in the Arab community about CSIS interviews was so intense that the community was accusing the service and the RCMP of stifling free expression through intimidation. Svend Robinson, the champion of the Arabs and Muslims during the war, jumped in after this acknowledgement and asked the CSIS head to elaborate on how targets were picked. "Are all Iraqi Canadians who still have relatives in Iraq the subject of questioning? Are other Arab Canadians who have relatives in other countries in the Arab world, in the Muslim world, also considered fair game for questioning by CSIS? What are the ground rules for questioning in these circumstances?" Morden dodged the question, saying the MP could hardly expect him to outline their operational methods. He then tried to change the topic by talking of CSIS helping to prevent Iraqi spies from blackmailing Iraqi Canadians. . . .

CSIS's Gerry Cummings later said they interviewed about two hundred people, which, he believes, is next to nothing given that there are more than two hundred and fifty thousand Arabs in Canada. James Kafieh of CAF believes, based on a formula utilized by the Ontario Human Rights Commission, that for every complainant there are about five who do not bother to complain and therefore that the interview subjects numbered somewhere between five hundred and one thousand.

And then there was the photography. Both James Kafieh and Rashad Saleh had numerous complaints about Arabs being visited and shown photographs of others. In some cases, the photographs were taken at peace demonstrations. Among others, Professor Harish Jain, co-chair of Hamilton's anti-racism group, heard several such complaints. "The war was a nightmare for Arab groups in terms of intolerance, and on top of that you have this kind of harassment. What are we living in, a dictatorship? These are people who ran away from countries that have this sort of thing, and they come here to face the same thing, you have CSIS and other agencies investigating you and asking questions they have no right to ask. It was that kind of thing that was going on, the line of questioning was very wrong."

Gerry Cummings was emphatic that CSIS did not target peace rallies and considered them legitimate dissent. And he insisted that just because people were interviewed, it did not mean there was a file on them. So far, so good, but under questioning he acknowledged other facts. For instance, what if a so-called legitimate target attended a peace rally? "If any individual who is our target attends a rally, we would be interested in knowing who he or she is mixing with, not the rally." In this case, the gloves would come off, and that portion of the rally showing the contacts would be photographed. And after that, the targets would multiply— they would now include the people the first target was in touch with to determine their relationship with the original.

When Cummings was asked about the filing of information on people interviewed, he denied that this was done in the sense of creating a file on the individual person. Nevertheless, information is input and cross-referenced on databases, and the information would include the name of the person interviewed. According to CSIS insiders, after this an entry could simply be made seeking all references to a person, and all the cross-referenced material would show up. In the case of the Vancouver technologist hounded by CSIS, it would even show which mosque he attends and how faithfully he follows Islam.

The scariest part of the security sweep was the targeting of people and the methods that were used to persuade them to talk. The RCMP were better at this, perhaps because Mounties are policemen with the power to arrest, while CSIS agents are civilians. The RCMP pulled out all the stops and implemented the National Emergency Operations Plan. Inspector Robert Norton was in charge of the implementation and co-ordination in Ottawa. The Mounties, he said, are forbidden to investigate groups, which is left to CSIS. They only investigate individuals and individual threats.

"We would receive information that an individual was planning to get together money and explosives to do something. If that individual happened to be an Arab, so be it. We would investigate that individual." "How would they get the tips?" he was asked. "We would get telephone calls; there would be citizens who approached the police and said they were aware of something or somebody. It would then be handled by the National Security Intelligence [Service]. We had a normal relationship with the FBI, and we got information from them, usually specific names."

But the majority of calls were from citizens, and these people put so much pressure on the Mounties that headquarters in Ottawa began to draft officers from other units, beginning with the Passport and Immigration section. Inspector Norton said officers worked tremendous overtime. They would be going off work, he said, and an anonymous call would come in, and it would have to be checked out. Since Canada was at war, tips were not screened; they were all investigated with equal zeal. According to a Metro Toronto police officer who was involved with the RCMP, it reached the point where one could call in about a neighbour one did not like and the family would come under police scrutiny.

Inspector Norton said the most common kind of tip was somebody calling in and saying he knew so and so was planning a terrorist act. In most such cases, he said,

the lead amounted to nothing, but it had to be checked out. He said there were liter-
ally hundreds of such calls—he lost count—all of which were checked out. . . .

Some of the leads that were investigated seem questionable. Majdi Hanoneh, a
twenty-six-year-old Palestinian, who was himself interviewed by CSIS about a non-
profit club he had set up, tells the following story. His uncle owns and operates a
donut shop in Thornhill, a Toronto suburb. One day in the first week of the war
the shopowner noticed two men who had coffee, paid, and left. An hour later, with
the donut shop more than half full, they were back. This time, they approached the
owner and flashed their badges. They were Mounties investigating a complaint that
he "may be a threat to the security of Canada." When he asked them to elaborate
on the complaint, one of them replied that a couple of customers had called the
RCMP to say that they were at the donut shop a day earlier and had heard "a group
of Arabs involved in lengthy discussions" relating to the war and that they felt the
group was planning something. The uncle replied with a smile that since the first
week of the war was barely underway, he would be surprised if his Arab customers
did not discuss the war; everybody else did.

The Mounties then demanded the owner's identification, which was clearly a
breach of his rights since he had not been charged with any offence. He protested.
He was angry because his customers were watching and listening to the conversation. They had watched the two men flash their badges and talk of security and terrorism. He warned them towards the end that what they had done was bad for the
store and for his business and that this sort of harassment had never happened to
him in his twelve years in Canada. The two then left. . . .

Rashad Saleh said similar incidents took place at two Arab restaurants in
Burlington, where business started dropping after the visits and the general tone of
reports in the media. In Cambridge, Ontario, a Palestinian who owns several auto
businesses and is very well placed financially was called up by a business associate of
his, who told him that the Mounties thought he was a terrorist. The RCMP had
been inquiring about his cash flow and the source of his funds. They were
approaching his bankers and others he had dealt with, but they never came to him.

This type of modus operandi shows the Mounties were themselves under pressure to keep the flow of information continuing steadily. Every morning, Inspector
Norton and his group would issue a summary of events that would go to the solicitor general and to the executive level of government, especially the cabinet security
committee. The extensive nature of this summary gave the government a basis for
announcing that the security forces had everything under control but that nevertheless vigilance was necessary still. And for all this effort, "In more than 99 per
cent of the cases, the end result of the inquiry was a BIG zero," according to
Inspector Norton.

Among the agencies involved with the government's security plan were Customs
and Immigration. They took their cue from the government, which announced
that visitors' visas would not be given to Iraqis and Palestinians. The agencies made
it clear that visitors from the Middle East could expect extra scrutiny. What they
did not mention was that all one needed to have was an Arab or Muslim name to
face this extraordinary scrutiny. . . .

The powers that the security forces were allowed to exercise during the Gulf War were extremely broad. The targeting of individuals was a violation of the Charter of Rights and Freedoms, which prohibits discrimination based on race, religion, and national origin. Not only did the two agencies violate civil rights, but also they managed to stifle dissent and free expression of belief. Many Arabs and Muslims did not attend demonstrations or any other meetings because they were afraid of being photographed and put under surveillance. In Mississauga, for example, the Muslim community had organized a fund-raising dinner for a centre it was building. It sold out all two hundred tickets. Only seventy people showed up.

The government, meanwhile, in a deliberate and irresponsible act, did not publicize the CSIS assessments that showed little risk of terrorism in Canada. Even a step such as this would have persuaded the non-Arab and non-Muslim population to view the minority group in a kinder light.

Instead, it sought to further its agenda of drumming up support for the war by continuing to play up the bogey of terrorism, although it had little chance of taking place in Canada. In addition, it unleashed the full force of the RCMP through the national emergency plan, not just overreacting, but overreacting to a non-existent threat—and that too in a racist manner. The signals that Ottawa sent out spread far and wide, affecting agencies such as Customs and Immigration, which began obstructing and humiliating not just suspected foreigners but even long-time Canadian citizens. If the idea of multiculturalism is to make new Canadians feel at home in the country and to help integrate them, the calendar had been set back by many, many years.

# PART VIII

# THE CONTINUING SURVEILLANCE STATE

*Democracy Street poster showing police pepper-spraying anti-*APEC *demonstrators* (Democracy Street, Vancouver). [Pearlston, chap. 21]

KAREN PEARLSTON

twenty-one ★ ★ ★

# APEC Days at UBC: Student Protests and National Security in an Era of Trade Liberalization

The consequences of the meeting still reverberate. At the November 1997 gathering of Asian Pacific Economic Cooperation (APEC), held on the University of British Columbia campus, the Canadian state took on the task of defending the "security" of the various visiting leaders from the member countries. On the first day of the meetings, Tuesday, November 27, a huge group of demonstrators of all sorts was in place to protest the gathering of eighteen heads of state, including Suharto, the notorious and now deposed Indonesian president. The resulting clash between protestors and police, with over seventy demonstrators arrested, became front-page news—though the events of that day alone were just the tip of the iceberg.

In connection with the subsequent RCMP Public Complaints Commission (PCC) hearing into police repression and violence on that day as well as in the months leading up to the event, thousands of pages of documents were released, many to great fanfare on the nightly news. The documents reveal that many activists whom the police acknowledged to be peaceful had been under surveillance for weeks or months prior to the event.[1] They also reveal substantial involvement by the Prime Minister's Office (PMO) for the purpose of avoiding embarrassment to the visiting leaders, especially Suharto.

Had it not been for the documents implicating the prime minister and his office, the press coverage of APEC would have undoubtedly been more limited. As the cover-up—and the story of the events that took place that day, and before—began to unravel, the government was driven to extreme measures.

## Introducing Security

During the APEC meetings I was at UBC, at Green College, a graduate student residence located on the edge of the campus, the distance of a city block away from the Museum of Anthropology, where the APEC leaders gathered. The Museum and the college were both inside the security zone established by the RCMP for the meetings, and it was in the street passing by Green College that some of the most notorious free-speech violations occurred. One Green College demonstrator, Craig

Jones, was wrestled to the ground, arrested, and held for fourteen hours for attempting to display signs reading "democracy," "free speech," and "human rights" while the motorcades went past. Others—Isabel Varela, Jodie Morris, and Mike Thoms— had signs taken away from them and were threatened with arrest. These Green College residents would sue the government of Canada and the RCMP for violating their rights as guaranteed in the Canadian Charter of Rights and Freedoms.

I was also threatened with arrest and had my posters taken down and carried away, but in my case the incident occurred on Saturday, November 22, *three days* before the leaders were scheduled to visit the campus.

That morning I was awakened in residence at 9 a.m. by a blast of music several minutes long, followed by many more minutes of metal-clanging noises. When I looked out my window, I saw that a security fence about ten or twelve feet high had gone up outside my building, blocking off the college from the roadway, Marine Drive. I decided it would be a good idea to make a few little posters and stick them up on the fence. At that point I had no idea that many other Green College residents would be moved to protest on the 25th. My posters attempted to make the connection between the larger APEC issues and the invasion of our residential space as symbolized by the fences.

I made ten posters, writing slogans in Magic Marker on the back of used Xerox paper. The slogans were along the lines of "APEC off campus" and "secret police off campus," and some of them played on the Green College motto, "Ideas and Friendship," with slogans like "Green College is for ideas and friendship NOT APEC." Then I went outside to tape the posters onto the fence. As soon as I began to put the first one up, a police officer drove up in a car and told me that I had to take the sign down and could not put up any more. I told him I was exercising my free-speech rights and was not going to stop. I walked ten feet or so down the fence and put up another poster. Before I could put up a third sign, three or four other cops arrived. We spoke for several minutes. During the course of the conversation they told me I would have to stop putting up the posters or they would arrest me. I told them, again, that I was exercising my rights of free speech. When they said that what I was doing was not "speech," I told them that yes, it was, according to the Supreme Court of Canada. I also made the mistake of telling them that I had attended law school, which only increased their hostility. One officer repeatedly demanded to see my bar card and did not seem to be willing to absorb my attempts to tell her that I had never been called to the bar. Instead, she accused *me* of attempting to intimidate *the cops*.

The police insisted that they would arrest me if I continued to put up posters, and they informed me that they would continue taking the posters down. I told them that it was illegal for them to take the posters down and it would be possible to obtain an injunction to stop them. They told me that there were orders from the PMO that there would be "no signs and no people" on the Green College side of Marine Drive, the road separating Green College from the rest of the campus. This discussion went on for several minutes. Finally they told me that if I kept it up they would arrest me. I asked on what charge, and one of the officers replied, "We'll make something up." I took him at his word and, since I was there by myself, I decided to leave.

I have to admit that I was shocked. After twenty or more years of participation in protest activities, I thought I had seen everything. I did not expect my signs to stay up for long, but it had never occurred to me that, three days before the arrival of the APEC leaders, the authorities would stop me from putting them up. If it had occurred to me, I would not have gone out there alone, without even a pencil and paper to write down police badge numbers.

I was also frightened. I well remembered the atmosphere around the 1988 G-7 Economic Summit in downtown Toronto: the helicopters and snipers, the threats that anyone who attempted to march would be arrested, and the phalanxes of riot cops and mounted police around the march that did finally and triumphantly occur. Green College residents had been informed towards the end of October that the "security zone" at the university would be closed from 6 p.m. on Monday, November 24, until 6 p.m. Tuesday the 25th, and that we would have to place our names on an RCMP access list in order to move in and out of the area during that time. I had decided even before we received that information that I would leave the college and stay with friends for the few days surrounding APEC. I knew that the college would be crawling with secret police from many countries, and I decided that the situation would be both unpleasant and potentially dangerous. (Later it was revealed that during pre-APEC discussions the Indonesian government had asked Canadian government officials whether it would be permissible for them to shoot protestors.) After the Saturday morning incident, I felt exposed and vulnerable in the knowledge that the police had already identified me as an agitator.

What happened to me was minor compared to the police violence that ensued, and the extensive harassment and surveillance of activists that have since been exposed. When I left the campus that Saturday I saw police and fences everywhere. But the overt repression that began that day and continued through to Tuesday evening was just the culmination of what I believe to have been a campaign of surveillance and repression conducted by the Prime Minister's Office, CSIS, the RCMP, and the Vancouver police—with the collusion of the university—for most of the preceding year.

### "Lunch with Dictators"—Pass the Pepper

I had first heard of APEC on September 1, 1997, the day I arrived at UBC from Toronto. As I took my first stroll across the beautiful campus, I saw that someone had been busy postering against something called APEC. I found the protest group, APEC-Alert!, at a table outside of the student centre. APEC-Alert! had formed the previous February, shortly after the announcement was made that the APEC leaders would gather at the university. The group had begun protesting almost immediately, writing a letter to the school's then-incoming president, Martha Piper, asking her to move APEC off campus. The letter was not answered. By July student members of the university Board of Governors had made an unsuccessful attempt to have APEC moved off campus, and the Graduate Student Society had passed a motion opposing the presence of APEC on campus. In June APEC-Alert! had held a vigil in commemoration of the Tiananmen Square massacre of 1989. The vigil was held at the Goddess of Democracy statue outside of the Student Union building. The statue was erected in memory of the massacre. On the same occasion APEC-Alert! members chalked graffiti at the Museum of Anthropology. At the end of July APEC-Alert! held a protest at the farewell party for the outgoing president David Strangway, who had made the deal to bring APEC to the campus. Members of the group handed out pamphlets and disrupted the event. Other groups, including student organizations, all of the unions on the campus, and university departments passed resolutions or wrote letters opposing APEC.

One exception was the Alma Mater Society, the undergraduate student government at UBC, which echoed the developing line of the administration that bringing APEC to campus was a good thing because it encouraged debate. Documents later released by the university in response to numerous Freedom of Information requests reveal that some elected members of the Alma Mater Society were actively co-operating with the administration in developing a view of APEC-Alert! as simultaneously trivial and threatening. In an August 8, 1987, memo, Chris Brown, an official of the Department of Foreign Aid and International Development, and who was seconded to co-ordinate APEC at the university, told President Martha Piper:

> In reflecting on the issues of APEC related security at UBC our strongest concerns rest not with the [APEC meeting] itself but with the series of meetings and events taking place on the campus earlier in the fall term. It is at these events that there is real potential for incidents which could be seriously disruptive. . . . To this end we will attempt to provide prior notification to all interested parties of any event or gathering where anti-APEC demonstrations are likely to take place. We will also cooperate directly with Campus Security to ensure that specific procedures are in place to deal with any incident.[2]

In a handwritten memo of August 8, 1997, Piper referred to Brown as "our security coordinator." Brown had been tracking APEC-Alert! since at least April 10.[3]

As the fall semester began, it became obvious that the UBC administration was not contributing to an atmosphere of calm. Information was almost impossible to come by. Meanwhile, it seemed like the administration was raising the stakes. APEC-Alert! began to hold weekly gatherings at which activists spray-painted an ever-larger series of concentric circles radiating out from the Goddess of Democracy statue. The circles denoted an APEC-free zone that activists anticipated would eventually encompass the Museum of Anthropology. In October two of the spray-painters were arrested. Activists also began to play ball hockey on the driveway of the president's official residence, where the APEC leaders were scheduled to have lunch. The house was undergoing a $400,000 renovation to make it suitable for what APEC-Alert! called the "lunch with dictators." There were no arrests, but police presence was heavy. On October 31, three other students were charged with criminal mischief for using water-soluble "glass chalk" to write slogans on windows. In the face of this repression, APEC-Alert! continued to educate, organize, poster, and hold graffiti actions. At the same time as it was having students arrested for spray-painting, the administration remained tight-lipped about specific plans for the days of APEC.

In contrast, APEC-Alert! was completely open with its information. It planned to establish a tent city, to hold teach-ins for the whole day before the summit, and, on the day itself, to crash the summit. The East Timor Alert Network announced that it planned to arrest Indonesian president Suharto for his crimes against humanity, including Indonesia's ongoing and genocidal occupation of East Timor and the murder of five hundred thousand leftists. On Monday, November 17, the tent city "Democracy Village" opened outside of the Student Union building. On the 20th a group from "DemoVille," as it became known, marched to the Museum of Anthropology and established a satellite camp, "Freedom's Outpost." On Saturday night, November 22, four students were arrested there. Journalists who followed and observed the arrests were threatened with the loss of their press credentials. Two more students at the Outpost were arrested on the next day. The people arrested were forced as a condition of their release to sign an undertaking that they would not "participate or be found in attendance at any public demonstration or rally that has gathered together for the sole purpose of demonstrating against the Asia Pacific Economic Cooperation or any nation participating in the so named conference."[4]

Later it was revealed that, under pressure from the government of Canada, the university had ceded control of the area inside of the security zone at 6 p.m. on November 22, forty-eight hours earlier than stated in the contract between UBC and the government. Brown had sent a memo to Piper the previous day, explaining that the federal Department of Justice was exploring "means by which they can unilaterally take over jurisdiction of the Museum area."[5] People who would be affected by this change of jurisdiction—for example, Green College residents and the staff members of Green College and other buildings inside of the security zone—were not informed of the early switch from the university to federal government control.

On Tuesday, the day that the APEC leaders came onto campus, the police repression led to the two incidents of pepper-spraying that would become so well known through repeated television clips. Less well known is the use of pepper-spray earlier, on the Monday. A spot known as the Rose Garden located across Marine Drive from the Museum of Anthropology, near the edge of the UBC campus, sports a very tall flagpole. On Monday afternoon a group of people went to the Rose Garden for the purpose of hanging a skull and crossbones flag from the flagpole. A group of students gathered. One person tried to climb the pole while another provided a distraction by making a speech. The speaker was arrested and the crowd was pepper-sprayed. An anonymous account written the following day stated that the speaker "was arrested—and I quote the RCMP Sergeant in charge— for 'saying foolish things.'" Later more protestors, including organizer Jaggi Singh, were arrested. "Many of the rest of us were threatened, roughed up and bitten by police dogs, all presumably for 'saying foolish things.'"[6]

The first of the now-famous Tuesday pepper-spray incidents occurred at the Rose Garden fence shortly after the arrival of a march of several thousand people. In addition to students, the crowd included working people, unemployed, and community activists representing the broad range of anti-APEC organizing in the Vancouver area (a large march also took place in downtown Vancouver on the same day). The crowd divided into people who wanted to engage in civil disobedience and people who were there to support that action and make a more general protest. When the first group approached the fence, it collapsed on them. They were pepper-sprayed, as were other protestors who approached the police lines. Unbeknownst to TV watchers, who have seen the video of that fence coming down over and over again in the news, the chain-link fencing was attached to the posts with plastic zip ties clearly insufficient for the purpose. That technicality went largely unexplained, and most people believe that the protestors did something aggressive to bring the fence down.

One of the most disturbing aspects of Tuesday's action on the main campus was the police strategy of seizing all communication devices (cell phones, walkie-talkies, bullhorns) and arresting all identifiable leaders. Despite these obstructions, activists did an amazingly good job of keeping the demonstration organized and motivated. After spending some time at the Rose Garden, the demonstration split into three groups, one for each potential motorcade exit. The three blockades remained solid until the end of the day. The blockade at the gate on the actual motorcade route provided the second famous pepper-spray incident of the APEC days: RCMP Staff-Sergeant Hugh Stewart (soon dubbed Sergeant Pepper) sounding his warning, then almost immediately letting loose with his huge canister of pepper-spray.

Documents released pursuant to the PCC hearing show that the government and police were, as many people suspected at the time, purposely trying to contain the protests by eliminating its organizers. For example, the arrest of Jaggi Singh at the Rose Garden flagpole was Singh's second arrest on the Monday. Earlier, when he was walking alone between two campus buildings, Singh had been arrested by three undercover cops who did not identify themselves. He was thrown to the ground, handcuffed, and carried to an unmarked car that soon sped away. Singh was charged with assaulting a UBC security officer—an incident that had allegedly occurred three weeks before the arrest. The officer claimed that the volume of a megaphone Singh was using was too loud and had injured his ear. Documents reveal that the warrant for Singh's arrest was processed on November 21, but deliberately delayed for entry onto police computers until the morning of his arrest, the day before the APEC meeting on campus.

Of the more than seventy people arrested in connection with anti-APEC protests at the university, only three had charges forwarded to crown counsel, and of those Singh was the only one who received a court date. One particular document, the "will-say" of RCMP Staff-Sergeant Lloyd Plante, a leader of the antiprotest forces at the APEC summit, reveals the lengths to which the government and police were willing to go to control an activist who avowed non-violence—and whom the security forces admitted to be non-violent. The document, released to the defence, is a summary of the testimony that Plante said he would give at Singh's criminal trial:

> Staff Sergeant Plante will say that the Report to Crown Counsel was forwarded with a view to eliminating some of the more high profile members of APEC-Alert!

from the UBC area. Staff Sergeant Plante will say that, some investigators believed that Mr. Singh should be charged with a "No go UBC" condition. Staff Sergeant Plante will say that, on November 22, 1997, he contacted Staff Sergeant Ken Handy, NSIS [National Security Intelligence Service], who indicated that Jaggi Singh was subject of a surveillance being conducted by the Vancouver Police Department Strike Force. The Staff Sergeant contacted Sergeant Evison of the Strike Force and decided that, considering that Singh would probably attend UBC on November 24, 1997, his arrest must occur prior to his attendance on campus. It was arranged that Sergeant Evison would affect the arrest and the UBC Detachment would be notified immediately. The Vancouver Police Department would transfer him to Richmond and Constable Lee would attend and process him. Constable Lee would be in contact with Crown Counsel would be seeking a condition that, considering the victim's employment, Mr. Singh should not attend UBC. Staff Sergeant Plante requested that the warrant be entered onto the CPIC [Canadian Police Information Computer] system at 0700 hours on November 24, 1997 with remarks to immediately advise Constable Lee or the Staff Sergeant upon arrest. Constable Lee's Continuation Report, dated November 24, 1997, indicates that on November 23, 1997, Staff Sergeant Plante advised him that Jaggi Singh had been located and would be arrested on November 24, 1997. On November 24, 1997, at 0700 hours, Constable Lee added the warrant of arrest for Mr. Singh to the CPIC. A copy of the CPIC entry, dated November 24, 1997, is on file. Staff Sergeant Plante's [*sic*] will say that, at 1115 hours, he advised Constables Howell and Labadie of NSIS that Jaggi Singh was observed at Brock Hall, however, he was to be arrested off campus or in an area of campus where his supporters would be unaware of his arrest so as to avoid making Mr. Singh a martyr.[7]

The charges against Singh were dropped in February 1999, two weeks before his scheduled trial and shortly after the PCC restarted with a new Commissioner appointed to conduct the hearings.

## The Aftermath

In the years after the main event, the APEC affair took many twists and turns. It now appears that under the rubric of Canada's national security, not only were lives and liberty endangered in November 1997 in hopes of avoiding embarrassment to Prime Minister Jean Chrétien's guests, but also careers and liberty became endangered in hopes of avoiding embarrassment to the prime minister himself.

The Canadian Broadcasting Corporation caved into government pressure by removing a veteran reporter from the APEC story. In response to a complaint from the PMO, Terry Milewski, who broke most of the APEC story on the nightly national newscast, was yanked from the story and punished with two suspensions, even though CBC executives publicly defended their reporter's accuracy and integrity. After a six-month investigation, during which Milewski was absent from *The National*, the CBC ombudsman issued a report that completely exonerated the correspondent. Nevertheless, CBC management refused to allow Milewski back on the story. Coverage of APEC became muted in his absence.

Meanwhile, Solicitor General Andy Scott was forced to resign after he was overheard on a plane telling his seatmate about the findings of the not yet convened RCMP Public Complaints Commission (PCC) hearing. The PCC hearing itself, which began on September 14, 1998, was brought to an abrupt halt in December, when its members resigned amid allegations of political interference. That the second commissioner, Ted Hughes, was a powerful retired judge gave the PCC new legitimacy in the eyes of the press and public. Adding to the aura of the legitimacy was the federal government's decision in February 1999 to fund legal counsel for the protestor complainants at the hearings. The government had refused to provide those funds during the first version of the PCC. The resulting spectacle of unrepresented and underrepresented protestors and their hard-working pro bono counsel placed up against numerous government-funded lawyers representing the federal government, the RCMP, and individual officers, projected an aura of palpable unfairness that was widely recognized by the public. But a lack of funding for protestors' lawyers was only one of the factors that threatened to turn the PCC hearings into a whitewash for the government.

One important issue was the release of federal documents relating to APEC. Many documents were withheld by government lawyers on the alleged ground of national security. The complainants argued that those documents, if released, "will reveal the extent and nature of the prime minister's involvement with APEC security."[8] There were also problems with censorship of the documents that the government did release. Some papers were so heavily censored that it was difficult to know what they contained.[9] The other and overarching problem was the limited scope of the hearings themselves. For the complainants and their supporters, APEC at UBC raised important issues of government interference in policing and the lengths to which the Canadian state would go to maintain its trade ties, which it has more and more come to identify with Canada's international position and security. Commissioner Hughes, however, made it clear that he viewed his mandate as being primarily concerned with individual allegations against individual RCMP officers who were "put under the cloud of complaint" and risked disciplinary action if the findings went against them. This narrow view of the PCC's mandate was of little interest to many of the complainants, who feared that their attempts to trace the actions of the PMO and other government officials would continue to be frustrated. Meanwhile, the government's continuing irresponsibility and heavy-handedness helped at the same time as it hindered, albeit at great cost.

When Prime Minister Chrétien returned to Vancouver on December 8, 1998, for the first time since the APEC meeting, two thousand demonstrators turned out to welcome him back. The peaceful demonstration was attacked by riot police, who claimed, once again, that demonstrators had rushed the barricades. According to one account:

> Police intimidation and brutality started well before the arrival of the riot police. During the demo, protesters who were blockading entrances had their hair pulled, necks twisted and had bikes shoved against them by police. . . . One person's nose was yanked by a Vancouver PD officer. Another person had his banner grabbed

away (for the record, it read: "Human need, not corporate greed"). Apparently, these actions served no other purpose than to try to provoke demonstrators.[10]

That day saw nine arrests, with five people hospitalized and an additional thirty to forty people aided on site by first-aid teams organized by the protestors.[11] Police defended their actions, claiming that the demonstrators had been violent and rushed police lines. In an ominous note, the CBC *National* reported, "Police say anyone standing near the front of a demonstration is taking a risk."[12] Demonstrators considered the police tactics to be an attempt to intimidate and frighten people away from protesting.

Since the APEC debacle at UBC, Vancouver police have taken to billing protest organizers for the cost of policing their demonstrations. The Vancouver International Women's Day Committee (IWDC) was charged over $6,000 for policing costs for its 1998 annual march. The IWDC was told that it was billed because it had refused to apply for a permit. However, the Canadian Federation of Students was billed thousands of dollars for a demonstration for which they *had* received a permit. The itemized bill included a charge for videotape used in police surveillance cameras. The tactic has also spread to the Vancouver suburbs. Organizers of a march to protest the killing of a Sikh temple caretaker by racist skinheads in Surrey had initially received city approval for the march. But the Surrey authorities later told them that because skinhead attacks on the march were expected, the organizers would be billed $28,000 for policing and other costs. The coalition was split over the issue, but the organizers that stuck with the project decided to go ahead with the march. In the end they were billed $17,000.[13]

Vancouver police have also used the threat of billing as a means of controlling march routes, and they have made a concerted effort to keep protests away from high traffic areas. Because the police force retains discretion over how policing is conducted and how many police are assigned to any event, and because the force issues its own bills, the police have a potentially unlimited means to impose de facto fines on demonstrations.[14]

With the billing of protestors and the notion that people who stand in the front line at demonstrations (and not everyone can take a place at the back) are voluntarily assuming a risk, a new neo-liberal leaf has been added to the old book of police brutality. The effect is familiar, though: intimidate and disrupt dissenting groups with threats of violence, surveillance, and financial ruin. The saga of the APEC protestors and their efforts in the hearing and court room and on the streets is emblematic of the struggle to defend the right to protest.

## Postscript

In the long months after the appointment of Ted Hughes on December 21, 1998, to head the PCC, and with the resumption of the inquiry, the interests served by the commission and the protestors continued to diverge. The Federal Court of Canada refused to order the release of relevant documents, and finally, on February 25,

2000, Hughes released a ruling stating that he did not have jurisdiction to sub-poena the prime minister or other members of the cabinet. Although the evidence presented at the hearing made it clear that officials from the Prime Minister's Office had indeed discussed security matters with RCMP personnel, instructions may not have been issued to the RCMP during those talks. Further, if instructions did issue, the inquiry could investigate them only insofar as they proved relevant to RCMP conduct:

> Even if I ultimately decide that improper orders or directions respecting security were given to the RCMP by the federal executive, I wish to make it abundantly clear that the RCMP Act does not clothe me with jurisdiction to go beyond the source of such orders or directions and inquire into their underlying rationale, be it political or otherwise. Indeed, the issue of why any such orders may have been made is beyond the scope of this hearing. My role is to inquire into RCMP con-duct. It is not to investigate and determine the underlying rationale, be it political or otherwise, for any orders or directions given by the federal executive, nor is it to weigh that rationale against the alleged infringement of the complainants' civil liberties.[15]

Although he was adamant that the PCC *could not order* the prime minister to appear, Hughes did invite and urge him to appear, pointing to the numerous occasions on which government officials had responded to questions about government interfer-ence at APEC by advising the questioner that the answers would be provided in due course by the PCC. Such statements, Hughes wrote, "have proliferated in the House of Commons and in the media, without apparent regard for the limits on the jurisdiction of this Commission." In consequence, he added, "It is entirely likely that many members of the general public believe that this hearing is intended, at least in part, to inquire into the conduct of the Prime Minister and the political rationale for his alleged actions."[16]

On February 29, the prime minister declined the invitation to appear. A day later three protestor complainants who had represented themselves with consider-able flamboyance throughout the hearings withdrew their complaints, issuing state-ments that condemned the narrow scope of the inquiry. Another group of complainants, these ones represented by counsel, said they would appeal the Hughes ruling. On March 7, Terry Milewski's grievance against the CBC was finally settled, allowing him to return to reporting on the APEC story, after it was almost over.[17] The inquiry soon wound down, hearing its final witnesses at the end of March, with several days reserved later on for closing arguments.

The scope of protest and repression demonstrated at the Vancouver APEC meeting would soon be dwarfed by other events, in particular the protests at the World Trade Organization talks in Seattle in November 1999 and then at the World Bank and International Monetary Fund meetings in Washington, D.C. in April 2000. Clearly, Western democracies will take strong measures to repress protests against the meetings of international trade bodies, while ever-larger num-bers of protestors are willing to take equally strong measures to disrupt those meet-ings. It is equally clear that the APEC inquiry will result in a report that failed to touch on the important issues of government interference. Once again we have seen that a government inquiry, rather than exposing the abuses of power, has covered them up. As one of the protestors said when he withdrew from the hearing, "A bunch of hyperactive Mounties ripping away protest banners is not nearly as serious a threat to our freedom as the apathy induced by channelling debate into inquiries like this."[18]

# Notes

1. "Police Had Photos of Protest Leaders," CBC Newsworld Online, Sept. 23, 1998.
2. UBC Document no. 393. This internal document was one of over a thousand released by the University of British Columbia, Vancouver, in early 1998 in response to many requests pursuant to the B.C. Freedom of Information and Privacy Act.
3. UBC Document nos. 394, 194.
4. W. Wesley Pue, ed., *Pepper in Our Eyes: The APEC Affair* (Vancouver: University of British Columbia Press, 2000), p.xiv.
5. UBC Document no. 679.
6. Anonymous, "Offense of Saying Foolish Things," Web page, "Canada, APEC, and the Rule of Law," faculty.law.ubc.ca/Pue/apec97/things.html.
7. Press release re the nabbing of an APEC-Alert! organizer and the RCMP surveillance of the group, APEC-Alert! Web page www.cs.ubc.ca/spider/fuller/apec/surv.html.
8. Democracy Street, "Court Grants Adjournment for APEC Students over Funding for Document Disclosure," press release, Feb. 25, 1999. See democracy-street.tao.ca/press-releases/feb25th.html.
9. "New Documents Heavily Censored," Feb. 25, 1999, CBC Newsworld Online.
10. Jaggi Singh, "Riot Police Bloody Protesters at Demonstration in Vancouver; 9 Arrests Made, Others Injured and Hospitalized," democracy-street.tao.ca/Dec8th/damnarticle.html.
11. "In a Chilling Echo of Apec '97, Demonstrators Attacked at Peaceful Protest," democracy-street.tao.ca.
12. Ian Hanomansing, *The National*, CBC-TV, Dec. 9, 1998.
13. "The Right to Protest Coalition Information Pamphlet," democracy-street.tao.ca.
14. Ibid.
15. Ted Hughes, "Ruling on Application to Call Additional Government Witnesses," RCMP Public Complaints Commission Web page www.pcc-cpp.gc.ca/eAPEC.asp.
16. Ibid.
17. "APECers Withdraw Complaints," APEC-Alert! Web page //fermi.phys.ualberta.ca/~jono/pcc/withdraw.html; "APEC Protesters Vow to Stick with Process," March 2, 2000, CBC Newsworld Online; Mark Hume, "CBC Settlement with Milewski Allows Him to Report on APEC," *The National Post*, March 7, 2000.
18. Jonathan Oppenheim, "Okay Ted, I'm Outa Here," *The Globe and Mail*, March 1, 2000, p.A15; see also "Re: My Resignation as Self- Appointed Court Jester," March 1, 2000 //fermi.phys.ualberta.ca/~jono/pcc/feb25withdraw2hughes.html.

GARY KINSMAN, WITH DIETER K. BUSE AND MERCEDES STEEDMAN

twenty-two ✶ ✶ ✶

# How the Centre Holds—National Security as an Ideological Practice

Through the long-time use of "national security" surveillance, many forms of state organization have taken action against persons and groups seen as threats to those in power. From being supposed enemies of those in power, these groups become transformed into enemies of the nation or enemies of the state.

The right of governments to use these "national security" procedures against opponents is generally enshrined in constitutions and in laws (and, in Canada, cabinet directives) that are mobilized in campaigns against "subversives" and "dissidents." Often these "security" campaigns have been waged against groups that are attempting to transform social relations and government policies through democratic forms of popular struggles. These are based on expanding and extending possibilities for people to have more control over their lives in political, economic, social, and sexual realms. Sometimes the campaigns take aim at individuals who refuse to fit the mould of the elite groups that control state agencies or serve dominant social and economic interests.

But surely people have a basic right to be different, to advocate for change, and to seek to expose the misguided, sometimes illegal, and often repressive actions of the state and its dominant classes and groups. The fundamental issues underlying secret police surveillance and systems of collaboration and informing on other people are rooted in the context of power relationships in contemporary capitalist and bureaucratic states and societies. The issues are based not merely in the practice of observing, monitoring, and keeping dossiers on individuals who protest, who have different cultures and sexualities, or who advocate social change; they are also based in the various ways in which the "different" are defined and in the official assumptions that are part of those definitions.

Nearly all dominant and state groups operate by making a distinction between the centre and the periphery, the "normal" and the "deviant." The concept of centre versus periphery, of mainstream versus the outside, are commonplace dichotomies in this schema. As anthropologist Mary Douglas once pointed out, the notion of a "natural" order depends upon the maintenance of firm boundaries separating the "normal" from the "deviant." The norm in the centre, which is "naturalized," also has about it an associated sense of moral cleanliness.[1] And usually surveillance systems employ methods to ensure the marginalization of those whom state agencies and those in power oppose or find threatening to their privileges. Individual people or groups who are placed ideologically at such supposed edges can easily be pushed to a place even further out, to the place, for instance, in which Jews found themselves in Nazi Germany, namely outside any form of legal or social protection. After all, the Nazi campaign against Jews, Gypsies, homosexuals, communists, and trade unionists was also carried out in the name of national security and national interest.

To take a Canadian example: in his history of the Communist Party of Canada, Ivan Avakumovic, a Canadian scholar, presents the party members as though they did not come from Canadian society's "mainstream" (which seems to mean white Anglo-Saxon males) and were, rather, people from the margins of society (or mostly non-Anglo-Saxon immigrants).[2] That type of thinking and categorizing reflects exactly what the RCMP and its political masters propounded not just in their project of monitoring communists, but also in constructing all opposition as being "foreign" or "marginal" in character. Why should new immigrants, who made up an important part of the membership of the early Communist Party, not have had just as much right to participate in the political and social actions of their choice as did any other members of Canadian society, whose families often only arrived a generation of two earlier—or even, perhaps, around the same time or later? The definition of new immigrants as "marginal," as not being full and "proper" Canadians, not only marginalizes a form of dissidence but also creates the prevailing image of a "normal," "proper" Canadian. The normal Canadians at the centre of society become "non-immigrants" (even if they did immigrate from England or Scotland), white, and usually Anglo-Saxon (and later, with the emergence of Quebec nationalism, as French-Canadian in some cases). "National security" therefore relies on a broad social consensus regarding "deviant" and "subversive" characterizations. The state's diffuse notion of "subversive" makes many people likely targets for surveillance.

In critically investigating the issues of national security, we need to destabilize and decentre the centre. We need to look at national security from the standpoints of those defined as being on the margins, of those defined as being subversive. What we can learn from these groups is key to what we need to know about national security. One thing we learn is that "national security" and "subversion" are social constructions developed to protect those in power. And, clearly, from our vantage point immigrants' cultural practices, people's sexualities, non-Aryan physical shapes, high-school student protests about curriculum, Native Studies programs, university study groups, and trade union advocacy and militancy should not be grounds for security surveillance. None of these groups, or their members, should have their rights of democratic expression curtailed. None should be defined as being marginal, and none should fall under surveillance by state, church, or the allies of the elites.

Democratic rights, if they are to be concrete rights, must be based on the expression of forms of social difference and the freedom of expression and association of oppressed groups. Unfortunately, national security in the Canadian and other contexts operates by precisely attacking the democratic rights of these groups.

## National Security as Ideology

There are two moments to the social construction of national security. The first is the "common-sense," hegemonic construction of national security, and the second is the more specific construction of national security within a state discourse that rests upon and shifts this earlier "common-sense" moment. National security is an *ideological* practice, and we use the concept of ideology here to signify a form of social organization of knowledge that attends to the ruling and managing of people's lives and that is not grounded in the social relations and practices that people engage in on their own.[3]

The Canadian national security campaigns were and are organized through the ideological concept of national security—a concept that is simply taken for granted within the relations of these campaigns. The concept of national security has a vague and mobile character. It can be extended and reduced in different historical periods. While the defence of Canada's national security was mandated at the highest levels of the Canadian state and organized through cabinet directives (and for the 1950s and 1960s through an interdepartmental Security Panel), the specifics of the field of operation were never clearly defined in any official state text. This is in part because of the flexible and elastic character of the concept itself, which allows those in power to expand or contract "security" at will in relation to various perceived threats.

Further, the elasticity has allowed the RCMP and later CSIS more room to manoeuvre on the ground in undertaking national security work. This freedom of activity resulted from the very secretive character of the social organization of national security work in Canada, a situation quite different from the more public character of national security campaigns in the United States. In Canada the secrecy and official vagueness of national security initiatives are crucial to how the operations have been organized.

In their history of the RCMP written for the RCMP, Carl Betke and S.W. Horrall point out that the elected officials of the state never did offer the RCMP any clear directives on what the Force was to consider as subversive, although cabinet representatives did provide some direction to the Security Panel.[4] This lack of definition could, in part, provide a justification for the RCMP to get itself off the hook when its actions were criticized. But the tendency to official vagueness also expresses an aspect of how national security work was organized in Canada. In 1959, when he asked the House of Commons to give an official definition of what was subversive, CCF MP Douglas Fisher received vague replies. Justice Minister E. Davie Fulton said that the government could not offer a standard definition. "It is for that reason," he said, "that the responsibility for judging as to the suitability or otherwise of the applicant for citizenship or for employment in the government service or by agency of employment—is left to the department or agency concerned." Fulton implied that the communists were so devious that you could not possibly pin them down. If the elected officials themselves could not decide on a standard for security, the operations in reality became a movable feast. The only guideline the RCMP had was "to discover and prevent attempts at subversion," leaving the distinct possibility that almost anyone could become a surveillance target.[5]

The concept of national security is crucial to the mobilization and survival of security campaigns. The security and national defence establishments in the United States and Britain and other countries, for instance, have shared a common national security discourse, with many similarities in methods of spying and surveillance despite differing forms of state organization.[6] In standard formal usage the concept of national security has at least two aspects. First, it can refer to "external" security: the military protection of the nation-states' borders. As part of this, it can also refer to the secret documents that, to help "protect" its own borders, a state has access to through security arrangements with other states, and to how it acts to protect these documents. Second, it can refer to "internal" security: the defence of the nation-state from "enemies within." For instance, many groups or individuals have been constructed as "other" and seen as the "enemy within" and therefore defined as being against the nation-state. This distinction between external/internal is rather arbitrary, because some of the "internal" security threats also get constructed through the external security arrangements that the Canadian state entered into in the context of the Cold War and more recently in the context of new international alliances such as APEC.

The standard discourse of the national security regime defined "national security" as a policy or approach that stood in opposition to "threats" from many different groups. The concept of "national security" rests on notions of the interests of the "nation," which is delimited by capitalist, racist, patriarchal, and heterosexist relations.[7] The features of Canadian state formation were historically based on the subordination of indigenous peoples, Québécois, and Acadians; and on alliances with the British Empire and later U.S. imperialism. The state's primary goal has never been to protect the security of Canadian working-class people, immigrants, lesbians, gay men, and women in general.

The constructs of "national interest" and "national security," then, cannot be taken for granted. We need to ask whose national security is being protected through these conceptualizations, and who is doing the defining. The danger is that once the hegemony of "national security" is established, the concept and the resulting practice can become very powerful. Under its regime, those who are defined as "security threats" can be excluded from regular human and citizenship rights.

During the years of the Cold War the standpoint of "national security" was defined by the security police, "national defence," and the anti-communist, anti-Soviet, and anti-Third World liberation alliance that the Canadian state was then engaged in under the leadership of the U.S. government and military. As the 1969 report of the Royal Commission on Security expressed it, "The United States is the leader of the western alliance."[8] The Canadian state participated in international security agreements in which, even for private-sector research clearances, the United States set the standards for Canadian researchers and firms involved in defence and security-related research. Canadian public servants often needed access to U.S. information, and they therefore had to conform to U.S. security standards. In 1948 the U.S. War Department was willing to share classified information with the Canadian Department of National Defence and other government agencies, providing that "all personnel handling such material had been cleared from a security standpoint."[9] The Security Panel recommended that full security precautions be taken in certain government branches to lead to this information transfer. There were also important security connections between the RCMP and the FBI, and the RCMP and the CIA, especially given that the Canadian state did not generally do its own spying outside the borders of Canada.

The Canadian national security campaigns were not simply a U.S. import, though. The earlier national security campaigns in Canada were built in opposition to the Communist Party, socialists, and the union movement and were motivated by ruling-class opposition to radical workers' movements and socialist organizing. Canadian state agencies and business interests have identified many groups as "internal" national security threats.

## On Reading the Royal Commission on Security

The report of the Royal Commission on Security, released in 1969, crystallized and used some of the formulations commonly deployed in security texts and revealed the conceptual basis of the construction of "national security." In October 1968 the Royal Commission on Security itself noted that material had been omitted or amended in the public version of the report "in the interest of national security."[10] It thereby mobilized the concept of "national security" to construct what would be public and available. If information is successfully constructed as being in "the interest of national security" it can be omitted from public documents and become a secret text. The report goes on to argue, "Neither does an individual have a right to confidence; on the contrary, access to classified information is a privilege which the state has a right and duty to restrict."[11] The state, then, protects and restricts access to "classified" security information. This practice continues to this day to organize the problems that researchers and activists experience in attempting to gain access to national security information.

The Royal Commission was mandated to make a full and confidential inquiry into the operations of Canadian security and procedures having to do with the security of Canada as a nation and the rights and responsibilities of individual persons.[12] The way in which this mandate was constructed is key. The text does not place individual rights and national security on an equal level. Instead, whenever a conflict arises the text would place national security rights above individual rights, superseding those rights and, indeed, the rights of groups of people if they are counterposed to the defence of "national security."

Under the title "Security, Privacy and the Individual" the report notes as well that the privacy rights of individuals need to be subordinated to the national security of the nation.[13] It defines the idea of citizenship as dependent not only on place of birth but also on loyalty to the state; and if a member of the nation is not "loyal" to the state, that person can be denied citizenship rights, thereby sanctioning surveillance and interrogation. But it is the state itself that determines if a citizen is loyal or not, and there is no recourse to challenge that finding. Furthermore, the targets of surveillance do not know if and when they become suspects and labelled "disloyal." Given this organization, the state security regime cannot be contested by those deemed suspect. The definition of "national security" is never open to public scrutiny, which in turn limits public debate over what constitutes loyalty and security "in the interests of national security."

## National Security as a "Cutting out" Device

This ideology maintains the hegemony of national security, which means that human and civil rights can be restricted. The curtailing of human and civil rights by the security regime was legitimized on the assumption that individuals or groups who pose a risk to national security forfeit their rights. When a successful claim is made against an individual or a group as "a threat to national security," that claim operates as a "cutting out" device, which is directed at denying people their human and civil rights and cutting them out of regular social interaction.[14] The hegemony of national security normalizes the undercutting and curtailing of human and civil rights. These processes of "inclusion" and "exclusion" from human and civil rights become key to the maintenance of the hegemony of the national security regime discourse and practice.

This exclusionary character shows up clearly in the Royal Commission report. It declares, for example: "Canada's requirement for immigrants must be balanced with the need to protect the safety and health of the state and its people by excluding certain classes of persons who appear to be undesirable."[15] The statement of this need to preserve "the safety and health of the state" by excluding those "who appear to be undesirable" is a revealing formulation, because it builds on constructions and practices of public health, in which some groups become "vectors of infection" of the "general population."[16] At the same time it constructs some people—in this case immigrants—as undesirable.

The hegemonic—"common-sense," "taken-for-granted"—character of "national security" makes it hard for people in their everyday lives to dispute the interests and security of a nation such as Canada. The concepts of the nation and national security draw in all those who identify with the nation of "Canada" and who therefore also by extension identify with Canadian "national security." On a common-sense level, the construction of Canadian national identifications has a certain consensual, unitary character. That is why nationalism can be such a useful hegemonic language and strategy. If someone identifies with "Canada" they will probably support the defence of its national security, especially if they have no basis in experience to be critical of that particular sphere of activity. The powerful emotional and moral symbol of "our country" becomes associated with a particular historical and social formation of nation and national security—with a particular strategy of state formation and with a particular ideological project.[17] Through this formulation and practice a unitary "national security" becomes naturalized. It seems just plain "common sense." As Antonio Gramsci pointed out, the process of common-sense naturalization is one of the main ways in which hegemony operates.[18]

At the same time, however, the formulation of "national" interest obscures social differences of class, sexuality, gender, race, ethnicity, age, language, and nation, especially regarding Quebec and the First Nations. The Canadian "nation" and state are constructed on the basis of these social differences, but this unitary national interest suppresses these social differences and polarizes them as "other" and as "threats" to national security.

## National Security as an Exclusionary and Inclusionary Device

In Canada, "nation" and "national security" are collecting categories that bring together a number of different social processes.[19] These concepts condense the interests of the "nation" with the maintenance of capitalist social relations, with participation in U.S.-led security arrangements, with notions of "proper" politics, gender, family, and sexuality, and of ethnicity and race (for instance, coding Canadian as "white").

This notion was deployed, for instance, against Japanese-Canadians in World War II, and official immigration and citizenship policies have been used against immigrants and refugees. The popular notion of the nation as "everyone" stands against a much narrower series of constructions that it draws upon. The state's definition of the nation and national security excludes many people from its confines at the same time as it includes some people. The excluded are thrown outside the boundaries of the nation to become "threats" to national security, with little recourse to challenge the hegemonic character of state security.

In undertaking historical explorations of the mobilization of "national security," then, we need to cast a critical eye on the contemporary uses of the concept. In our research and in our struggles for social justice and greater democracy we need to consistently defend the rights of those who are "excluded." If we are to move in the direction of a more democratic and socially just society, we need to challenge the state's right to deny people their democratic rights; and defending the democratic rights of the marginalized and excluded requires that we challenge and deconstruct the rhetoric and practices of "national security."

## Notes

Some material for this chapter was taken from: Gary Kinsman and Patrizia Gentile with the assistance of Heidi McDonell and Mary Mahood-Greer, "'In the Interests of the State': The Anti-Gay, Anti-Lesbian National Security Campaign in Canada," Laurentian University, Sudbury, 1998. It has since been transformed by the contributions of Mercedes Steedman and Dieter K. Buse, and by our reflections on the chapters in this book.

1.  See Mary Douglas, *Purity and Danger* (London: Routledge and Kegan Paul, 1979), and *Natural Symbols* (New York: Penguin, 1973).
2.  See Ivan Avakumovic, *The Communist Party in Canada: A History* (Toronto: McClelland and Stewart, 1975).
3.  As Bologh expresses it, "Ideology refers to all forms of knowledge that are divorced from their conditions of production (their grounds)." See Roslyn Bologh, *Dialectical Phenomenology: Marx's Method* (Boston: Routledge and Kegan Paul, 1979), p.19. See also the work of Dorothy E. Smith, including *The Everyday World as Problematic: A Feminist Sociology* (Toronto: University of Toronto Press, 1987), *The Conceptual Practices of Power: A Feminist Sociology of Knowledge* (Toronto: University of Toronto

Press, 1990), and *Texts, Facts and Femininity: Exploring the Relations of Ruling* (London and New York: Routledge, 1990); and Himani Bannerji, *Thinking Through: Essays on Feminism, Marxism and Anti-Racism* (Toronto: Women's Press, 1995) and her articles on the ideological construction of India: "Beyond the Ruling Category to What Actually Happens: Notes on James Mill's Historiography in *The History of British India*," in *Knowledge, Experience and Ruling Relations: Studies in the Social Organization of Knowledge*, ed. Marie Campbell and Ann Manicom (Toronto: University of Toronto Press, 1995), pp.49–64, and "Writing 'India,' Doing Ideology," *Left History*, 2,2 (Fall 1994), pp.5–17.

4.  Carl Betke and S.W. Horrall, *Canada's Security Service: An Historical Outline, 1864–1966* (Ottawa: RCMP Historical Section, 1978), especially chap. 6, "From Royal Commission on Espionage to Royal Commission on Security, 1946–1966," Document No. 20, File 117-90-107, CSIS Access 117-90-107.

5.  Canada, *House of Commons Debates*, June 25, 1959, pp.5144–5166.

6.  See Reg Whitaker and Gary Marcuse, *Cold War Canada: The Making of a National Insecurity State, 1945–1957* (Toronto: University of Toronto Press, 1994); and Larry Hannant, *The Infernal Machine: Investigating the Loyalty of Canada's Citizens* (Toronto: University of Toronto Press, 1995); and chapter 1 here.

7.  On this see Cynthia Enloe, *Does Khaki Become You? Militarization and Women's Lives* (London: Pluto, 1983); Enloe, *Bananas, Beaches and Bases: Making Feminist Sense of International Politics* (London: Pandora, 1989); and some of the articles in Andrew Parker et al., *Nationalisms and Sexualities* (New York: Routledge, 1992).

8.  Canada, *Report of the Royal Commission on Security* [Mackenzie Commission] (Ottawa: Queen's Printer, 1969), p.8.

9.  Cited in Daniel Robinson and David Kimmel, "The Queer Career of Homosexual Security Vetting in Cold-War Canada," *Canadian Historical Review* 75,3 (September 1994), pp.325–26, quoting from Security Panel Meeting, April 6, 1948, PCO series 18, vol. 103, file S-100-M.

10. Canada, *Report of the Royal Commission on Security*.

11. Ibid., p.28.

12. Ibid., pp.27–44.

13. Ibid.

14. On cutting out operations, see Dorothy E. Smith, "K Is Mentally Ill," in *Texts, Facts and Femininity*, pp.30–32, 43.

15. Canada, *Report of the Royal Commission on Security*, p.45, s.119.

16. See Alan Sears "'To Teach Them How to Live': The Politics of Public Health From Tuberculosis to AIDS," *Journal of Historical Sociology* 5,1, (1992), pp.61–83; and "Before the Welfare State: Public Health and Social Policy," *The Canadian Review of Sociology and Anthropology* 32,2 (May 1995), pp.169–88.

17. On state formation as an ideological project, see Philip Corrigan and Derek Sayer, *The Great Arch: English State Formation as Cultural Revolution* (London: Basil Blackwell, 1985), pp.7–9.

18. See Antonio Gramsci, *Selections from the Prison Notebooks*, ed. and trans. Quinton Hoare and Geoffrey Nowell Smith (New York: International Publishers, 1971).

19. Collecting categories are the official mandated courses of action or concepts through which a series of unrelated practices are brought together so that they can be regulated together through common administrative classifications. Our use of it comes from the work of Philip Corrigan. See his "On Moral Regulation," *Sociological Review* 5,29 (1981), pp.313–16.

# Index

Abbott, Douglas, 77, 83
Acadians, 281
access to information (on national security issues), not in public domain, 2; electronic, 5; in Europe, 14–15; in National Archives, 223–27, 229–32; in CSIS visiting room, 229. *See also* Access to Information and Privacy Act
Access to Information and Privacy Act (ATIP), 6, 74, 110, 223–24, 247, 270; value to researchers, 18, 21; information on "human sources" protected, 28, 96; motion on, 212; experience with, 213–14, 220–21, 229–32; exemption of information, 217; and CUPW experience, 247, 249–50, 252–53
Adams, Mary Louise, 57
*agents provocateurs*, 236, 239, 252
AIM. *See* American Indian Movement
Akens, Lee, 123
Alberta, 113
Allan Memorial Institute (McGill University), 11
Allard, A.B., 26
Alliance Quebec, 244
American Civil Liberties Union, 179
American Federation of Labor, 48
American Indian Movement (AIM), 5, 111–13, 218
Andrews, A.J., 25
Anicinabe Provincial Park, 112
anti-communism, 19–20, 61, 64–68, 74–83, 132, 155, 160–64, 179, 180. *See also* Communist Party of Canada, communism
APEC. *See* Asian Pacific Economic Cooperation
APEC-Alert!, 269–71
Aquash, Anna Mae, 218
Arab Canadians, 4, 256–63
Archdiocese of Toronto. *See* Catholic Church
Arland, Anne, 80
Armitage, Robson, 23
Asian Pacific Economic Cooperation (APEC), 4, 7, 267–77, 281
Association of United Ukrainian Canadians, 75, 81
ATIP. *See* Access to Information and Privacy Act
atom bomb, 206–7
Atomic Energy Commission, 207
Austria, 12
Avakumovic, Ivan, 39, 279

Bachand, François Mario, 225
Baldwin, Roger, 179
Barkway, Michael, 157
Baron, Sam, 241–42
B.C. Carpenters Union, 246
Beatty, Edward, 235
beauty contests, 131–36
Bebel, August, 13
Bellecourt, Clyde, 111
Bengough, Percy, 240
Bennett, R.B., 20–21, 93

Benoit, Paul, 238
Benton Banai, Eddie, 111
Berthiaume-Du Tremblay family, 237
Betke, Carl, 56, 280
Bill of Rights, 176–77, 181–82
birth control, 121
Black, Mervyn, 29
black activists, 1, 91, 124–25; in Nova Scotia, 4–5; in United States, 98–99
Black Panther Party (U.S.), 4, 97, 99, 111, 125
Boer War, 22, 23, 28
Bohlen, Charles, 207
Boisvert, Paul, 249
Boivin, Marc-André, 246, 252
Bolshevism (Soviet Union), 14, 19, 20, 21
Borden, Robert, 20, 29
Boudreau, Alexandre, 63–64
Bourassa, Robert, 242
Bourgeois, M. Claude, 237
Bourne, Robin, 248, 249
Bourque, Deborah, 247
Bowman, Dave, 95
Boyle, Jean, 201
*Boy's Life*, 191
Bracken, John, 78
Brand, Johanna, 112–13
Brands, H.W., 195
Bristow, Grant, 247, 252, 253
Britain. *See* United Kingdom
British Columbia, 214–15
British Columbia Federation of Labour, 246
Brown, Chris, 270, 271
Budd, Ruth, 219
Buck, Tim, 39, 81
Buhay, Becky, 93

Cahagan Douglas, Helen, 194
Cahan, C.H., 20, 29–30
Calgary, 24–25, 29, 134
*Call Northside 777*, 203
Callwood, June, 157–58, 221
Cameron, Don, 83
Canada Council, 1
Canada Evidence Act, 174
Canada Pension Plan, 215
Canada Unity Information Office, 227
Canadian Arab Federation (CAF), 259
Canadian Association of Consumers, 81
Canadian Association of Social Workers, 159
Canadian Association of University Teachers (CAUT), 96, 110, 114, 115
Canadian Auto Workers, 246
*Canadian Bar Review, The*, 175
Canadian Broadcasting Corporation (CBC), 159, 273
Canadian Cancer Society, 62
Canadian Citizenship Branch, 159, 161

287

**AGMV** Marquis

MEMBER OF THE SCABRINI GROUP

Quebec, Canada
2000